The Intermediate Guide to
Microsoft Excel 2010
Microsoft Office Specialist Exam 77-882 Study Guide

another
Computer
Mama
Guide

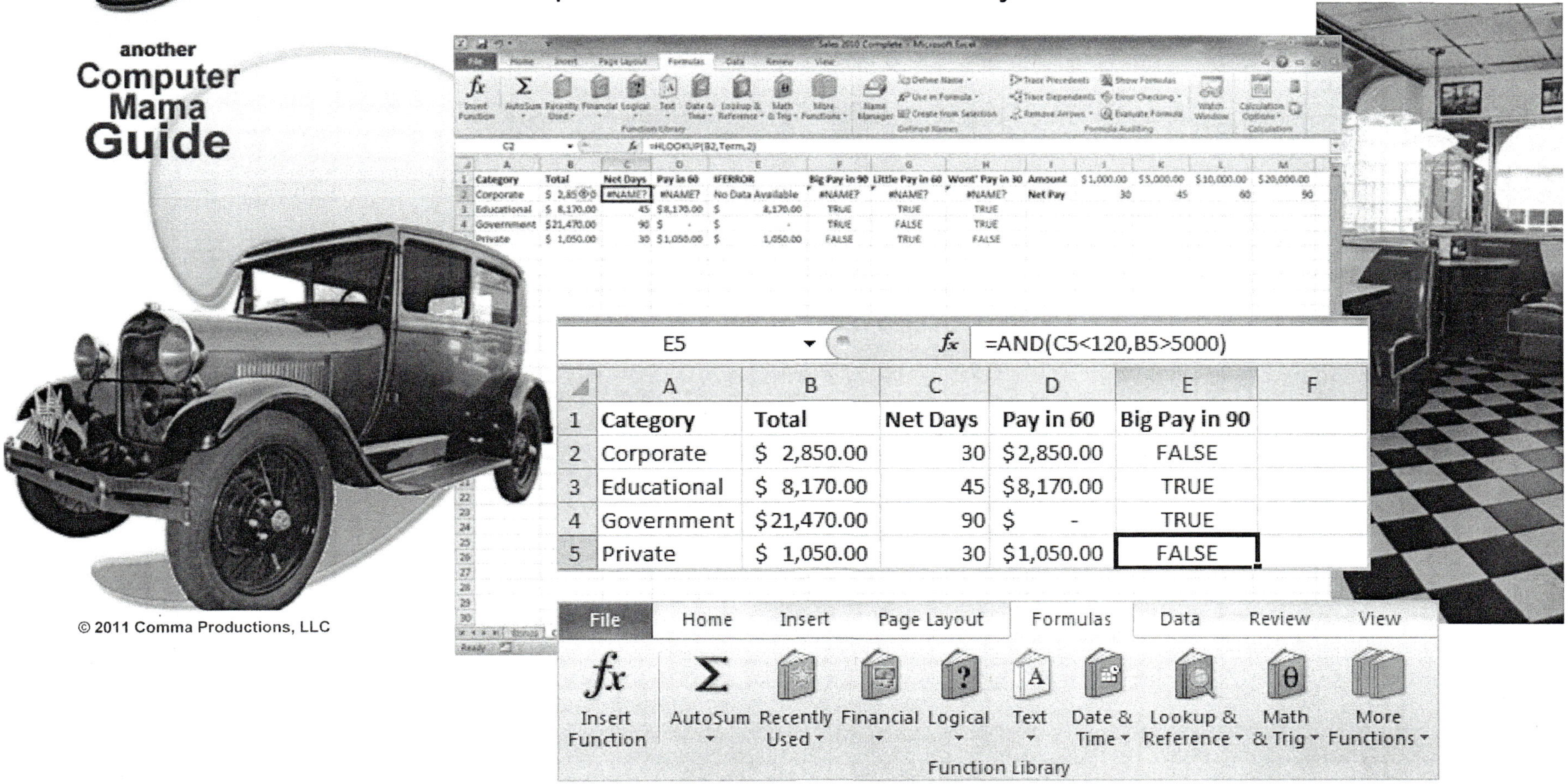

© 2011 Comma Productions, LLC

	A	B	C	D	E	F
				fx	=AND(C5<120,B5>5000)	
1	Category	Total	Net Days	Pay in 60	Big Pay in 90	
2	Corporate	$ 2,850.00	30	$2,850.00	FALSE	
3	Educational	$ 8,170.00	45	$8,170.00	TRUE	
4	Government	$21,470.00	90	$ -	TRUE	
5	Private	$ 1,050.00	30	$1,050.00	FALSE	

File	Home	Insert	Page Layout	Formulas	Data	Review	View

fx Insert Function | Σ AutoSum | Recently Used | Financial | Logical | Text | Date & Time | Lookup & Reference | Math & Trig | More Functions

Function Library

another
Computer
Mama
Guide

Intermediate Guide to Microsoft Excel 2010

© 2011 Comma Productions
9090 Chilson Road
Brighton, MI 48116
978-0-9838917-4-1

Trademark and Copyright

Limit of Liability/Disclaimer of Warranty:

Intermediate Guide to Microsoft Excel 2010

Microsoft Office Specialist Certification

What is the Microsoft Office Specialist Certification?

The Microsoft Office Specialist certification validates through the use of exams that you have obtained specific skill sets within the applicable Microsoft Office programs and other Microsoft programs included in the Microsoft Office Specialist Program. The candidate can choose which exam(s) they want to take according to which skills they want to validate.

CertiPort is the premier provider for validating technology skills.

The **Microsoft Office Specialist** tests are offered at authorized testing centers.

For more information on the MOS exam topics or to find a testing center near you please contact: **www.certiport.com**

What is the Microsoft Office Specialist Certification Program?

The **Microsoft Office Specialist (MOS) Certification Program** enables candidates to show that they have something exceptional to offer – proven expertise in Microsoft Office programs. Recognized by businesses and schools around the world, millions of certifications have been obtained in over 100 different countries. The **Microsoft Office Specialist (MOS) Certification Program** is the only Microsoft-approved certification program of its kind.

The Microsoft Office Specialist Certification Series

Core Certification: Pass any 1 test:
Word 2010 Core: Exam 77-881
Excel® 2010 Core: Exam 77-882
PowerPoint® 2010: Exam 77-883
Access® 2010: Exam 77-885
Outlook® 2010: Exam 77-884

Expert Certification: Pass either test:
Word 2010 Expert: Exam 77-887
Excel® 2010 Expert: Exam 77-888

Master: Pass 3 required and 1 elective test:
Required
Word 2010 Expert: Exam 77-887
Excel® 2010 Expert: Exam 77-888
PowerPoint® 2010: Exam 77-883

Elective
Access® 2010: Exam 77-885 or
Outlook® 2010: Exam 77-884

Please Note: Comma Productions, LLC. is independent from Microsoft Corporation, and not affiliated with Microsoft in any manner. While the Complete Computer Guides may be used in assisting individuals to prepare for a Microsoft Office Specialist Certification exam, Microsoft, its designated program administrator, and Comma Productions, LLC. do not warrant that use of these Complete Computer Guides will ensure passing a Microsoft Office Specialist Certification exam.

The Benefits of Certification

For More Information:
www.certiport.com
www.microsoft.com

Why Get Certified?

For employers, the certification provides skill-verification tools that not only help assess a person's skills in using Microsoft Office programs but also the ability to quickly complete on-the-job tasks across multiple programs in the Microsoft Office system. (http://www.microsoft.com/learning/en/us/certification/mos.aspx). Certification proves a certain level of advanced competency with the programs in question. Employers don't have to wonder if the skills stated on the resume are honest and without exaggeration. This can lead to further employment opportunities and increased pay.

A person holding Microsoft Office Certification shows not just a level of skill, but an ability to quickly complete tasks, due to familiarity with the program and it's many time-saving features. The hard work that goes into learning Microsoft Office programs to the level of proficiency necessary for successful completion of the Certification Exams also indicates a desire on behalf of the student to learn and succeed.

The Benefits: Earn More, Find Jobs Quicker

Research indicates that employees with Microsoft Certification earn more and find jobs quicker than those employees without certification. Furthermore, employees with certification report a greater feeling of confidence. These things translate into greater job satisfaction. (http://www.microsoft.com/learning/en/us/certification/mos.aspx)

Research also shows that individuals with certification make up to 12% more than those without certification. In addition, 82% of Microsoft Office Specialists report a salary increase after receiving certification. Managers like the skills proven and the ability demonstrated by those with Microsoft Office Certifications.
http://www.certiport.com/Portal/desktopdefault.aspx?page=common/pagelibrary/mos2003.html

About Our Certification Program

Books in this Series:
Beginning Guide to
Microsoft® Excel 2010

Intermediate Guide to
Microsoft® Excel 2010

Advanced Guide to
Microsoft® Excel 2010

Microsoft Office Specialist (MOS) Certification for Excel 2010

Overview: Our Microsoft Office Specialist certification program for Word 2010 has three levels of mastery: Beginning, Intermediate and Advanced. In general, the CORE exam topics are demonstrated in the Beginning and Intermediate Guides. EXPERT concepts are included where relevant, with the Advanced Guide only covering EXPERT concepts

Our Approach: In designing these Guides, we found that it made more sense to write the lessons based on the Ribbons and Tasks. For example, the Beginning Guide to Microsoft Excel 2010 shows all of the Picture Tools: CORE and EXPERT. The beginning of each lesson provides an overview of the Ribbons and Tasks covered.

The Beginning Guide to Microsoft Excel 2010 demonstrates the following Ribbons: **Home, Formula, Insert, Picture Tools, Drawing Tool, SmartArt Tools: Design, Chart Tools, Chart Tools: Layout: Labels** The lesson activities focus on basic data and formula entry as well as inserting and formatting graphics and charts.

The Intermediate Guide to Microsoft Excel 2010 demonstrates the following Ribbons: **Formulas, Page Layout, Insert, Sparkline Tools.** The lesson activities focus on additional formulas as well as page options, finishing with the use of Sparklines.

The Advanced Guide to Microsoft Excel 2010 demonstrates the following Ribbons: **Table Tools, Table Tools, Data, PivotTable Tools: Design, PivotTable Tools: Options, PivotChart Tools: Design, PivotChart Tools: Analyze, Review, Developer.** The lesson activities further explore presentation with advanced Table options as well as PivotCharts and PivotTables, finishing with sharing and form controls.

Course Prerequisites: Students who enroll in Microsoft Office Specialist (MOS) program should have basic computer skills including how to turn on the computer, how to use an Internet browser and how to select commands from a menu. Students should know how to save files and send attachments by email as well.

Microsoft Excel 2010 Study Guide: Intermediate Excel

Microsoft Office Specialist (MOS): Exam 77-882 for Excel 2010

Keep going...There's more...

Microsoft Excel 2010 Study Guide: Intermediate Excel
Microsoft Office Specialist (MOS): Exam 77-882 and 77-888 for Excel 2010

 **About the Authors**

Microsoft Office Specialist (MOS): Exam 77-882 for Excel 2010

Elizabeth Ann Nofs

Elizabeth is the Computer Mama. She developed the teaching methodology in the Complete Computer Guide series using breakthrough research in gender balanced training. Elizabeth has taught several thousand men and women from government, manufacturing, small business, and education in both online and hands-on classrooms.

She is the author of the Complete Computer Guides as well as a Microsoft Certified Office Specialist. She earned a BA in Biology from the University of Michigan.

Alex Sergay, Senior Instructional Designer

For more than 20 years, Alex has made complex technology easy to understand. Alex has developed instructional multimedia software for educational websites including the Sounds of English, a linguistics-training tool that earned a <u>*ComputerWorld/Smithsonian Laureate.*</u>

Alex earned his Masters of Educational Technology from the University of Michigan, Ann Arbor.

Clair Dickson, Student Services

Clair works with adult learners in online, face-to-face and hybrid classroom settings. She is considered "highly qualified" to teach introductory computers, including Microsoft Office.

Clair has a Graduate Certificate in Educational Media and Technology, an program that explored ways to infuse technology into the learning experience so that learning is interactive. She has earned Microsoft Office 2007 Master Certification. She also holds a BS in Secondary English Education from Eastern Michigan University.

Leo Michael Nofs, Technical Writing and Quality Control

Leo is a Microsoft Certified Professional and an Access database designer. He uses his exemplary attention to detail for copy editing the computer instructions for accuracy and clarity.

Traci DeRosiers Nofs, Photography and Photo Editing

Traci has been photographing children and nature since 2000. She works freelance out of her home, including weddings, engagements, and particularly children's photography. She has further enhanced her photos by use of image manipulation, focusing on light and color.

M. Jeanette McCrickard, Office Manager

Jeanette has years of experience as an office manager, including the increasing use of computer-related tasks. Her excellent attention to detail has lead her to work as an Access database administrator and a copy editor.

All of my books

are dedicated to

Fr. Paul Cummings

who taught me

computers.

Love, eBeth

How To Use This Guide
Microsoft Office Specialist Certification Training

The Comma Method
Observation is a perceptual strategy that asks: why am I doing this and which tools would be most effective? Each lesson begins with a discussion of the purpose and the objectives.

Orientation helps students start at the right place. The screen shots in the *Complete Compute Guides* show the entire window as well as a close up of the particular button or command.

Notation There are "breadcrumbs" above each screen image. Like Hansel and Gretel, the breadcrumbs show the pathway to a button or option. Our notation uses the following convention:
Ribbon->Group->Button->Options

Menu Maps
The Comma Method recognizes that there is a difference in how men and women navigate the menus. Men typically have the ability to see the map first. This method of acquiring knowledge is called *Breadth-first.* [1] Women tend to work with the details first. They learn several commands, such as copy, cut, and paste, then they put those concepts under the label, "edit." This method of learning is called *Depth-first.*

The Comma Method uses menu mapping to assist men and women to see both the Breadth and the Depth. An example of the menu map is can be seen here.

[1] Ford, Nigel, Sherry Chen, Matching/mismatching revisited: An Empirical Study of Learning and Teaching Styles. British Journal of Educational Technology v.32 no1 (Jan. 2001)

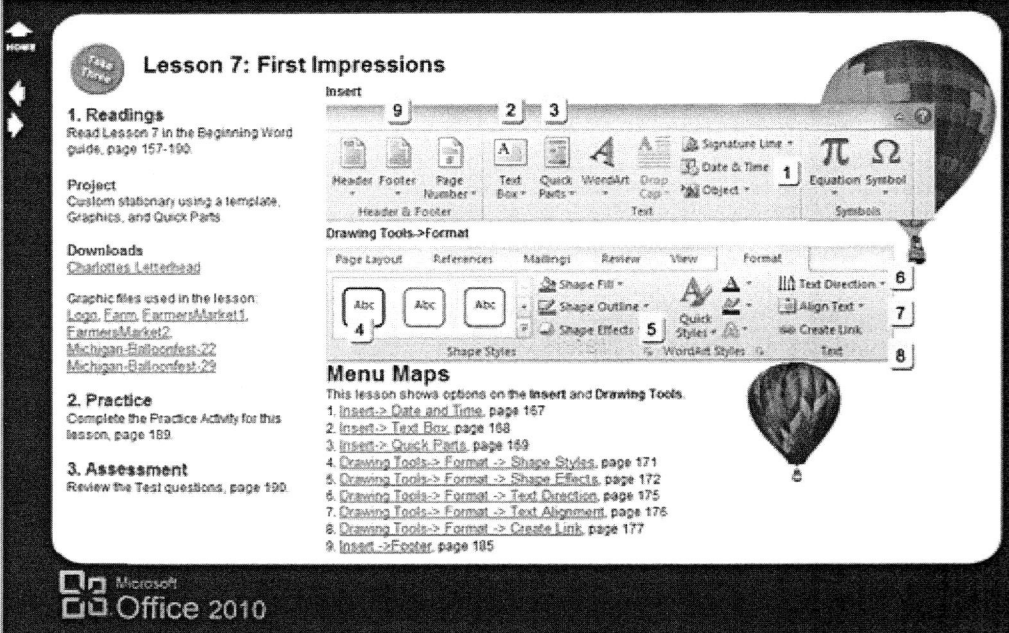

Data-> Data Tools

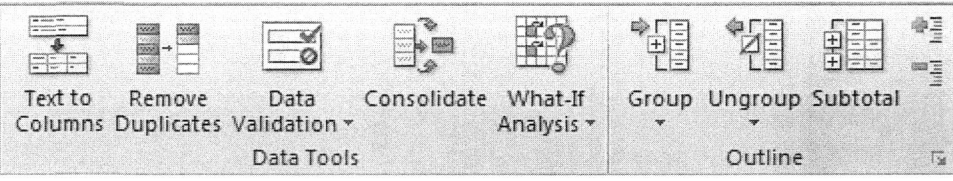

Excel 2010: Business Spreadsheets

Legs, Eggs and Pigs in a Basket

Intermediate Excel Objectives
In this lesson, you will learn how to:
1. Format data and content
2. Fill a series with AutoFill
3. Learn how to calculate revenue with a formula
4. Summarize the data
5. Identify Relative References
6. Identify errors and troubleshoot equations
7. Use the Auditing Toolbar

E25			f_x	=SUM(E6:E24)
	A	B	C	D	E
1	Price	3.25			
2	Start	100			
3	Increment	5			
4					
5	Date	Product	Net	Quantity	Revenue
6	June 1, 2011	Pigs	$ 3.25	100	$ 325.00
7	June 2, 2011	Pigs	$ 3.25	105	$ 341.25
8	June 3, 2011	Pigs	$ 3.25	110	$ 360.00
9	June 6, 2011	Pigs	$ 3.25	115	$ 373.75
10	June 7, 2011	Pigs	$ 3.25	120	$ 390.00
11	June 8, 2011	Pigs	$ 3.25	125	$ 406.25

 # Lesson 1: Legs, Eggs and Pigs in a Basket

1. Readings
Read Lesson 1 in the Intermediate Excel guide, page 11-48.

Project
A spreadsheet that calculates the daily sales for three products and adds up the total on a summary spreadsheet.

Downloads
Legs Eggs Pigs 2010.xlsx

2. Practice
Complete the Practice Activity on page 49.

3. Assessment
Review the Test questions on page 50.

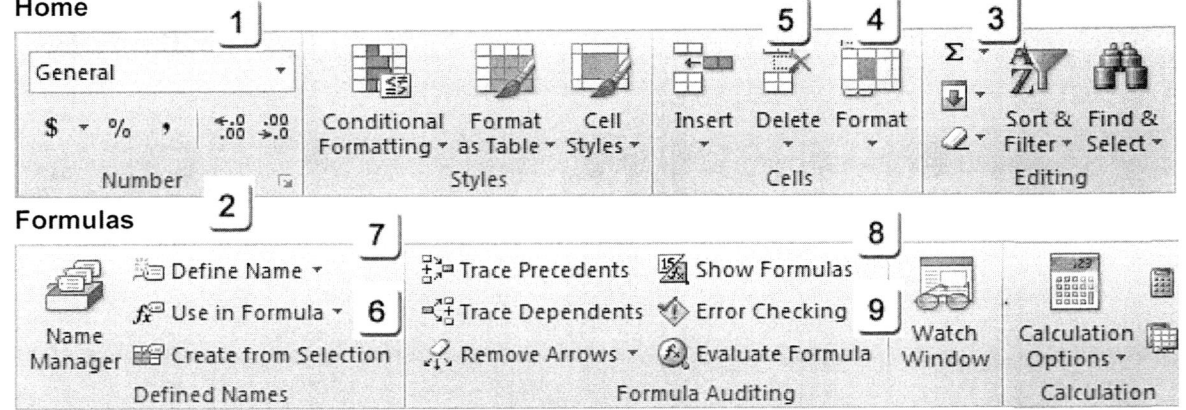

Menu Maps

This lesson demonstrates options on the **Home** and **Formulas** Ribbons.

1. Home->Number->Date, page 15
2. Home->Numbering->Format Cells, page 17
3. Home->Editing->AutoSum, page 24
4. Home->Cells->Format, page 27
5. Home->Cells->Delete, page 29
6. Formulas -> Formula Auditing->Trace Dependents, page 41
7. Formulas -> Formula Auditing->Trace Precedents, page 42
8. Formulas -> Formula Auditing->Show Formulas, page 44
9. Formulas -> Formula Auditing->Error Checking, page 46

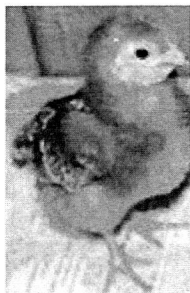

Calculating Sales

Our little online farmer's market is growing. Supply can hardly keep up with demand at Charlotte's Web Site. We're counting the chickens before they are hatched. Is there a way to forecast what we might sell, say Wednesday two weeks from now? Yes, there is. We can set up a spreadsheet that will calculate our sales on any given day.

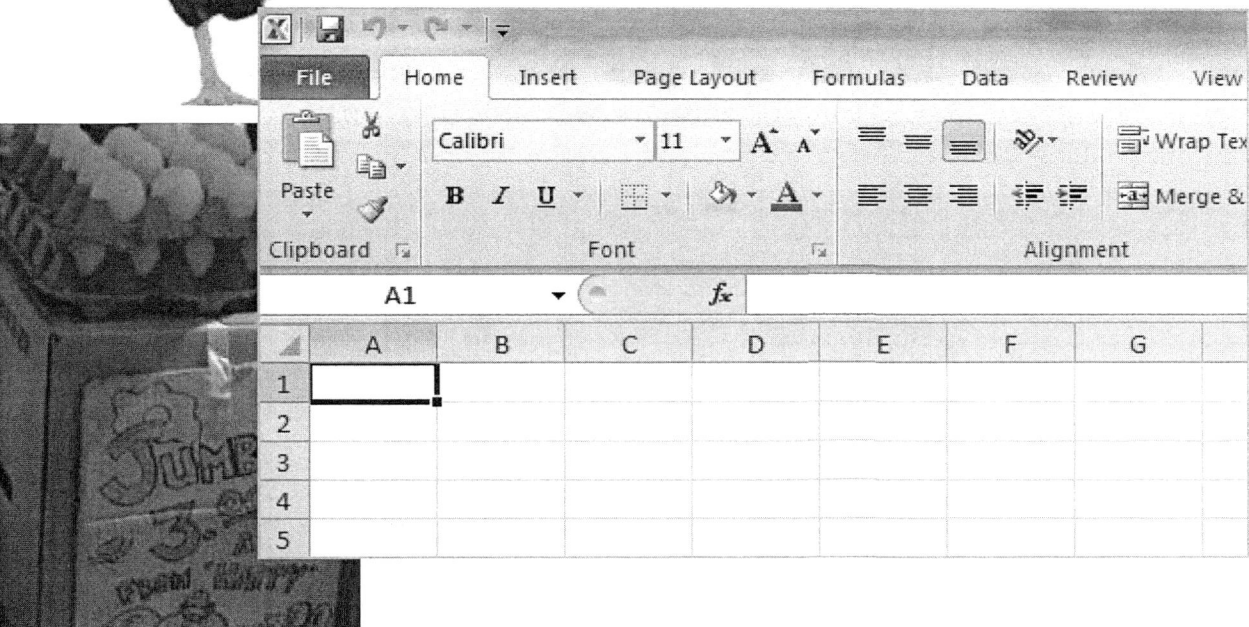

Start the Program Microsoft Excel

What Do You See? Is there a blue Title Bar that says Microsoft Excel? Yes.

Is there a Home Ribbon with the Clipboard, Font, Alignment and Number Groups? Yes.

If your screen looks similar to the example on this page, then you are ready to get started.

Enter the Labels

Hello, Excel. There are only three parts to a spreadsheet: **labels**, **data**, and **formulas**. Start with the labels.

1. Try This: Enter the Labels

Click on Cell A1 and type: Date
In Cell B1 type: Product
In Cell C1 type: Net
In Cell D1 type: Quantity
In Cell E1 type: Revenue

If these are **labels**--and they are-- select Row 1 and make them **Bold**.

Keep going...

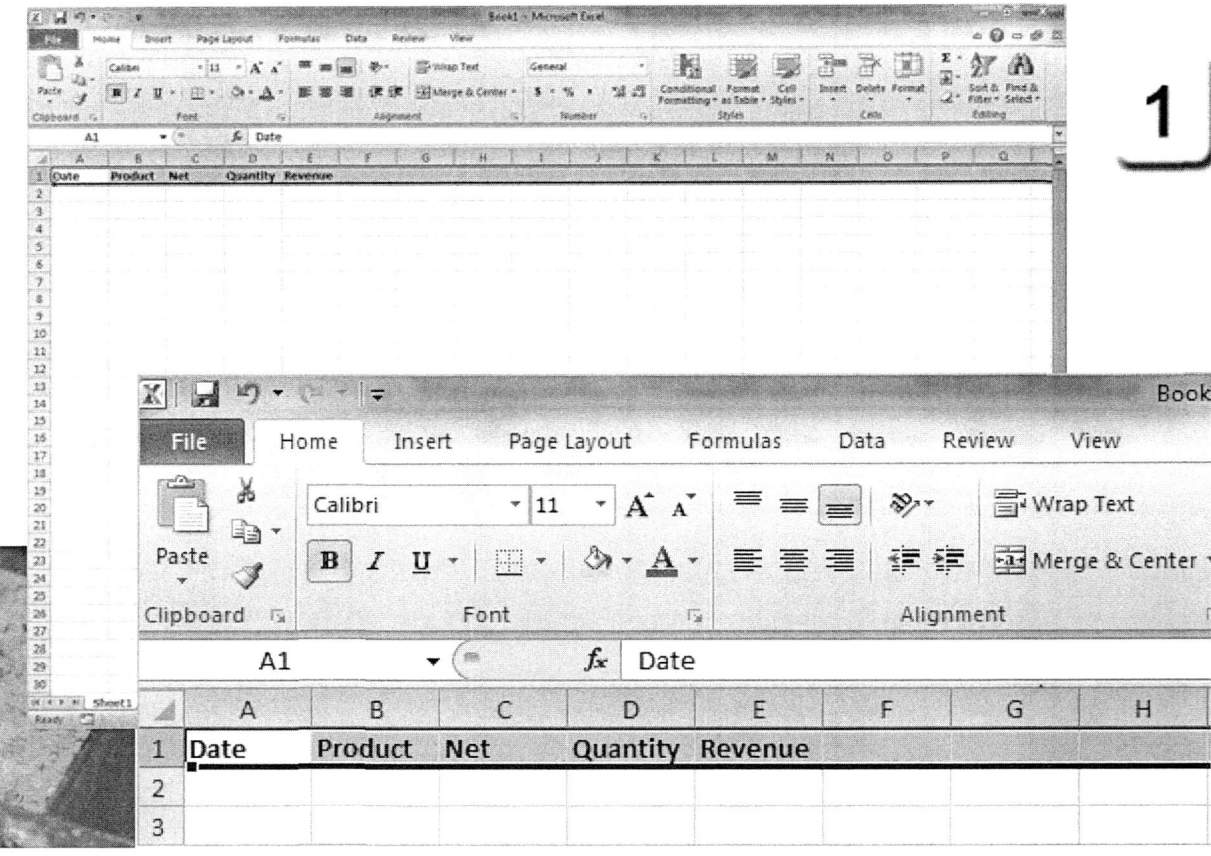

1

Exam 77-882: Microsoft Excel 2010 Core
3. Formatting Cells and Worksheets
3.6. Create and apply cell styles

Enter the Date

2. Try This: Enter the Date
Select Cell A2 and type: June 1, 2011.
Click ENTER on the keyboard.

What Do You See? The date in Cell A2
is displayed as **6/1/11.** This is the
default date format: d/m/yy. Keep
going...

Home -> Number

	A2	▼		f_x	6/1/2011	
	A	B	C	D	E	F
1	Date	Product	Net	Quantity	Revenue	
2	6/1/2011					
3						
4						
5						

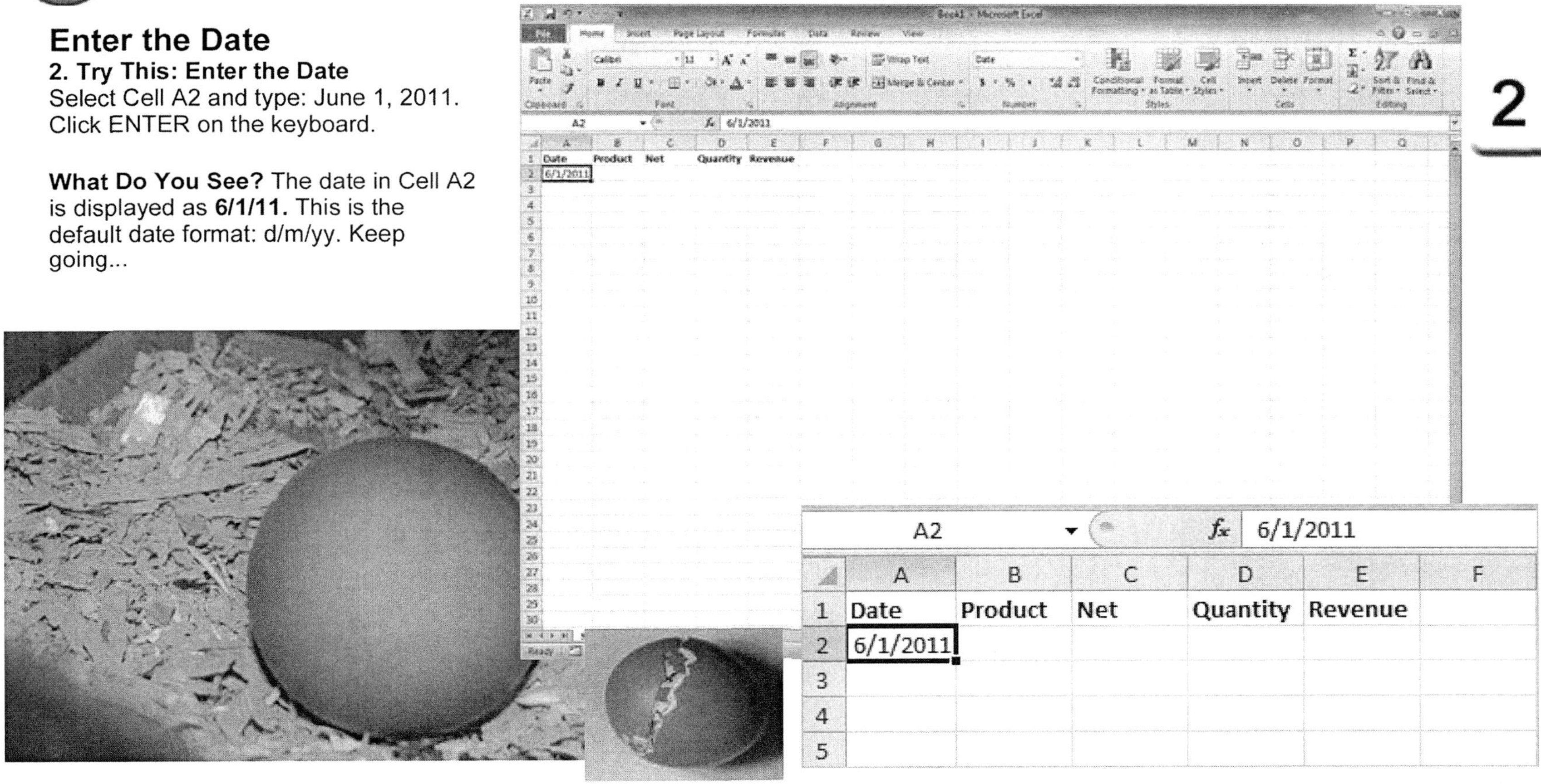

Exam 77-882: Microsoft Excel 2010 Core
3. Formatting Cells and Worksheets
3.6. Create and apply cell styles: Format the Date

Format Date and Time

Many companies work with people from around the world. When you select a format that displays the names of the months, it makes it clear whether 2/1/11 is January 2nd or February 1st. Please format this column for date and time.

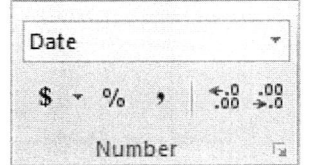

3. Try This: Change The Date Format
Select Column A, first.
Go to **Home->Number.**
The default number format is **General.**
Select: **Long Date.**

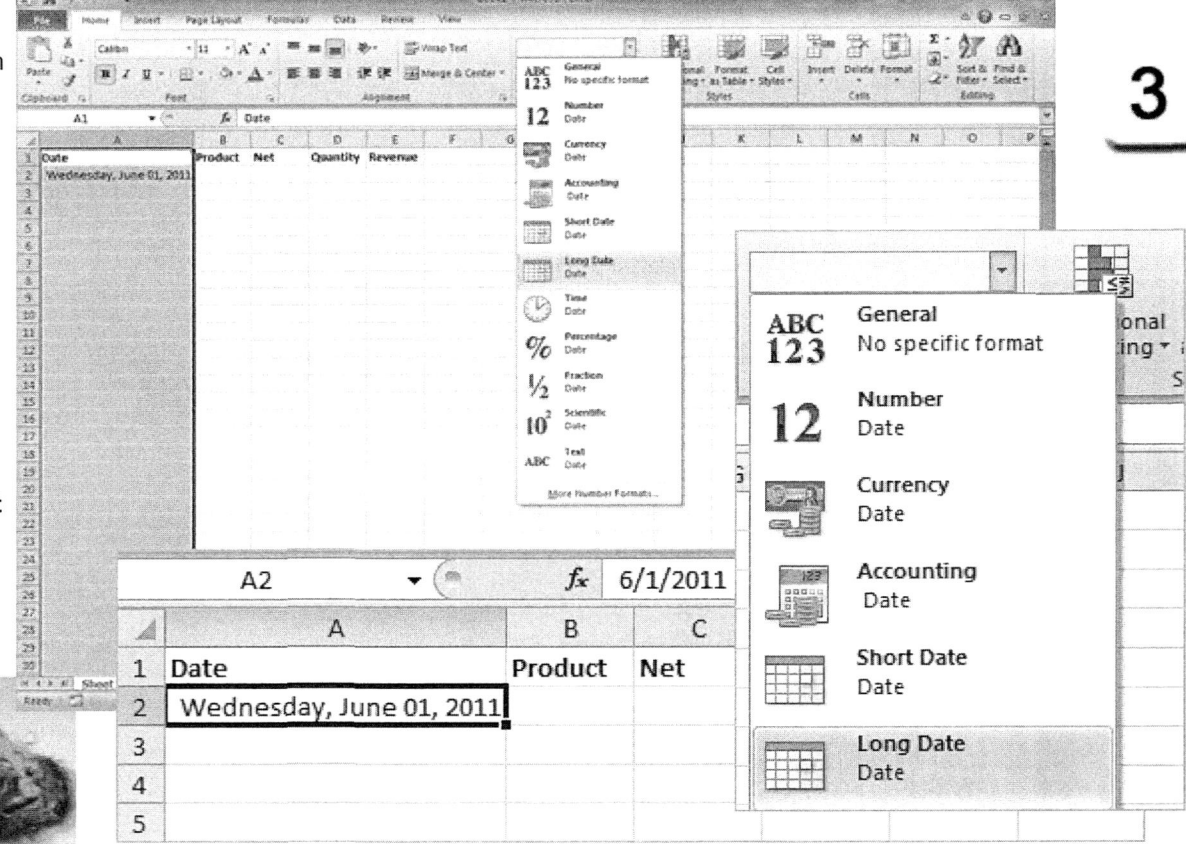

Exam 77-882: Microsoft Excel 2010 Core
3. Formatting Cells and Worksheets
3.6. Create and apply cell styles: Format the Date

Format Cells

4. Try This, Too: Custom Date Formats

There are additional formats in the Number Group. These options can be found by clicking on the **Option arrow** in the lower right corner.

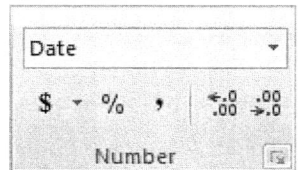

What Do You See? There are several pages of formatting options. On the **Number** page, select the **Date** category and select the Medium Date format: March 14, 2001.

Memo to Self: You can create a Custom format if you wish.

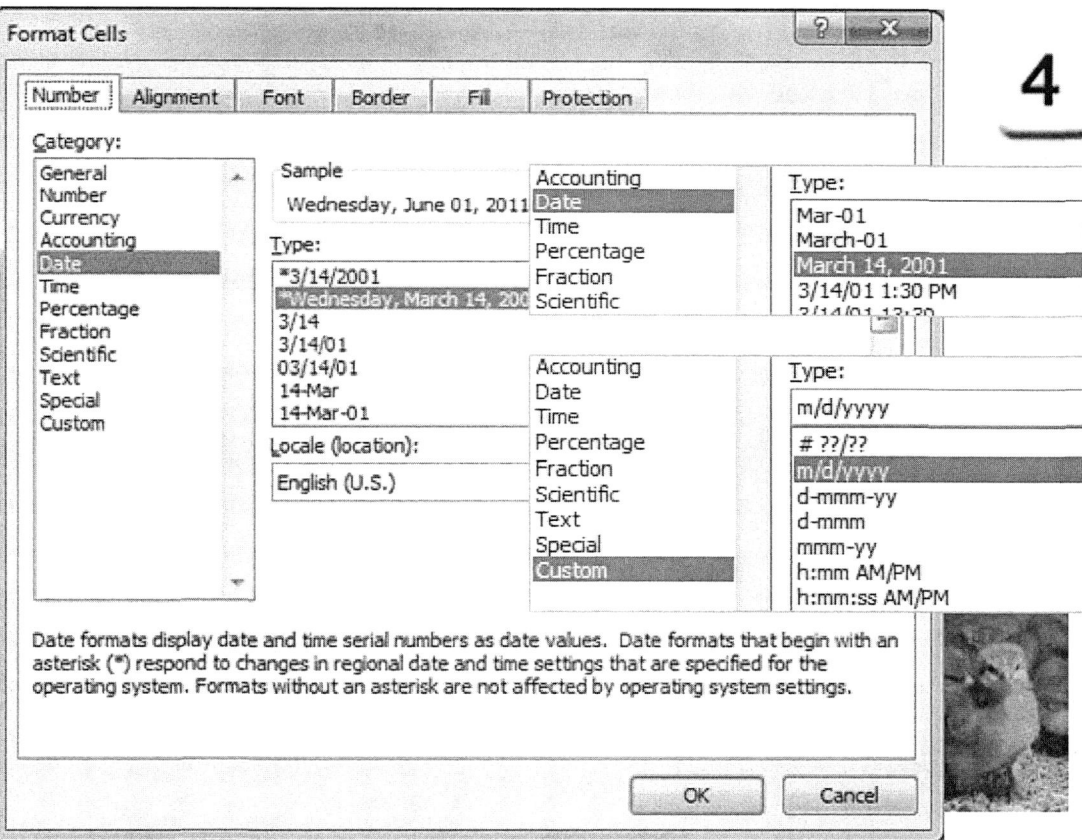

Exam 77-882: Microsoft Excel 2010 Core
3. Formatting Cells and Worksheets
3.6. Create and apply cell styles: Format the Date

Take One

Fill a Series with AutoFill

Now, one way to put in the dates for the next month would be to type them all. Do you want to know a faster way? **AutoFill** is a quick method for filling in data. It is not quite the same as copy and paste.

5. Try This: Use The AutoFill
Please select Cell A2, first.
Look at the bottom right corner of Cell A2.
The AutoFill Handle is a black square. When you run your mouse over the Handle, your mouse will become a thin black cross.

Hold the **AutoFill** handle and drag down to Row 20.

What Do You See? The dates will increment (add another day to each Row) as you Fill Down Cell A2.

Keep going...

Home -> Number ->Format Cells

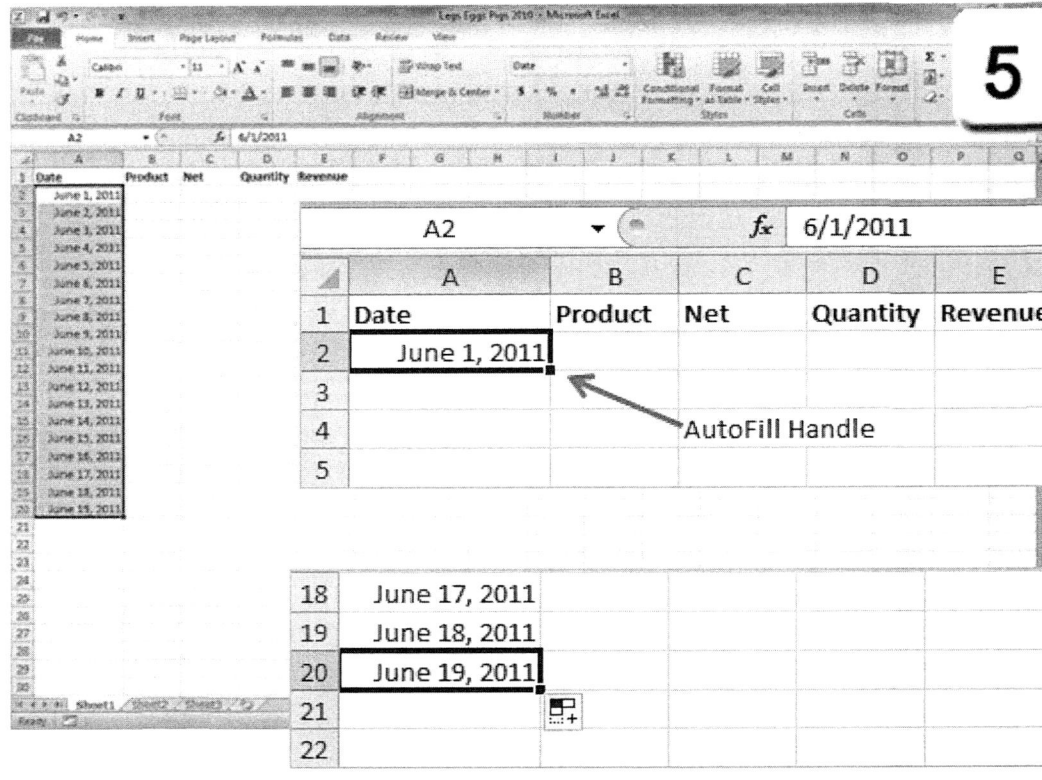

	A	B	C	D	E
1	Date	Product	Net	Quantity	Revenue
2	June 1, 2011				
3					
4					
5					

AutoFill Handle

	A	B	C	D	E
18	June 17, 2011				
19	June 18, 2011				
20	June 19, 2011				
21					
22					

Exam 77-882: Microsoft Excel 2010 Core
2. Creating Cell Data
2.2. Apply AutoFill: Fill a Series

AutoFill Options

What Else Do You See? Look by the AutoFill handle in Cell A20. There is a little option box that you can click. The **AutoFill Options** are:
Copy Cells
Fill Series
Fill Formatting
Fill Without Formatting
Fill Days
Fill Weekdays
Fill Months
Fill Years.

The **Day**, **Month** and **Year** formatting displays only that portion of the date that you entered in the Cells. You can choose to Fill the Cells with or without the Cell **Formatting**, too.

Fill Weekdays looks up the dates in your **Series** and enters only the days from Monday to Friday. No weekends-sweet.

Memo to Self: The example on this page is formatted with the Medium Date format and shows only the Weekdays.

AutoFill Options

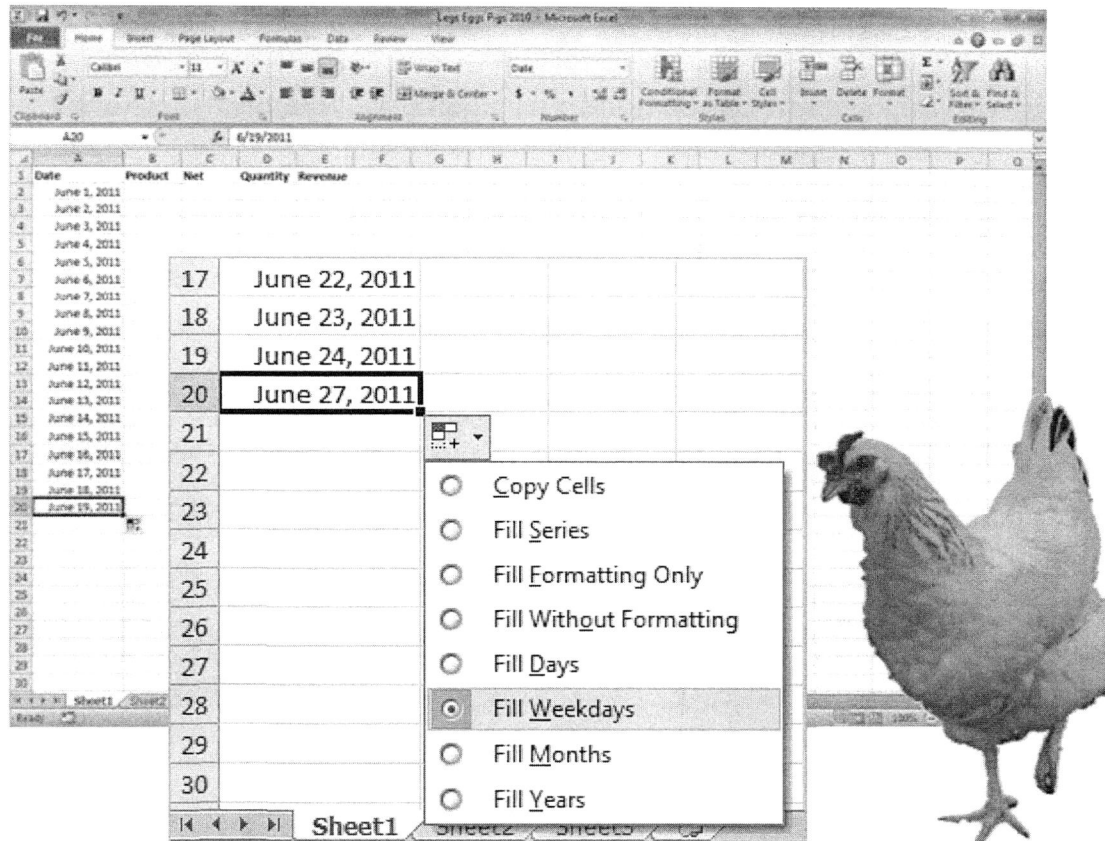

Exam 77-882: Microsoft Excel 2010 Core
2. Creating Cell Data
2.2. Apply AutoFill: Select from the Options List

Copy the Data with AutoFill
Charlotte's Website sells eggs, chicken wings, and little sausages wrapped in pastry. Eggs, Legs, and Pigs in a Basket. **AutoFill** works here, as well.

6.Try This, Too: Copy a Series
Select Cell B2 and type: Eggs.
Now, click once on Cell B2 to select it.
Double click the AutoFill handle on Cell B2.

What Do You See? AutoFill copies the word Eggs and fills all the way down to Row 20.

Look Again: AutoFill copied the data down as far as the column to the left. So don't worry, it won't go on beyond zebra.

AutoFill Options

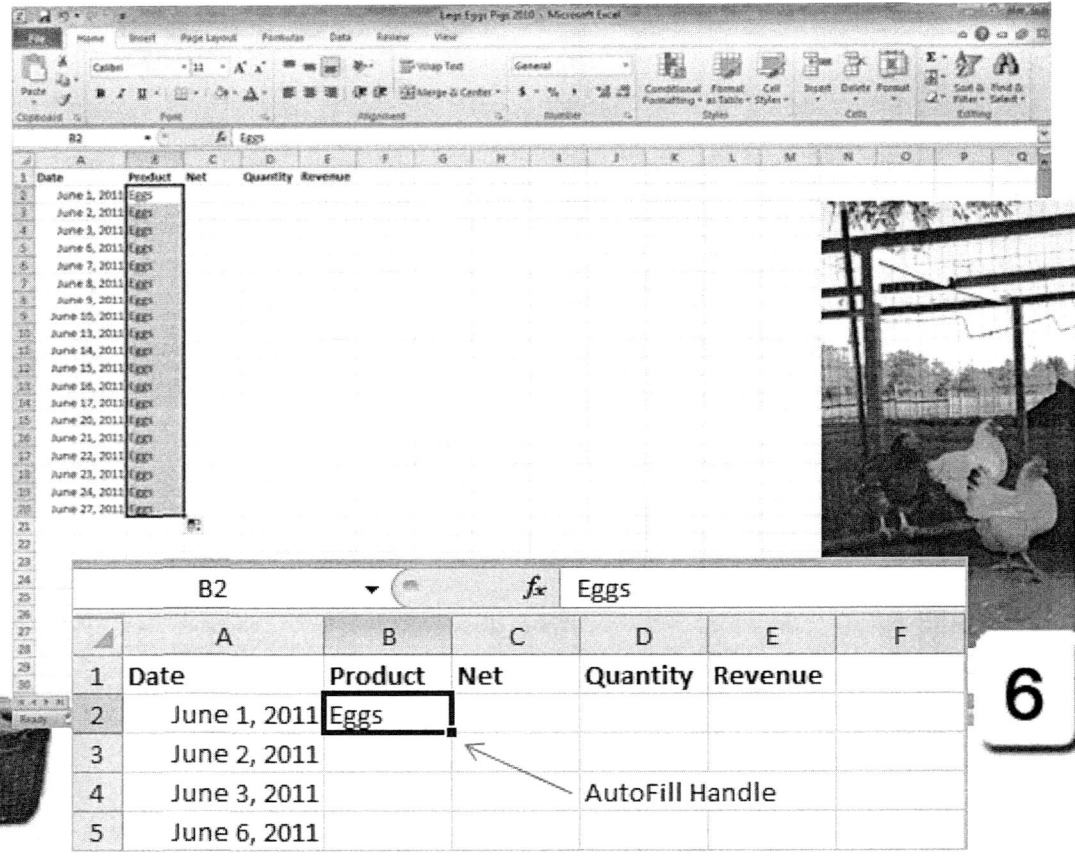

Exam 77-882: Microsoft Excel 2010 Core
2. Creating Cell Data
2.2. Apply AutoFill: Copy Data

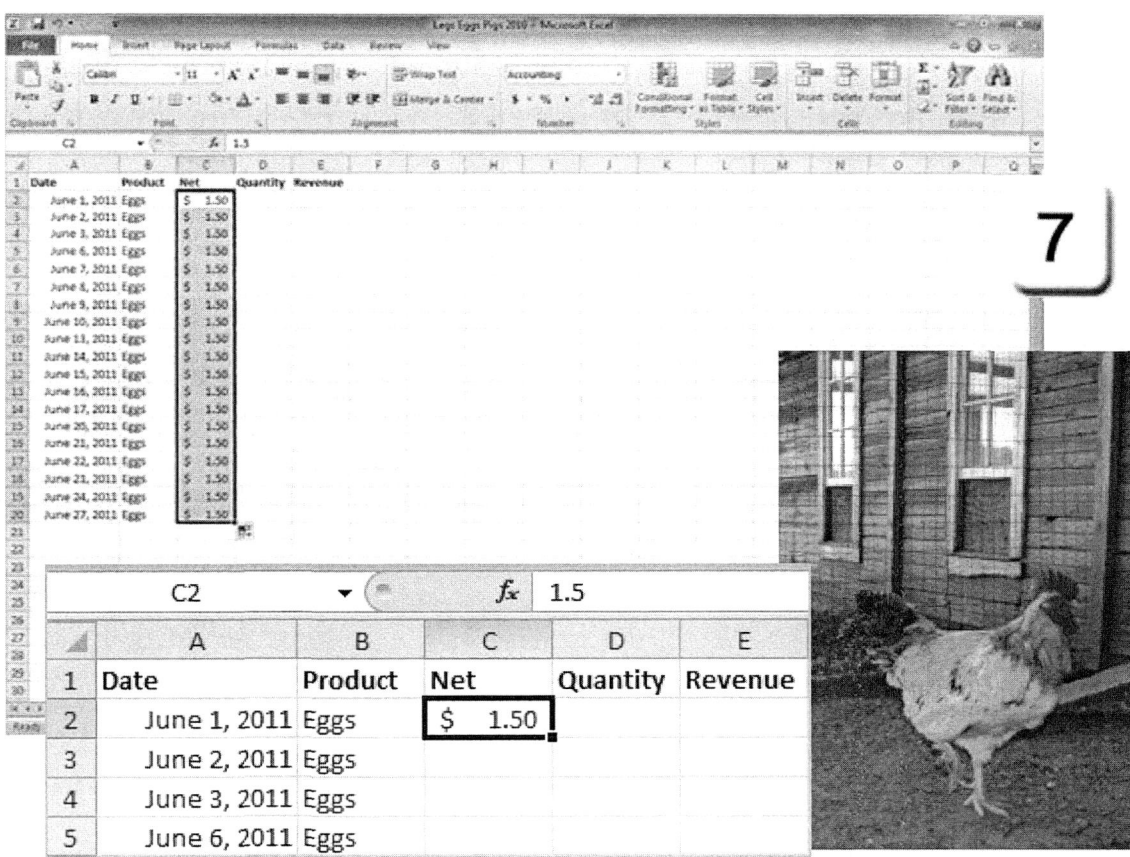

Edit and Format the Money

Say the net profit on a dozen eggs is $1.50 after shipping and handling. Pretend these are gourmet eggs, sold on the Internet. You don't need to type the dollar sign. We're going to format the Column for currency.

7. Try This: Enter the Data
Select Cell C2 and type: 1.50.

Try This, Too: Format the Cells
Select Column C.
Go to **Home->Number.**
Select **Accounting** (dollar sign) in the Number group. Excel formats Cells so the dollars and cents line up.

And Try This: AutoFill the Data
Select Cell C3 and AutoFill the $1.50 by double clicking on the little black handle.

What Do You See? The money should be copied all the way down to Cell C20.

	A	B	C	D	E
1	Date	Product	Net	Quantity	Revenue
2	June 1, 2011	Eggs	$ 1.50		
3	June 2, 2011	Eggs			
4	June 3, 2011	Eggs			
5	June 6, 2011	Eggs			

Exam 77-882: Microsoft Excel 2010 Core
3. Formatting Cells and Worksheets
3.1. Apply and modify cell formats: Apply number formats

AutoFill a Series

This little web site sells about 100 egg baskets a day. Suppose we sold another 5 baskets every day. What would the sales revenue be?

8. Try This: Enter the Data
In Cell D2 type 100.
In Cell D3 type 105.

And Do This: AutoFill a Series
Select Cell D2 AND D3: both the 100 and the 105. Now you have selected enough of a **Range** for Excel to recognize that this is a **Series**, incrementing by 5s.

Double click the **AutoFill** handle and the **Series** will fill down to match Column C on the left.

What Do You See? When you **AutoFill** this Series, Microsoft Excel adds 5 more to the quantity in each Row.

AutoFill Options

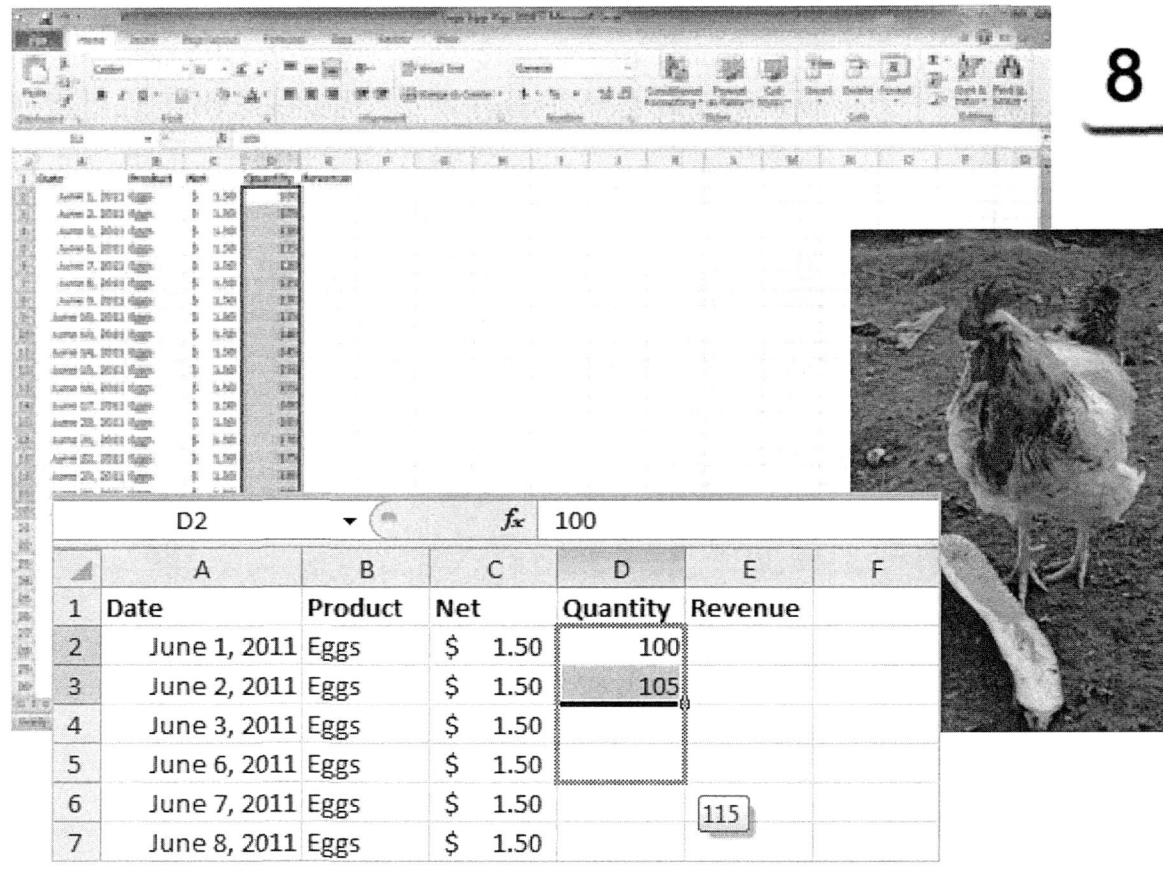

	A	B	C	D	E	F
1	Date	Product	Net	Quantity	Revenue	
2	June 1, 2011	Eggs	$ 1.50	100		
3	June 2, 2011	Eggs	$ 1.50	105		
4	June 3, 2011	Eggs	$ 1.50			
5	June 6, 2011	Eggs	$ 1.50			
6	June 7, 2011	Eggs	$ 1.50		115	
7	June 8, 2011	Eggs	$ 1.50			

Exam 77-882: Microsoft Excel 2010 Core
2. Creating Cell Data
2.2. Apply AutoFill: AutoFill a Series

Calculate Revenue

Labels and Data. Now all we need are the formulas. Think about the math: revenue equals net times quantity.

9. Try This: Create a Formula

Select Cell E2 and type in the equal sign. All good equations begin with "=."
Select Cell C2—the Net is $1.50.
Type the times symbol (the asterisk key).
Select Cell D2—the Quantity is 100.

The completed equation is =C2*D2

Hit the **Enter** key on your keyboard. Excel won't calculate until you leave the Cell.

What Do You See? There it is. $1.50 times 100 equals $150.00. OK, go to Cell E2 and double click on the **AutoFill** handle to fill in the equations.

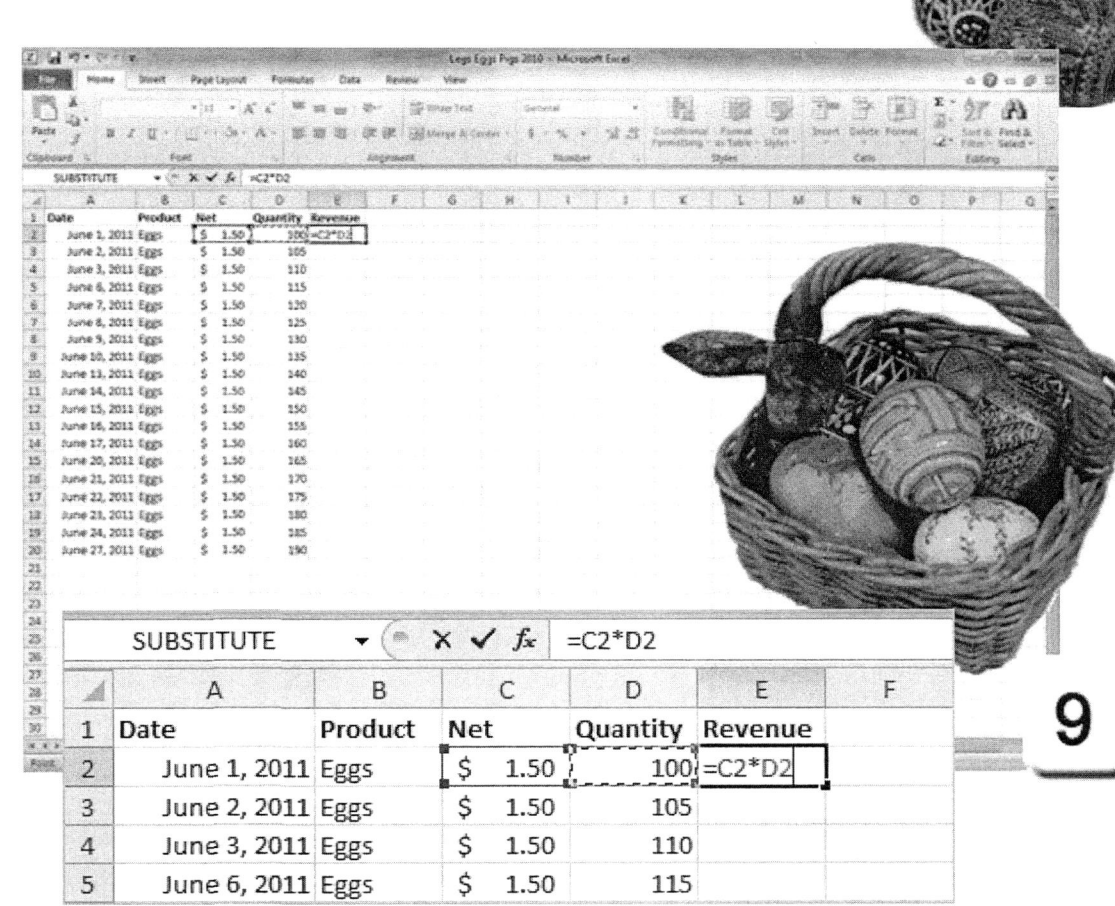

Take One

AutoSum the Total Sales

What is the sum of all the products sold? Here are the steps to calculate the total sales.

Try it: AutoSum the Revenue
Select Cell E21
Go to **Home ->Editing->AutoSum.**

Excel will enter the formula:
=SUM(E2:E20)

Click ENTER on your keyboard.

What Do You See? In the example on this page the Sum is $4,132.50.

Home ->Editing->AutoSum

	A	B	C	D	E	F	G
1	Date	Product	Net	Quantity	Revenue		
2	June 1, 2011	Eggs	$ 1.50	100	$ 150.00		
3	June 2, 2011	Eggs	$ 1.50	105	$ 157.50		
4	June 3, 2011	Eggs	$ 1.50	110	$ 165.00		
5	June 6, 2011	Eggs	$ 1.50	115	$ 172.50		
6	June 7, 2011	Eggs	$ 1.50	120	$ 180.00		
7	June 8, 2011	Eggs	$ 1.50	125	$ 187.50		
8	June 9, 2011	Eggs	$ 1.50	130	$ 195.00		
9	June 10, 2011	Eggs	$ 1.50	135	$ 202.50		
10	June 13, 2011	Eggs	$ 1.50	140	$ 210.00		
11	June 14, 2011	Eggs	$ 1.50	145	$ 217.50		
12	June 15, 2011	Eggs	$ 1.50	150	$ 225.00		
13	June 16, 2011	Eggs	$ 1.50	155	$ 232.50		

18	June 23, 2011	Eggs	$ 1.50	180	$ 270.00
19	June 24, 2011	Eggs	$ 1.50	185	$ 277.50
20	June 27, 2011	Eggs	$ 1.50	190	$ 285.00
21					=SUM(E2:E20)
22					SUM(**number1**, [number2], ...)
23					

18	June 23, 2011	Eggs	$ 1.50	180	$ 270.00
19	June 24, 2011	Eggs	$ 1.50	185	$ 277.50
20	June 27, 2011	Eggs	$ 1.50	190	$ 285.00
21					$4,132.50
22					

Exam 77-882: Microsoft Excel 2010 Core
5. Applying Formulas and Functions
5.1. Create formulas: Use SUM, COUNT, COUNTA, AVERAGE, MIN, and MAX

Copy the Spreadsheet

OK, that takes care of the eggs. Let's name the spreadsheet and move on.

1. Rename the Spreadsheet
Double click the Sheet1 tab.
Type: Eggs

2. Copy the Spreadsheet
Right mouse click the "Eggs" label.
Select **Move or Copy.**

3. Check Create a copy.

4. What Do You See? There should be a new sheet called Eggs (2).

Memo to Self: This method copied everything: labels, data, and formulas. Saves time, doesn't it?

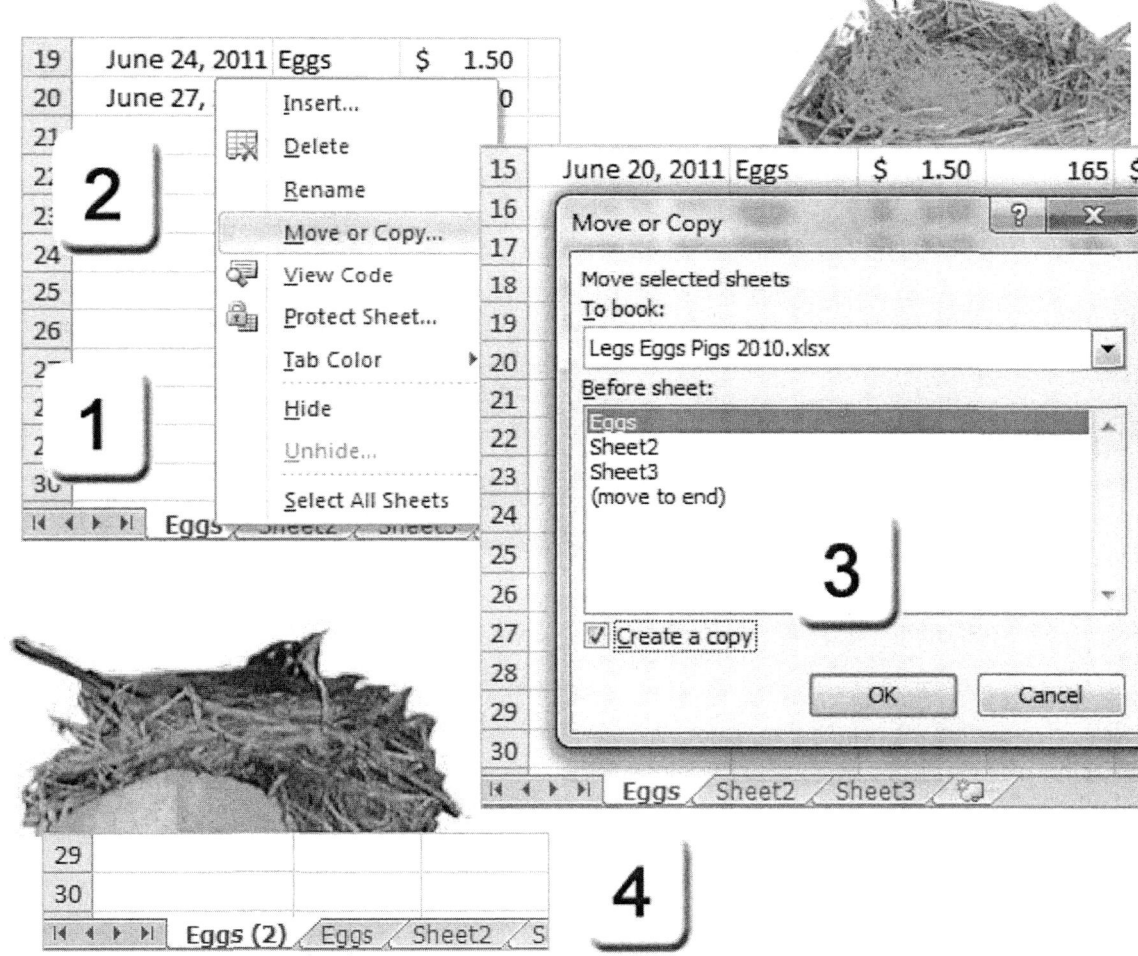

Exam 77-882: Microsoft Excel 2010 Core
4. Managing Worksheets and Workbooks
4.1. Create and format worksheets: Copy a worksheet

Change the Variables
Next Step: Change a few variables, please.

Rename the Spreadsheet
Double click on the tab for Eggs (2).
Rename this spreadsheet: Legs.

Update the product data
Go to Cell B2 and change Eggs to Legs.
AutoFill Cell B2 to the bottom of Column B.

Change the Net
The net for chicken legs is 3.25.
Enter that amount and AutoFill.

Change the Quantity
The quantity starts at 50 and adds 5 per day.
In Cell D2 type: 50.
In Cell D3 type: 55.
Select D2 and D3 and AutoFill.

The work on the Pig's page is similar. Copy the Eggs sheet. Rename the new Eggs(2) sheet to Pigs. Change the product to Pigs. The Net is 4.75 and the quantity starts at 200 but only adds one more per day.

	A	B	C	D	E	F
1	Date	Product	Net	Quantity	Revenue	
2	June 1, 2011	Legs	$ 3.25	50	$ 162.50	
3	June 2, 2011	Legs	$ 3.25	55	$ 178.75	
4	June 3, 2011	Legs	$ 3.25	60	$ 195.00	
5	June 6, 2011	Legs	$ 3.25	65	$ 211.25	

	A	B	C	D	E	F
1	Date	Product	Net	Quantity	Revenue	
2	June 1, 2011	Pigs	$ 4.75	200	$ 950.00	
3	June 2, 2011	Pigs	$ 4.75	201	$ 954.75	
4	June 3, 2011	Pigs	$ 4.75	202	$ 959.50	
5	June 6, 2011	Pigs	$ 4.75	203	$ 964.25	

HOME

AutoFit the Columns

What Do You See? Column E may display #####. Why are there pound signs? That's Excel's way of saying that the column is too narrow.

The Computer Mama sez that means you have too much money.

Try it: Format the Column Width
Select Column E.
Go to **Home->Cells_> Format**.
Select **AutoFit Column Width**.

Here's another way:
Place your cursor between the E and F Column header—right on the line. Your cursor will change from a white plus sign to a black double-headed arrow. Double click and Column E will be resized as wide as it needs to be.

Home ->Cells ->Format ->AutoFit Column Width

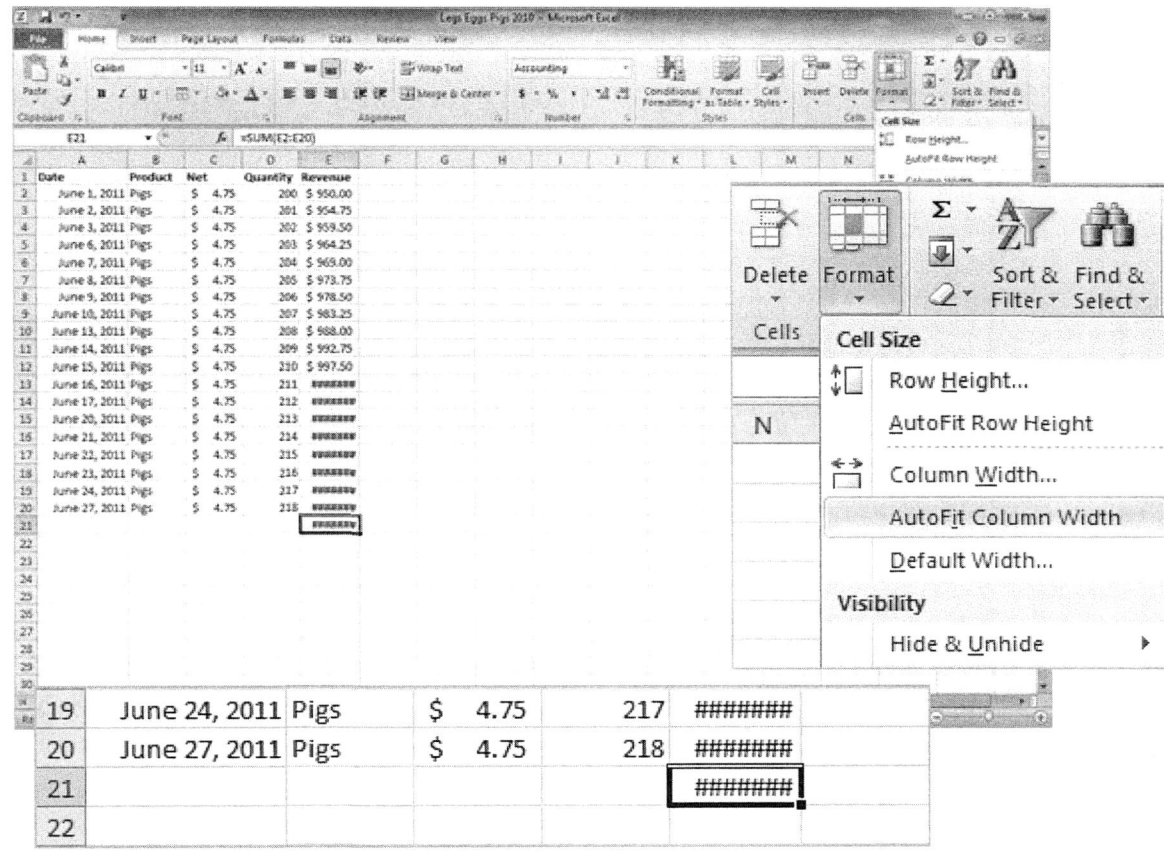

Exam 77-882: Microsoft Excel 2010 Core
4. Managing Worksheets and Workbooks
4.1. Create and format worksheets: AutoFit Column Width

Create a Summary Sheet

1. Make a copy of the "Eggs" spreadsheet
Right Click the Eggs Tab.
Select **Move or Copy.**
When the little Options window pops up,
Check to Create a copy.

2. Rename the Spreadsheet
Double click the tab.
Type: Summary

3. Edit the Data
Select Cell B2 and type: All Products.
AutoFill Cell B2.

Keep going, please...

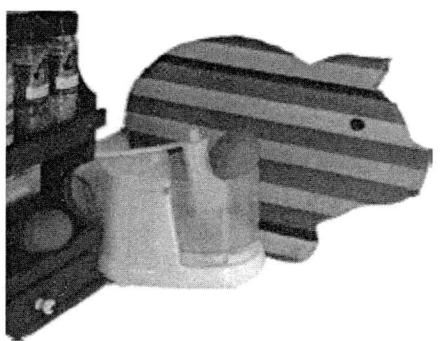

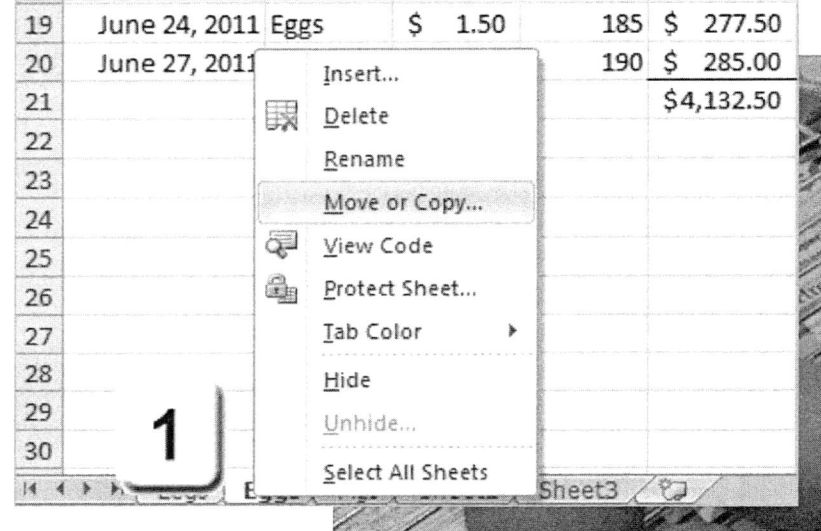

1

19	June 24, 2011	Eggs	$	1.50	185	$	277.50
20	June 27, 2011				190	$	285.00
21							$4,132.50
22							
23							
24							
25							
26							
27							
28							
29							
30							

Context menu:
Insert...
Delete
Rename
Move or Copy...
View Code
Protect Sheet...
Tab Color ▶
Hide
Unhide...
Select All Sheets

2

| 29 | | | | |
| 30 | | | | |

Summary / Legs / Eggs / Pigs / Sheet2 / Sheet3

3

1	Date	Product	Net		Quantity	Revenue
2	June 1, 2011	All Products	$	1.50	100	$ 150.00
3	June 2, 2011	All Products	$	1.50	105	$ 157.50

Exam 77-882: Microsoft Excel 2010 Core
4. Managing Worksheets and Workbooks
4.1. Create and format worksheets: Copy and Rename Worksheets

Create a Summary Sheet, Continued

4. Delete Column C and D

Select Column C and D.

Go to **Home->Cells->Delete**.

Click on **Delete Sheet Columns**.

What Do You See? The equations in the Revenue column now read: #REF!. The equation doesn't have the data for Net and Quantity anymore. It has nothing to reference, hence the error message.

Go ahead: select those cells and hit the delete key to clear the busted equations.

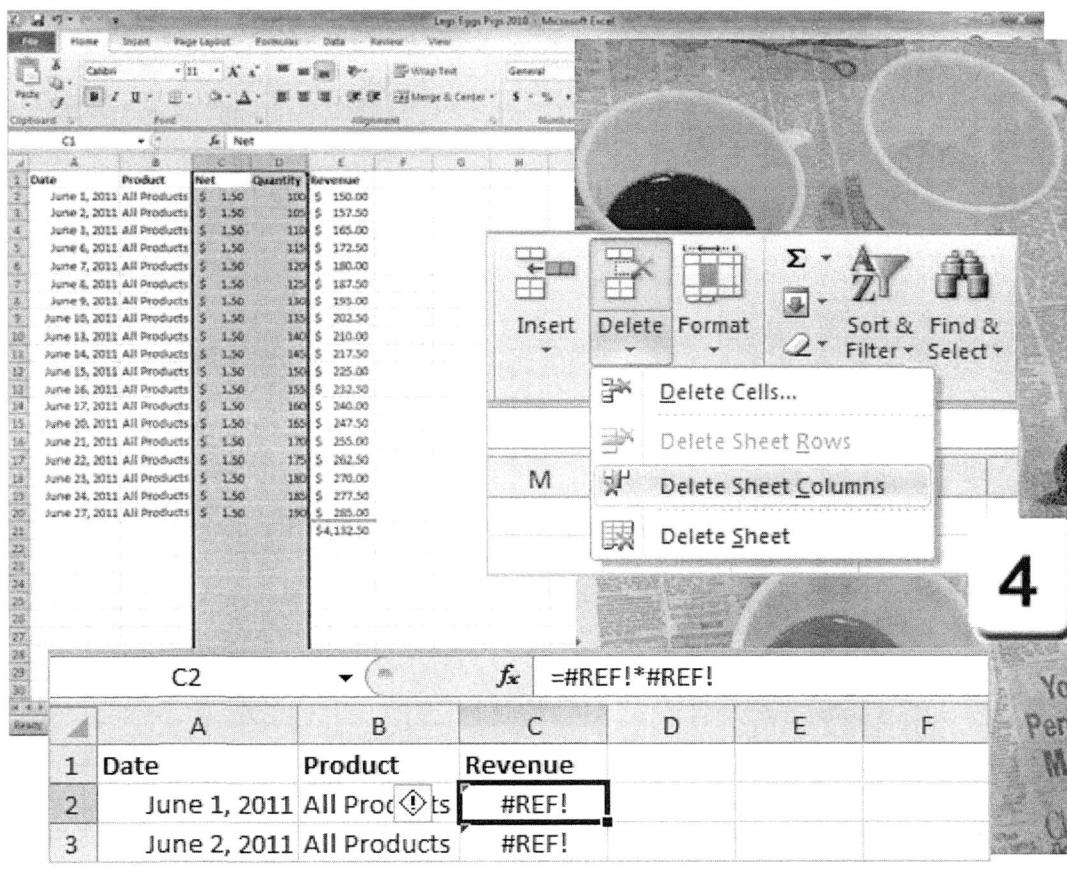

Exam 77-882: Microsoft Excel 2010 Core
5. Applying Formulas and Functions
5.3. Apply cell references in formulas: Troubleshoot a formula

The Grand Total
This equation will link the Summary sheet to each of the product sheets: Legs, Eggs, and Pigs.

Try it: Create reference links
1. Start on the **Summary** Sheet
Select Cell C2 type: =.
All good equations begin with "="

2. Go to the **Legs** sheet
Select Cell E2.
Type + (to add the next variable)

3. Go to the **Eggs** sheet
Select Cell E2.
Type + (to add the next variable)

Keep going, please...

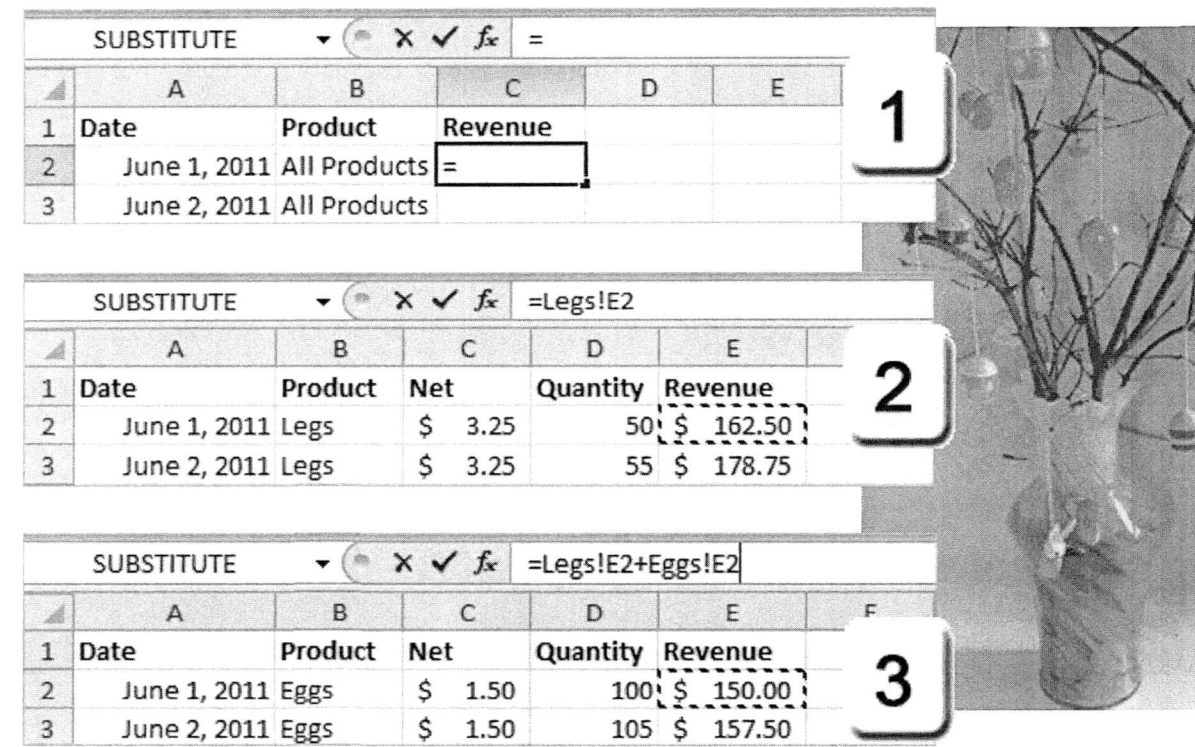

1

SUBSTITUTE	▼	× ✓ fx	=	
	A	B	C	D	E
1	Date	Product	Revenue		
2	June 1, 2011	All Products	=		
3	June 2, 2011	All Products			

2

SUBSTITUTE	▼	× ✓ fx	=Legs!E2	
	A	B	C	D	E
1	Date	Product	Net	Quantity	Revenue
2	June 1, 2011	Legs	$ 3.25	50	$ 162.50
3	June 2, 2011	Legs	$ 3.25	55	$ 178.75

3

SUBSTITUTE	▼	× ✓ fx	=Legs!E2+Eggs!E2	
	A	B	C	D	E	F
1	Date	Product	Net	Quantity	Revenue	
2	June 1, 2011	Eggs	$ 1.50	100	$ 150.00	
3	June 2, 2011	Eggs	$ 1.50	105	$ 157.50	

Exam 77-882: Microsoft Excel 2010 Core
5. Applying Formulas and Functions
5.3. Apply cell references in formulas: Reference data from other worksheets or workbooks

The Grand Total

4. Lastly, go to the **Pigs** sheet
Select Cell E2
Hit Enter on your keyboard...

5. You will be taken back to Cell C2 in the Summary spreadsheet.

6. **AutoFill** this equation and you've got a formula that adds all of the sales for each product. Well done.

What Do You See? The formula says:
=Spreadsheet!Cell
where Legs, Eggs, and Pigs are the names of our spreadsheets.

| SUBSTITUTE | ▾ | ✗ ✓ ƒx | =Legs!E2+Eggs!E2+Pigs!E2 |

	A	B	C	D	E	F
1	Date	Product	Net	Quantity	Revenue	
2	June 1, 2011	Pigs	$ 4.75	200	$ 950.00	
3	June 2, 2011	Pigs	$ 4.75	201	$ 954.75	

4

| C2 | ▾ | | ƒx | =Legs!E2+Eggs!E2+Pigs!E2 |

	A	B	C	D	E	F
1	Date	Product	Revenue			
2	June 1, 2011	All Products	$ 1,262.50			
3	June 2, 2011	All Products	$ 1,291.00			

5

18	June 23, 2011	All Products	$ 1,718.50
19	June 24, 2011	All Products	$ 1,747.00
20	June 27, 2011	All Products	$ 1,775.50
21			$ 28,861.00

6

|◄ ◄ ► ►| **Summary** / Legs / Eggs / Pigs / Sheet2 / Sheet3 / ⬚⤶

Exam 77-882: Microsoft Excel 2010 Core
5. Applying Formulas and Functions
5.3. Apply cell references in formulas: Reference data from other worksheets or workbooks

Cell References

When you created the sales spreadsheet, you selected a **range of cells** to **AutoFill**. If we put 100 for the quantity in the first cell and 105 in the next, Excel fills down the series and add 5 more to each cell. If you wanted a different forecast you could enter new quantities in the first and second cells and use the AutoFill again.

This could get old very fast. It is also a rather inflexible method of changing the data.
There is a better method: **reference cells**.

Reference cells set up one place to enter the data. All of the other equations and spreadsheets that depend on that data look it up in the reference cells.

D2		▾	f_x	100		
	A	B	C	D	E	F
1	Date	Product	Net	Quantity	Revenue	
2	June 1, 2011	Eggs	$ 1.50	100		
3	June 2, 2011	Eggs	$ 1.50	105		
4	June 3, 2011	Eggs	$ 1.50			
5	June 6, 2011	Eggs	$ 1.50			
6	June 7, 2011	Eggs	$ 1.50		115	
7	June 8, 2011	Eggs	$ 1.50			

Exam 77-882: Microsoft Excel 2010 Core
5. Applying Formulas and Functions
5.3. Apply cell references in formulas

Create the Reference Cells

Before You Begin: Go to the Pigs sheet. Please select Row 1 and **Insert** four more **Rows**. This will give us room to work.

1. Try This: Enter the Labels and Data
In Cell A1 type: Price
In Cell A2 type: Start
In Cell A3 type: Increment

In Cell B1 type: 3.25.
Format Cell B1 for Accounting.
Keep going, please..

Memo to Self: This lesson continues with the Legs Eggs and Pigs spreadsheet:
Legs Eggs and Pigs.xlsx

Home->Cells ->Insert

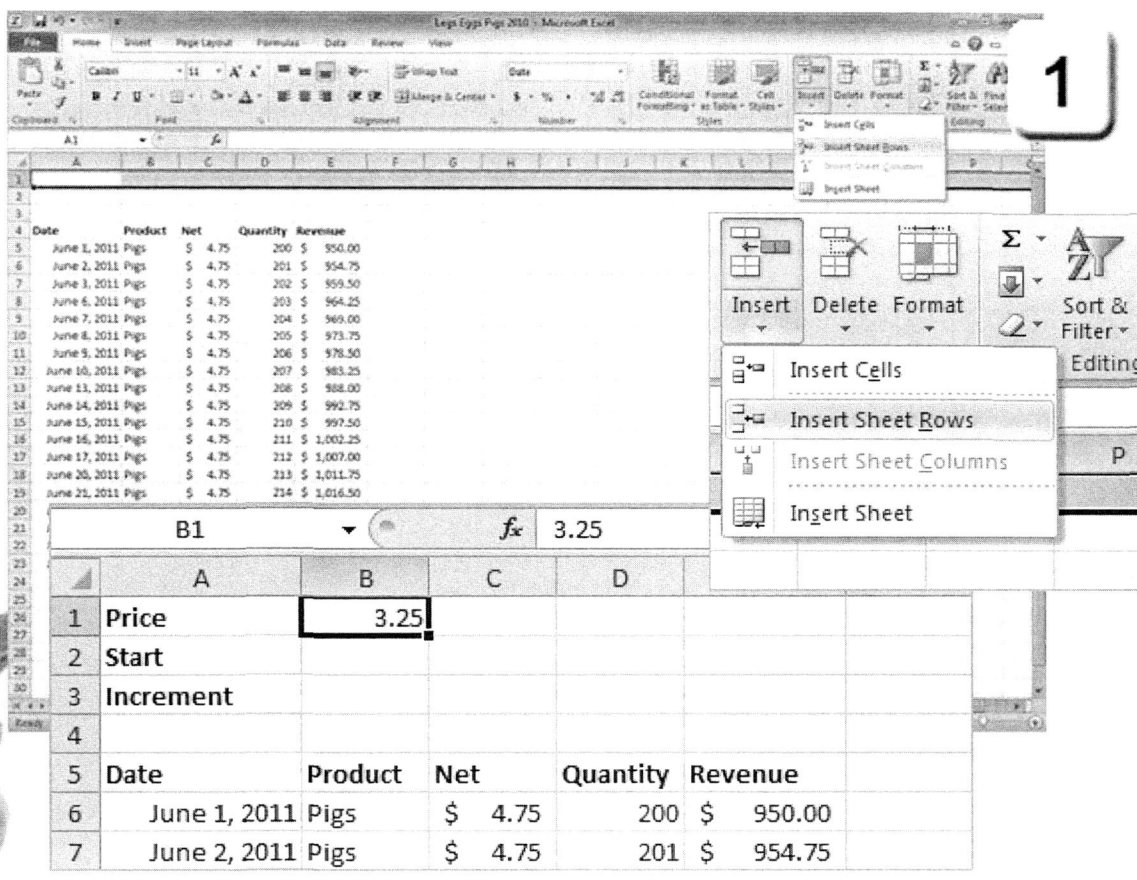

Exam 77-882: Microsoft Excel 2010 Core
5. Applying Formulas and Functions
5.3. Apply cell references in formulas

HOME

Take One

Create a Relative Reference

2. Try This, Too: Create a Relative Reference
All good equations begin with "equals."
Select Cell C6 and type: =
Click on Cell B1.
Type: ENTER on the keyboard.

What Do You See? The formula in Cell C6 says that C6 equals B1. If you change the number in Cell B1, it should automatically update in Cell C6.

Test Your Formula: Change the Data
Select Cell B1 and type: 4.75
Type: ENTER on the keyboard.
Select Cell B1 and type: 3.25
Type: ENTER on the keyboard.

What Else Do You See? The number in Cell C6 should update as soon as you hit the ENTER key.

The other Cells in Column C will NOT update at this time: those Cells do not have a formula, yet.

Keep going...

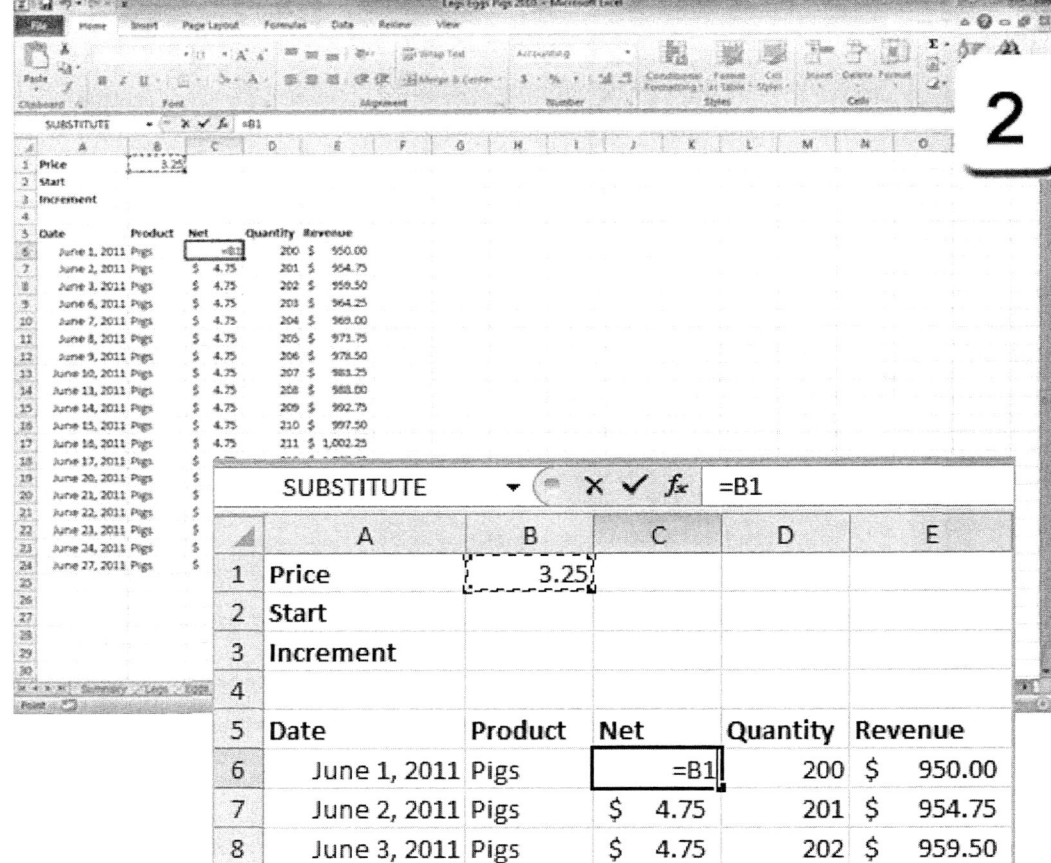

Exam 77-882: Microsoft Excel 2010 Core
5. Applying Formulas and Functions
5.3. Apply cell references in formulas: Relative Cell References

Autofill a Relative Reference

In the previous page we created an equation in Cell C6 and tested it. Please **Autofill** that equation to all of the dates in Column C.

3. Try This: Autofill a Relative Reference
Select Cell C6. Double Click the **AutoFill** handle in the lower right corner of the Cell.

What Do You See? The formula in Cell C6 will be copied to all of the dates in Column C. However, instead of copying $3.25, the price in Cell B1, Cell C10 says "Product" and Cell C11 says "Pigs."

What Else Do You See? The numbers in Column E also indicate a problem. The first equation in Cell E6 calculates correctly.

#VALUE means the data doesn't make any sense: there may be a **mismatch**. In this example, Excel can't multiply Pigs*205 (**Text** times a **Number**).

Keep going...

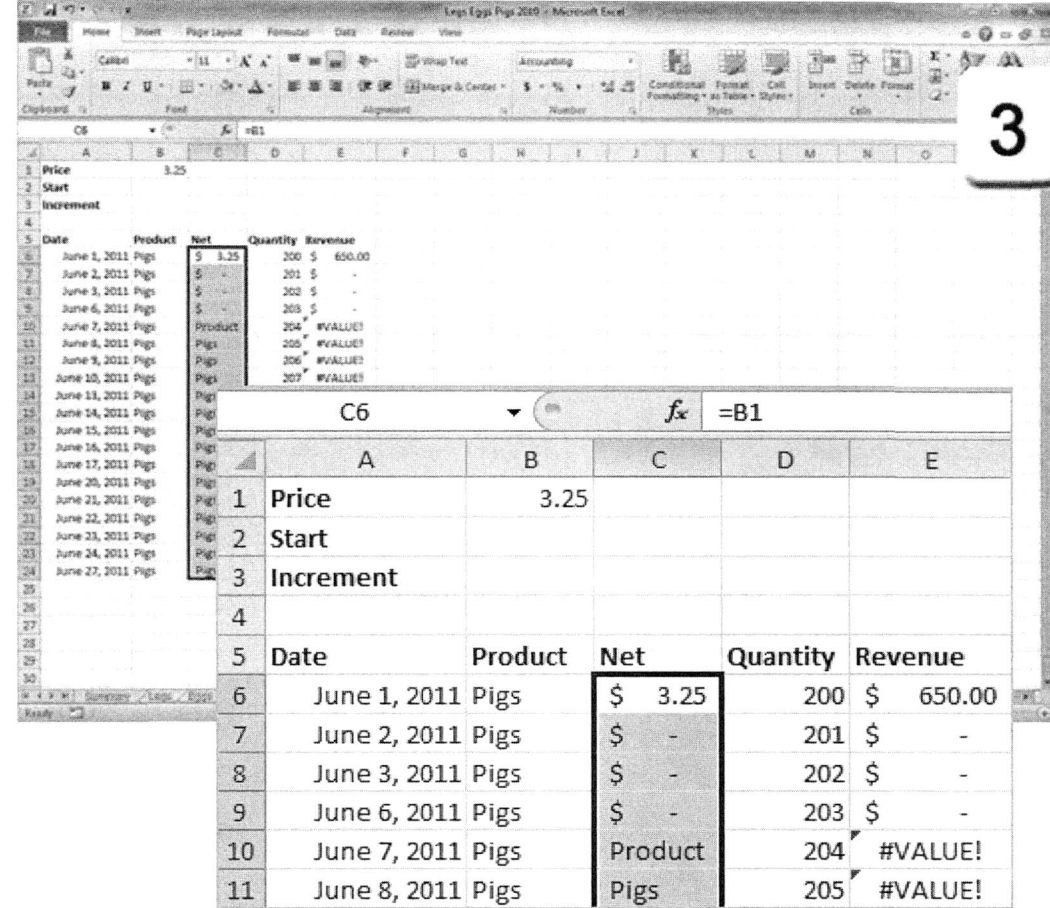

Exam 77-882: Microsoft Excel 2010 Core
5. Applying Formulas and Functions
5.3. Apply cell references in formulas: Relative Cell References

Review the Relative References

You can double click any Cell that has a formula and see an outline of the Cell (s) that are used in that equation.

Let's **audit** this spreadsheet.

4. Try This: Audit a Relative Reference
Double Click Cell C6. You should see the formula displayed in the Formula Bar at the top of the spreadsheet. Cell B1 is outlined in Blue.

Double Click Cell C10. Cell B5 is outlined.

What Does That Mean? The formula in Cell C6 was =B1. Instead of copying $3.25, the formula (=B1) was AutoFilled.

What Else Do You See? When the formula in Cell C6 was AutoFilled, the Cell Reference was updated for each Row.

This is an example of a **Relative Cell Reference**. It is Relative because it was updated for each Row.

Keep going...

SUBSTITUTE	▾	✕ ✓ ƒx	=B1	

	A	B	C	D	E
1	Price	3.25			
2	Start				
3	Increment				
4					
5	Date	Product	Net	Quantity	Revenue
6	June 1, 2011	Pigs	=B1	200	$ 650.00
7	June 2, 2011	Pigs	$ -	201	$ -

SUBSTITUTE	▾	✕ ✓ ƒx	=B5	

	A	B	C	D	E
1	Price	3.25			
2	Start				
3	Increment				
4					
5	Date	Product	Net	Quantity	Revenue
6	June 1, 2011	Pigs	$ 3.25	200	$ 650.00
7	June 2, 2011	Pigs	$ -	201	$ -
8	June 3, 2011	Pigs	$ -	202	$ -
9	June 6, 2011	Pigs	$ -	203	$ -
10	June 7, 2011	Pigs	=B5	204	#VALUE!
11	June 8, 2011	Pigs	Pigs	205	#VALUE!

Exam 77-882: Microsoft Excel 2010 Core
5. Applying Formulas and Functions
5.3. Apply cell references in formulas: Relative Cell References

Create an Absolute Reference

There is another way to manage copying formulas so that they point to the right data.

An **Absolute Reference** is defined an a specific Row or Column. The Absolute Reference will NOT update if it is copied to another Row with Autofill.

5. Try This: Create an Absolute Reference
Select Cell C6.
Click your cursor in the Formula Bar on B1.
On your keyboard, click on F4.

What Do You See? The formula in Cell C6 is now: =$B$1, where the dollar $ sign means that it is Absolute.

Try This Too: AutoFill the Absolute Reference
Select Cell C6.
Double click the Autofill handle.

It looks like it worked this time.

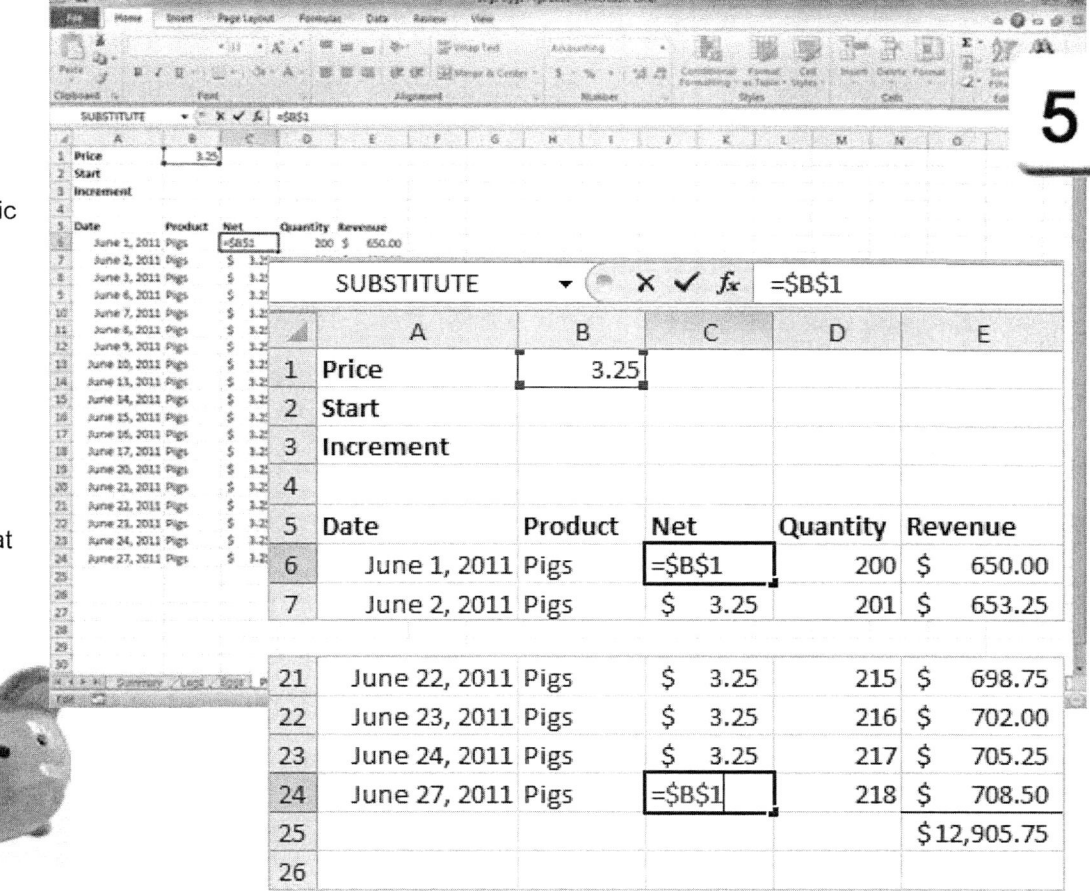

	A	B	C	D	E
1	Price	3.25			
2	Start				
3	Increment				
4					
5	Date	Product	Net	Quantity	Revenue
6	June 1, 2011	Pigs	=$B$1	200	$ 650.00
7	June 2, 2011	Pigs	$ 3.25	201	$ 653.25
21	June 22, 2011	Pigs	$ 3.25	215	$ 698.75
22	June 23, 2011	Pigs	$ 3.25	216	$ 702.00
23	June 24, 2011	Pigs	$ 3.25	217	$ 705.25
24	June 27, 2011	Pigs	=$B$1	218	$ 708.50
25					$12,905.75
26					

Exam 77-882: Microsoft Excel 2010 Core
5. Applying Formulas and Functions
5.3. Apply cell references in formulas: Absolute Cell References

Using Reference Cells

The next task is to calculate the daily sales. In this example, we will make one Cell Reference in the formula Relative and the other Absolute.

Before You Begin: Edit the Data
In Cell B2 type: 100
In Cell B3 type: 5

Thoughts to Consider
Cell D6 is the initial quantity sold.
Cell D7 should be whatever we sold on the first day, plus the quantity we are forecasting for each day's sales increment.

6. Try it: Create the Formulas
Select Cell D6 and enter this equation:
=B2

Select Cell D7, and enter this equation:
=D6 +B3

Try This, Too: AutoFill the Formula
Select **Cell D7** and double click the **AutoFill** handle to fill down the formula. Keep going...

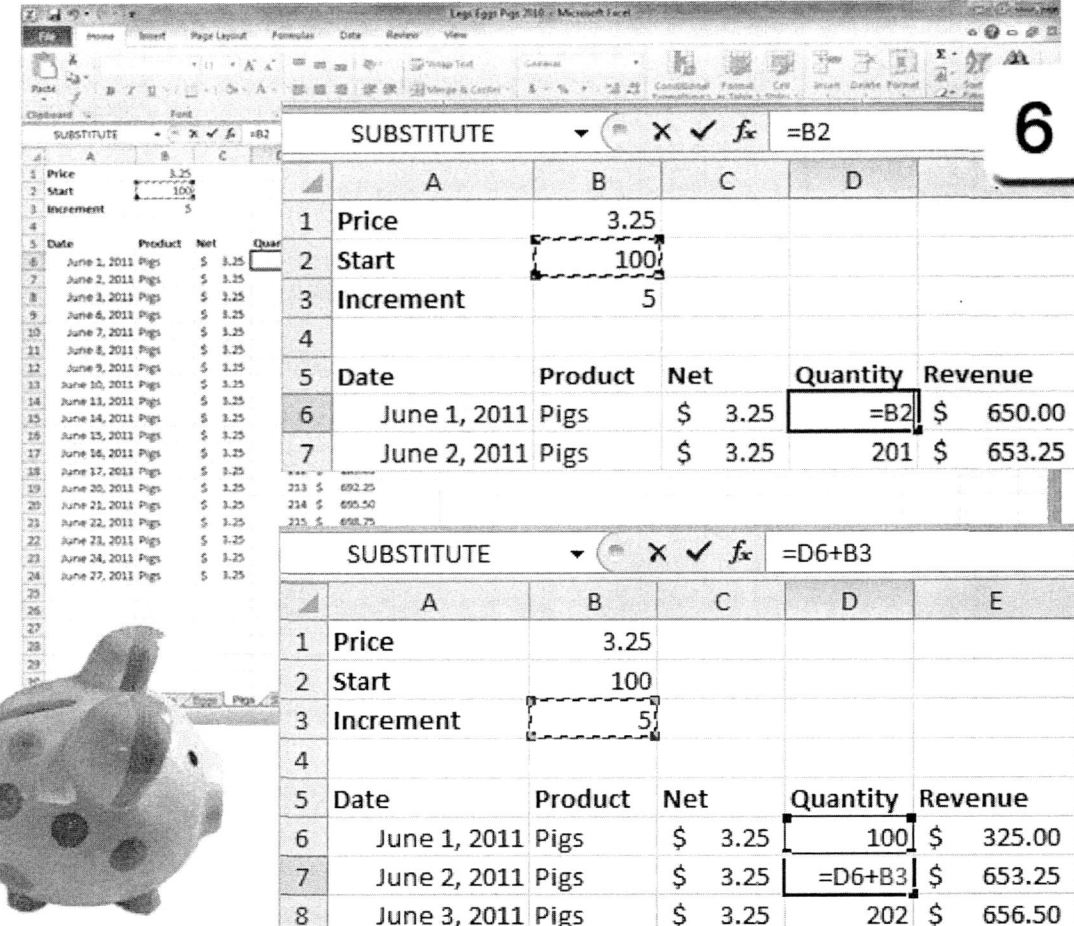

6

	A	B	C	D	
1	Price	3.25			
2	Start	100			
3	Increment	5			
4					
5	Date	Product	Net	Quantity	Revenue
6	June 1, 2011	Pigs	$ 3.25	=B2	$ 650.00
7	June 2, 2011	Pigs	$ 3.25	201	$ 653.25

SUBSTITUTE =B2

SUBSTITUTE =D6+B3

	A	B	C	D	E
1	Price	3.25			
2	Start	100			
3	Increment	5			
4					
5	Date	Product	Net	Quantity	Revenue
6	June 1, 2011	Pigs	$ 3.25	100	$ 325.00
7	June 2, 2011	Pigs	$ 3.25	=D6+B3	$ 653.25
8	June 3, 2011	Pigs	$ 3.25	202	$ 656.50

Exam 77-882: Microsoft Excel 2010 Core
5. Applying Formulas and Functions
5.3. Apply cell references in formulas: Using Relative and Absolute Cell References

Troubleshoot the Formulas

What Do You See? The **#Value!** means that there is an error. Please audit the spreadsheet. Double click on **Cell D9.** Excel highlights the cells in this formula: =D8+B5

How Did That Happen? Part of the formula is still correct. It equals yesterday's sales—the Cell above me—and adds to it.

Most formulas automatically use **Relative References**. A Relative Reference adjusts the the cell references when you copy or fill it down.

In our example, **=D8+B5** becomes **=D9+B6** in the next Row down.

In **Cell D9**, the formula adds a number to a label. Hence, the error **#Value!**

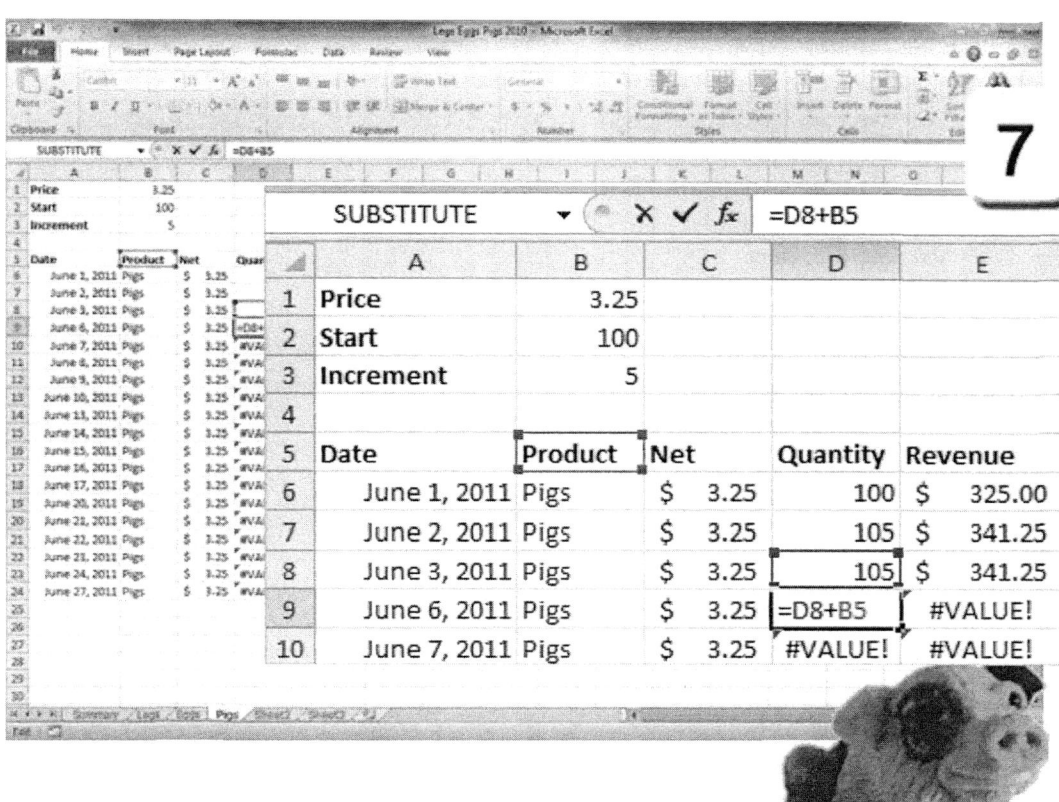

	A	B	C	D	E
	SUBSTITUTE		X ✓ *fx*	=D8+B5	
1	Price	3.25			
2	Start	100			
3	Increment	5			
4					
5	Date	Product	Net	Quantity	Revenue
6	June 1, 2011	Pigs	$ 3.25	100	$ 325.00
7	June 2, 2011	Pigs	$ 3.25	105	$ 341.25
8	June 3, 2011	Pigs	$ 3.25	105	$ 341.25
9	June 6, 2011	Pigs	$ 3.25	=D8+B5	#VALUE!
10	June 7, 2011	Pigs	$ 3.25	#VALUE!	#VALUE!

Exam 77-882: Microsoft Excel 2010 Core
5. Applying Formulas and Functions
5.3. Apply cell references in formulas: Troubleshoot a formula

Absolute References

When you need to work with one particular cell you need an **Absolute Reference**.

Try it: Create an Absolute Reference
Select **Cell D7**.
The Formula bar shows =D6+B3.
Go to the Formula Bar and click on B3.
Click the **F4 function key** on the top row of the keyboard.

What Do You See? The cell reference becomes $B$3. This means "go to B3 only, and no place else," to get the data.

Try This, Too: AutoFill the Formula
Select **Cell D7** and **AutoFill** the revised equation to the rest of the rows.

A **Mixed Reference** uses Absolute and Relative cell references.

SUBSTITUTE ▼ X ✔ fx =D6+$B$3

	A	B	C	D	E
1	Price	3.25			
2	Start	100			
3	Increment	5			
4					
5	Date	Product	Net	Quantity	Revenue
6	June 1, 2011	Pigs	$ 3.25	100	$ 325.00
7	June 2, 2011	Pigs	$ 3.25	=D6+$B$3	$ 341.25
8	June 3, 2011	Pigs	$ 3.25	105	$ 341.25
9	June 6, 2011	Pigs	$ 3.25	#VALUE!	#VALUE!

Exam 77-882: Microsoft Excel 2010 Core
5. Applying Formulas and Functions
5.3. Apply cell references in formulas: Use Absolute and Relative cell references

Audit Your Work

You can double click on a cell to **trace** the references in the formula. Here is a better way to audit your spreadsheet.

Try This: Trace the Dependants
Select Cell B3.
Go to **Formulas->Formula Auditing.**
Click on **Trace Dependents**.

What Do You See? There are some useful tools for **Formula Auditing:**

Trace Precedents
Finds the cells that have an affect on the cell you selected

Trace Dependents
Locates the formulas that use this cell in their equations

Remove Arrows

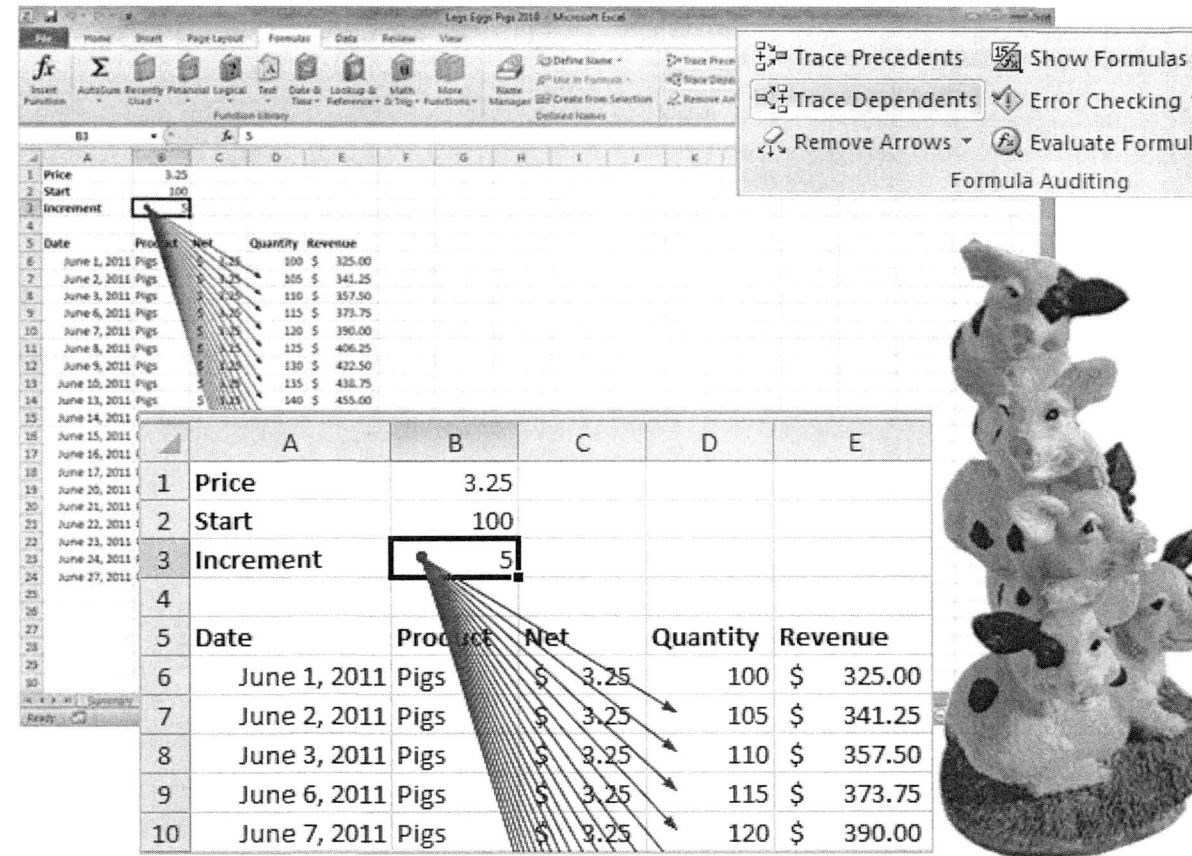

Exam 77-888: Microsoft Excel Expert 2010
2. Applying Formulas and Functions
2.1. Audit formulas: Trace Dependents

HOME

Formula Auditing

Try it: Trace Precedents
Select Cell E25.
Go to **Formulas->Formula Auditing.**
Click **Trace Precedents.** You will see an arrow from Cell E25 to Cell E6.

Click **Trace Precedents** again.
You should see arrows in each Row that trace the formulas.

Click **Trace Precedents** a third time.
You will see a call out to each variable in Cells B1, B2 and B3.

Please click on Remove Arrows to take off the tracings.

Formulas -> Formula Auditing->Trace Precedents

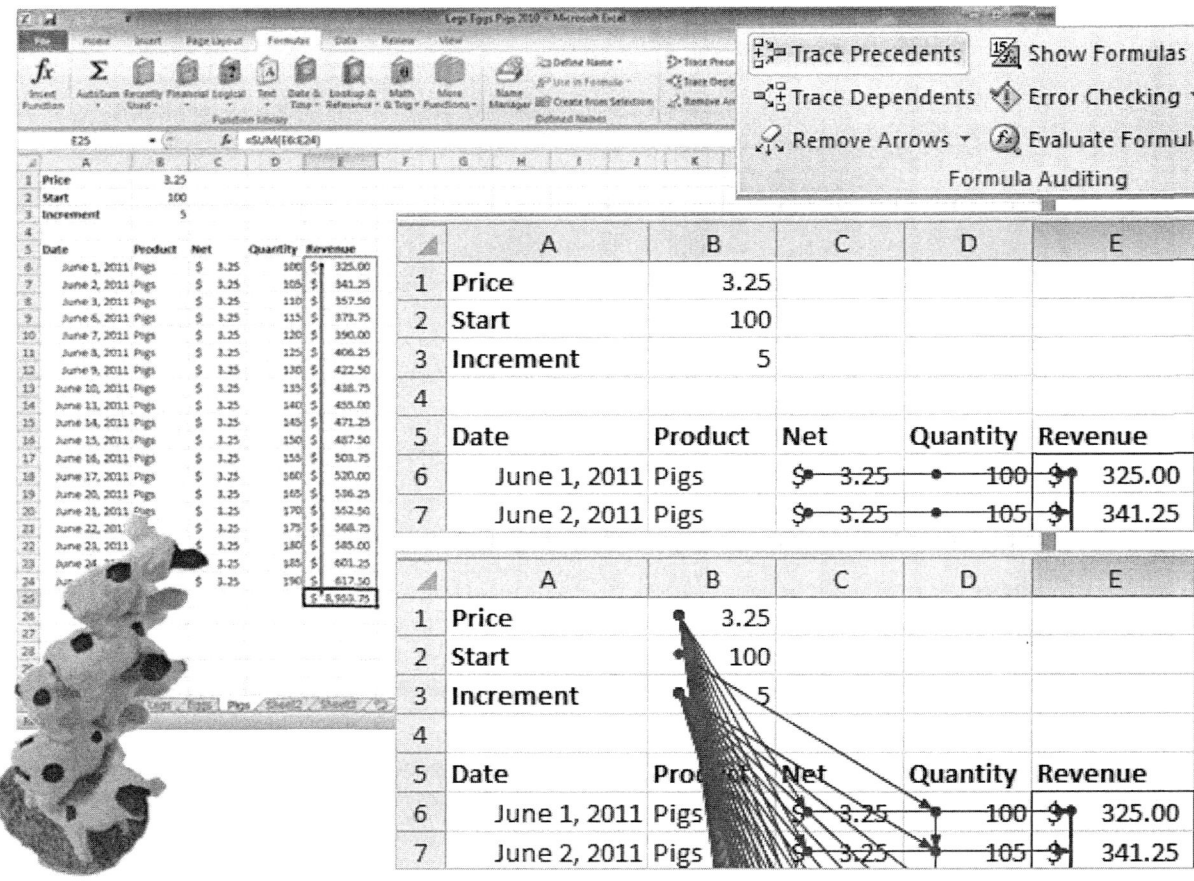

Exam 77-888: Microsoft Excel Expert 2010
2. Applying Formulas and Functions
2.1. Audit formulas: Trace Precedents

Tracing Errors
What Does an Error Look Like? Here is a simple example we can try.

Before You Begin: Setup a Mistake
Select **Cell E8** and type: 360
Now Cell E8 does NOT have a formula. Yet, how would you know?

Try This: Trace the Precedents
Select Cell E25.
Go to **Formulas->Formula Auditing**.
Click **Trace Precedents.** You will see an arrow from Cell E25 to Cell E6.

Click **Trace Precedents** again.

What Do You See? You should see arrows in each Row that trace the formulas. You should see a "gap" in the tracings. This gap indicates that there is no formula in Cell E8.

Formulas -> Formula Auditing->Trace Precedents

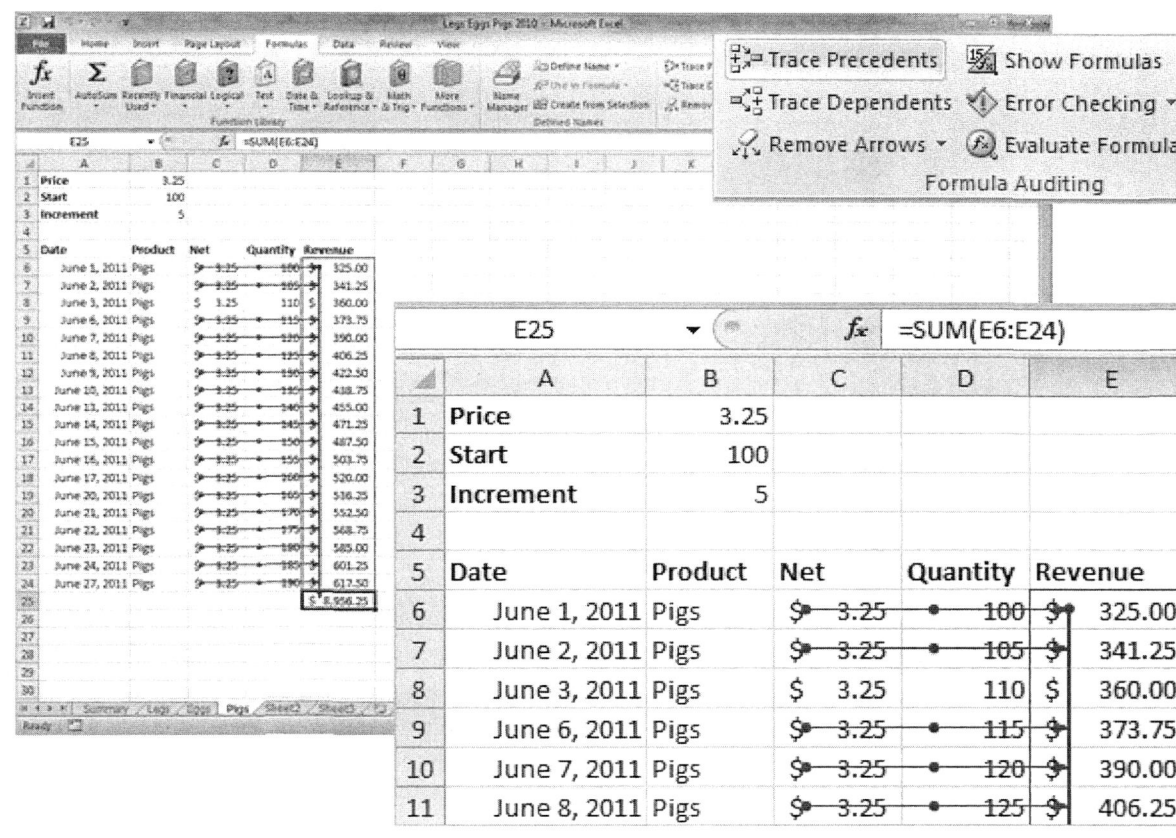

	A	B	C	D	E
1	Price	3.25			
2	Start	100			
3	Increment	5			
4					
5	Date	Product	Net	Quantity	Revenue
6	June 1, 2011	Pigs	$ 3.25	100	$ 325.00
7	June 2, 2011	Pigs	$ 3.25	105	$ 341.25
8	June 3, 2011	Pigs	$ 3.25	110	$ 360.00
9	June 6, 2011	Pigs	$ 3.25	115	$ 373.75
10	June 7, 2011	Pigs	$ 3.25	120	$ 390.00
11	June 8, 2011	Pigs	$ 3.25	125	$ 406.25

Exam 77-888: Microsoft Excel Expert 2010
2. Applying Formulas and Functions
2.1. Audit formulas: Trace Precedents

HOME

Show Formulas
Sometimes, it helps to looooook at the formulas. Here are the steps:

Before You Begin: Remove the arrows

Try it: Show Formulas
Select Cell E8.
Go to **Formulas->Formula Auditing.**
Click **Show Formulas.**

What Do You See? All of the cells that have formulas are displayed. Cell E8 has a number that we typed in earlier in this lesson: no formula.

You can click on **Show Formulas,** again, to turn off the formulas display.

Formulas -> Formula Auditing->Show Formulas

Net	Quantity	Revenue
=$B$1	=B2	=C6*D6
=$B$1	=D6+$B$3	=C7*D7
=$B$1	=D7+$B$3	360
=$B$1	=D8+$B$3	=C9*D9
=$B$1	=D9+$B$3	=C10*D10
=$B$1	=D10+$B$3	=C11*D11
=$B$1	=D11+$B$3	=C12*D12

Exam 77-888: Microsoft Excel Expert 2010
2. Applying Formulas and Functions
2.1. Audit formulas: Show Formulas

Error Checking

Error Checking works like Spell Checking. Errors can be marked and corrected one at a time, or Live, as you work on your formulas.

Before You Begin: Make a Mistake
Select Cell E8.
Enter this formula: =C7*D8.

What Do You See? This formula does NOT match the formula above or below it. So, Cell E8 has a error mark, a small triangle in the upper left corner.

Keep going, please...

Formulas -> Formula Auditing->Error Checking

5	Date	Product	Net		Quantity	Revenue	
6	June 1, 2011	Pigs	$	3.25	100	$	325.00
7	June 2, 2011	Pigs	$	3.25	105	$	341.25
8	June 3, 2011	Pigs	$	3.25	110	=C7*D8	
9	June 6, 2011	Pigs	$	3.25	115	$	373.75
10	June 7, 2011	Pigs	$	3.25	120	$	390.00

7	June 2, 2011	Pigs	$	3.25	105	$	341.25
8	June 3, 2011	Pigs	$	3.25	110	$	357.50
9	June 6, 2011	Pigs	$	3.25	115	$	373.75

Exam 77-888: Microsoft Excel Expert 2010
2. Applying Formulas and Functions
2.1. Audit formulas: Error Checking

Error Checking Options

Try This: Run Error Checking
Select Cell E8.
Go to **Formulas -> Formula Auditing**.
Go to **Error Checking->Trace Error**.

What Do You See? The Error Checker found that the formula in Cell E8 is inconsistent: it is not the same as the formula in the Row above.

The Error Checking Options include:
Copy Formula from Above
Help on this error
Ignore Error
Edit in Formula Bar.

If you have a LOT of problems with your formulas you can use the Previous and Next buttons to navigate through your Error Checking.

Formulas -> Formula Auditing->Error Checking

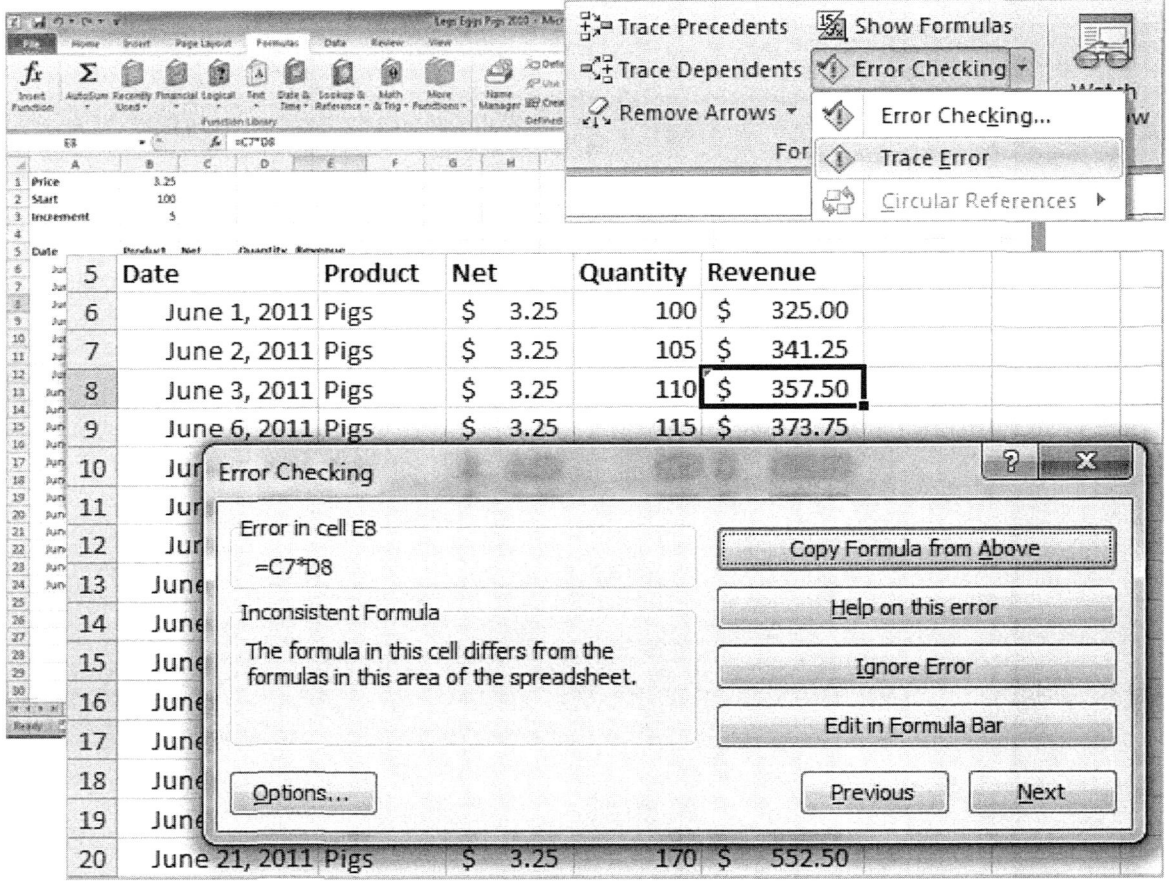

Exam 77-888: Microsoft Excel Expert 2010
2. Applying Formulas and Functions
2.1. Audit formulas: Error Checking

Error Checking Rules

Error Checking Rules can be found by clicking on the Options button when you are in the Error Checker.

Try This: Review the Options
Go to **Formulas -> Formula Auditing-> Error Checking.**
Click on **Options.**

What Do You See? Error Checking is enabled by default.

The Error checking rules include:
Cells that result in an error
Inconsistent formulas in tables
Years that are only 2-digits
Numbers formatted as Text
Formulas which omit cells
Unlocked cells which have formulas
Formulas that refer to empty cells
Data that is invalid

Formulas -> Formula Auditing->Error Checking->Options

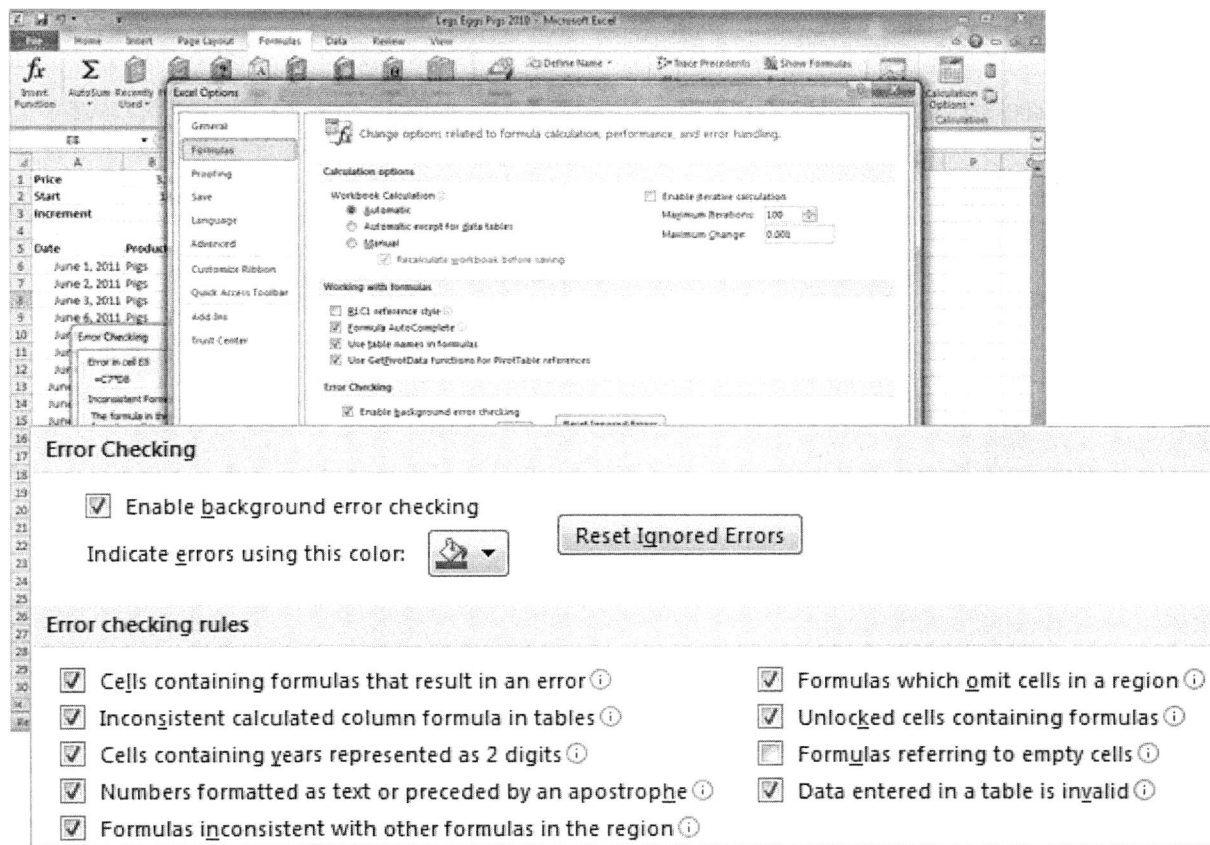

Exam 77-888: Microsoft Excel Expert 2010
2. Applying Formulas and Functions
2.1. Audit formulas: Error Checking

Summary

This lesson introduced **Formulas** and **Formula Auditing**. The focus of each exercise was on the **Cell References**. We looked at the differences between **Relative** and **Absolute** Cell References.

Well, you done good.
You get the cookie. <grin>

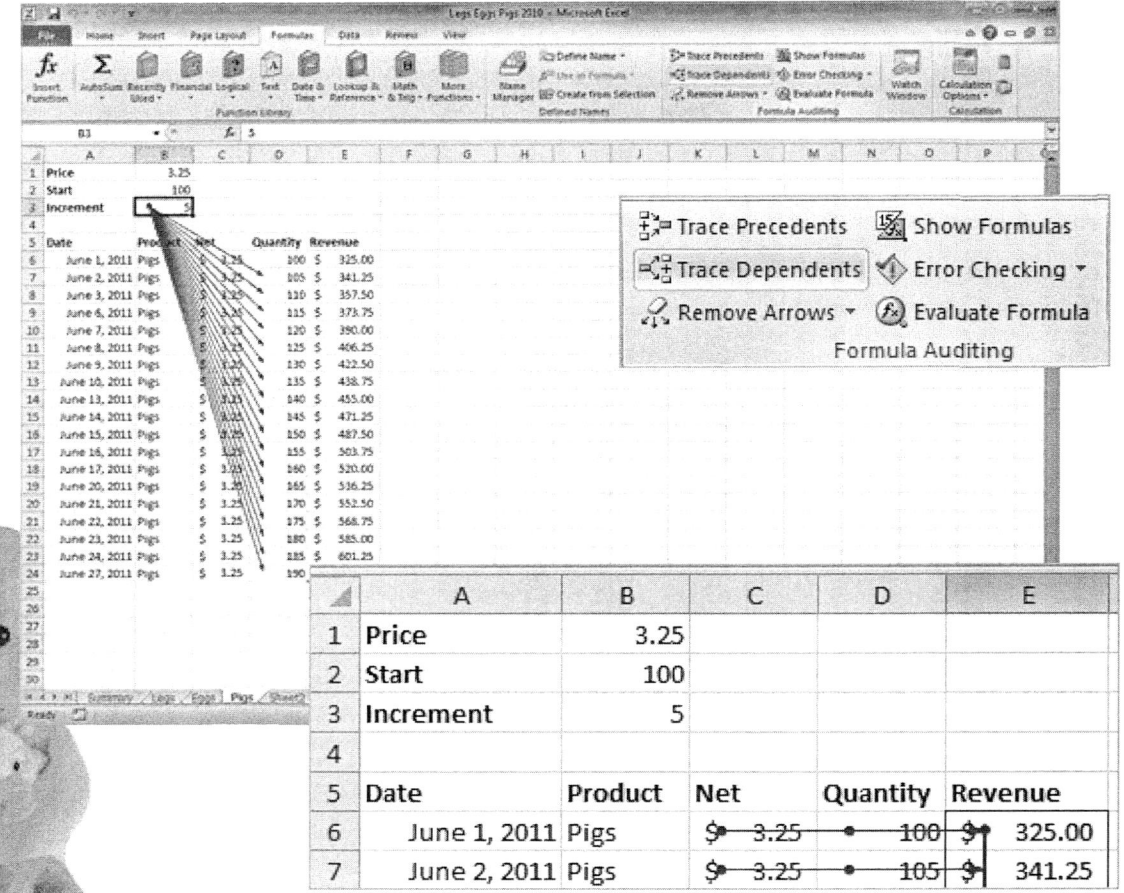

Practice Activities

Lesson 1: Legs, Eggs and Pigs

Before You Begin: Start Microsoft Excel 2010. You should see a new, blank spreadsheet.

Try This: Do the following steps

1. Enter the following labels in Row 1, beginning with Cell A1: Date, Location, Sales, Profit. Format Row 1 as Bold.
2. Select A2. Enter: January
3. Select A2. Use the AutoFill command to fill January through December in Column A.
4. Select B2. Enter the location as Ann Arbor. Use the AutoFill command to fill the location through December
5. Select D2. Enter the formula for Profit. Profit is 25% of the Sales. Use the AutoFill to fill the Formula from D2:D13.
6. Go to the bottom of Columns C and D, use the AutoSum command to find the total Sales and total Profit for the year.
7. Copy Sheet 1 two times.
8. Rename Sheet 1 to Ann Arbor.
9. Rename Sheet 2 to Detroit. Change the Location to Detroit and AutoFill.
10. Rename Sheet 3 to Lansing. Change the Location to Lansing and AutoFill.
11. Adjust the column widths where necessary to fit the contents.
12. Go to the Ann Arbor sheet. Enter the sales for January as $10,000. Format the column to be Accounting. Enter the sales for February as $11,000. AutoFill down. The increment is an increase of sales each month.
13. Go to the Detroit sheet. Insert 3 blank rows at the top of the sheet. Add labels in column A for **Start** and **Increment**. Enter the value $15,000 for start. For increment enter 5,000. Enter the formula in the Sales. January is $15,000, the starting point. February and beyond will be start plus increment. Create an Absolute Reference for the Increment. Use AutoFill and fill down.
14. Go to the Lansing sheet. Insert 3 blank rows at the top of the sheet. Add labels in column A for **Start** and **Increment**. Enter the value $20,000 for start. For increment enter 110%. Enter the formula in the Sales. January is $20,000, the starting point. February and beyond will be start times the increment. Create an Absolute Reference for the Increment. Use AutoFill and fill down.
15. Insert a new blank sheet in the workbook. Rename the sheet Totals.
16. Enter the following labels on the Totals sheet: Month, Sales, Profits
17. Enter the date as January and AutoFill through December.
18. Enter the formula for Sales to add the three locations (make sure you select January across all three sheets—remember that Detroit and Lansing have the reference rows at the top.)
19. Use the AutoSum to add the total sales and total profit on the Totals sheet.
20. SAVE as YOUR NAME Legs Eggs and Pigs Practice.

Test Yourself

1. Where is the command that formats the Date & Time?
a. Insert Ribbon
b. Format Ribbon
c. Home Ribbon
d. Cells Ribbon
Tip: Intermediate Excel, page 16

2. AutoFill for dates is the same as Copy and Paste.
a. True
b. False
Tip: Intermediate Excel, page 18

3. You can rename a sheet in Excel from Sheet 1 to Eggs.
a. True
b. False
Tip: Intermediate Excel, page 25

4. What does it mean when Excel displays #######?
a. The data doesn't make sense (such as adding text to numbers)
b. The column is too narrow
c. Nothing for the formula to reference (such as a blank cell)
d. You made an error
e. Unspecified Error
Tip: Intermediate Excel, page 27

5. What does it mean when Excel displays #REF!
a. The data doesn't make sense (such as adding text to numbers)
b. The column is too narrow
c. Nothing for the formula to reference (such as a blank cell)
d. You made an error
e. Unspecified Error
Tip: Intermediate Excel, page 29

6. Which is NOT a valid formula?
a. =B1
b. B1
c. =B1*B3
d. =SUM(B1:B20)
Tip: Intermediate Excel, page 34

7. What does it mean when Excel displays #VALUE ?
a. The data doesn't make sense (such as adding text to numbers)
b. The column is too narrow
c. Nothing for the formula to reference (such as a blank cell)
d. You made an error
e. Unspecified Error
Tip: Intermediate Excel, page 35

8. Which is true about Relative & Absolute References? (Select all correct answers)
a. When the fill command is used, a relative reference updates each row to match the new location
b. The F4 key turns a Relative Reference into an Absolute Reference.
c. A mixed reference has both Relative and Absolute References
d. $A$4 is an Absolute Reference
Tip: Intermediate Excel, page 37

9. Which command shows the formulas?
a. View-> Formulas-> Show
b. Formulas-> Formula Auditing-> Show Formulas
c. Formulas-> Reveal Formulas
Tip: Intermediate Excel, page 44

Excel 2010: Business Spreadsheets

This Little Piggy Goes to Market

Intermediate Excel Objectives
In this lesson, you will learn how to:

1. Practice modifying cell contents and formats

2. Use the Paste Special options

3. CONCATENATE (combine) data with a formula

4. Modify and format TEXT with formulas

5. Use DATE and TIME formulas

6. Use FINANCIAL formulas to calculate a payment

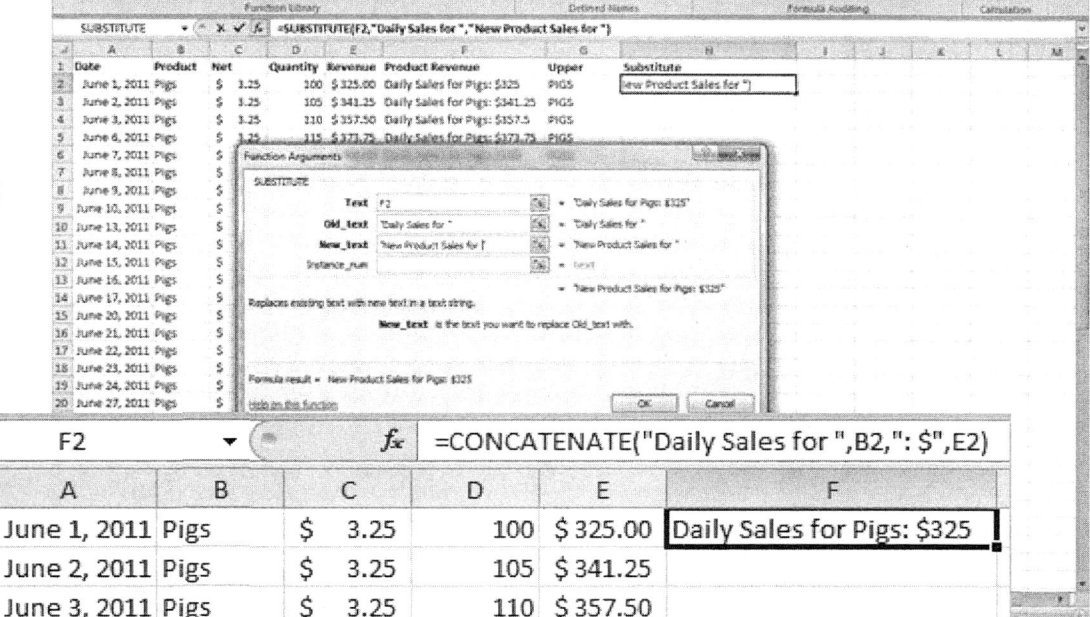

 # Lesson 2: Little Piggy Goes to Market

Formulas

1. Readings

Read Lesson 2 in your Intermediate Excel Guide, page 51-81.

Project

Use formulas to format and modify TEXT, DATE, and TIME. Use FINANCIAL formulas to calculate a car payment..

Downloads

Legs Eggs Pigs 2010.xlsx
Counting Chickens 2010.xlsx
Brown Bag Sales Data 2010.xlsx

2. Practice

There is no Practice Activity for this lesson.

3. Assessment

Review the Test Yourself questions on page 82.

Menu Maps

This lesson introduces the **Formulas** Ribbon.
1. Formulas -> Function Library->Text ->Concatenate, page 62
2. Formulas -> Function Library->Text ->UPPER, page 65
3. Formulas -> Function Library->Text ->SUBSTITUTE, page 67
4. Formulas->Function Library->Date->MONTH, page 69
5. Formulas->Function Library->Date->NETWORKDAYS, page 71
6. Formulas->Function Library->Financial->PMT, page 79

Formulas

In the previous lesson, the focus was on naming the cells that are included in a formula. We looked at the difference between **Relative** and **Absolute Cell References**. This lesson will use formulas to calculate, compare and format Text. We will also use formulas to summarize the data.

I know, I know: the mere thought of formulas sends folks out the door. I believe that math is taught very poorly and that most people do NOT have a comfortable understanding of the rules and options. This lesson will include a discussion of the math as well as what the spreadsheet software can do.

Start -> All Programs ->Microsoft Office -> Excel

What Do You See? Is there a Title Bar that says Book 1-Microsoft Excel? Yes.

Is there a **Home** Ribbon with the Clipboard, Font and Alignment Groups? Yes.

If your screen looks similar to the example on this page, then you are ready to get started.

Before You Begin

This discussion begins by creating a sample spreadsheet that combines all of the dates and product sales forecast from three different spreadsheets. This lesson introduces a common copy/paste error, and methods for correcting it.

1. Try it: Create a Sample Spreadsheet

Open the spreadsheet you created in the previous lesson: Legs Eggs Pigs 2010.xlsx
Go to the **Pigs** spreadsheet.
Select Row 5 through Row 24.
(Do not include the Total in Row 25.)
Go to **Home->Copy**.

Go to a new spreadsheet.
Select Cell A1.
Go to **Home->Paste**.
Keep going...!
*You can use the **sample spreadsheet** or enter your own data if you wish.*

Home->Copy

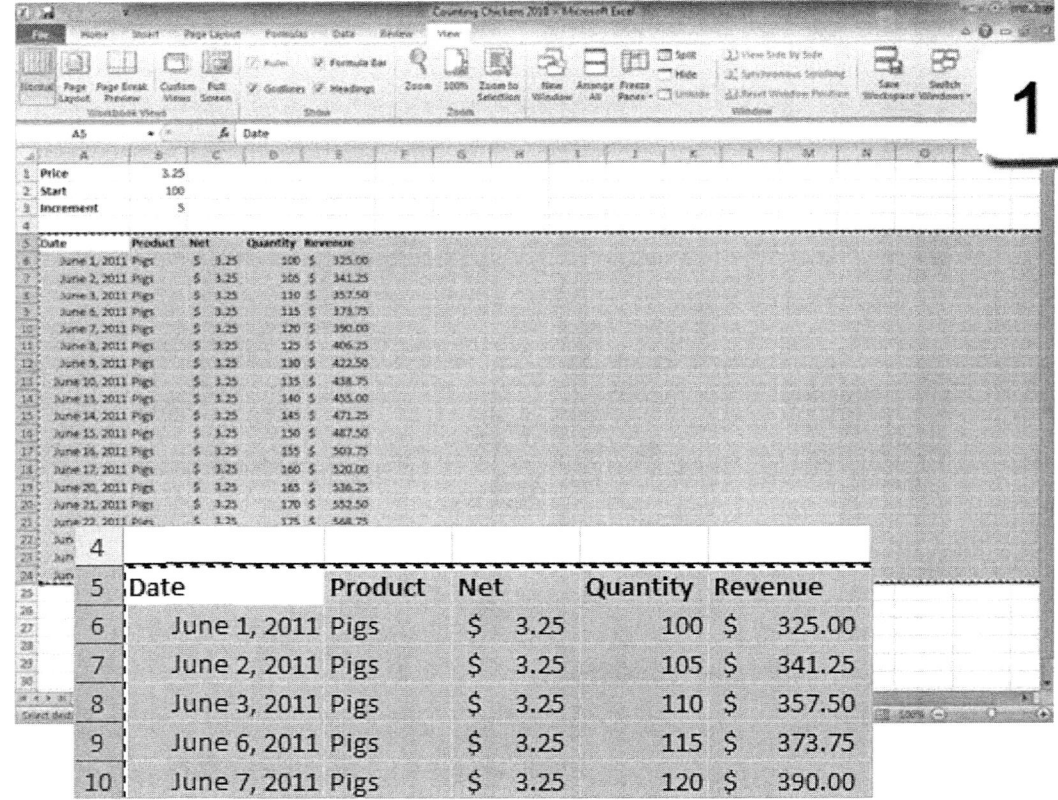

	Date	Product	Net	Quantity	Revenue
5	Date	Product	Net	Quantity	Revenue
6	June 1, 2011	Pigs	$ 3.25	100	$ 325.00
7	June 2, 2011	Pigs	$ 3.25	105	$ 341.25
8	June 3, 2011	Pigs	$ 3.25	110	$ 357.50
9	June 6, 2011	Pigs	$ 3.25	115	$ 373.75
10	June 7, 2011	Pigs	$ 3.25	120	$ 390.00

Exam 77-882: Microsoft Excel 2010 Core
2. Creating Cell Data
2.1. Construct cell data

Take Two

Paste Between Worksheets
What Do You See? When you copy and paste data into a new spreadsheet, you may see many error messages. That's Excel's way of asking, "Where's the data?"

2. Try This: Review the #REF Errors
Click on any cell that says **#REF!**
You will see that the formulas are still there.
This example shows: **D3=D2+$B$3.**
When you paste formulas into a new spreadsheet, the cell references may become meaningless. In this example, there is no **Reference Cell**, $B$3, so there is nowhere to look up the quantity.

3. Try This: Review the #VALUE! Errors
Click on any cell that says **#VALUE!**
You will see that the formulas are still there.
This example shows: **E3=C3+D3.**

In this example C3 has Text, not Numbers. How do you multiply Text times Numbers? Hence, the error **#value!**

Keep going, please...

Home->Paste

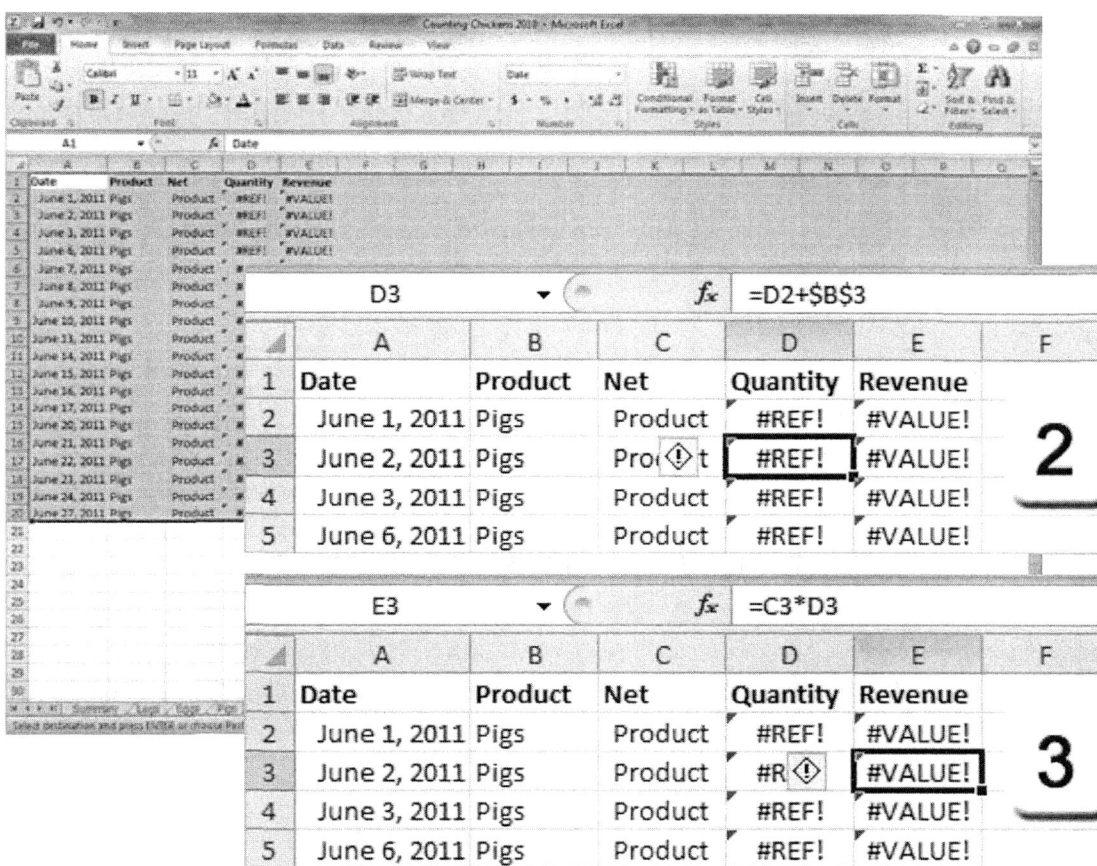

Exam 77-882: Microsoft Excel 2010 Core
2. Creating Cell Data
2.1. Construct cell data: Paste Special

Paste Errors

4. What Else Do You See? Look next to the **#REF!** message: There is an exclamation point that flags the error. This error has been identified as an **Invalid Cell Reference**.

The Error options include:
Help on this error
Trace Error
Ignore Error
Edit in the Formula Bar
Error Checking Options

This **#REF!** error comes from pasting data from one spreadsheet to another, but the new spreadsheet does not include all of the Cells that the formulas **reference**. Keep going...

Home->Paste

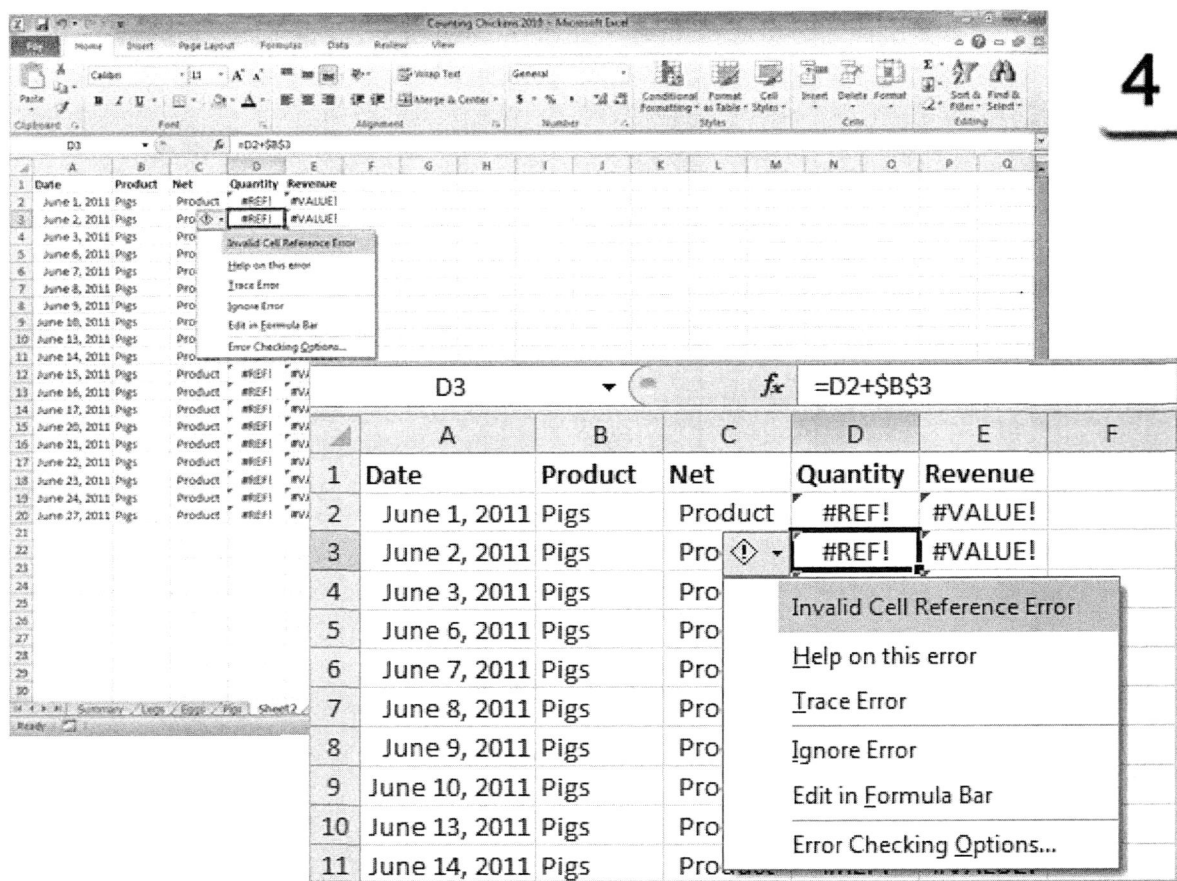

4

Exam 77-882: Microsoft Excel 2010 Core
2. Creating Cell Data
2.1. Construct cell data: Paste Special

Paste Special Options

There is another method of pasting the **Values**, without the formulas.

Before You Begin: Delete the data that you just pasted. We are going to start over.

5. Try it: Paste Special
Go to the **Pigs** spreadsheet.
Select Row 5 through Row 24.
(Do not include the Total in Row 25.)
Go to **Home->Copy.**

Go to a new spreadsheet, Sheet 2.
Select Cell A1.
Go to **Home->Paste Special.**

What Do You See? There are four rows of **Paste Options**. You can choose whether to keep the formatting, formulas, or values.

What Else Do You See? The **Other Paste Options** include **Paste Link**, so you can link the data from one workbook or spreadsheet to another and synchronize the data.
Keep going, there's more. ;-)

Home->Paste ->Paste Special

Exam 77-882: Microsoft Excel 2010 Core
2. Creating Cell Data
2.1. Construct cell data: Paste Special

Home->Paste ->Paste Special ->Values

Paste Special

6. What Do You See? Paste Special lets you choose what you want to paste. The default options include: All (everything), Formulas, Values, Formats, Comments, or Validation, only.

Options to Remove Formatting
Paste Special can get rid of Formats, Themes, Borders or blanks you may have copied from the original sheet.

Options to Select Operation
You can select the math you want to paste: Add, Subtract, Multiply, Divide, or none at all.

Keep going...

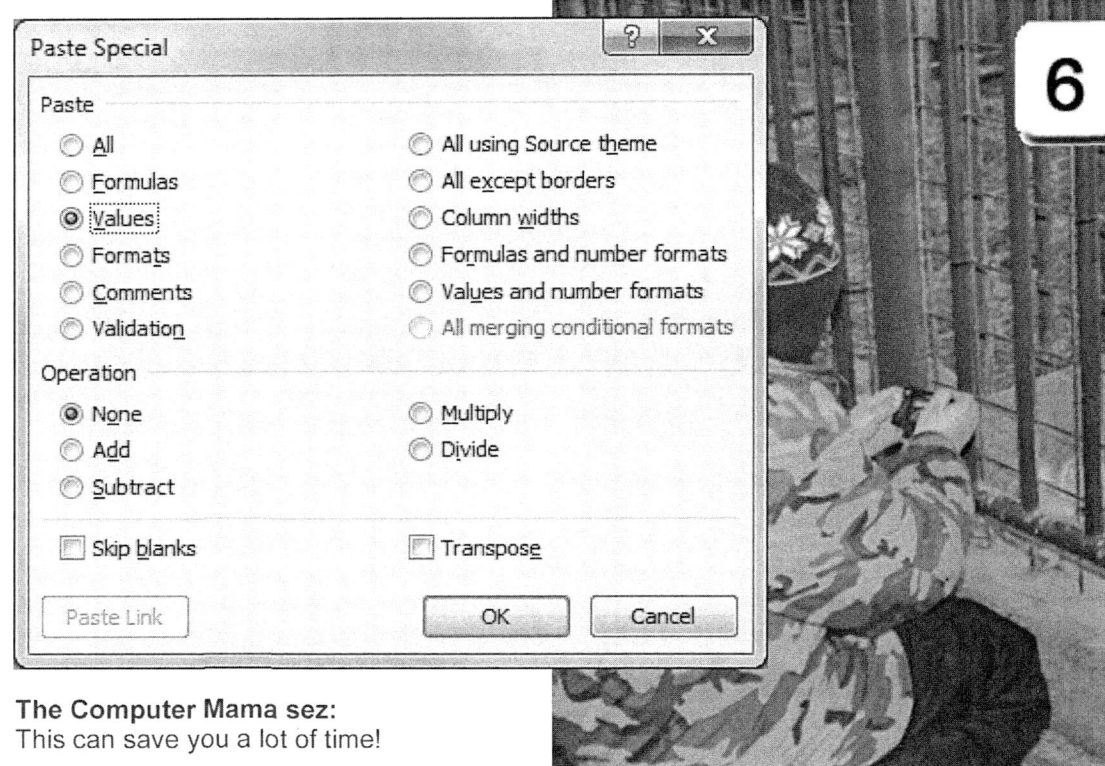

The Computer Mama sez:
This can save you a lot of time!

Exam 77-882: Microsoft Excel 2010 Core
2. Creating Cell Data
2.1. Construct cell data: Paste Special

Home->Paste ->Paste Special ->Values

Paste Special: Values

7. Try it: Paste the Sample Data
Go to the **Eggs** spreadsheet.
Select Row 1 through Row 20.
(Do not include the Total in Row 21.)
Go to **Home->Copy.**
Go to the new spreadsheet, Sheet 2.
Select Cell A21. Go to **Home->Paste Special->Values and number formats..**

Go to the **Legs** spreadsheet.
Select Row 1 through Row 20.
Go to **Home->Copy**.
Go to the new spreadsheet, Sheet 2.
Select Cell A40. Go to **Home->Paste Special->Values and number formats.**

Try This, Too: Rename the spreadsheet
Double-click the tab for this spreadsheet. Type:
Original Data for TEXT Formulas.

8. Try This: Save the Spreadsheet
Go to **File->Save.**
Go to your **Documents** folder, if you wish.
Type the Name: **Counting Chickens 2010.**
Click on **SAVE.**

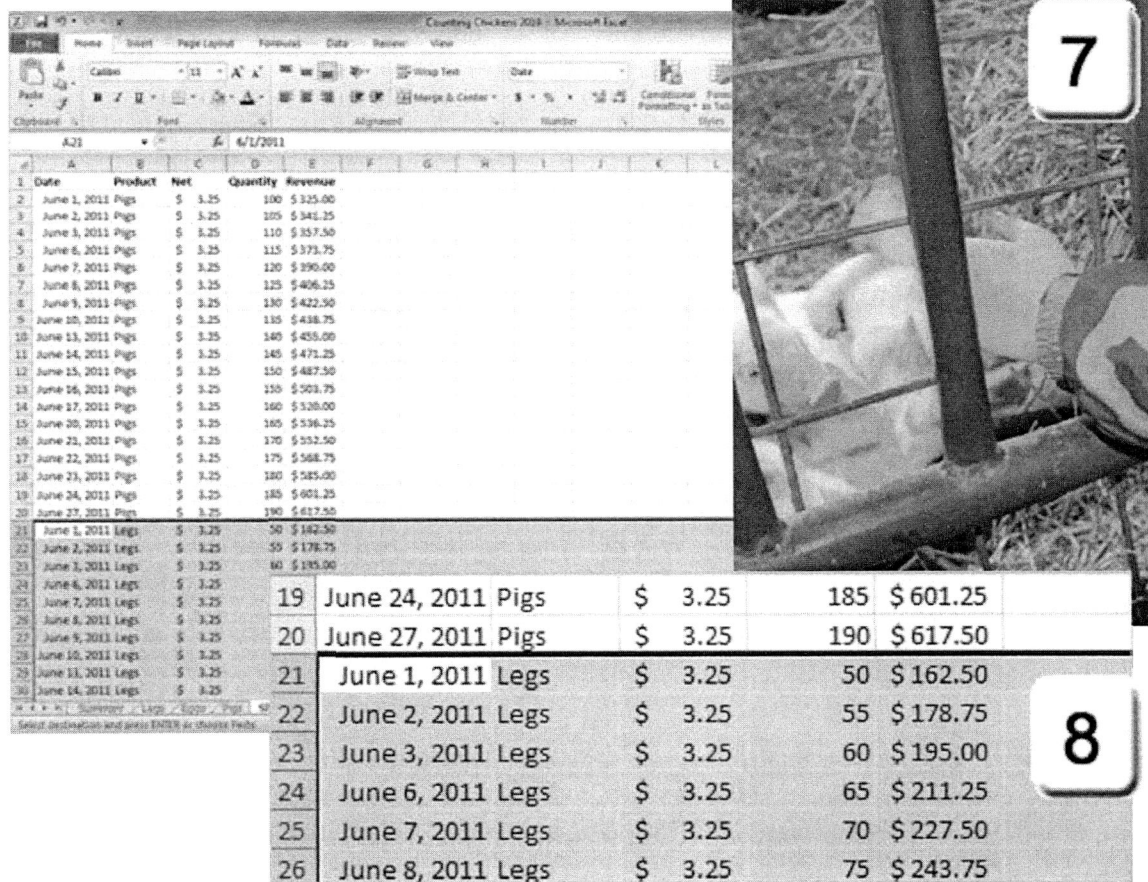

Exam 77-882: Microsoft Excel 2010 Core
2. Creating Cell Data
2.1. Construct cell data: Paste Special

Format TEXT with Formulas

The next lesson demonstrates the TEXT functions. Each example creates a **Cell Reference**, and uses **Arguments** to create the formulas.

The TEXT functions include:
CONCATENATE (combining fields)
UPPER/LOWER
SUBSTITUTE

1. Before You Begin: Open the file: <u>Counting Chickens 2010.xlsx</u>.

There should be a spreadsheet called **Original Data for TEXT Formulas**.

File->Open

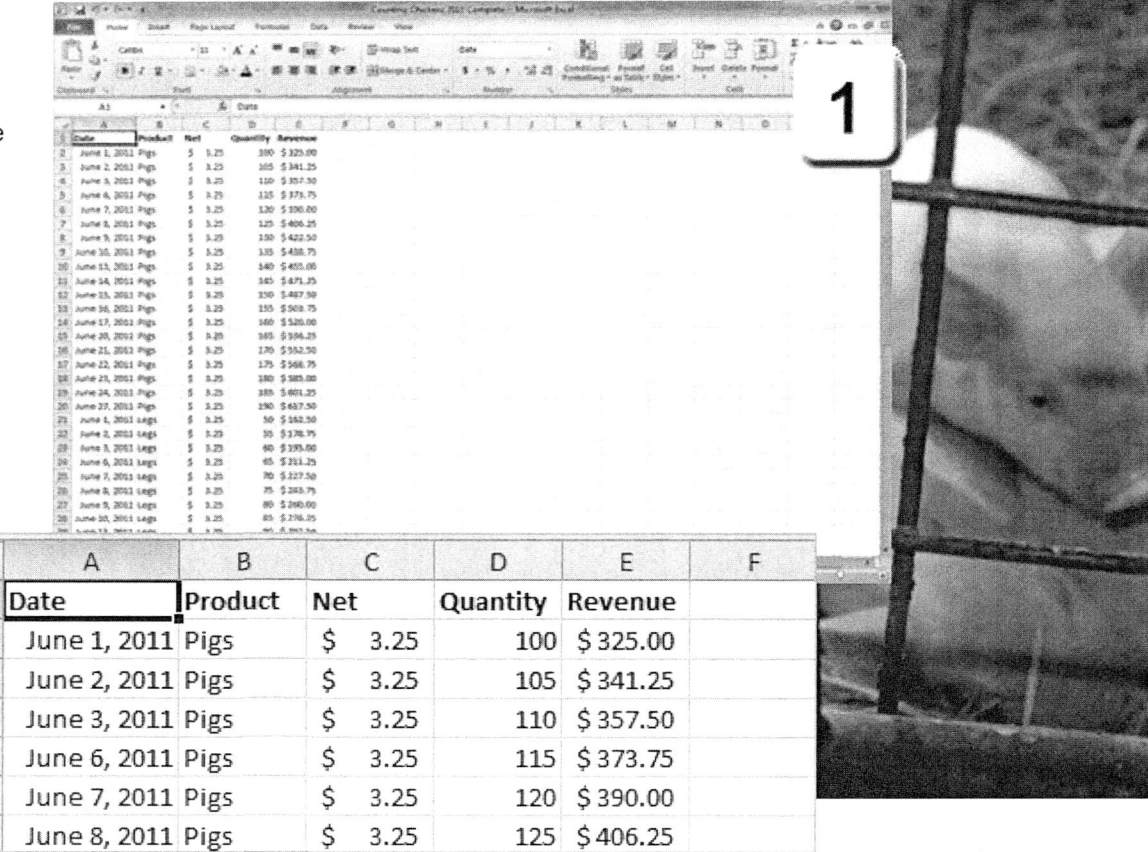

	A	B	C	D	E	F
1	Date	Product	Net	Quantity	Revenue	
2	June 1, 2011	Pigs	$ 3.25	100	$ 325.00	
3	June 2, 2011	Pigs	$ 3.25	105	$ 341.25	
4	June 3, 2011	Pigs	$ 3.25	110	$ 357.50	
5	June 6, 2011	Pigs	$ 3.25	115	$ 373.75	
6	June 7, 2011	Pigs	$ 3.25	120	$ 390.00	
7	June 8, 2011	Pigs	$ 3.25	125	$ 406.25	

Exam 77-888: Microsoft Excel Expert 2010
2. Applying Formulas and Functions
2.4. Apply functions in formulas: TEXT Functions

Text Formulas

Text as well as numbers can be edited by formulas. One useful Text function combines the data from several cells.

This function also has a cool name: **Concatenate**.

2. Try This: Make a Copy
Select the Original Data sheet.
Right click and make a **Copy**.
Name the new sheet: Text Functions.

And Try This: Add a Label
Select Cell F1.
Type: Product Revenue

Keep going....

19	June 24, 2011	Pigs	$	3.25	185	$ 601.25
20	June 27, 2011	Pigs	$	3.25	190	$ 617.50
21	June 1, 2011	Legs	$	3.25	50	$ 162.50
22	June 2, 2011	Legs	$	3.25	55	$ 178.75
23	June 3, 2011	Legs	$	3.25	60	$ 195.00
24	June 6, 2011	Legs	$	3.25	65	$ 211.25
25	June 7, 2011	Legs	$	3.25	70	$ 227.50
26	June 8, 2011	Legs	$	3.25	75	$ 243.75
27	June 9, 2011	Legs	$	3.25	80	$ 260.00
28	June 10, 2011	Legs	$	3.25	85	$ 276.25
29	June 13, 2011	Legs	$	3.25	90	$ 292.50
30	June 14, 2011	Legs	$	3.25	95	$ 308.75

Insert...
Delete
Rename
Move or Copy...
View Code
Protect Sheet...
Tab Color ▶
Hide
Unhide...
Select All Sheets

Summary / Legs / Eggs / Pigs / Original Data for TEXT formulas / Sheet3

2

Exam 77-882: Microsoft Excel 2010 Core
4. Managing Worksheets and Workbooks
4.1. Create and format worksheets: Move or Copy

Take Two

Formulas -> Function Library-> Text ->Concatenate

3

Text Function: Concatenate

3. Try It: Concatenate the Text
Select **Cell F2.**
Go to **Formulas->Function Library-> Text.**
Click on: **Concatenate.**

Text

Keep going...

File	Home	Insert	Page Layout	Formulas	Data	Review	View

Insert Function | AutoSum | Recently Used ▾ | Financial ▾ | Logical ▾ | Text ▾ | Date & Time ▾ | Lookup & Reference ▾ | Math & Trig ▾ | More Functions ▾

Functio

F2   fx

BAHTTEXT
CHAR
CLEAN
CODE
CONCATENATE
DOLLAR
EXACT
FIND

	A	B	C	Q		F	G
1	Date	Product	Net			Revenue	
2	June 1, 2011	Pigs	$ 3.25				
3	June 2, 2011	Pigs	$ 3.25				
4	June 3, 2011	Pigs	$ 3.25				
5	June 6, 2011	Pigs	$ 3.25				
6	June 7, 2011	Pigs	$ 3.25				

Exam 77-888: Microsoft Excel Expert 2010
2. Applying Formulas and Functions
2.4. Apply functions in formulas: TEXT Functions CONCATENATE

Formulas -> Function Library-> Text ->Concatenate

Text Formula Options

This formula combines two cells: B2, the name of the Product, with E2, the calculated revenue.

4. Try It: Edit the Text Function
Start by entering the cell references.

Edit Text1: B2
Edit Text2: E2

What Do You See? The formula is
=CONCATENATE(B2,E2)

This TEXT formula did, indeed, combine the fields. However, this result needs some improvements. Keep going...

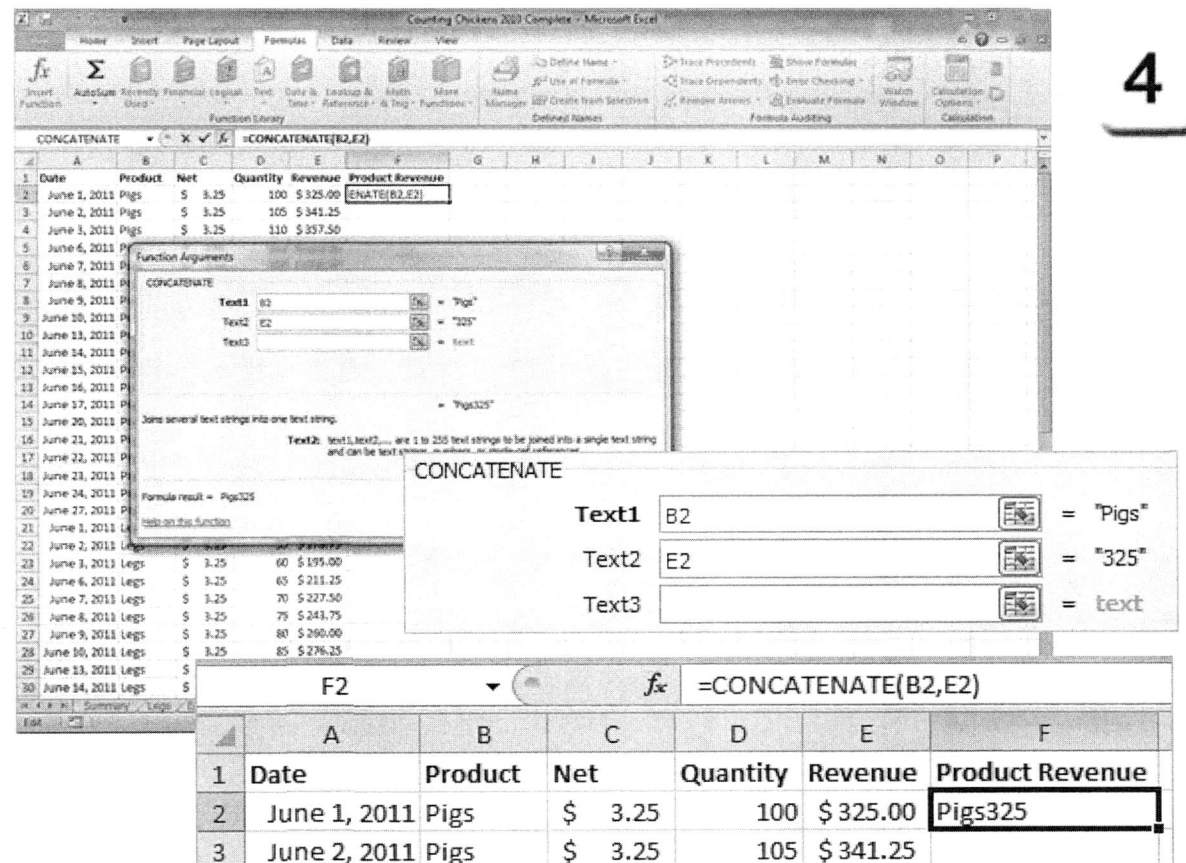

4

Exam 77-888: Microsoft Excel Expert 2010
2. Applying Formulas and Functions
2.4. Apply functions in formulas: TEXT Functions CONCATENATE

Additional Text Fields

If you add additional Text fields, you can include labels and punctuation if you wish.

5. Try This: Use Additional Text Fields
Select **Cell F2** and delete the formula.
Select **Cell F2**, again.
Go to **Formulas -> Function Library-> Text.**
Click on **Concatenate.**
Edit Text1: "Daily Sales for "
Edit Text2: B2
Edit Text 3: ": $ "
Edit Text 4: E2

Try This, Too: AutoFill the Formula
Select Cell F2.
AutoFill Cell F2 to the bottom of Column F.

What Do You See? Does your formula include the additional Text fields in the Concatenation?

Memo to Self: Whatever is in quotes will be placed in the answer. If you need a space between the "$" sign and the number, then add a space to Text3 between the quotes.

Formulas -> Function Library-> Text ->Concatenate

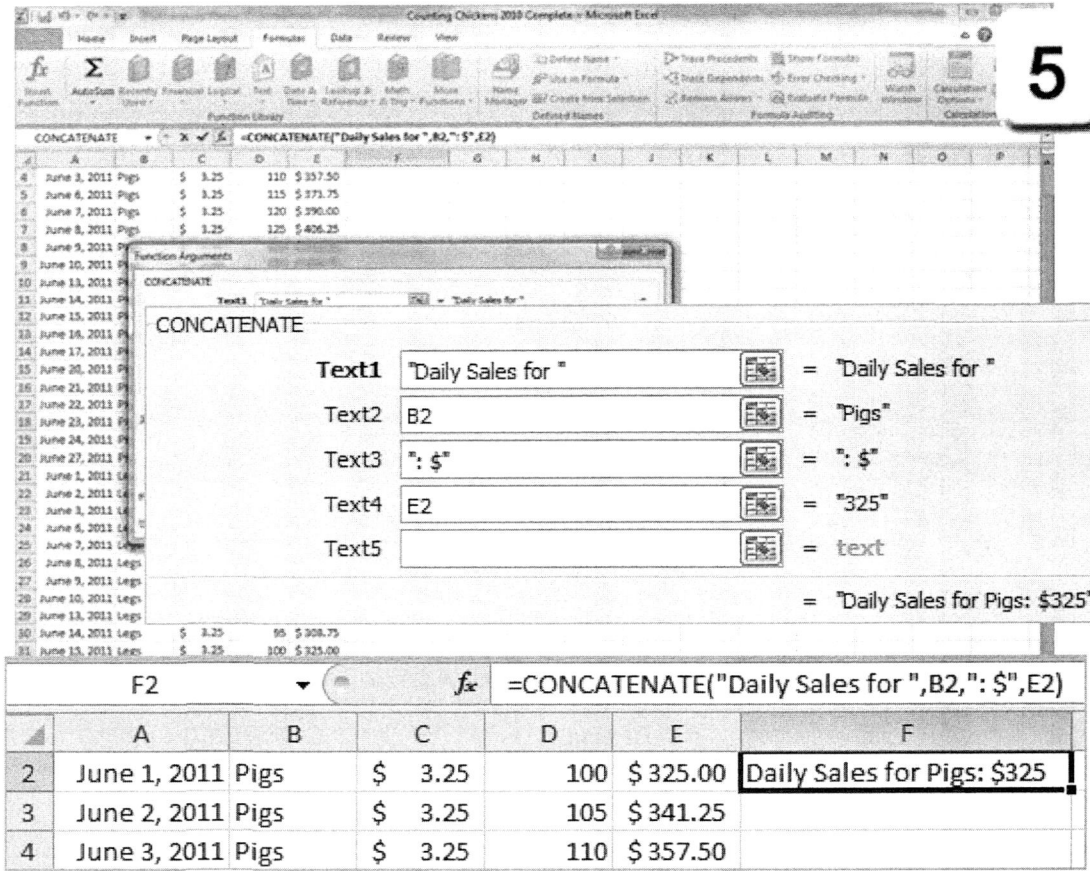

	A	B	C	D	E	F
2	June 1, 2011	Pigs	$ 3.25	100	$ 325.00	Daily Sales for Pigs: $325
3	June 2, 2011	Pigs	$ 3.25	105	$ 341.25	
4	June 3, 2011	Pigs	$ 3.25	110	$ 357.50	

Exam 77-888: Microsoft Excel Expert 2010
2. Applying Formulas and Functions
2.4. Apply functions in formulas: TEXT Functions CONCATENATE

Formulas -> Function Library-> Text ->UPPER

TEXT Functions: UPPER

Look at the text in any spreadsheet. The data entry may not be consistent. Some people never use capital letters, and some folks make every word begin with a capital letter. You can create a formula that formats the Text: **UPPER, LOWER, PROPER.**

1. Try It: Add a Label
Go to the Text Function spreadsheet.
Select **Cell G1**.
Type the label: UPPER

2. Try It: Use the UPPER Text Function
Select **Cell G2**.
Go to **Formulas->Function Library-> Text.**
Click on **UPPER.**

Keep going, please.

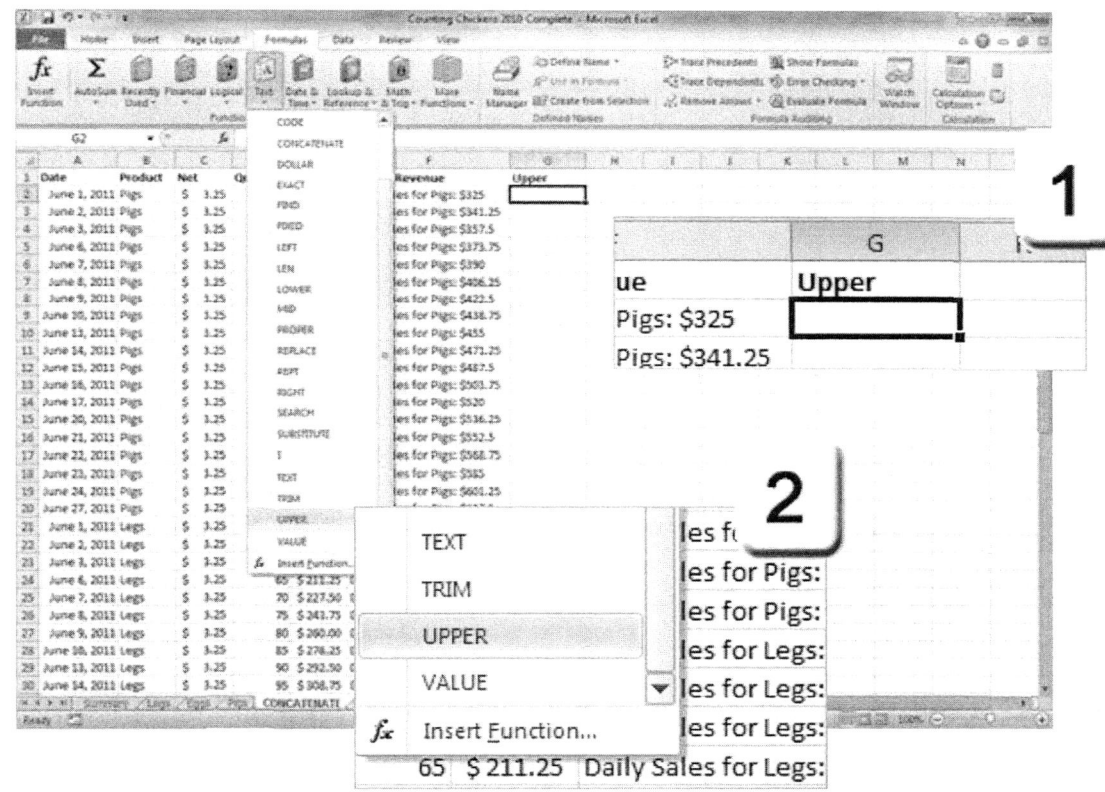

Exam 77-888: Microsoft Excel Expert 2010
2. Applying Formulas and Functions
2.4. Apply functions in formulas: TEXT Functions UPPER

UPPER Text Arguments

3. Try This: Edit the Function Arguments
Edit the Text:B2.

You should see a preview of the data in all capital letters, "PIGS".
Click **OK**.

Try This, Too: AutoFill the Formula
Use the **AutoFill** handle to fill down this formula in Column G.

Memo to Self: The **LOWER** text function converts the text to all lowercase letters.

The **PROPER** Text function begins each word with a capital letter.

Formulas -> Function Library-> Text ->UPPER

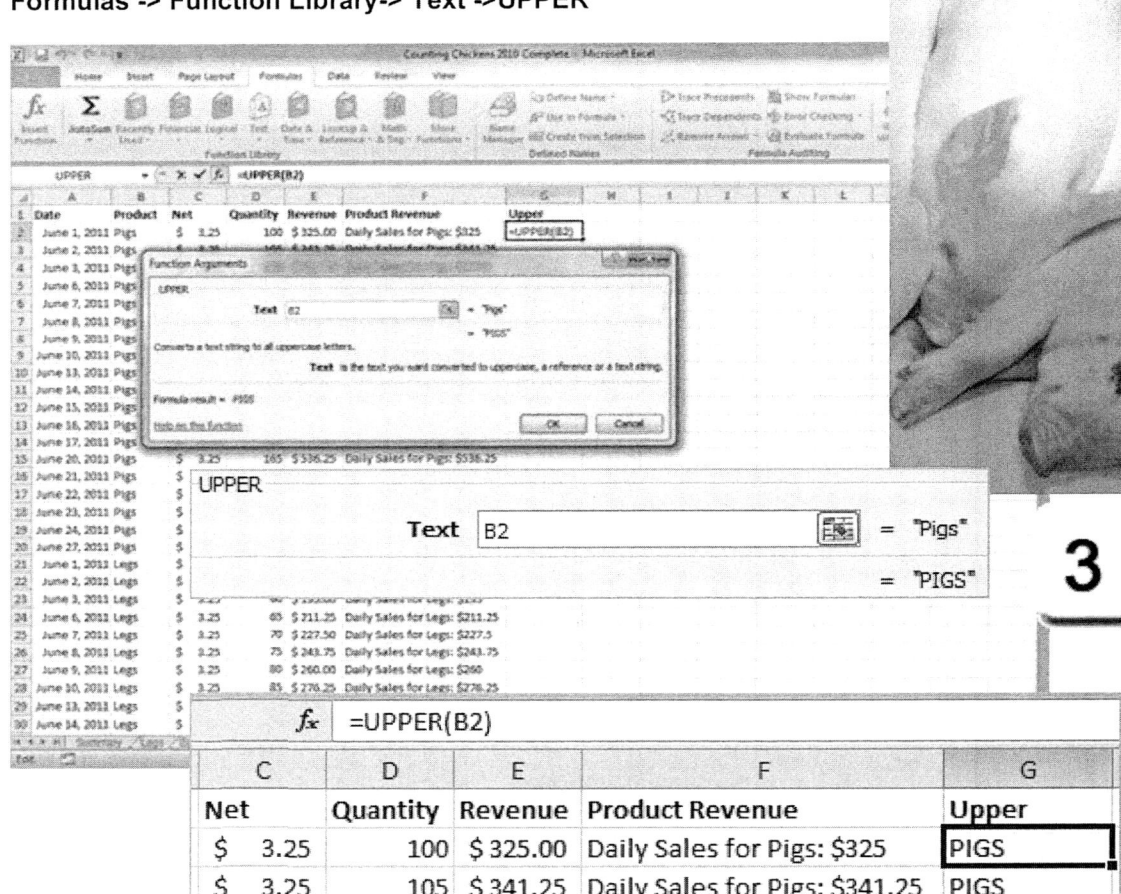

	Net	Quantity	Revenue	Product Revenue	Upper
fx =UPPER(B2)					
	$ 3.25	100	$ 325.00	Daily Sales for Pigs: $325	PIGS
	$ 3.25	105	$ 341.25	Daily Sales for Pigs: $341.25	PIGS

3

Exam 77-888: Microsoft Excel Expert 2010
2. Applying Formulas and Functions
2.4. Apply functions in formulas: TEXT Functions UPPER

Formulas -> Function Library-> Text ->SUBSTITUTE

Text Functions: SUBSTITUTE

The **Substitute** Text function can find and edit specific words or phrases.

For example, you can compare the formula in Column F and **Substitute** "New Product Sales" for "Daily Sales."

1. Try This: Add a Label
Go to the Text Functions sheet.
Select **Cell H1**.
Type the following label: Substitute

2. Try This, Too: Substitute the Text
Select **Cell H2**.
Go to **Formulas->Function Library-> Text**.
Click on: **SUBSTITUTE**.

Keep going...

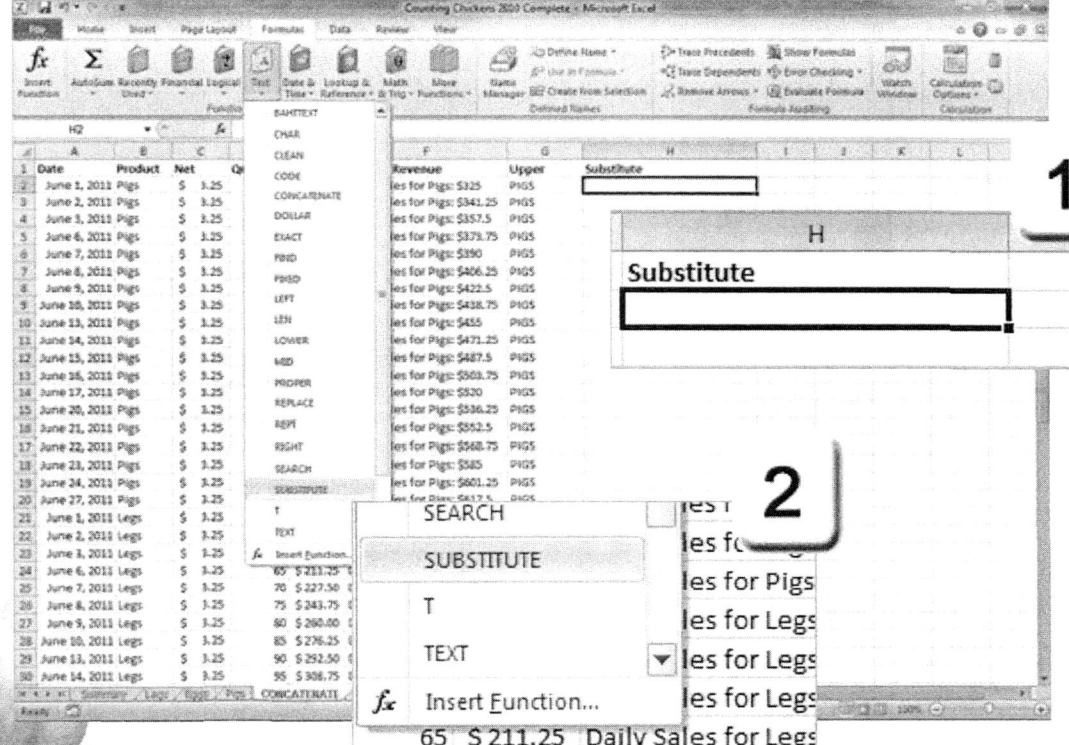

Exam 77-888: Microsoft Excel Expert 2010
2. Applying Formulas and Functions
2.4. Apply functions in formulas: TEXT Functions UPPER

SUBSTITUTE Arguments

3: Try This: Enter the Arguments
Text: F2

Old_text: "Daily Sales for"
Microsoft Excel will compare the text in your cell, F2. and determine if your data matches this Old_text.

New_text: "New Product Sales for"
This is the text that Microsoft Excel will substitute when it finds a word or phrase that matches.

You should see a preview of the data to the right of the Argument.

Click **OK**.

Try This, Too: AutoFill the Formula
Use the **AutoFill** handle to fill down this formula in Column H.

Formulas -> Function Library-> Text ->SUBSTITUTE

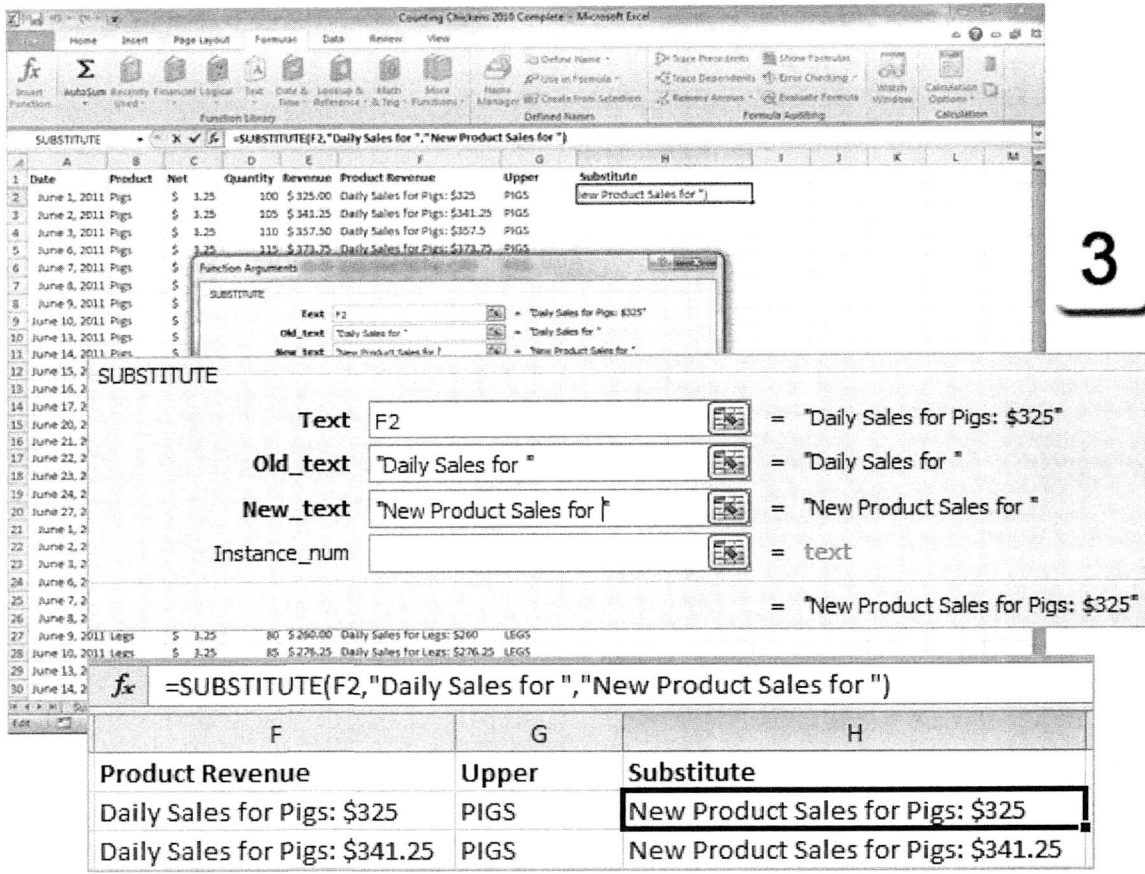

	Text	F2		=	"Daily Sales for Pigs: $325"
	Old_text	"Daily Sales for "		=	"Daily Sales for "
	New_text	"New Product Sales for "		=	"New Product Sales for "
	Instance_num			=	text
				=	"New Product Sales for Pigs: $325"

fx =SUBSTITUTE(F2,"Daily Sales for ","New Product Sales for ")

F	G	H
Product Revenue	**Upper**	**Substitute**
Daily Sales for Pigs: $325	PIGS	New Product Sales for Pigs: $325
Daily Sales for Pigs: $341.25	PIGS	New Product Sales for Pigs: $341.25

Exam 77-888: Microsoft Excel Expert 2010
2. Applying Formulas and Functions
2.4. Apply functions in formulas: TEXT Functions SUBSTITUTE

Date Functions: Month

Businesses are "date driven." Bills need to be paid on time. The **DATE** functions can be used to format as well as calculate.

Before You Begin: Make a Copy
Select the Original Data sheet.
Right click and make a **Copy**.
Name the new sheet: Date Functions.

1. Try This: Add a Label
Go to the Date Functions sheet.
Select **Cell F1**.
Type the following label: Date: Month

2. Try This, Too: Use a Date Function
Select **Cell F2**.
Go to Formulas->Function Library-> Date&Time.
Click on: **MONTH**.

Date & Time ▼

Keep going...

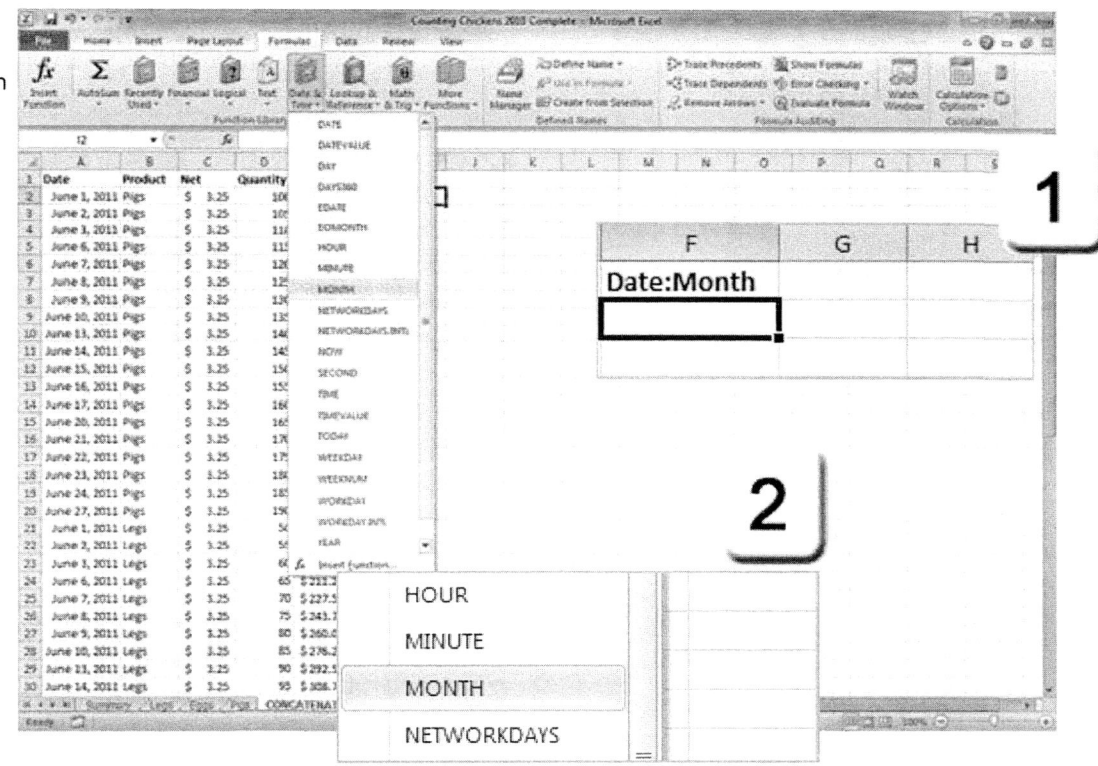

Exam 77-888: Microsoft Excel Expert 2010
2. Applying Formulas and Functions
2.4. Apply functions in formulas: DATE Functions MONTH

The MONTH Arguments

The purpose of the MONTH function is to read the date, figure out which month it is, and return a number for the month. In this example, the date is the Column A.

3. Try it: Edit the Serial_Number
Edit the Serial_Number: A2.
You should see a preview of the data to the right of the Arguments.
Click **OK.**

4. Try This, Too: AutoFill the Formula
Use the **AutoFill** handle to fill down this formula in Column F.

Formulas->Function Library-> Date & Time->MONTH

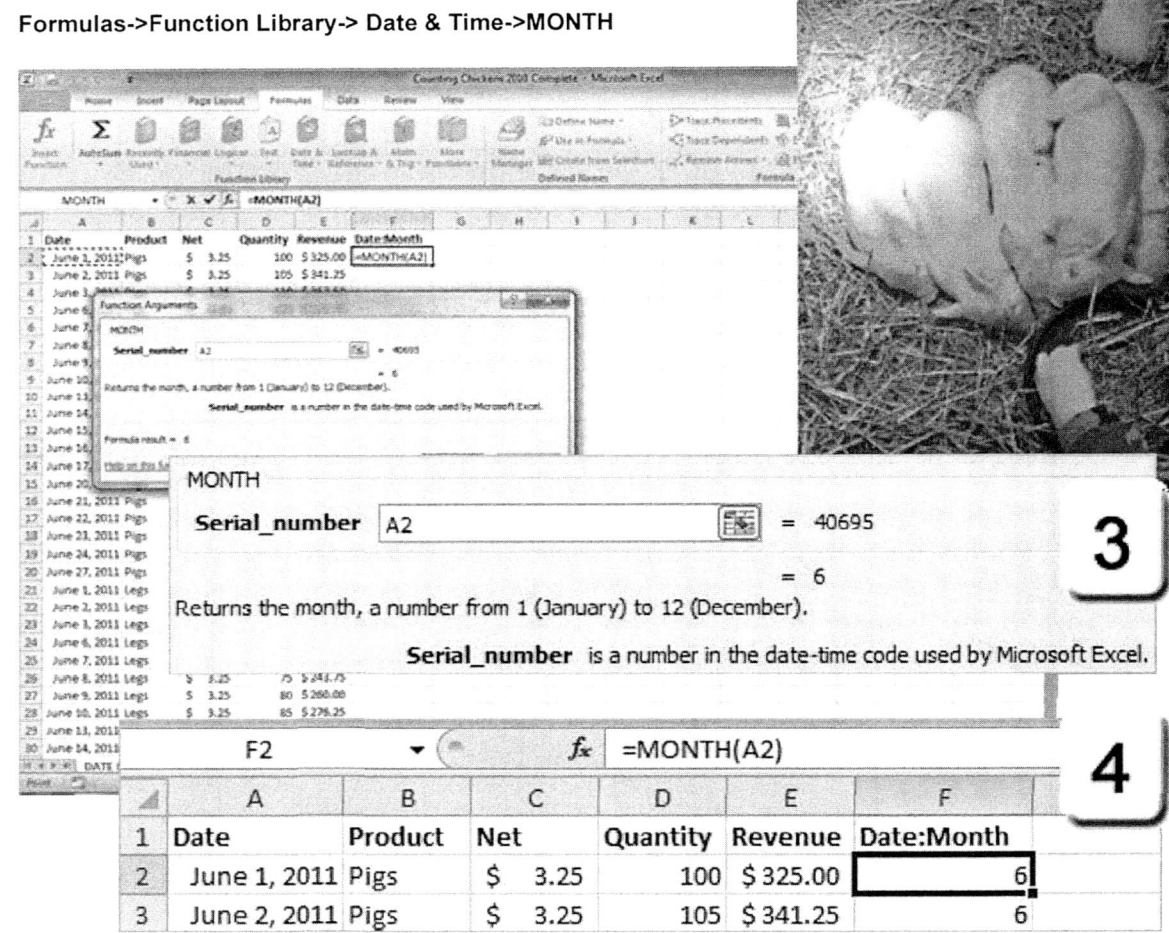

MONTH

Serial_number A2 = 40695

= 6

Returns the month, a number from 1 (January) to 12 (December).

Serial_number is a number in the date-time code used by Microsoft Excel.

3

F2 f_x =MONTH(A2)

4

	A	B	C	D	E	F
1	Date	Product	Net	Quantity	Revenue	Date:Month
2	June 1, 2011	Pigs	$ 3.25	100	$ 325.00	6
3	June 2, 2011	Pigs	$ 3.25	105	$ 341.25	6

Exam 77-888: Microsoft Excel Expert 2010
2. Applying Formulas and Functions
2.4. Apply functions in formulas: DATE Functions MONTH

Calculating the Date

Many businesses need to calculate the difference between the current date and the date on the transaction. For example, a movie rental business may charge more if the movie is returned 3 days late.

Microsoft Excel has a function called **NETWORKDAYS.**

1. Before Your Begin: Enter the Date
Select Cell G1 and type: Today's Date

Select Cell G2 and type: July, 1, 2011. Copy and Paste Cell G2 to G58 (all of the Rows in this example)

What Do You See? In this example every Cell in Column G has the same date: July 1, 2011.

Keep going...

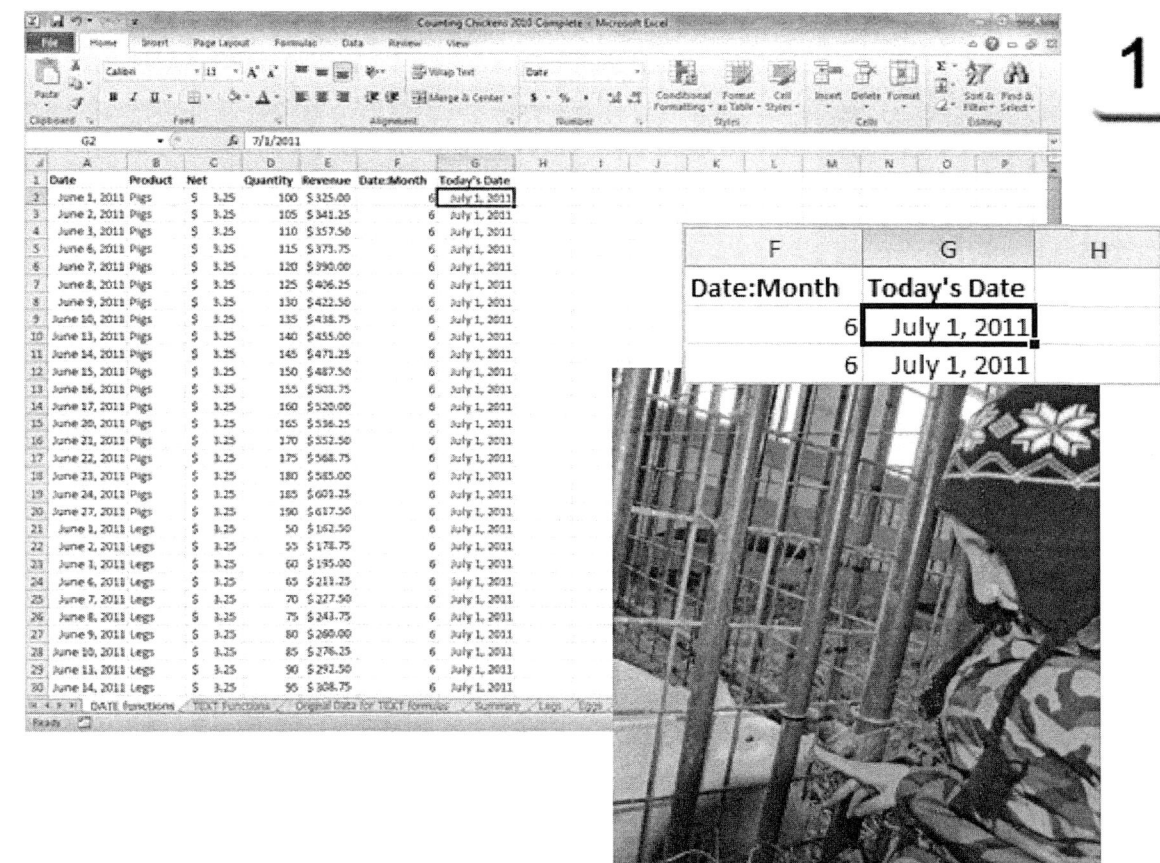

F	G	H
Date:Month	Today's Date	
6	July 1, 2011	
6	July 1, 2011	

Exam 77-888: Microsoft Excel Expert 2010
2. Applying Formulas and Functions
2.4. Apply functions in formulas: DATE Functions NETWORKDAYS

Date Functions: NETWORKDAYS

2 Try This: Add a Label
Go to the Date Functions sheet.
Select Cell H1.
Type the following label: Net Work Days

3. Try This, Too: Use a Date Function
Select **Cell H2**.
Go to **Formulas->Function Library-> Date&Time**.
Click on: **NETWORKDAYS**.
Keep going...

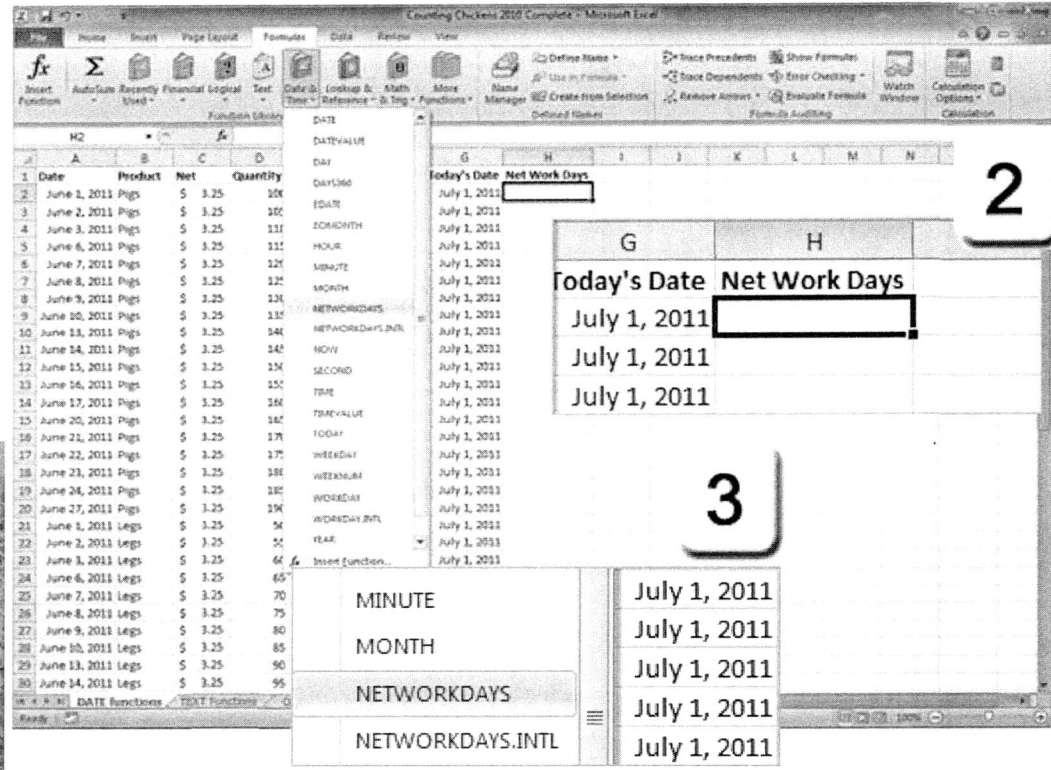

Exam 77-888: Microsoft Excel Expert 2010
2. Applying Formulas and Functions
2.4. Apply functions in formulas: DATE Functions NETWORKDAYS

NETWORKDAYS Arguments

4. Try it: Edit the NETWORKDAYS
Edit the Start_Date: A2.
Edit the End_Date:G2
You should see a preview of the data to the right of the Arguments.
Click **OK**.

5. Try This, Too: AutoFill the Formula
Use the **AutoFill** handle to fill down this formula in Column H.

Memo to Self: The date that is displayed in the Preview is a SERIAL NUMBER. After you edit the Arguments, the work days will be displayed as a whole number.

Formulas->Function Library-> Date & Time->NETWORKDAYS

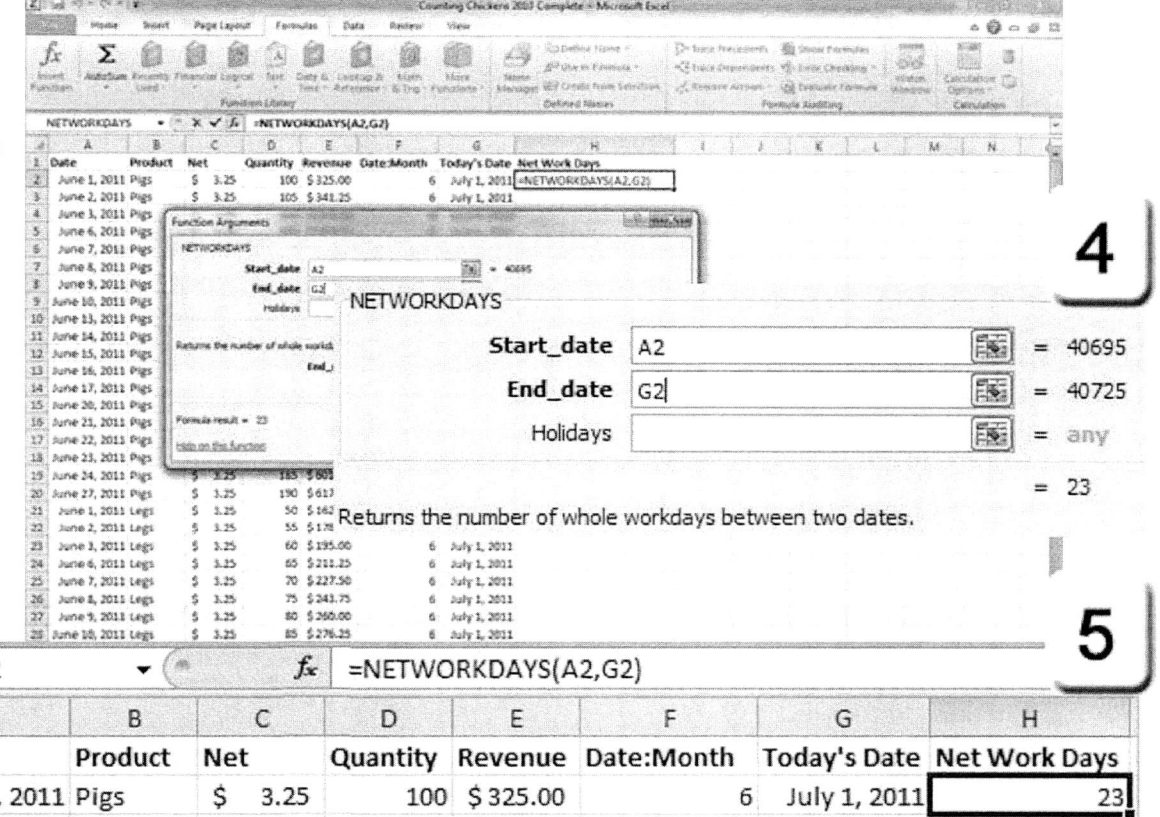

	Start_date	A2	= 40695
	End_date	G2	= 40725
	Holidays		= any
			= 23

Returns the number of whole workdays between two dates.

4

5

	H2	▼	f_x	=NETWORKDAYS(A2,G2)			
	A	B	C	D	E	F	G	H
1	Date	Product	Net	Quantity	Revenue	Date:Month	Today's Date	Net Work Days
2	June 1, 2011	Pigs	$ 3.25	100	$ 325.00	6	July 1, 2011	23
3	June 2, 2011	Pigs	$ 3.25	105	$ 341.25	6	July 1, 2011	22

Exam 77-888: Microsoft Excel Expert 2010
2. Applying Formulas and Functions
2.4. Apply functions in formulas: DATE Functions NETWORKDAYS

Time Functions

How many hours or minutes are there between the Start Time and the End Time? Here are the steps to figure it out.

1. Before You Begin: Enter the Data
Select Cell J1 and type: Start Time.
Select Cell K1 and type: End Time.
Select Cell L1 and type: Duration.
Format Cells J1, K1 and L1 **BOLD**.

Select Columns J and K.
Go to **Home->Numbers.**
Select the **Time** format.
Select Cell J2 and type: 8:30 AM
Select Cell K2 and type: 5:00 PM

2. Copy the Data
Copy and Paste Cell J2 to J58
Copy and Paste Cell K2 to K58
(all of the Rows in this example)

What Do You See?
The Cells in Column J have: 8:30:00 AM.
The Cells in Column K have: 5:00:00 PM
OK, keep going...

Home->Numbers->Time

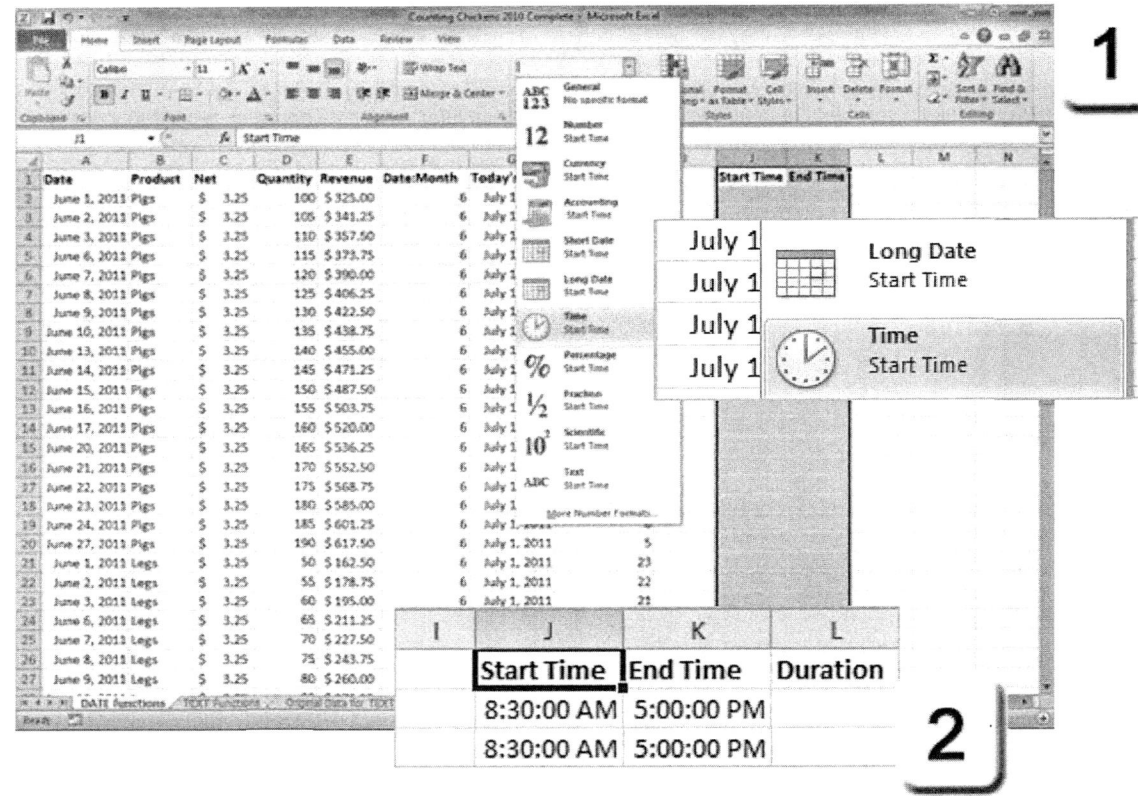

Exam 77-888: Microsoft Excel Expert 2010
2. Applying Formulas and Functions
2.4. Apply functions in formulas: TIME Functions

Calculate the Duration

Duration is the number of hours, minutes and seconds from the Start Time to the End Time.

3. Try it: Calculate the Duration

Select Cell L2 and type:=K2-J2,
Where K2 is the End Time and J2 is the Start Time.

Please **AutoFill** this formula from L2:L58. (all of the Rows in this example)

4. What Do You See? The formula and
the answer are correct. However, the formatting--8:30:00 AM--is confusing.

Keep going...

Home->Numbers->Time

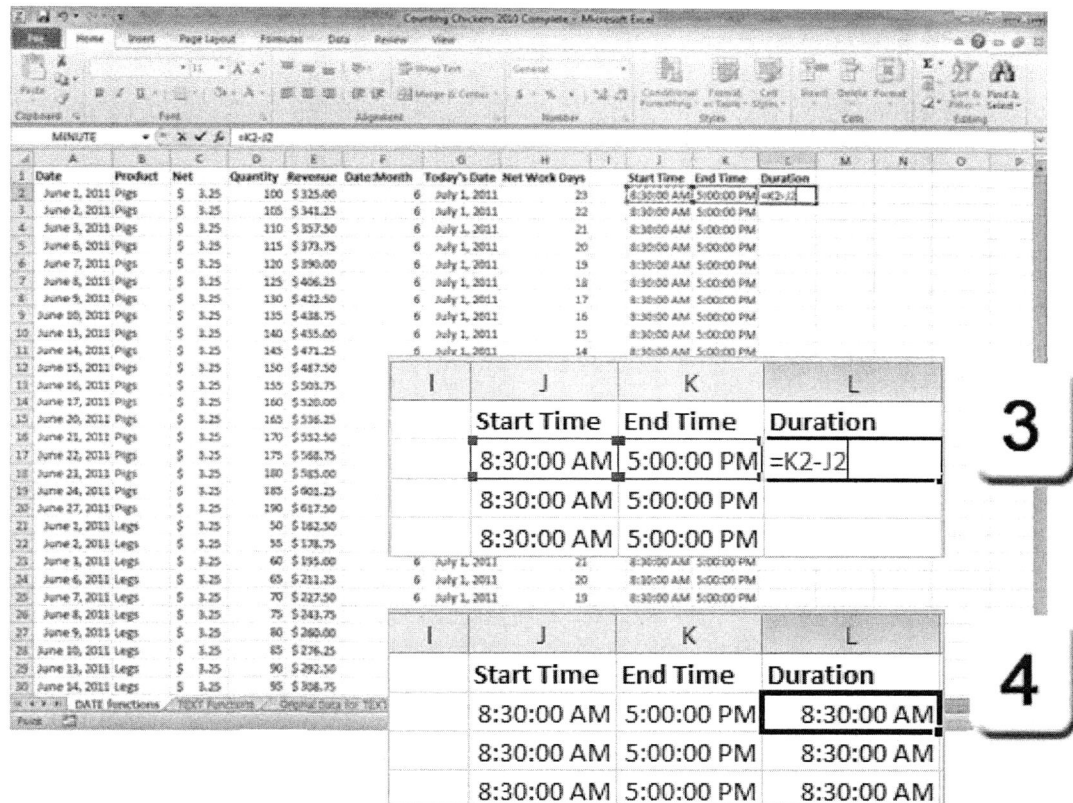

Exam 77-888: Microsoft Excel Expert 2010
2. Applying Formulas and Functions
2.4. Apply functions in formulas: TIME Functions

Format the Time

5. Try it: Format the Time
Select Column L.
Go to **Home->Number->More**.
(the little arrow in the bottom right corner)

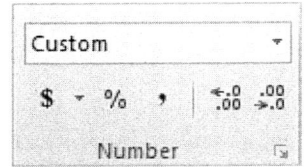

Go to the **Number** Tab.
Select the **Custom Category**.
Choose: h:mm

6. What Do You See? The Duration will
be formatted as Hours and Minutes.

Save Your Spreadsheet.
Very good.

Home->Number->More

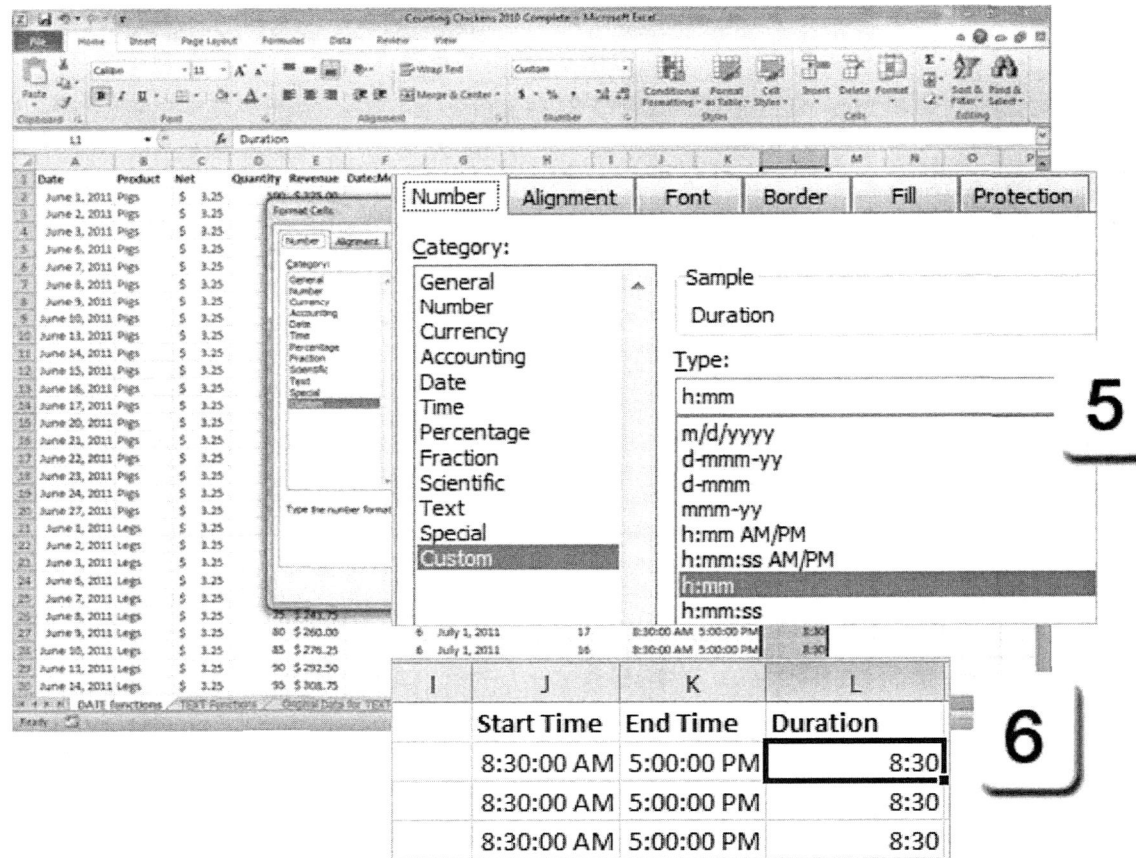

	Start Time	End Time	Duration
	8:30:00 AM	5:00:00 PM	8:30
	8:30:00 AM	5:00:00 PM	8:30
	8:30:00 AM	5:00:00 PM	8:30

Exam 77-882: Microsoft Excel 2010 Core
3. Formatting Cells and Worksheets
3.6. Create and apply cell styles: Apply Custom Format

Financial Functions

Microsoft Excel has a robust library of **Financial Functions**. Let's say that our little company, Charlotte's Website, needs a car. How would you calculate the car payments? Here are the steps.

1. Before You Begin: Enter the Labels
Open a new, blank spreadsheet.
Select Cell A1 and type: Present Value
Select Cell A2 and type: Number of Payments
Select Cell A3 and type: Interest Rate
Select Cell A4 and type: Payment

If these are labels, and they are, they should be selected and formatted BOLD.

Keep going...

Home->Font->Bold

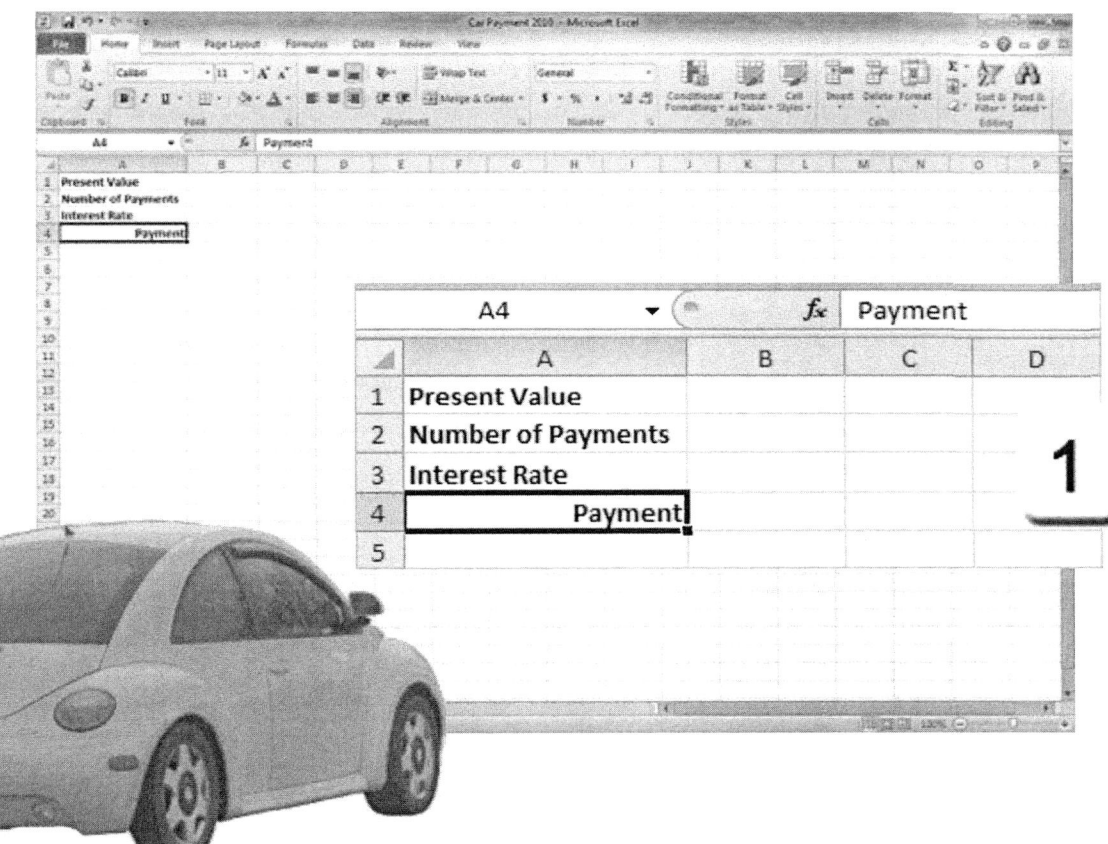

Exam 77-888: Microsoft Excel Expert 2010
2. Applying Formulas and Functions
2.4. Apply functions in formulas: FINANCIAL Functions

Enter and Format the Data

2. Try it: Enter the Data
Select Cell B1 and type: 20000
Go to **Home->Number** and select **Accounting**.
This is the **Present Value** of the car. **(Pv)**

Select Cell B2 and type: 36
This is the number of payment periods. **(Nper)**

Select Cell B3 and type: .04
Go to **Home->Number** and select **Percent**.
This is the **Interest Rate** for the loan. **(Rate)**

Keep going...

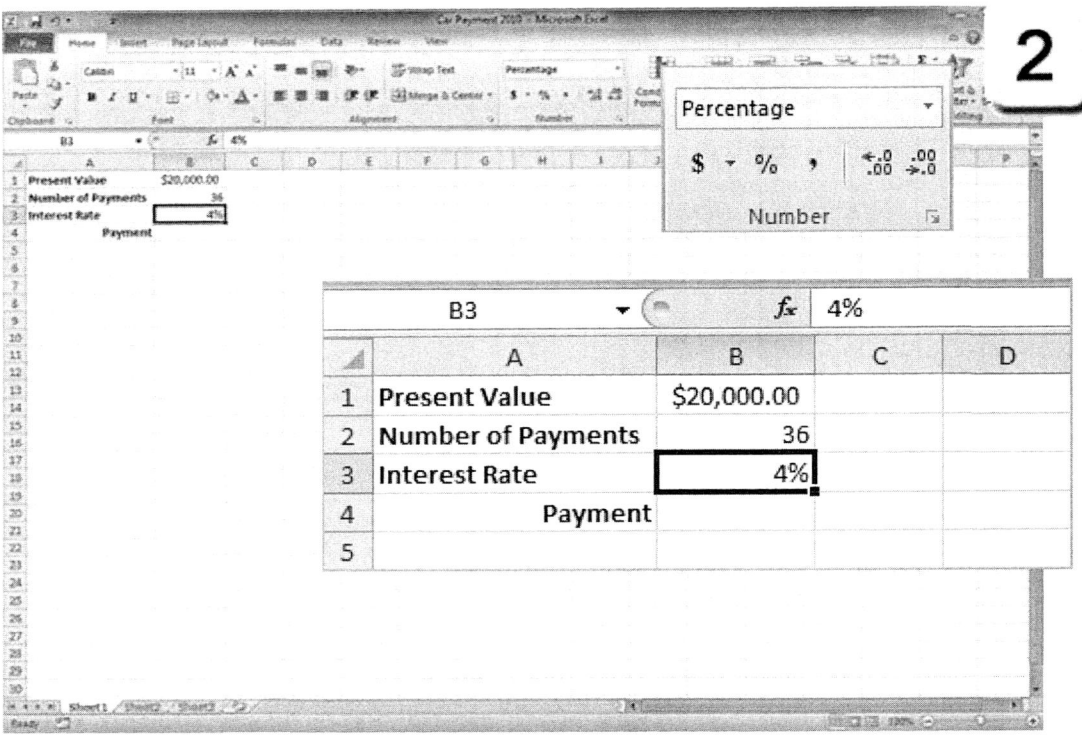

	A	B	C	D
1	Present Value	$20,000.00		
2	Number of Payments	36		
3	Interest Rate	4%		
4	Payment			
5				

Exam 77-888: Microsoft Excel Expert 2010
2. Applying Formulas and Functions
2.4. Apply functions in formulas: FINANCIAL Functions PMT

Financial Function: PMT
3. Try it: Use a Financial Function
Select Cell B4.
Go to **Formulas->Function Library.**
Go to **Financial.** Click on **PMT**.

Financial

When you see the Function Arguments:
Edit the **Rate**: B3/12
Edit the **Nper**: B2
Edit the **Pv**: B1
Keep going, please...

Memo to Self: The Yearly Rate is divided by 12 to get the Monthly Rate

Formulas-> Function Library-> Financial-> PMT

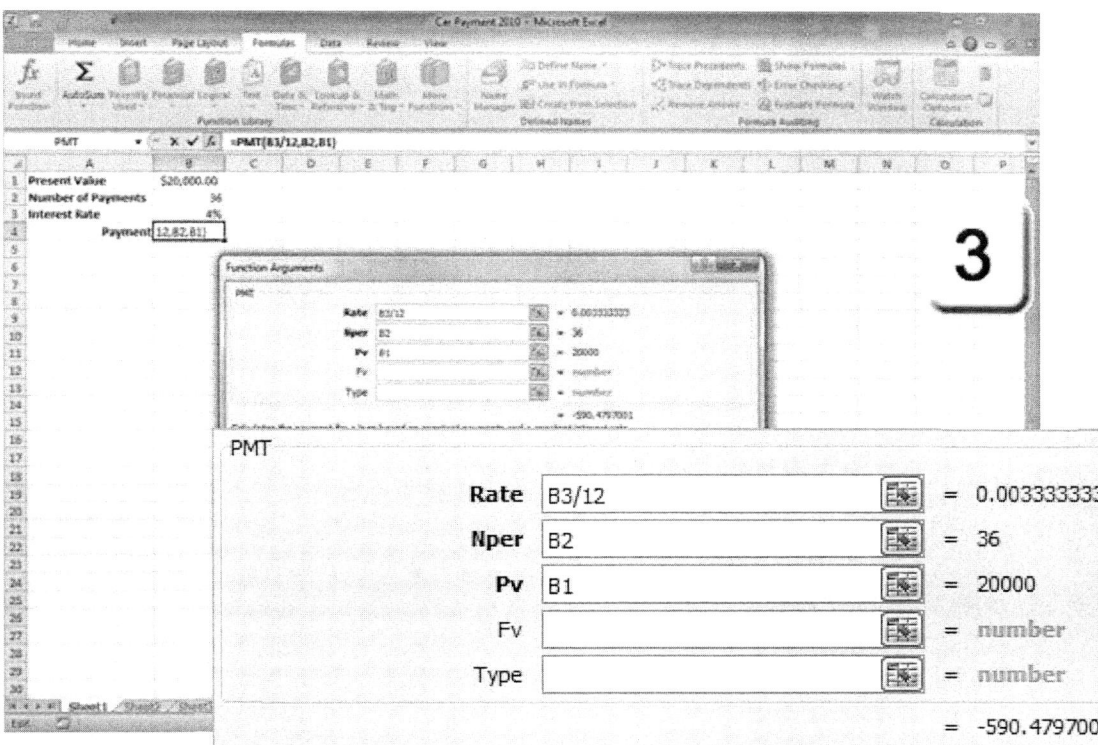

Rate	B3/12	= 0.003333333
Nper	B2	= 36
Pv	B1	= 20000
Fv		= number
Type		= number

= -590.479700:

Calculates the payment for a loan based on constant payments and a constant interest rate.

Exam 77-888: Microsoft Excel Expert 2010
2. Applying Formulas and Functions
2.4. Apply functions in formulas: FINANCIAL Functions PMT

PMT Arguments

4. What Do You See? In the example on this page, the payment on a $20,000 car would be $590.48 per month for 36 months.

What Else Do You See? A payment is a negative number: that means money is taken away from your bank account.

Very well, that was a simple example of a financial formula. Microsoft Excel has many formulas for calculating the value of investments, Tbills, price, rate and yield.

Formulas->Function Library->Financial->PMT

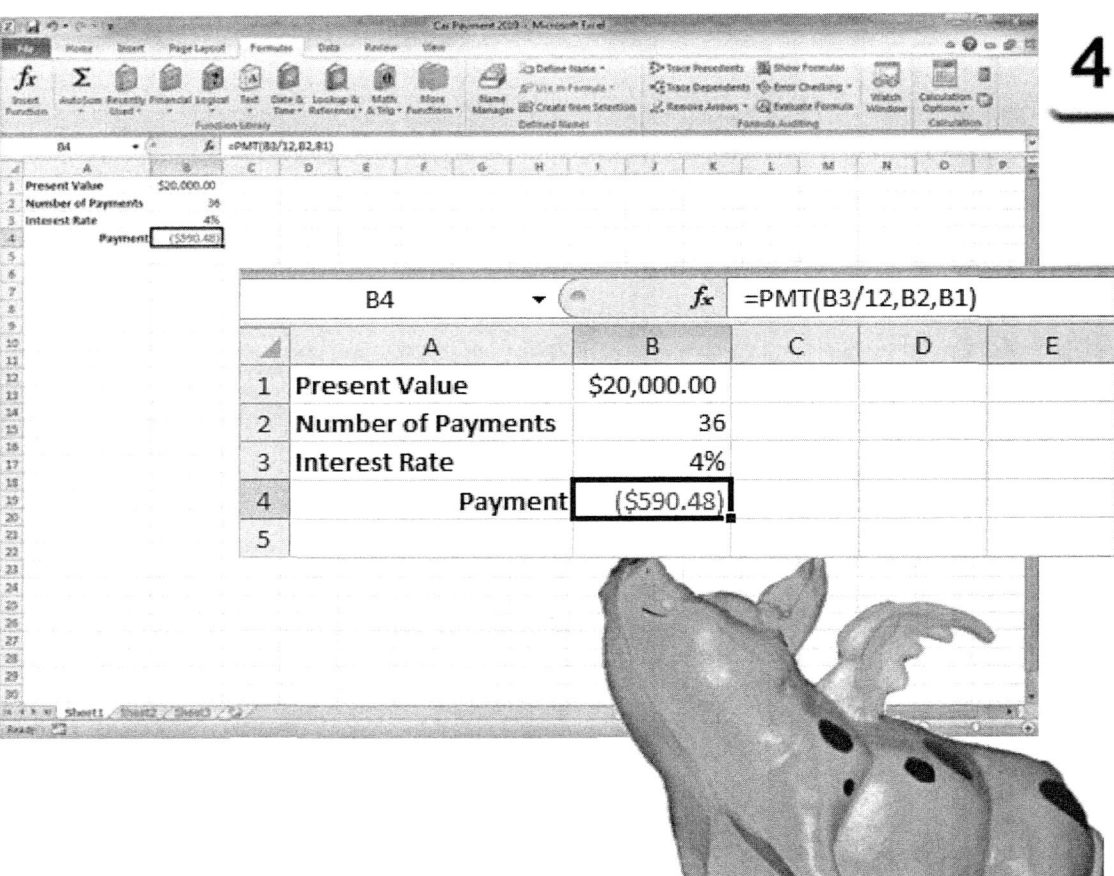

B4		f_x =PMT(B3/12,B2,B1)		
	A	B	C	D	E
1	Present Value	$20,000.00			
2	Number of Payments	36			
3	Interest Rate	4%			
4	Payment	($590.48)			
5					

Exam 77-888: Microsoft Excel Expert 2010
2. Applying Formulas and Functions
2.4. Apply functions in formulas: FINANCIAL Functions PMT

Summary

The purpose of the exercise was to use formulas, formulas, formulas. The lesson began with formulas that worked with TEXT: formatting text, combining text, and manipulating text.

We also looked at formulas that work with DATE and TIME.

The last pages demonstrated a very simple FINANCIAL formula.

Allez Allez in Free.
You done good. You get the cookie.

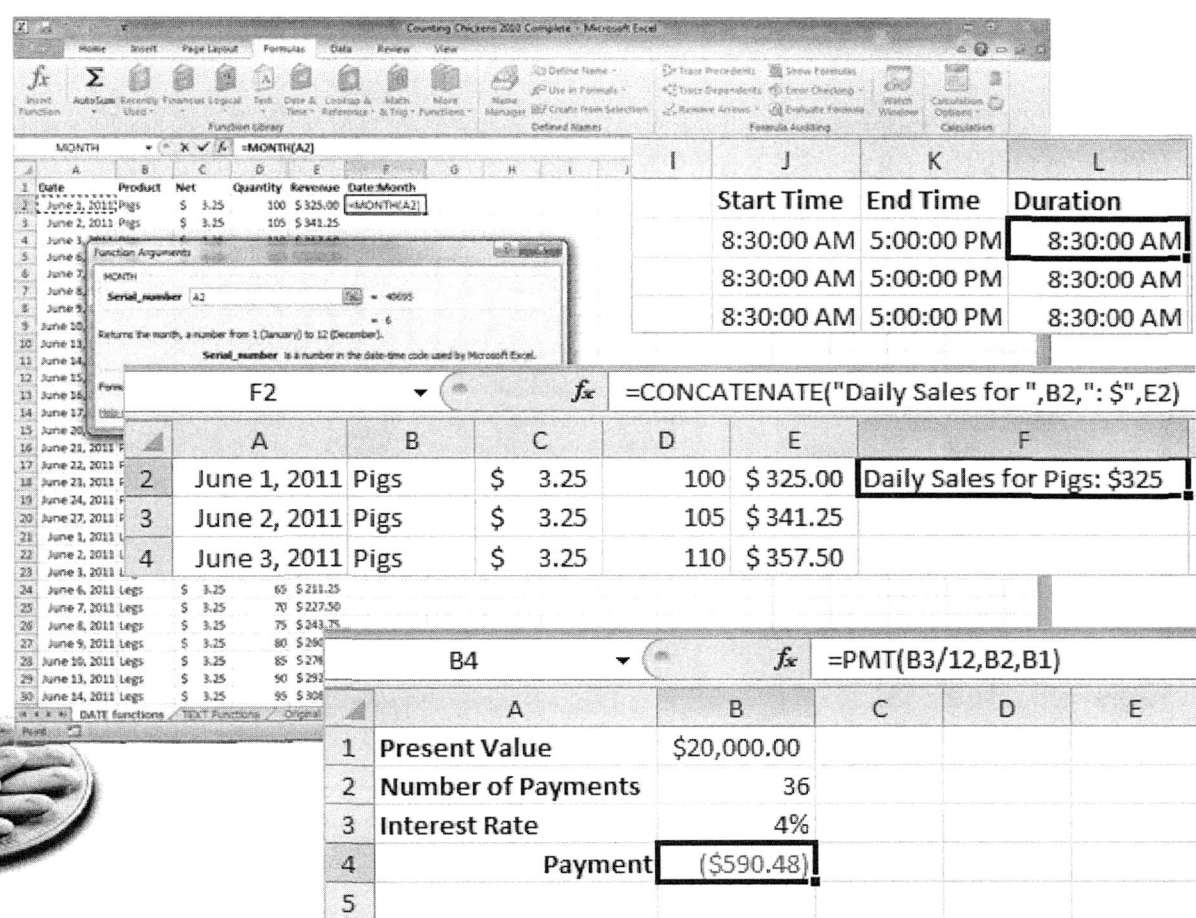

Practice Activities

Lesson 2: Piggy Goes to Market

Before You Begin: Download the sample file:
Brown Bag Sales Data 2010.xlsx.

Try This: Do the following steps

1. Open the sample: **Brown Bag Sales Data 2010.xlsx**

2. Select Column A: Sort by Date (not alphabetically)

3. Select Cell H1 and enter the label: UPPER

4. Select Cell H2 and create a Text Formula that references Cell B2 and formats the Text as UPPER.

5. AutoFill the TEXT formula from H2:H69

6. Select Cell I1 and enter the label: CONCATENATE
7. Select Cell I2 and create a Text Formula that combines Cell B2 and Cell D2.
Hint: You can use Row 2 to add the following ": "
8. AutoFill the TEXT formula from I2:I69.
9. Save this as YOUR NAME Piggy Practice.

Test Yourself

1. Which of the following are Paste Special Options?
(Select all correct answers.)
a. Values
b. Formulas
c. Formats
d. Paste All
Tip: Intermediate Excel, page 58

2. What does the Concatenate command do?
a. Combines the values of the selected cells
b. Concentrates and compresses the data
c. Filters the data
Tip: Intermediate Excel, page 61

3. Which command changes the formatting so each word starts with an upper case letter?
a. Upper
b. Change Case
c. Proper
d. Sentence Case
Tip: Intermediate Excel, p 66

4. Which of the following are text formulas?
(Select all correct answers)
a. Upper
b. Substitute
c. Concatenate
d. Sum
Tip: Intermediate Excel, page 61, 68

5. Excel can calculate the number of workdays between two given dates.
a. True
b. False
Tip: Intermediate Excel, page 72

6. Excel can calculate the amount of time elapsed.
a. True
b. False
Tip: Intermediate Excel, page 74

7. Which is the correct command for calculating payments on a car?
a. Formulas-> Calculate-> Car Payment
b. Formulas-> Financial-> Car Payment
c. Formulas->Financial-> PMT
Tip: Intermediate Excel, page 79

Excel 2010: Applying Formulas and Functions

Name that Tune

Intermediate Excel Objectives
In this lesson, you will learn how to:
1. Select and Name a RANGE of Cells
2. Use the Named Range in a formula
3. Use the Name Manager
4. Use Defined Names in a formula
5. Create Conditional Formulas
6. Identify errors

© 2011 Comma Productions

Lesson 3: Name that Tune

1. Readings

Read Lesson 3 in the Intermediate Excel guide, page 83-108.

Project

A spreadsheet that uses Defined Names in formulas to conditionally summarize data.

Downloads

Counting Chickens 2010 Complete.xlsx
Using Named Ranges.xlsx
Employee Data.xlsx

2. Practice

Complete the Practice Activity on page 108.

3. Assessment

Do the Test Yourself questions on page 108.

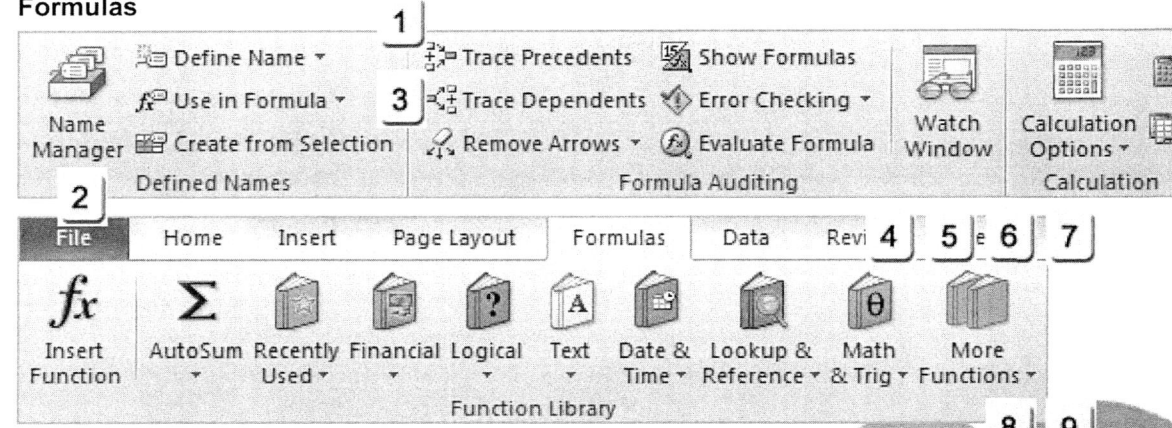

Menu Maps

This lesson demonstrates options on the **Formulas** Ribbon.

1. Formulas->Defined Names->Define Name, page 89
2. Formulas->Defined Names->Name Manager, page 93
3. Formulas->Defined Names ->Use in Formula, page 97
4. Formulas->Function Library->Math and Trig -> SUMIF, page 98
5. Formulas->Function Library->Math and Trig -> SUMIFS, page 99
6. Formulas->Function Library->More Functions ->Statistical ->COUNTIF, page 101
7. Formulas ->Function Library->More Functions -> Statistical ->COUNTIFS, page 102
8. Formulas ->Function Library->More Functions -> Statistical ->AVERAGEIF, page 103
9. Formulas ->Function Library->More Functions -> Statistical ->AVERAGEIFS, page 104

Using Names in Formulas

The Intermediate Guide to Excel focuses on References. The first lesson looked at **Cell References**: Relative and Absolute Cell References. The second lesson used the **Cell References in a Formula**. The lesson demonstrated formulas that modified and formatted Text, Date and Time. This third lesson will show how to select a RANGE of cells and use a **Named Range in a Formula**.

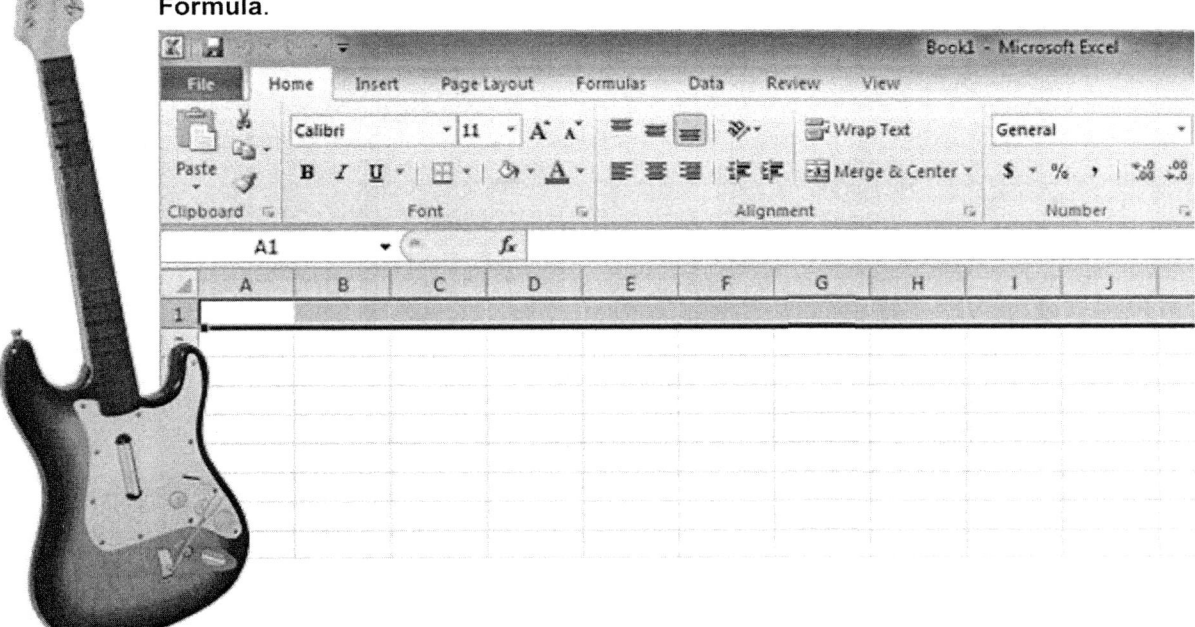

Start the Program Microsoft Excel.

What Do You See? Is there a Title Bar that says Book1 - Microsoft Excel? Yes.

Is there a **Home** Ribbon with the Clipboard, Font, Alignment and Number Groups? Yes.

If your screen looks similar to the example on this page, then you are ready to get started.

Before you Begin

This example uses the same spreadsheet that was created in the previous lesson. You can continue with the one you saved or download a new sample if you wish.

Try This: Open a Sample Spreadsheet
Open a sample spreadsheet:
Using Named Ranges.xlsx
Go to the Original Data sheet.

What Do You See? This sheet shows the net product sales for three products: Legs, Eggs, and Pigs. The data includes:

Date (Number, formatted as Medium Date)
Product (Text)
Net (Number, formatted as Accounting)
Quantity (Number)
Revenue (Number, formatted as Accounting)

Memo to Self: You do not have to MATCH the numbers shown on these pages. It is more important that you begin with some data and *understand* the options.

File -> Open

	A	B	C	D	E	F	G
1	Date	Product	Net	Quantity	Revenue		
2	June 1, 2011	Pigs	$ 3.25	100	$ 325.00		
3	June 1, 2011	Legs	$ 3.25	50	$ 162.50		
4	June 1, 2011	Eggs	$ 1.50	100	$ 150.00		
5	June 2, 2011	Pigs	$ 3.25	105	$ 341.25		
6	June 2, 2011	Legs	$ 3.25	55	$ 178.75		
7	June 2, 2011	Eggs	$ 1.50	105	$ 157.50		

Select a Range

By definition, a **RANGE** is a one or more cells on a spreadsheet. The cells may be adjacent or not. There are a couple of ways to select a **Range of Cells**.

Before You Begin: The sample spreadsheet, Using Named Ranges.xlsx should be open.
Go to the Original Data spreadsheet.

1. Try This: Select a Range with a Mouse
Select Cells E1:E58
(the last row with data in this example.)

Keep going...

E1				f_x	Revenue	
	A	B	C	D	E	F	G
1	Date	Product	Net	Quantity	Revenue		
2	June 1, 2011	Pigs	$ 3.25	100	$ 325.00		
3	June 1, 2011	Legs	$ 3.25	50	$ 162.50		
4	June 1, 2011	Eggs	$ 1.50	100	$ 150.00		
5	June 2, 2011	Pigs	$ 3.25	105	$ 341.25		
6	June 2, 2011	Legs	$ 3.25	55	$ 178.75		

Exam 77-882: Microsoft Excel 2010 Core
5. Applying Formulas and Functions
5.6. Apply cell ranges in formulas: Select a Range

Define a Range

The **Name Box** is a special tool in the top left corner by the Formula bar. You can use the Name Box to **Define a Range,** instead of selecting the cells with your mouse.

2. Try This, Too: Define a Range

Place your cursor in the **Name Box.**
Type: E1:E58
Hit the ENTER key on your keyboard.

What Do You See? The RANGE of cells from Cell E1 through Cell E58 are selected and highlighted blue.

Keep going, please...

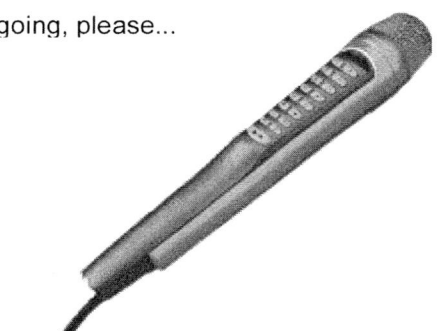

Formulas -> Define Name

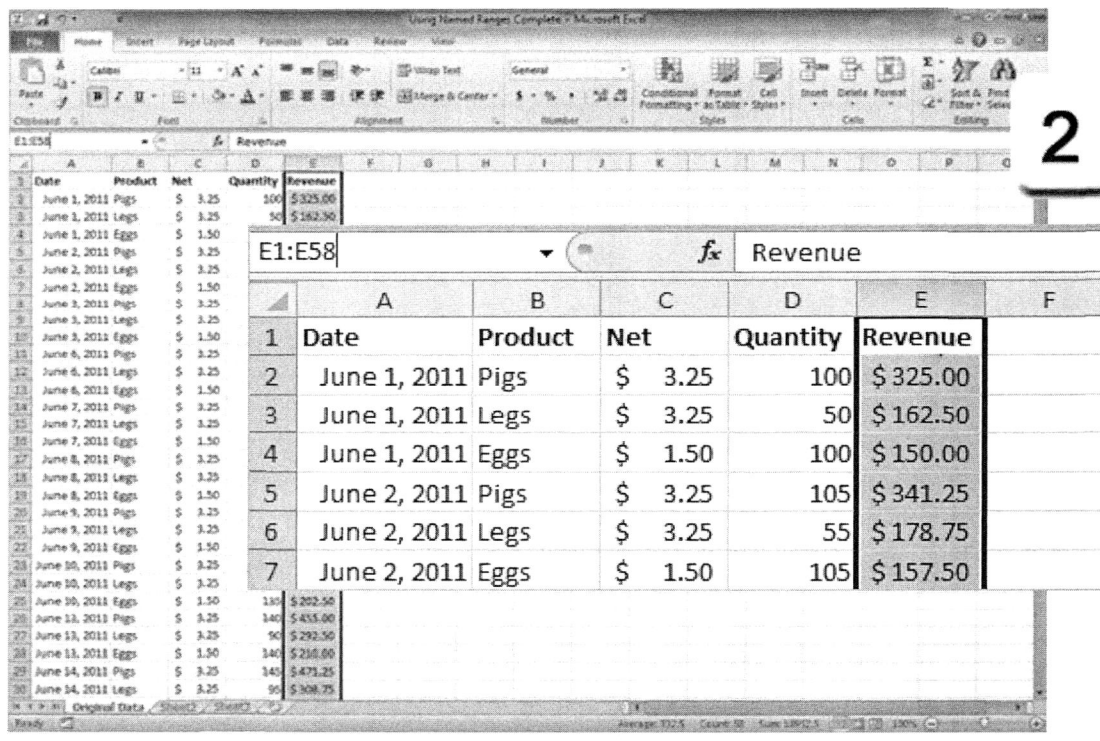

	A	B	C	D	E	F
1	Date	Product	Net	Quantity	Revenue	
2	June 1, 2011	Pigs	$ 3.25	100	$ 325.00	
3	June 1, 2011	Legs	$ 3.25	50	$ 162.50	
4	June 1, 2011	Eggs	$ 1.50	100	$ 150.00	
5	June 2, 2011	Pigs	$ 3.25	105	$ 341.25	
6	June 2, 2011	Legs	$ 3.25	55	$ 178.75	
7	June 2, 2011	Eggs	$ 1.50	105	$ 157.50	

Exam 77-882: Microsoft Excel 2010 Core
5. Applying Formulas and Functions
5.6. Apply cell ranges in formulas: Name a Range

Name a Range

So far so good. The goal is to select a RANGE of cells and then name it. The example on this page shows how to create a **Defined Name** with the **Formula** Ribbon.

3. Try This: Name a Range

The sample spreadsheet is open to the Original Data. Cells E1:E58 are selected

Go to **Formulas->Defined Names**.

Click on **Define Name.**

What Do You See? You will be prompted to enter a Name. By default, Microsoft Excel chose the label from Cell E1.

What Else Do You See? The New Name **Refers to:** ='Original Data'!$E$1:$E$58

All good formulas begin with equals: =

'Original Data' is the name of the sheet.

The Range of Cells, **$E$1:$E$58** is defined with **Absolute** Cell References.

Formulas -> Defined Names->Define Name

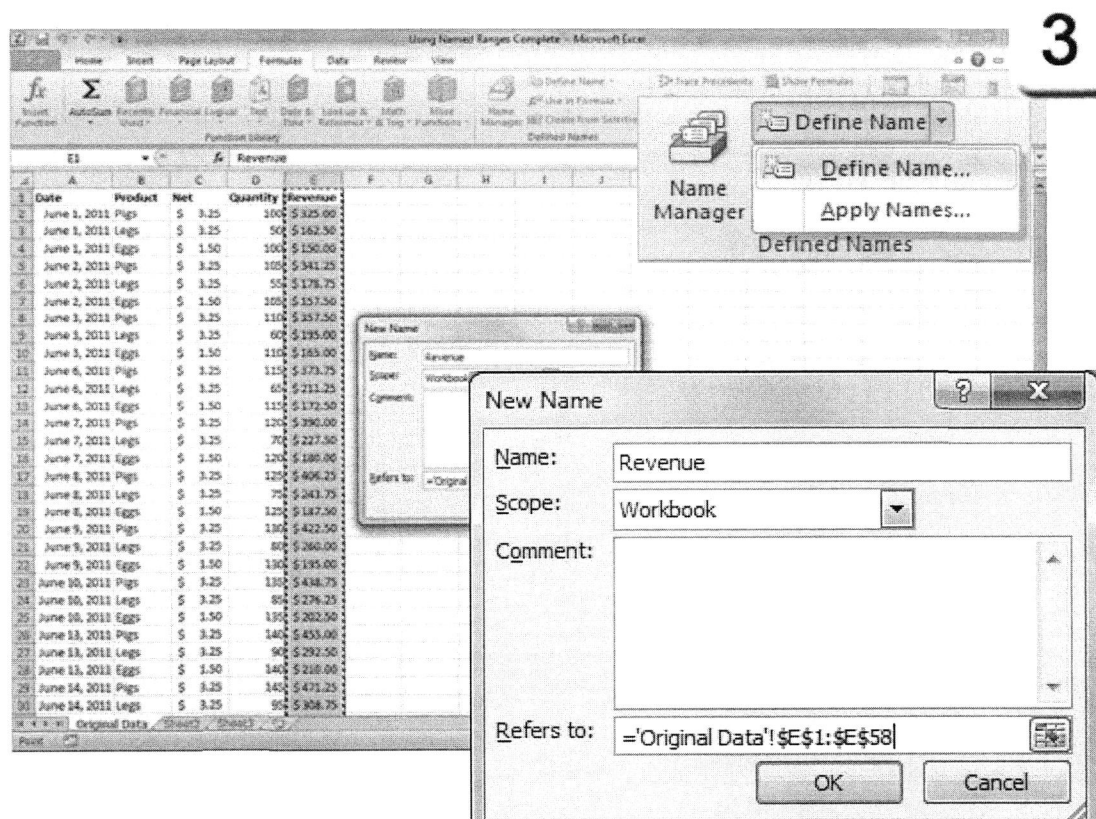

3

Exam 77-882: Microsoft Excel 2010 Core
5. Applying Formulas and Functions
5.3. Apply cell references in formulas: Use Absolute and Relative cell references

Another Way to Name a Range

You can use the **Name Box** to select and name a Range. Here are the steps.

4. Try This: Define a Named Range

The sample spreadsheet is open.
Go to the Original Data sheet.
Place your cursor in the **Name Box**.
Type: D1:D58
Hit the ENTER key on your keyboard.
The data in Column D should be selected.

5. Try This, Too: Name a Range

Place your cursor in the **Name Box**.
Type: QuantitySold
Hit the ENTER key on your keyboard.

What Do You See? The **QuantitySold** should be in the **Name Box**.

Keep going...

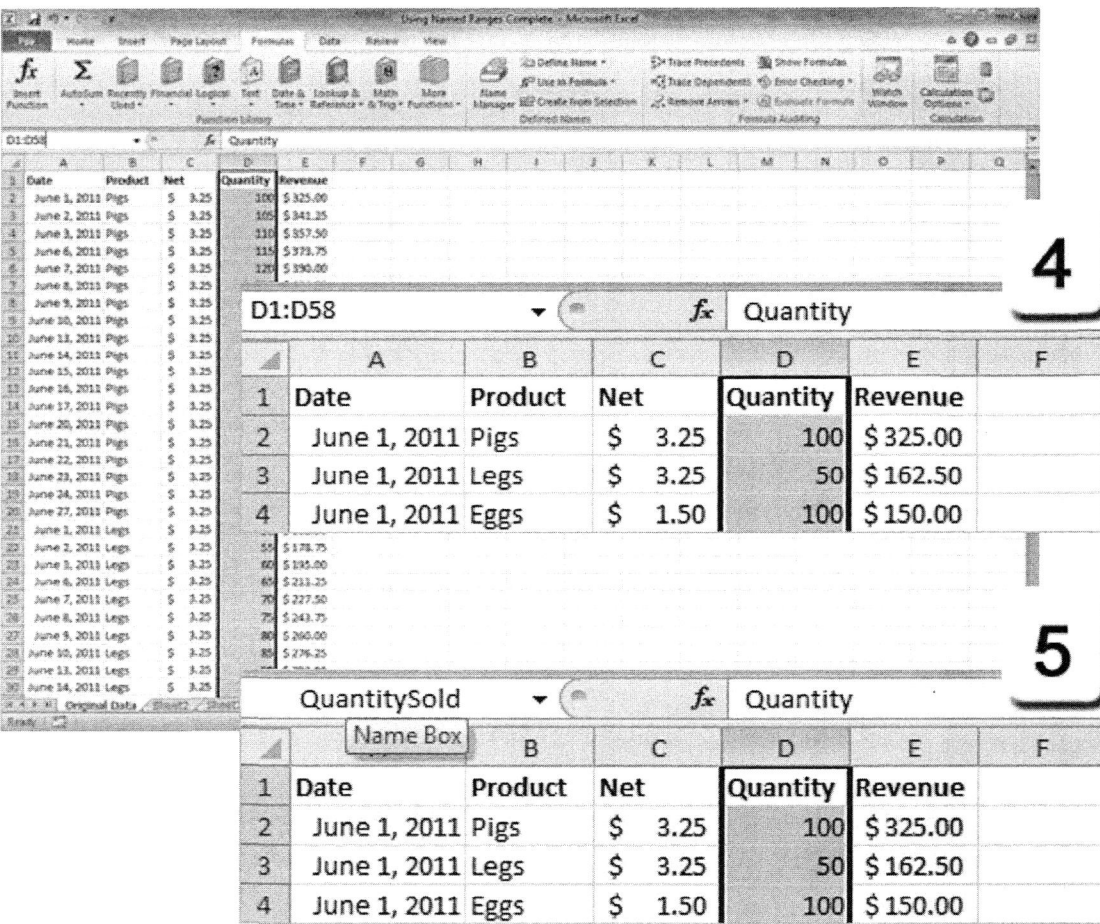

Exam 77-882: Microsoft Excel 2010 Core
5. Applying Formulas and Functions
5.6. Apply cell ranges in formulas: Define a Named Range

HOME

Take One

Formulas -> Defined Names->Define Name

Rules for Defined Names

There was a Dr. Seuss story about a Mrs. McCave who had 23 sons and named them all "Dave." She could have named one "Buffalo Bill" and one "Buffalo Bluff",...and one "Zanzibar Buck-Buck McFate." But she didn't, and now it's too late.

It was a good story about names. Let's talk about names. The **Defined Names** should make sense if someone else is trying to edit or update your spreadsheet. There are also rules for what is and is not allowed for names.

Syntax Rules for Defined Names

The first character must be a letter. The next characters can be text, numbers, periods and underscores. Names can be up to 255 characters. **Names cannot include Cell References**. For example, a Name cannot be $B$1. Names cannot include "C", "c", "R", or "r" because they are used as shorthand for selecting Columns and Rows in the Name Box.

Spaces are not allowed.

QuantitySold f_x Quantity

Name Box

	A	B	C	D	E	F
1	Date	Product	Net	Quantity	Revenue	
2	June 1, 2011	Pigs	$ 3.25	100	$ 325.00	
3	June 1, 2011	Legs	$ 3.25	50	$ 162.50	
4	June 1, 2011	Eggs	$ 1.50	100	$ 150.00	
5	June 2, 2011	Pigs	$ 3.25	105	$ 341.25	
6	June 2, 2011	Legs	$ 3.25	55	$ 178.75	
7	June 2, 2011	Eggs	$ 1.50	105	$ 157.50	

Exam 77-882: Microsoft Excel 2010 Core
5. Applying Formulas and Functions
5.6. Apply cell ranges in formulas: Define a Named Range

Select a Named Range

You can use a Named Range to find and select the data. This is also a good way to proof your Ranges.

Before You Begin: Go to a blank sheet. Select Cell A1.

1. Try This: Select a Named Range
Go to the down arrow on the **Name Box.**
Select: Revenue.

2. What Do You See? You will be taken to the Original Data spreadsheet. The Revenue Range, Cells E1:E58, should be selected and highlighted.

Formulas -> Defined Names->Define Name

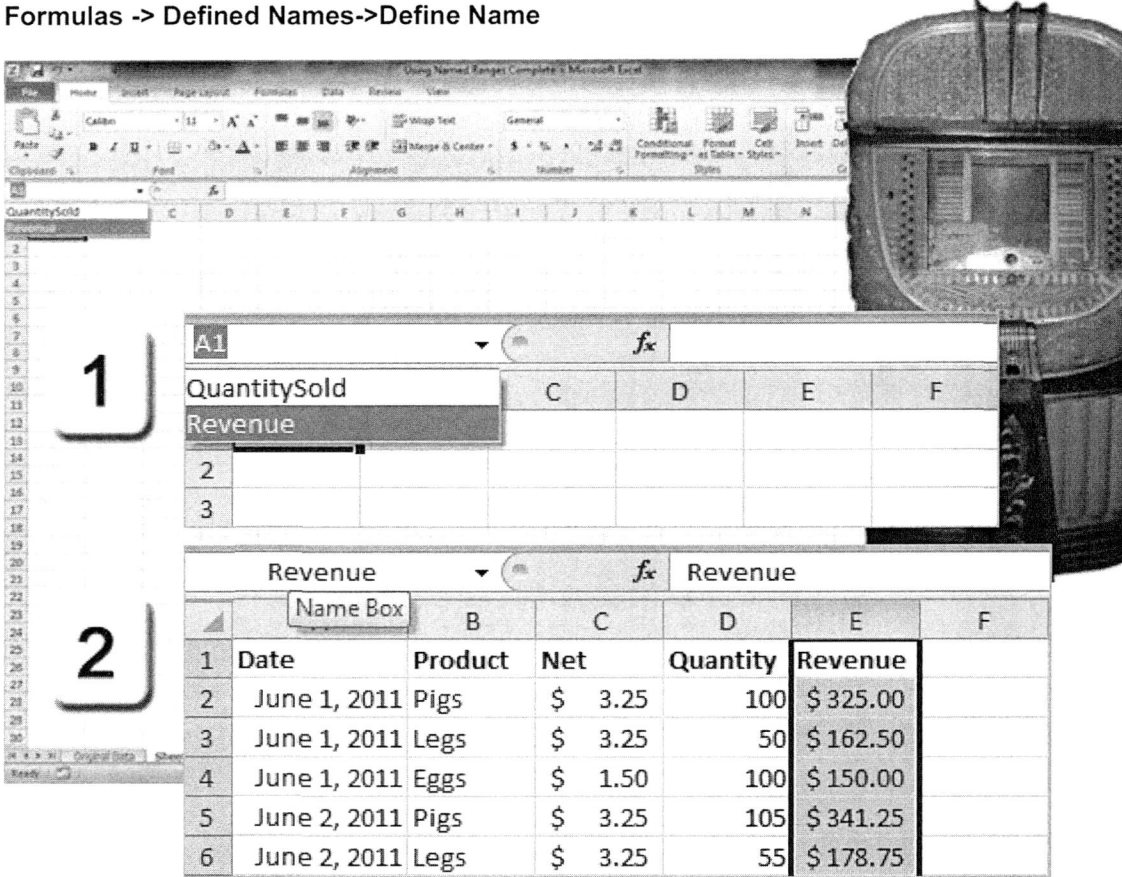

Exam 77-882: Microsoft Excel 2010 Core
5. Applying Formulas and Functions
5.6. Apply cell ranges in formulas: Select a Named Range

Take One

Formulas ->Defined Names-> Name Manager

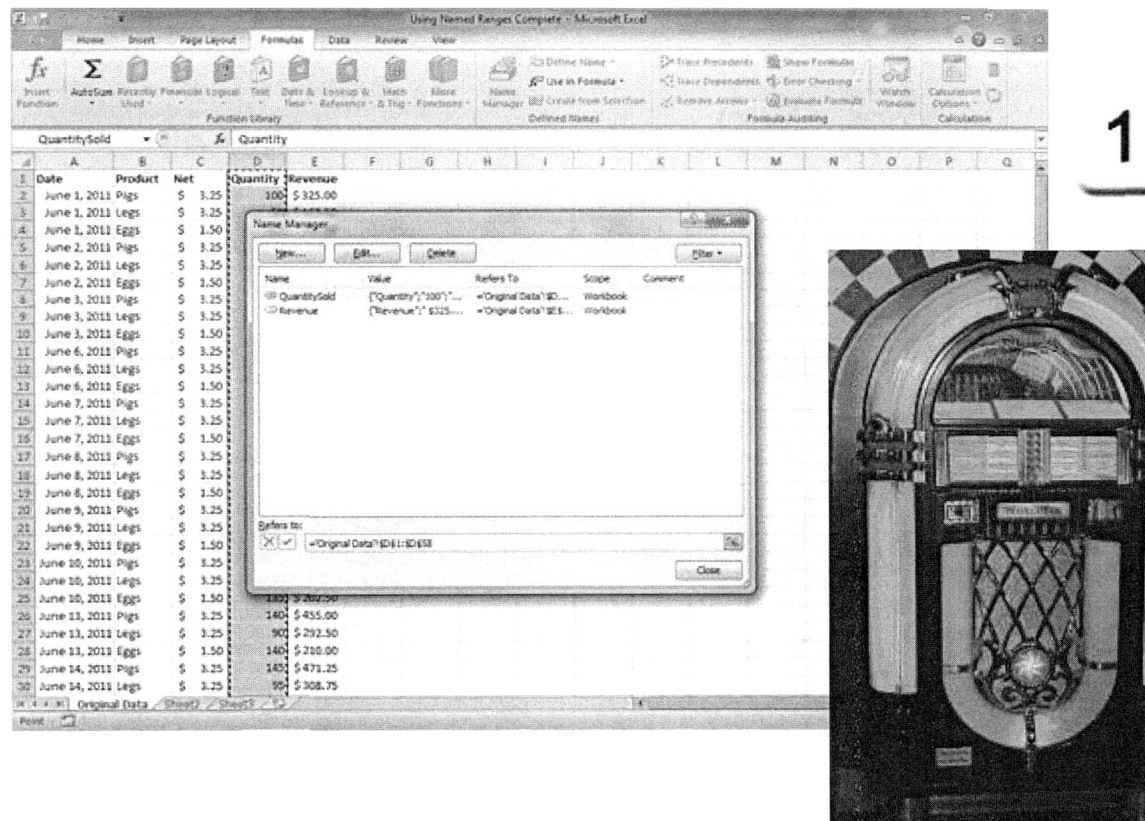

1

The Name Manager

A **Named Range** is a selection of cells that you can define and name with the **Name Box**. Each of these Defined Names can be found in the **Name Manager**.

1. Try This: Work With Defined Names
Go to **Formulas ->Defined Names.**
Select **Name Manager**.

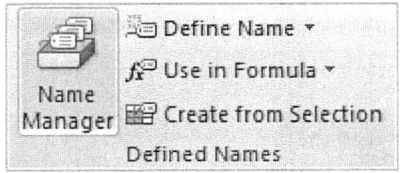

What Do You See? The Name Manager will display all of the Defined Names in this Spreadsheet.

Keep going...

Exam 77-882: Microsoft Excel 2010 Core
5. Applying Formulas and Functions
5.6. Apply cell ranges in formulas: Use the Name Manager

Manage the Ranges

The **Name Manager** simplifies the task of finding and editing the Defined Names in an Excel workbook. You can use the Name Manager to create, edit and delete Defined Names.

2. Try It: Review the Defined Names
Go to **Formulas->Defined Names**.
Click on Name Manager.
Select a Name: QuantitySold

What Do You See? This Defined Name Refers to the Original Data sheet. This is an Absolute Reference to Cells $D$1 through $D$58.
Keep going...

Formulas ->Defined Names->Name Manager

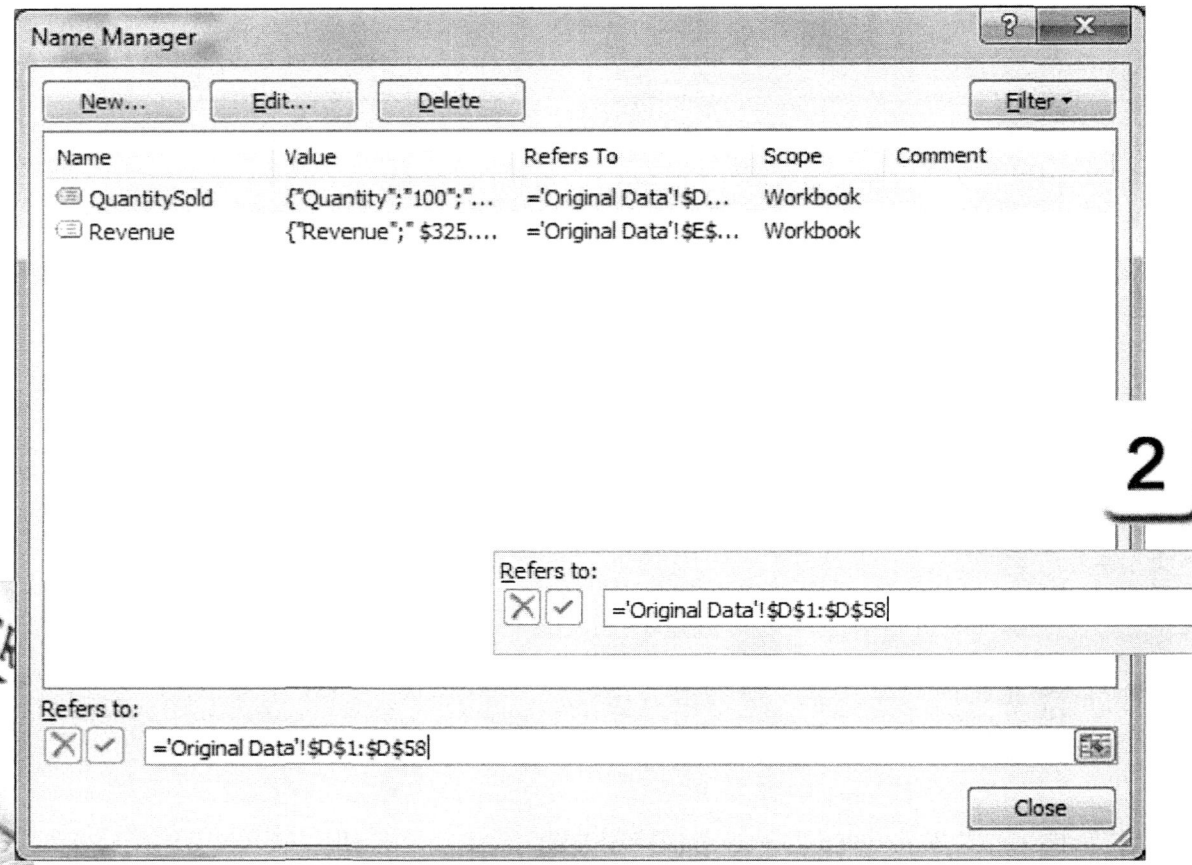

2

Exam 77-882: Microsoft Excel 2010 Core
5. Applying Formulas and Functions
5.6. Apply cell ranges in formulas: Use the Name Manager

Intermediate Excel 2010 Page 94 of 230

Take One

Edit a Name

Say you wanted to add or modify one of your Names. You can use the Name Manager to edit the name and the range. You can also add a comment to document your changes if you wish.

3. Try This: Create or Edit a Name

Go to **Formulas->Defined Names->Name Manager.** Click on **New.**

The **New Name** window will open.

Enter a **Name**: Product

Enter the **Scope**: Workbook

Click on **Lookup** (the red, white and blue button)

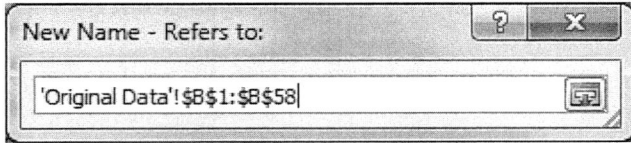

Go to the Original Data spreadsheet.
Select Cells B1 through B58.
Click on **Lookup** to return **New Name** window. Click on **OK** to return to the **Name Manager**.
This process added another **Defined Name** to the **Name Manager**.

Formulas ->Defined Names->Name Manager ->New

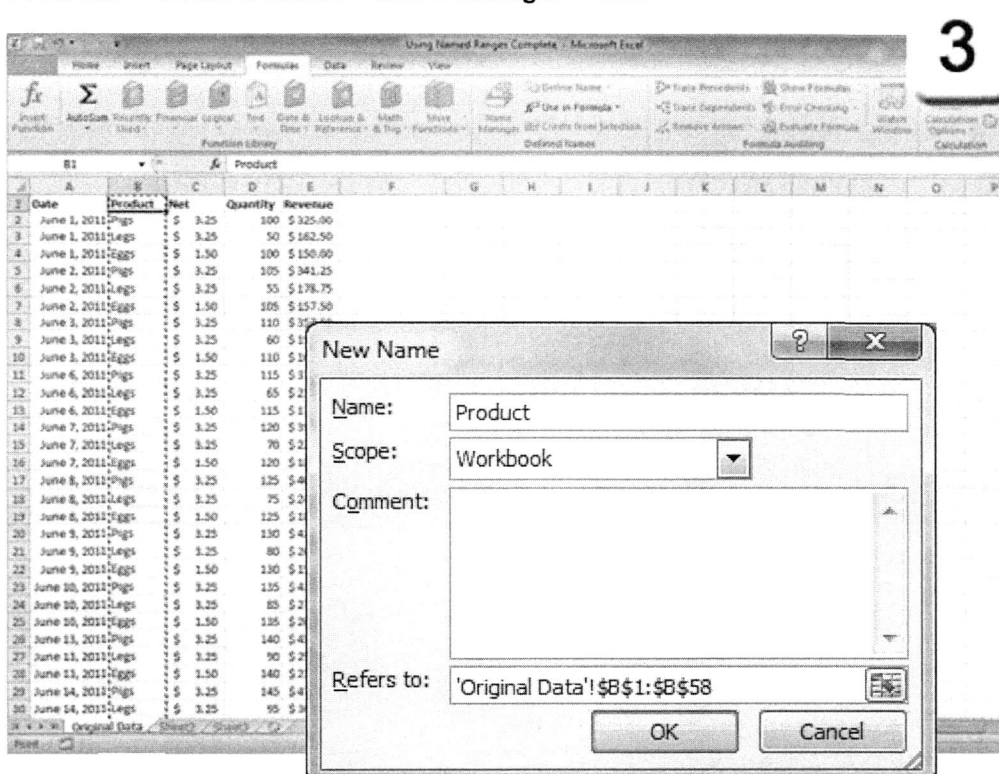

Exam 77-882: Microsoft Excel 2010 Core
5. Applying Formulas and Functions
5.6. Apply cell ranges in formulas: Use the Name Manager to Edit a Name

Name Manager Options
A good working spreadsheet may have dozens of Named references.

One of the best tools is the **Filter**. The Filter lets you choose which Defined Names you would like to see. You can limit the list of Names to the Names in just one worksheet, or view all of the Names in the workbook.

Try It: Filter the Names
Go to **Formulas->Defined Names.**
Select **Name Manager**.
Click on **Filter.**

What Do You See? The options are:
Names Scoped to a Worksheet
Names Scoped to a Workbook
Name with Errors
Names without Errors
Defined Names
Table Names

Please close the **Name Manager** and save your work.

Formulas ->Defined Names->Name Manager->Filter

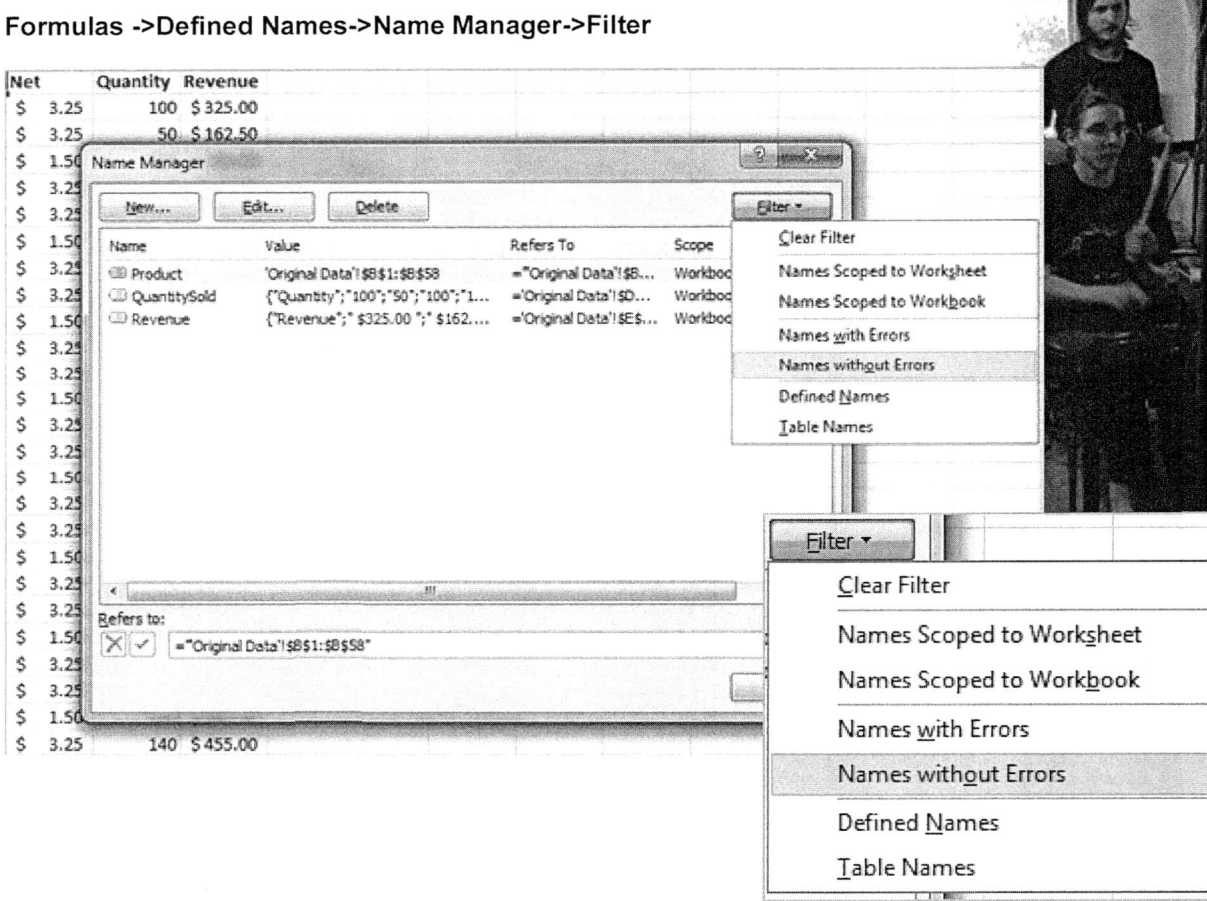

Exam 77-882: Microsoft Excel 2010 Core
5. Applying Formulas and Functions
5.6. Apply cell ranges in formulas: Use the Name Manager

Use the Names in a Formula

The purpose of creating these Defined Names is to use the references in a formula. The following pages will demonstrate how to **conditionally summarize** data with formulas.

A **Conditional Summary** means: show me the data that matches my **Criteria**. At the basic level, a Conditional Summary is a filter. Say you had three products: legs, eggs and pigs. A filter asks: show me the eggs sales. A **Conditional Summary** asks: show me the eggs sales that were greater than $500.00 per day. Which days?

1. Try This: Create a Sample Formula
Select Cell F1 and type: Sample Formula
Select Cell F2.
Go to **Formulas ->Defined Names.**
Go to **Use in Formula.**
Select: **Revenue.**

2. What Do You See? The formula is: =Revenue. The formula bar displays the Defined Name and the correct Range of Cells is selected.

Please **UNDO** this practice and keep going...

Formulas ->Defined Names Use in Formula ->Use in Formula

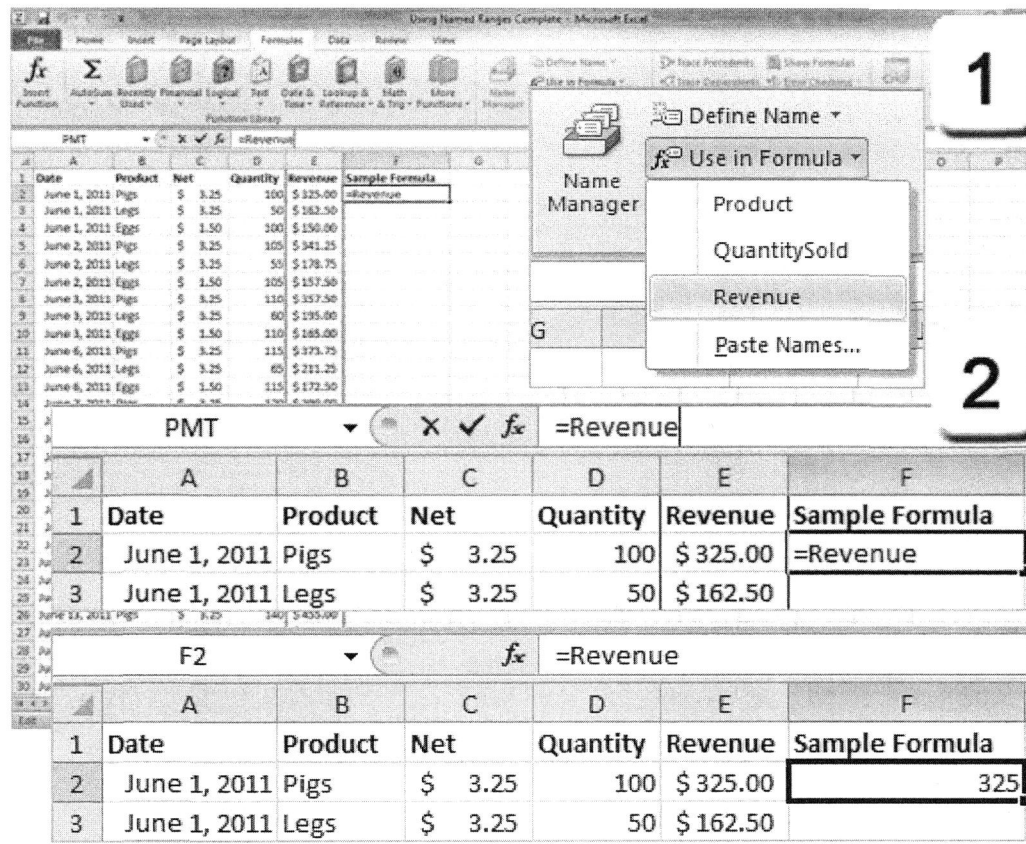

Exam 77-888: Microsoft Excel Expert 2010
2. Applying Formulas and Functions
2.3. Data summary: SUMIF, SUMIFS, COUNTIF, COUNTIFS, AVERAGEIF, and AVERAGEIFS

Summarize the Data

What is the sum of the product sales if you look at the Eggs, only?

Try This: SUMIF
Add a label to Cell D59: SUMIF eggs
Select Cell E59.
Go to **Formulas -> Function Library.**
Go to **Math and Trig->SUMIF**.
Enter the **Range**: Product
Enter the **Criteria**: Eggs
(Microsoft Excel will add quotes because this is Text)
Enter the **Sum_range**: Revenue.
Click **OK**.

What Do You See?
The **SUMIF** function calculates the sum based on your criteria. In this example, the **Criteria** is the product: Eggs.

The **Sum_range** is Revenue. Excel will look in Column E, Cells E1:E58, and SUM the money.

Formulas -> Function Library->Math and Trig -> SUMIF

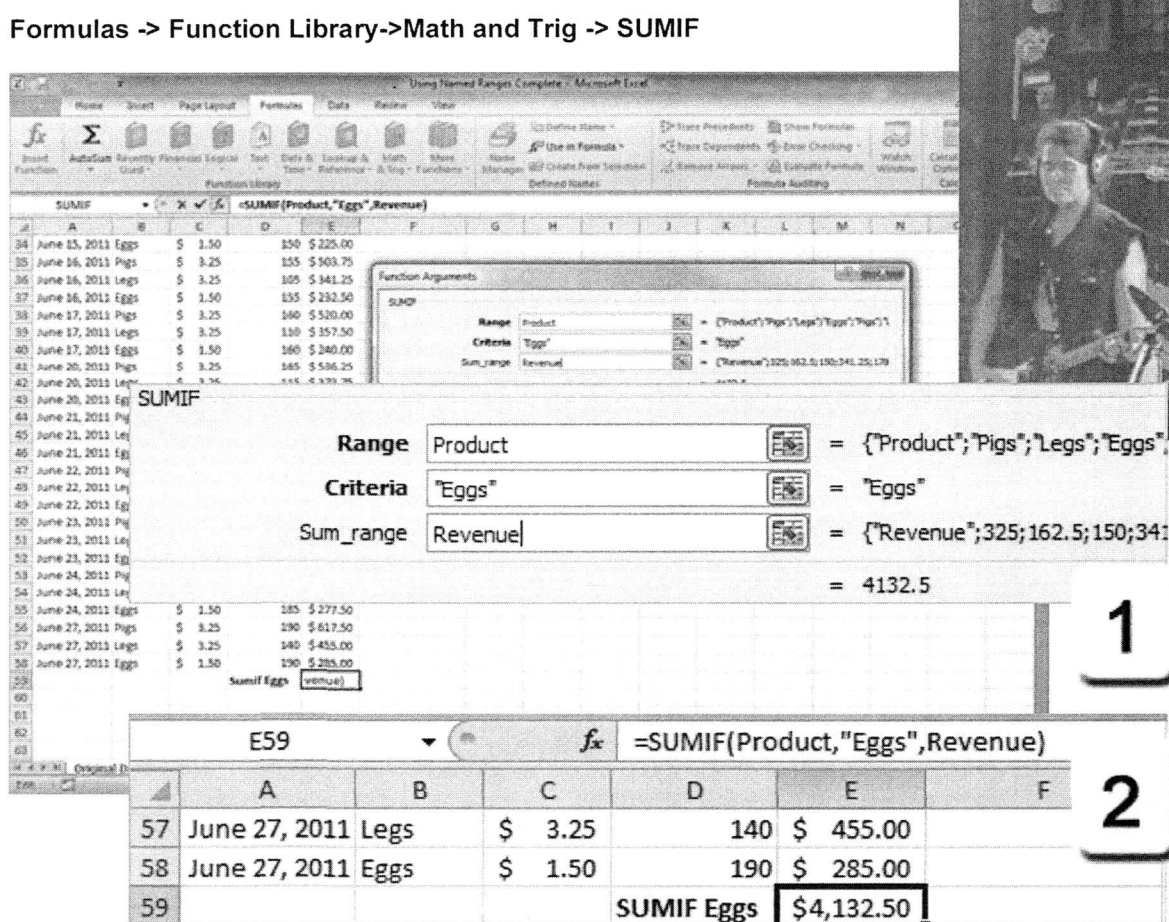

Exam 77-888: Microsoft Excel Expert 2010
2. Applying Formulas and Functions
2.3. Data summary: SUMIF, SUMIFS, COUNTIF, COUNTIFS, AVERAGEIF, and AVERAGEIFS

SUMIFS Function

What is the SUM of the products with more than $500.00 in sales each day?

SUMIFS lets you use several **Criteria** in the formula. This function works with the numbers, not the text.

1. Try This: SUMIFS

Select Cell D60.
Type: SUMIFS All Sales Greater than $500. Format the Cell to Wrap Text.
Select Cell E60.
Go to **Formulas -> Function Library.**
Go to **Math and Trig->SUMIFS.**
Enter the **Sum_Range:** Revenue
Enter the Criteria_range1: Revenue
Enter Criteria1: >500.

2. What Do You See? The formula is;
=SUMIFS(Revenue,Revenue,">500")

Keep going....

Formulas -> Function Library->Math and Trig -> SUMIFS

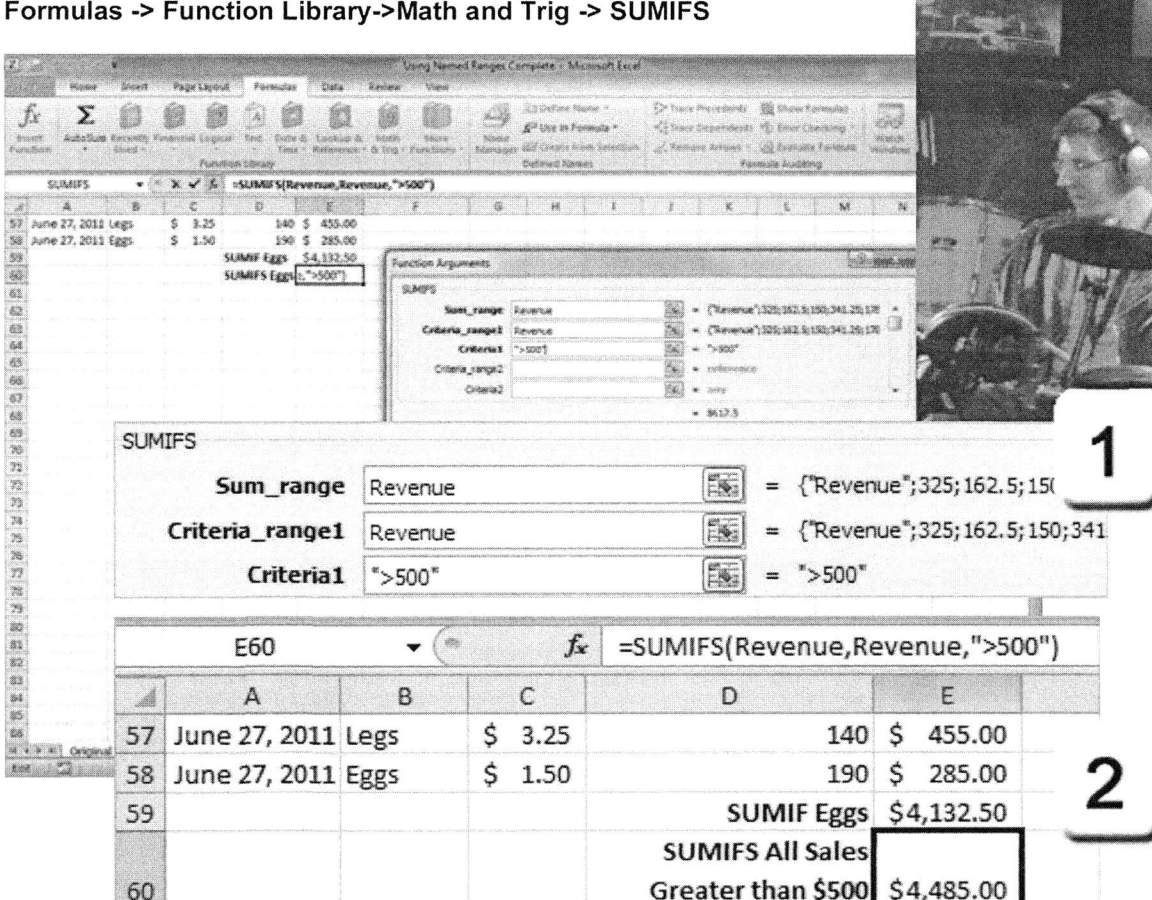

Exam 77-888: Microsoft Excel Expert 2010
2. Applying Formulas and Functions
2.3. Data summary: SUMIF, SUMIFS, COUNTIF, COUNTIFS, AVERAGEIF, and AVERAGEIFS

Formulas -> Function Library->Math and Trig -> SUMIFS

SUMIFS: Add Another Criteria
What is the sum if you added sales greater than 500 AND less than 1000?

3. Try This: Add Another Criteria
Select Cell D61.
Type: SUMIFS All Sales Greater than $500 and Less than $1000
Select Cell E61.
Go to **Formulas -> Function Library.**
Go to **More Functions->Math and Trig** .
Select **SUMIFS**.
Enter the **Sum_Range:** Revenue
Enter **Criteria_range1**: Revenue
Enter **Criteria1**: >500.

Add another Criteria:
Enter **Criteria_range2**:Revenue
Enter **Criteria2**: <1000

3. What Do You See?
The formula in this example is:
 =SUMIFS(Revenue,Revenue,">500", Revenue,"<1000")

Memo to Self: The formula has no line breaks.

	A	B	C	D	E	F
				SUMIFS All Sales		
				Greater than $500 and		
61				Less Than $1000	$4,485.00	

fx =SUMIFS(Revenue,Revenue,">500",Revenue,"<1000")

E61

3

4

Exam 77-888: Microsoft Excel Expert 2010
2. Applying Formulas and Functions
2.3. Data summary: SUMIF, SUMIFS, COUNTIF, COUNTIFS, AVERAGEIF, and AVERAGEIFS

Intermediate Excel 2010 Page 100 of 230

COUNTIF Function

How many products had more than $500.00 in sales each day?

COUNTIF lets you count the products based on your criteria. This function works with the numbers in the Revenue data in Column E.

1. Try This: COUNTIF

Add a label to Cell D62: COUNTIF greater than $500. Format the Cell to Wrap Text.

Select Cell E62.

Go to **Formulas -> Function Library.**

Go to **More Functions->Statistical** .

Select **COUNTIF.**

Enter the Range: Revenue

Enter the Criteria: >500

2. What Do You See? The formula is:

=COUNTIF(Revenue,">500")

Go to Formulas -> Function Library-> More Functions -> Statistical ->COUNTIF

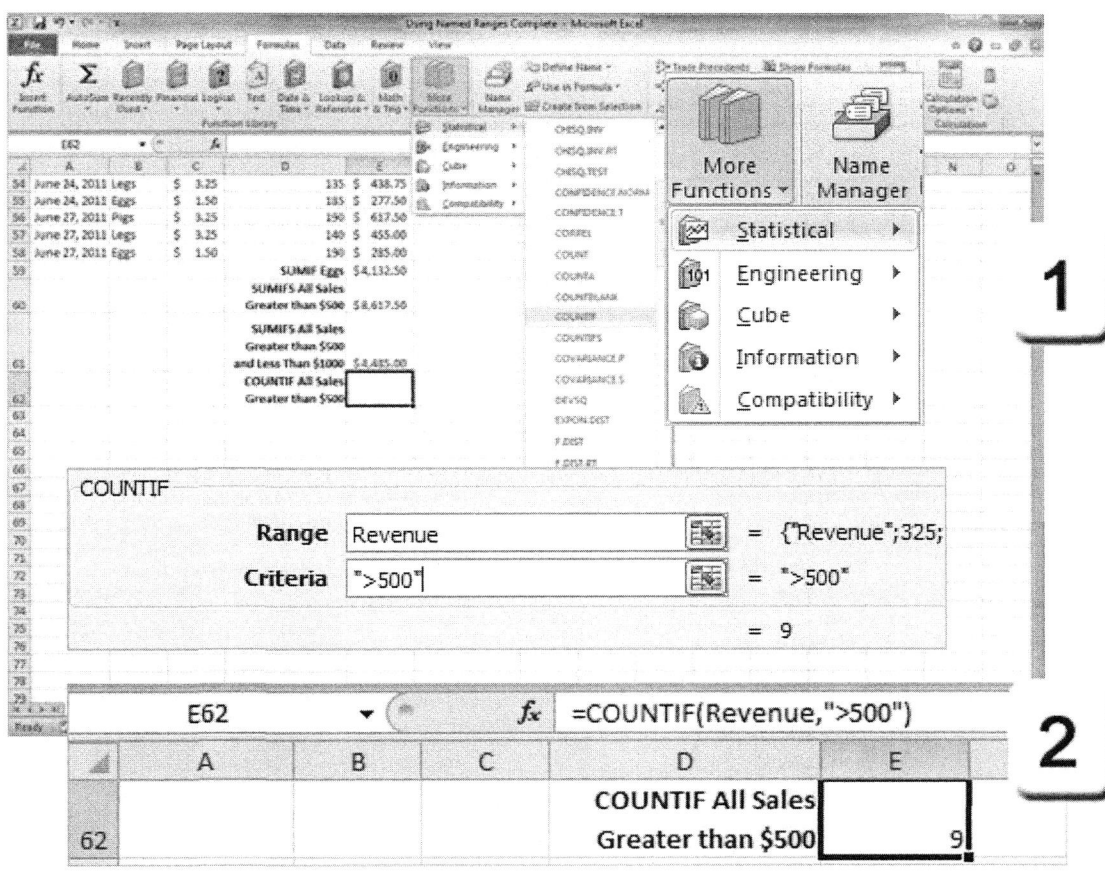

Exam 77-888: Microsoft Excel Expert 2010
2. Applying Formulas and Functions
2.3. Data summary: SUMIF, SUMIFS, COUNTIF, COUNTIFS, AVERAGEIF, and AVERAGEIFS

COUNTIFS Function

How many cheap products are less than $3.50, net more than $500.00 in daily sales?

COUNTIFS lets you calculate the answer based on two (or more) conditions: the net price and the daily sales.

1. Try This: COUNTIFS

Select Cells: $C$1:$C$58

Name the Range: Net.
In Cell D63 type: COUNTIFS for Cheap Products with sales greater than $500.

Now, select Cell E63.
Go to **Formulas -> Function Library** .
Go to **More Functions->Statistical**
Select **->COUNTIFS**.

Enter Criteria_range1: Net
Enter Criteria1: <3.50
Enter Criteria_range2: Revenue
Enter Criteria2: >500

2. What Do You See? The formula is:
=COUNTIFS(Net,"<3.50",Revenue,">500")

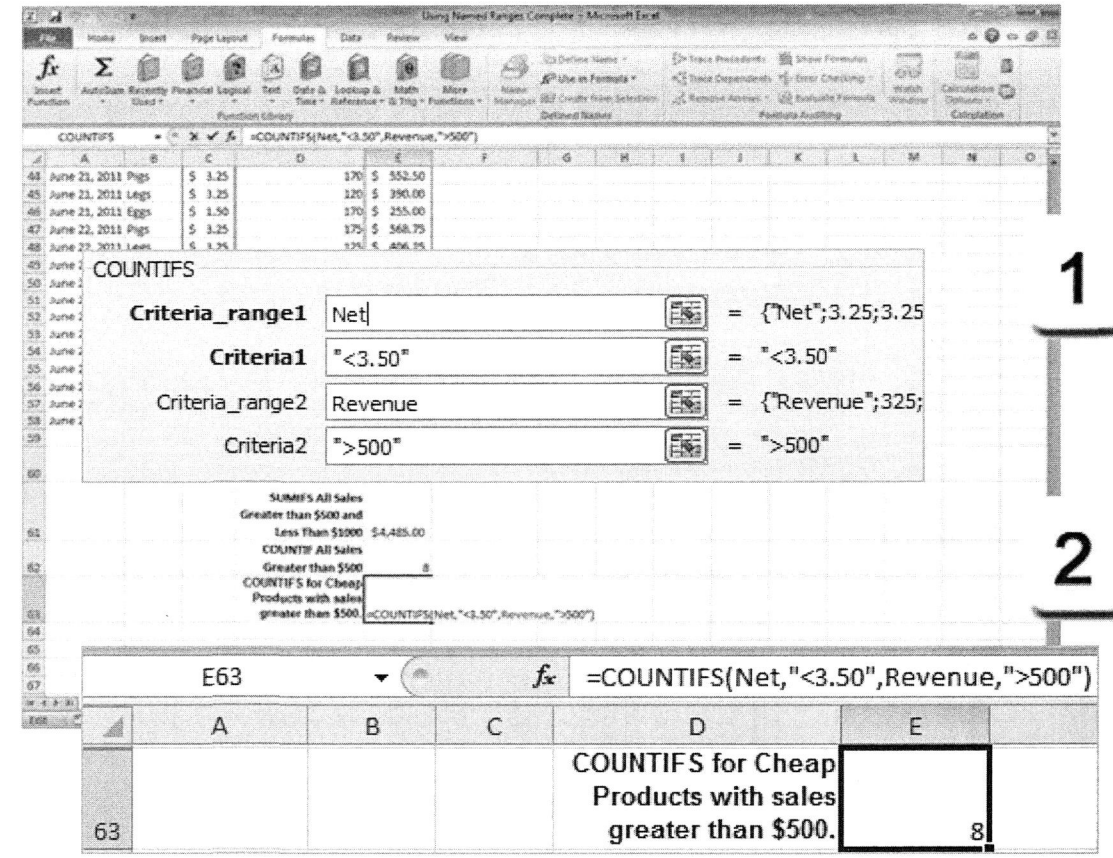

Exam 77-888: Microsoft Excel Expert 2010
2. Applying Formulas and Functions
2.3. Data summary: SUMIF, SUMIFS, COUNTIF, COUNTIFS, AVERAGEIF, and AVERAGEIFS

AVERAGEIF Function

What is the Average daily sales for the cheap products?

AVERAGEIF lets you figure the average based on your criteria. This formula will look up a number in a **Range** of prices: that's the Filter. The cells that you select to calculate the Average is called the **Average_Range** .

1. Try This: AVERAGEIF
In Cell D64 type: Average Daily Sale for Cheap Products.

Now, select Cell E64.
Go to **Formulas -> Function Library.**
Go to **More Functions>Statistical.**
Select **AVERAGEIF.**

Enter the Range: Net
Enter the Criteria: <3.50
Enter the Average_range: Revenue

2. What Do You See? The formula is =AVERAGEIF(Net,"<3.50",Revenue)

Formulas -> Function Library->More Functions -> Statistical ->AVERAGEIF

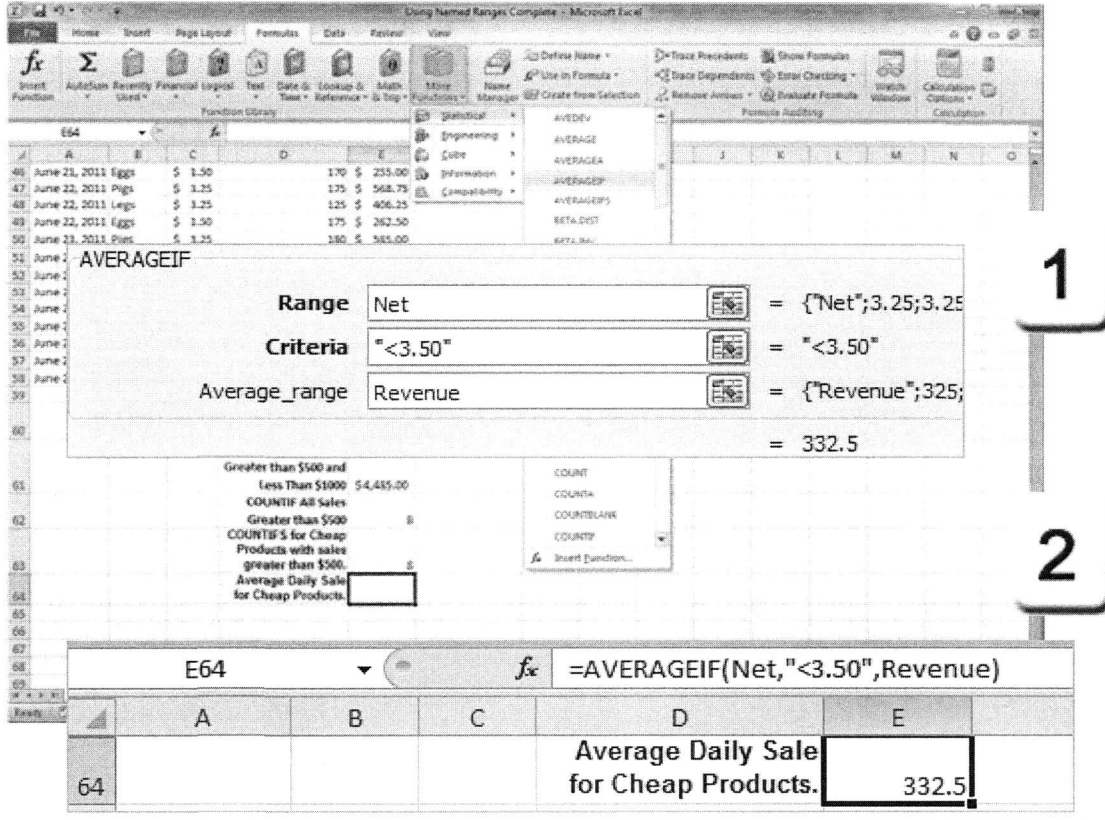

Exam 77-888: Microsoft Excel Expert 2010
2. Applying Formulas and Functions
2.3. Data summary: SUMIF, SUMIFS, COUNTIF, COUNTIFS, AVERAGEIF, and AVERAGEIFS

b

AVERAGEIFS Function

One last question: What is the Average sales for the cheap products that sold more than $500 per day?

AVERAGEIFS lets you calculate the average based on two or more conditions: the example on this page uses the net and the revenue.

1. Try This: AVERAGEIFS

In Cell D65 type: Average Daily Sale for Cheap Products greater than $500.

Now, select Cell E65.
Go to **Formulas ->Function Library.**
Go to **More Functions->Statistical.**
Select **AVERAGEIFS.**
Enter the Average_range: Revenue
Enter Criteria_Range1: Revenue
Enter the Criteria1: >500
Enter Criteria_Range2: Net
Enter the Criteria2: <3.50

2. What Do You See? The formula is
=AVERAGEIFS
(Revenue,Revenue,">500",Net,"<3.50")

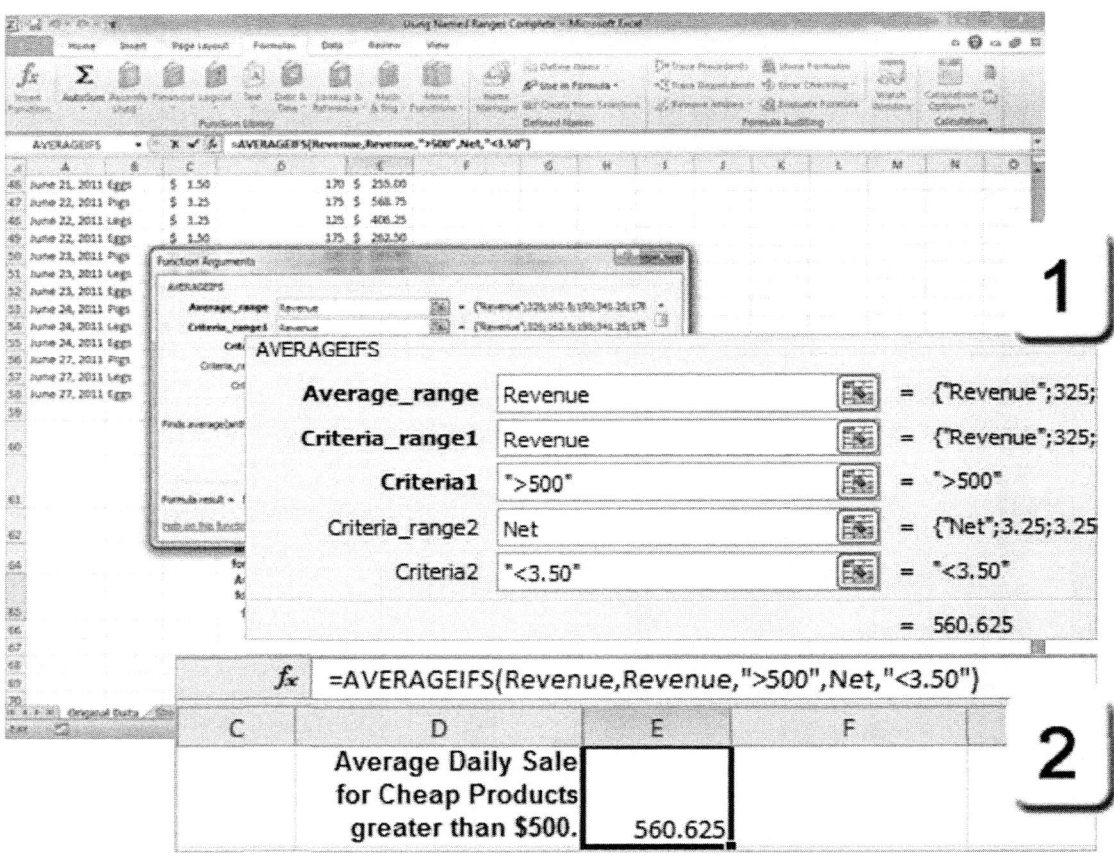

Exam 77-888: Microsoft Excel Expert 2010
2. Applying Formulas and Functions
2.3. Data summary: SUMIF, SUMIFS, COUNTIF, COUNTIFS, AVERAGEIF, and AVERAGEIFS

What If It Doesn't Work?

Computer books are very good if everything works and all of the steps are correct.

What happens when it doesn't work? (Besides the usual cussing and complaining...) Here are steps you can take to troubleshoot these formulas.

1. Try It: Audit the Formulas
Double Click Cell E63.

2. What Do You See? The formula will be displayed in Cell E63. Each of the Named Ranges is shown in color. The Range that was defined by the Name should be outlined with the matching color.

Keep going, please...

Memo to Self: The FORMAL way to look for problems is with Formula Auditing.

Formula -> Formula Auditing ->Trace Precedents

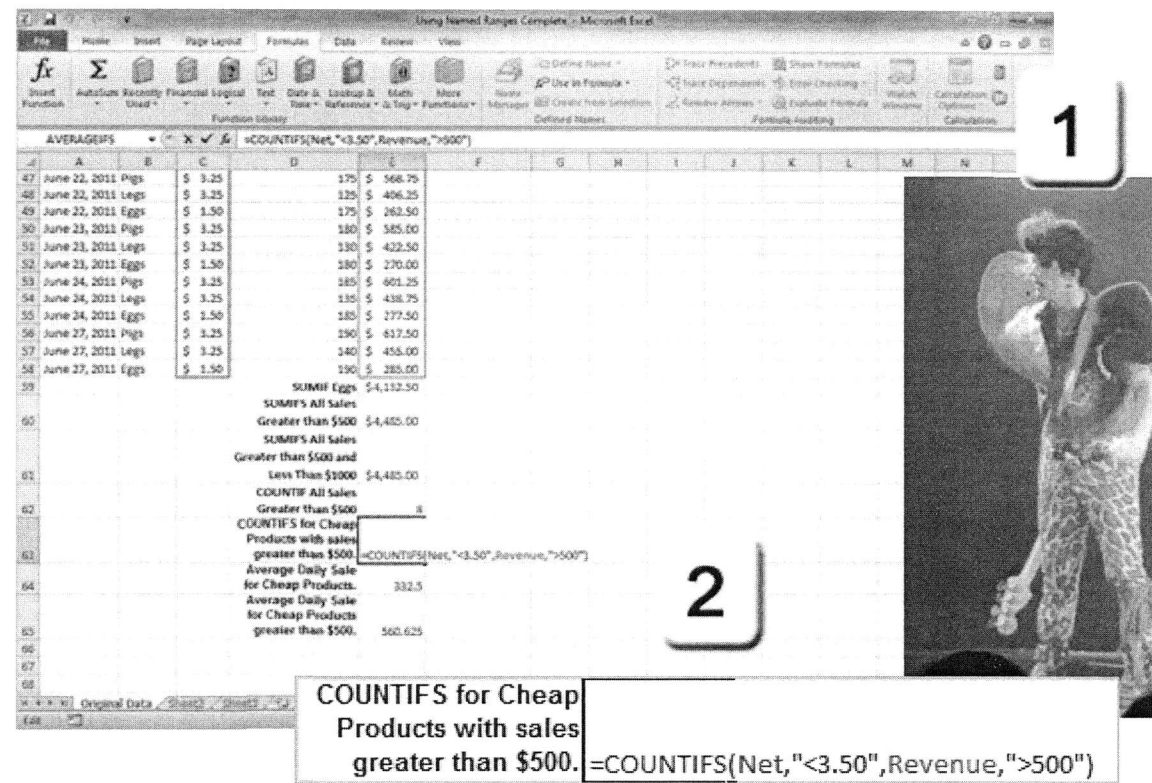

COUNTIFS for Cheap Products with sales greater than $500. =COUNTIFS(Net,"<3.50",Revenue,">500")

Exam 77-888: Microsoft Excel Expert 2010
2. Applying Formulas and Functions
2.1. Audit formulas.

Find the Mistakes

3. Here is an example of an error
In the example on this page, the Range for the Revenue is wrong. It is E1:E59. The Range should be E1:E58. You can re-create this error if you wish by editing the REVENUE with the Name Manager.

What Do You See? When the Range is wrong, you may see: "#VALUE!"

What Else Do You See? You may also see an Information (!) alert.

4. Try This: Audit the Formula
When you select the Cell that says #VALUE! you should see an outline of the data that is used in this calculation.

In this mistake, the RANGE for the REVENUE includes the formula in Cell E59. This is called a **Circular Reference**: where one formula requires the result from another, but that formula needs the result from the first.

Formula -> Formula Auditing ->Trace Precedents

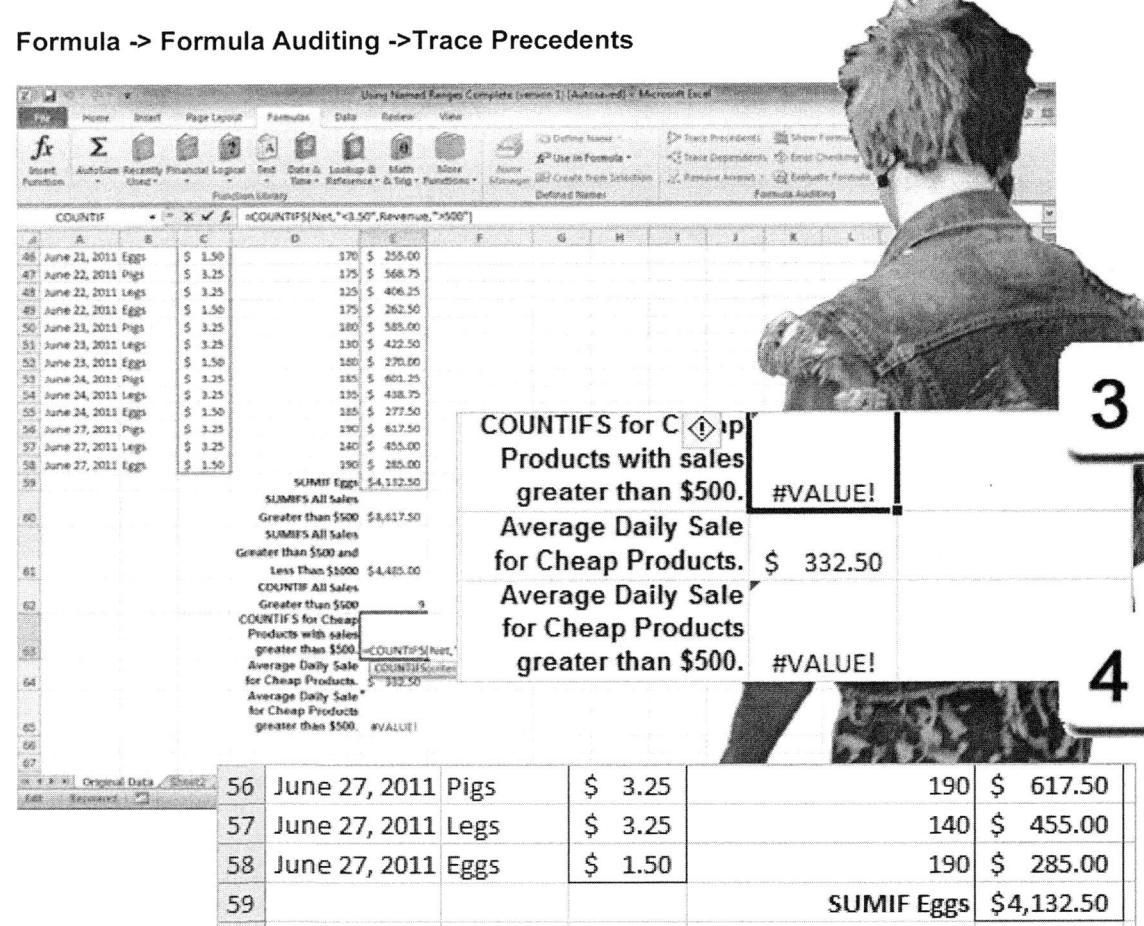

56	June 27, 2011	Pigs	$ 3.25		190	$ 617.50
57	June 27, 2011	Legs	$ 3.25		140	$ 455.00
58	June 27, 2011	Eggs	$ 1.50		190	$ 285.00
59					SUMIF Eggs	$4,132.50

Exam 77-888: Microsoft Excel Expert 2010
2. Applying Formulas and Functions
2.1. Audit formulas.

Intermediate Excel 2010 Page 106 of 230

Summary

This lesson demonstrated how to select a RANGE of cells and use a Named Range in a Formula.

This is just a small sample of the formulas that are available in Microsoft Excel. The purpose of this lesson is to show the advantages of using Defined Names to reference the data.

Very good.
You get the cookie. Take two!

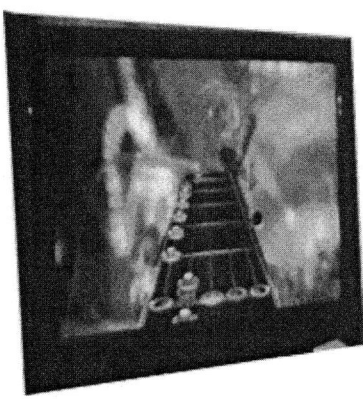

Formulas -> Function Library

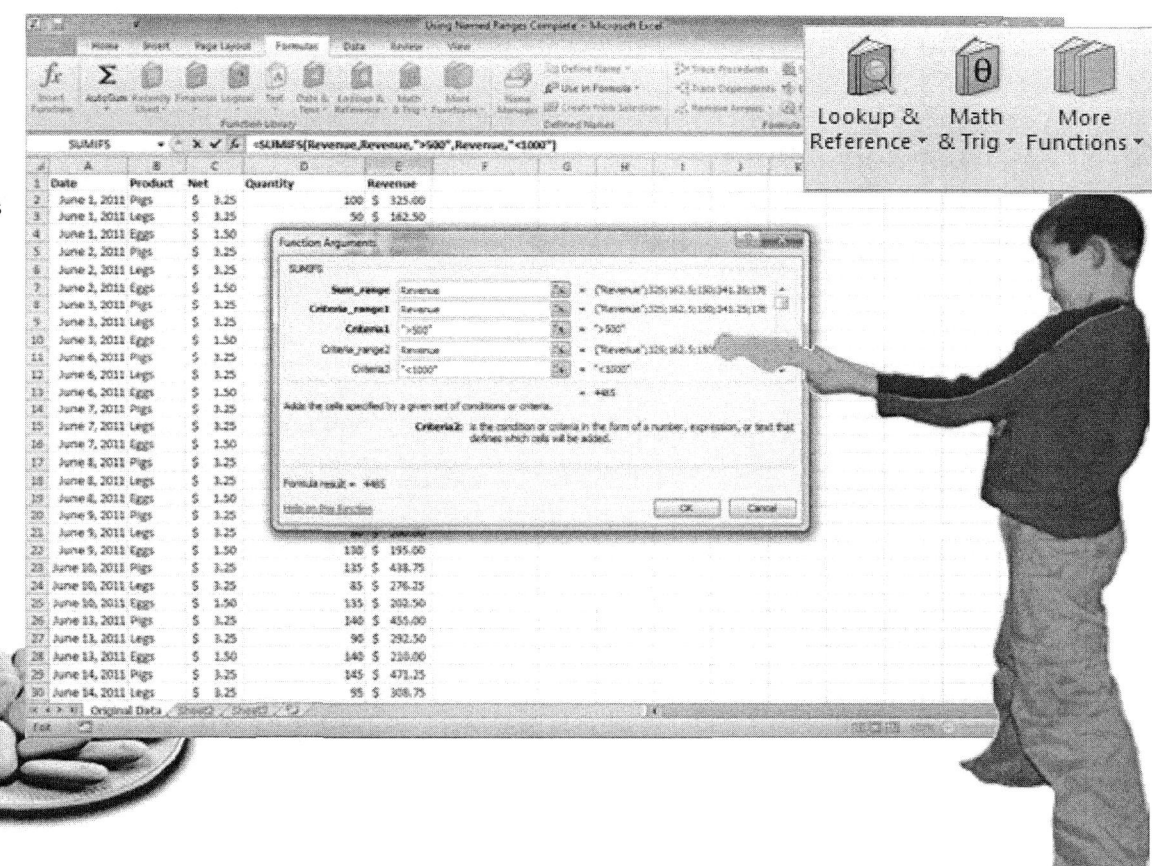

Practice Activities

Lesson 3:Name That Tune

Before You Begin: Download the sample file:

Employee Data.xlsx.

Try This: Do the following steps

Open the spreadsheet Employee Data.xlsx.

1. Format the labels Big, Bold, and Blue

2. Name the Range B1:B9: Education

3. Name Range D1:D9: Bonus

4. Name the Range C1:C9: Location

5 Name the Range A1:A9: Employee

6. In Cell E11, use the SUMIF function to add the bonuses earned at the Detroit Location

7. In Cell E12, use the SUMIF function to add the bonuses earned at the Ann Arbor Location

8. In Cell E13, use the SUMIF function to add the bonuses earned at the Lansing Location

9. Save your spreadsheet as:

YOUR NAME Name that Tune Practice

Test Yourself

1. Which is true about a Range?
(Select all correct answers.)
a. It is one or more cells in a spreadsheet
b. It can be given a name
c. Named Ranges can be used in a formula
Tip: Intermediate Excel, page 87, 88, 92

2. How do you Name a Range?
(Select all correct answers.)
a. Formulas-> Defined Name
b. Type name in the Name Box
Tip: Intermediate Excel, page 89, 90

3. Which is true about the rules for naming Ranges?
a. Can be text, numbers, periods, and underscores
b. Can include spaces
c. Can be up to 255 characters
d. Cannot include cell references such as B1
e. The first character must be a letter
Tip: Intermediate Excel, page 91

4. Which task can be completed in the Name Manager? (Select all correct answers.)
a. Create a new named Range
b. Edit an existing named Range
c. Delete a defined Range
Tip: Intermediate Excel, page 94

5. Which of the following is true?
(Select all correct answers.)
a. SUMIF adds values based on only one criteria
b. SUMIFS adds values based on only one criteria
c. SUMIF adds values based on more than one criteria
d. SUMIFS adds values based on more than one criteria
Tip: Intermediate Excel, page 98
6. Which is true about auditing a formula?
(Select all correct answers)
a. Double-clicking the cell is a shortcut to display the formula
b. The formula will be color coded with colored outlines around the cells matching colored cell names or Ranges in the formula
c. The command is Formula-> Formula Auditing> Trace Precedents
Tip: Intermediate Excel, page 105, 106

Excel 2010: Applying Formulas and Functions

Sound Advice

Intermediate Excel Objectives
In this lesson, you will learn how to:

1. Create a Lookup Table

2. Name the Lookup Table

3. Use a VLookup Table in a Formula

4. Use an HLookup Table in a Formula

5. Use Logical Functions: IF, AND, OR, NOT

6. Use a Logical Function to find an error: IFERROR

Lesson 4: Sound Advice

1. Readings
Read Lesson 4 in your Intermediate Excel Guide, page 109-140.

Project
Use Named Ranges to create Lookup tables. Use a formula to lookup the best answer.

Downloads
Sales 2010.xlsx
Student Records.xlsx

2. Practice
Complete the Practice Activity on page 141.

3. Assessment
Review the Test Yourself questions on page 142.

Formulas

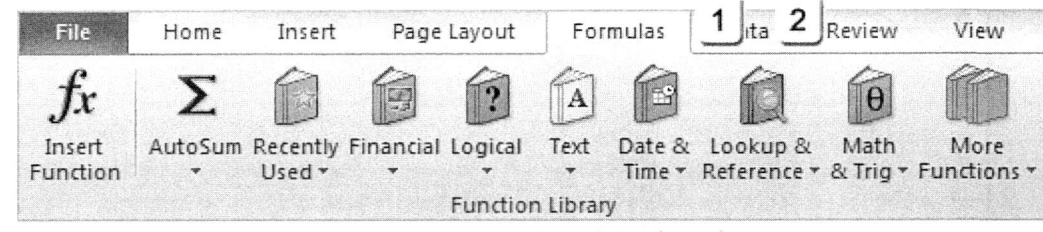

Menu Maps
This lesson introduces the **Formulas** Ribbon.

1. Formula -> Function Library>Lookup & Reference->VLookup, page 115
2. Formula -> Function Library>Lookup & Reference->HLookup, page 125
3. Formula ->Function Library ->Logical ->IF, page 131
4. Formula ->Function Library ->Logical ->AND, page 133
5. Formula ->Function Library ->Logical ->OR, page 135
6. Formula ->Function Library ->Logical ->NOT, page 136
7. Formula ->Function Library ->Logical ->IFERROR, page 137

When in Doubt, Look it Up

Every job has something that you need to look up. In automotive design there are lists and more lists of parts, part numbers, sizes and tolerances. In medical and dental care, there are lists of procedure codes. You can use Microsoft Excel to look up the right answer.

In our little company, Charlotte's Website, we need to calculate the commission for our sales representatives. The spreadsheet should compare the sales amount to the numbers in a Bonus table. The key to this formula is creating and naming a Lookup Table. This lesson will demonstrate Vlookup and HLookup Tables.

Start -> All Programs ->Microsoft Office -> Excel

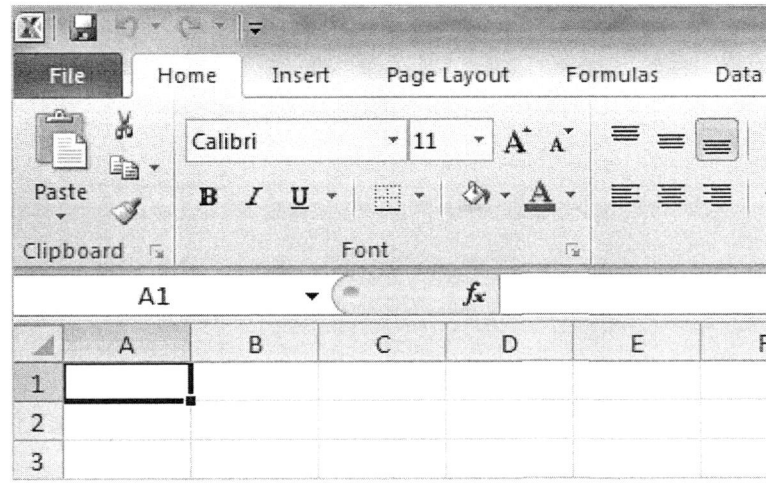

What Do You See? Is there a Title Bar that says Book 1-Microsoft Excel? Yes.

Is there a **Home** Ribbon with the Clipboard, Font and Alignment Groups? Yes.

If your screen looks similar to the example on this page, then you are ready to get started.

Before You Begin

This discussion begins by creating a sample spreadsheet that shows sales data for four reps.

1. Try it: Open a Sample Spreadsheet
Open the spreadsheet you created in the previous lesson: Sales 2010.xlsx
Go to the **Sales Subtotal by Rep** spreadsheet.

What Do You See? The spreadsheet Subtotals the amount for each Sales Rep.

Keep going, please...
Memo to Self: You can use the **sample spreadsheet** or enter your own data on the next page if you wish.

Another Memo: We will learn how to summarize data with Subtotals and PivotTable reports in the Advanced Guide to Excel 2010.

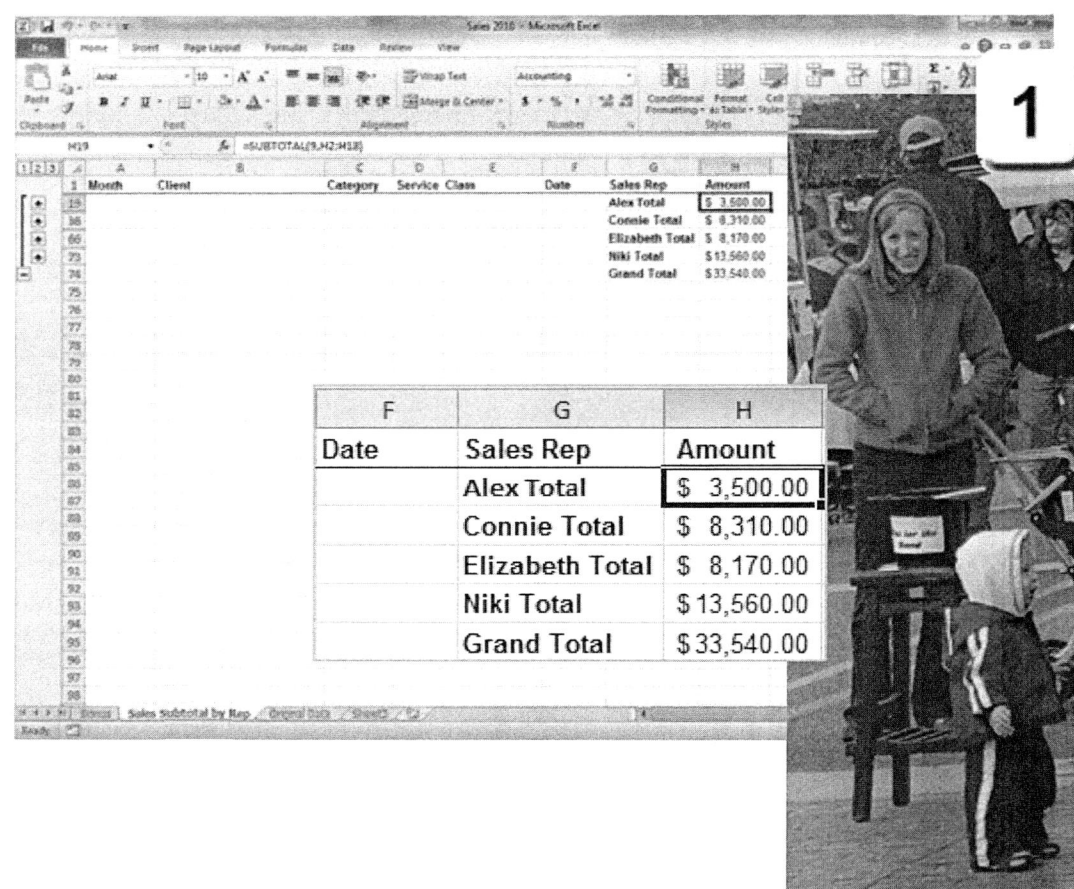

Date	Sales Rep	Amount
	Alex Total	$ 3,500.00
	Connie Total	$ 8,310.00
	Elizabeth Total	$ 8,170.00
	Niki Total	$ 13,560.00
	Grand Total	$ 33,540.00

Create a Bonus Spreadsheet

We will create a new Bonus spreadsheet that will look up the sales data from the **Sales Subtotal by Rep** spreadsheet.

2. Try it: Create a Bonus Sheet
Go to a new blank spreadsheet.
Double-click the tab.
Rename the spreadsheet: Bonus.

Add the following labels:
Select Cell A1 and type: Sales Rep.
Select Cell B1 and type: Total.
If these are labels (and they are) they need to be formatted BOLD.
Select Row 1. Go to **Home->Font->Bold.**

Select Cell A2 and type: Alex
Select Cell A3 and type: Connie
Select Cell A4 and type: Elizabeth
Select Cell A5 and type: Nikki

Keep going...
You can use the **sample spreadsheet** *or enter your own data if you wish.*

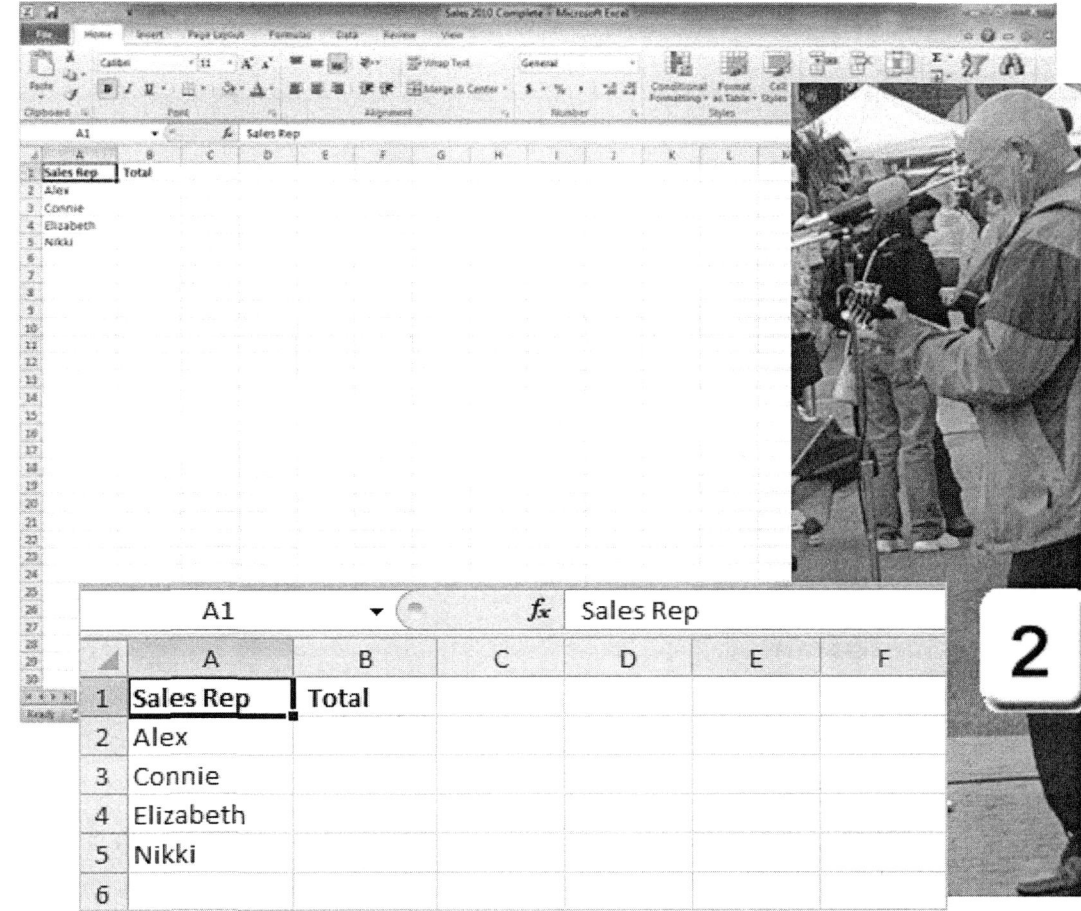

Exam 77-882: Microsoft Excel 2010 Core
2. Creating Cell Data
2.1. Construct cell data

Create the Formulas

The next steps use a simple formula to create a Relative Cell Reference that links the data from the **Sales Subtotal by Rep** spreadsheet that Subtotals each Reps sales.

3. Try it: Create the Formulas
Start on the **Bonus** spreadsheet.
All equations begin with equals.

Select Cell B2 and type: =.
Go to the **Sales Subtotal by Rep** sheet and click on the amount for Alex in the H column.

Select Cell B3 and type: =.
Go to **Sales Subtotal by Rep** and click on the amount for Connie in the H column.

Please create formulas for Elizabeth and Nikki as well. Keep going...!
Memo to Self: *You can use the sample spreadsheet or just type the data that you see on this page if you wish.*

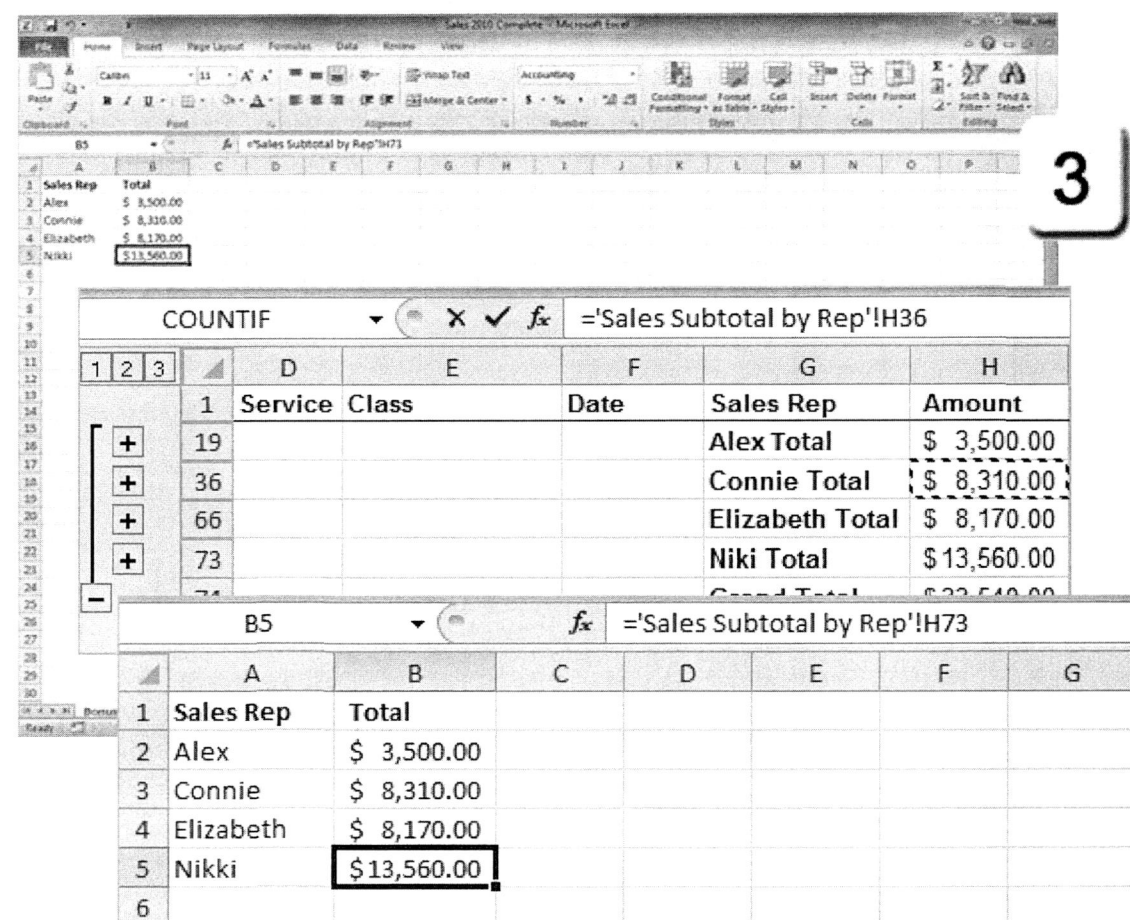

Exam 77-882: Microsoft Excel 2010 Core
5. Applying Formulas and Functions
5.1. Create formulas

The Lookup Function

Say your company offers a bonus for meeting sales goals. The bonus will be calculated as a percent of the sales.

The best way to calculate the bonus is to look up the answer in a table. Excel calls this the Lookup function. A vertical, or **VLookup** uses the values in the columns. A horizontal, or **HLookup**, uses the data in rows.

1. Try it: Create a VLookup Table
Go to the Bonus spreadsheet.
Add the following labels:
In cell C1, type Commission
In cell D1, type Bonus
In cell F1, type Sales
In cell G1, type Percent

Format the Labels **Bold**.
Format Column F for Accounting.
Format Column G for Percentage.

Keep going.

Home -> Number

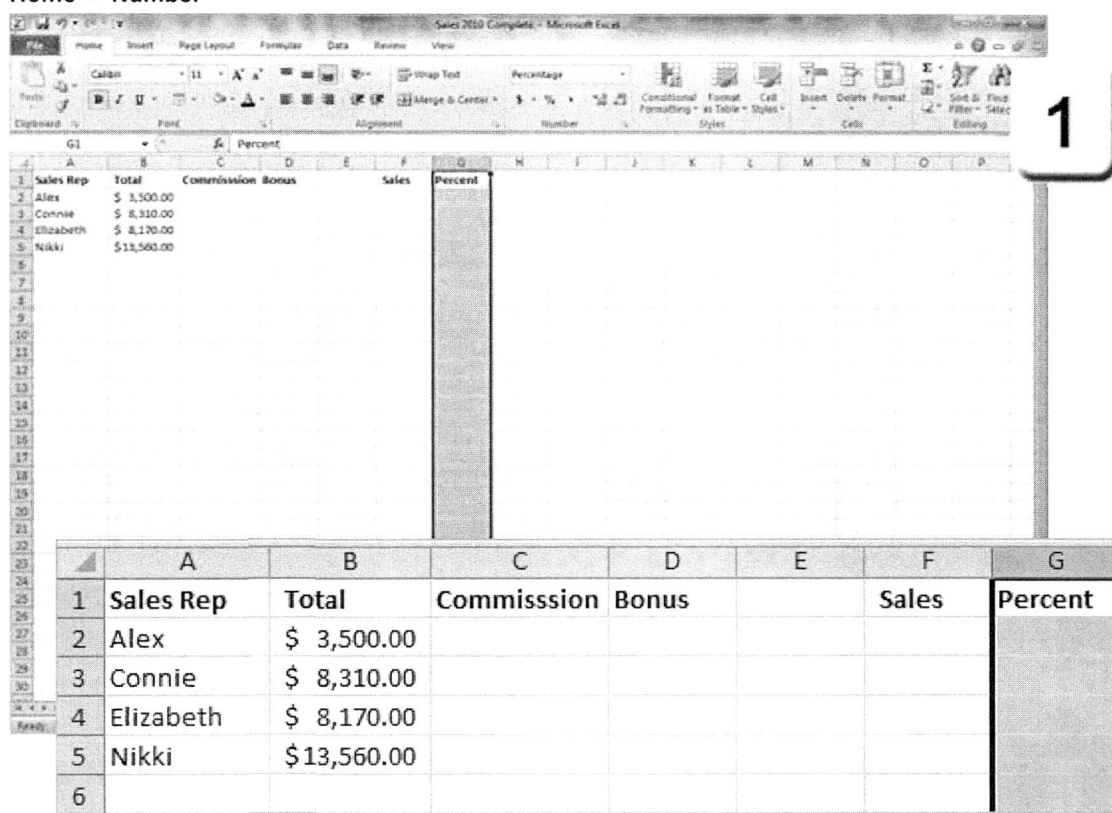

	A	B	C	D	E	F	G
1	Sales Rep	Total	Commisssion	Bonus		Sales	Percent
2	Alex	$ 3,500.00					
3	Connie	$ 8,310.00					
4	Elizabeth	$ 8,170.00					
5	Nikki	$13,560.00					
6							

Exam 77-882: Microsoft Excel 2010 Core
5. Applying Formulas and Functions
5.1. Create formulas

Create the Lookup Table

This Lookup table has two columns: Sales and Percent.

2. Try it: Add data to the table

Enter the following values:

Sales	Percent
$ 2,500.00	5%
$ 5,000.00	10%
$ 7,500.00	15%
$10,000.00	20%

Keep going, please...

	A	B	C	D	E	F	G
1	Sales Rep	Total	Commisssion	Bonus		Sales	Percent
2	Alex	$ 3,500.00				$ 2,500.00	5%
3	Connie	$ 8,310.00				$ 5,000.00	10%
4	Elizabeth	$ 8,170.00				$ 7,500.00	15%
5	Nikki	$13,560.00				$10,000.00	20%
6							

Exam 77-882: Microsoft Excel 2010 Core
5. Applying Formulas and Functions
5.1. Create formulas: VLookup

Name That Tune
In Excel, you can name a cell, or a range of cells. Using names makes it easy to go to a particular place. It also simplifies cell references when you create equations.

3. Try it: Name the Range
Select Cells F1 through G5.
Go to **Formula->Define Names**.
Select **Define Name**.

What Do You See? The New Name screen will pop up. The Name, **Sales**, came from the label in Cell F1.

Refers to: Show the name of the spreadsheet, Bonus. The Range of data can be found in cell F1 through G5.

Click OK and continue...

Formula -> Defined Names->Define Names

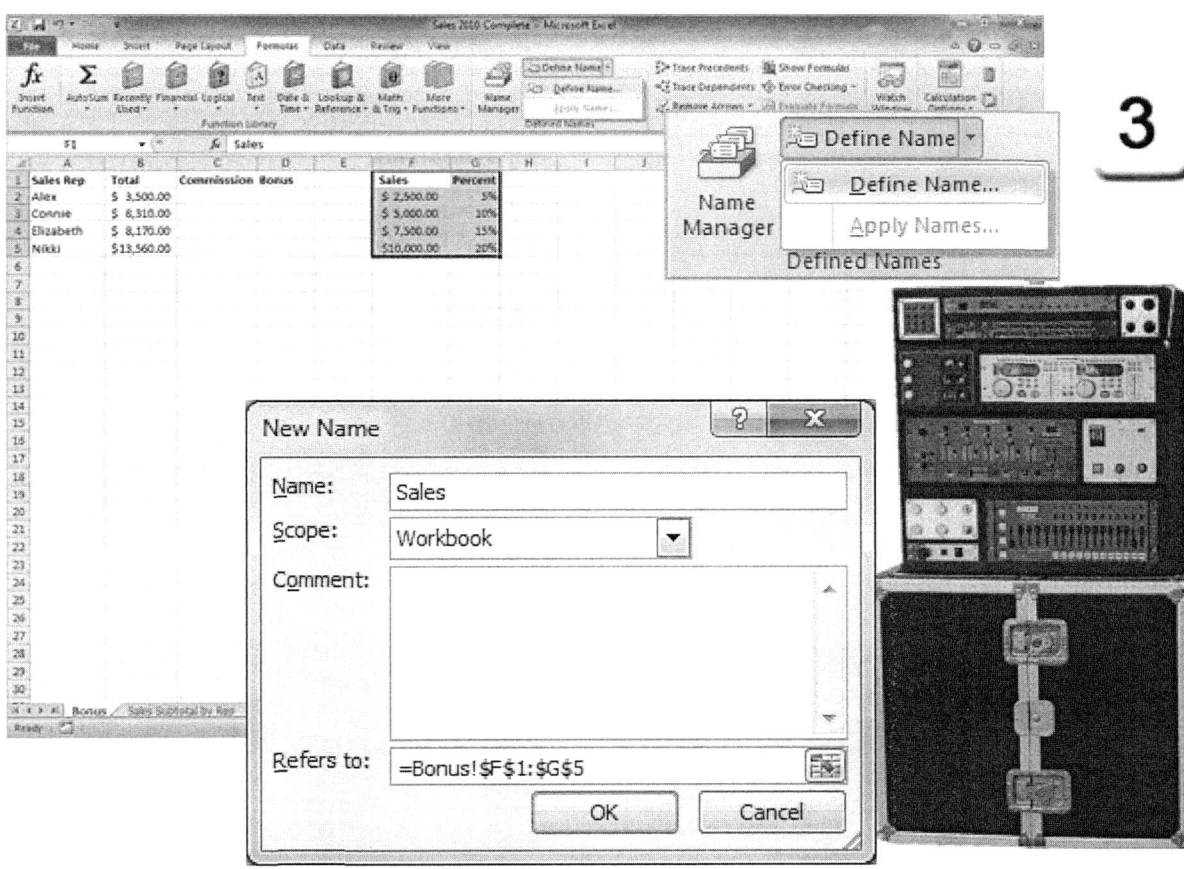

Exam 77-882: Microsoft Excel 2010 Core
5. Applying Formulas and Functions
5.5. Apply named ranges in formulas

Formula -> Function Library>Lookup & Reference->VLookup

The Lookup Function

Microsoft Excel has a a collection of Lookup and Reference Functions in the Function Library. Here are the steps to create a VLookup formula.

4. Try This: Insert a VLookup Function
Select Cell C2.
Go to **Formula -> Function Library**.
Go to **Lookup and Reference**.
Select **VLookup** from the function list.

Please keep going...

| File | Home | Insert | Page Layout | Formulas | Data | Review | View |

Insert Function | AutoSum | Recently Used | Financial | Logical | Text | Date & Time | Lookup & Reference | Math & Trig | More Functions | **4**

Function Library

C2   fx

	A	B	C	D	E	F	G
1	Sales Rep	Total	Commisssion	Bonus		Sales	Percent
2	Alex	$ 3,500.00				$ 2,500.00	5%
3	Connie	$ 8,310.00				$ 5,000.00	10%
4	Elizabeth	$ 8,170.00				$ 7,500.00	15%
5	Nikki	$13,560.00				$10,000.00	20%
6							
7							
8							
9							
10							

Exam 77-882: Microsoft Excel 2010 Core
5. Applying Formulas and Functions
5.1. Create formulas: VLookup

VLookup Arguments

5. What Do You See? Excel will prompt you to fill in the **Function Arguments.** Here are some answers.

Lookup_Value: The first argument asks, "Where is the data?" In our example, Alex's total is in cell B2. Click on cell **B2**.

Table_array: The second argument wants to know, "Where is the lookup table?" You can type the name, **sales**, for the range or use the red, white and blue lookup button to go to highlight cells F1 through G5.

Col_index_num: The third argument needs to identify where the answers are. In our two column Sales array, the percents are located in **Column 2**.

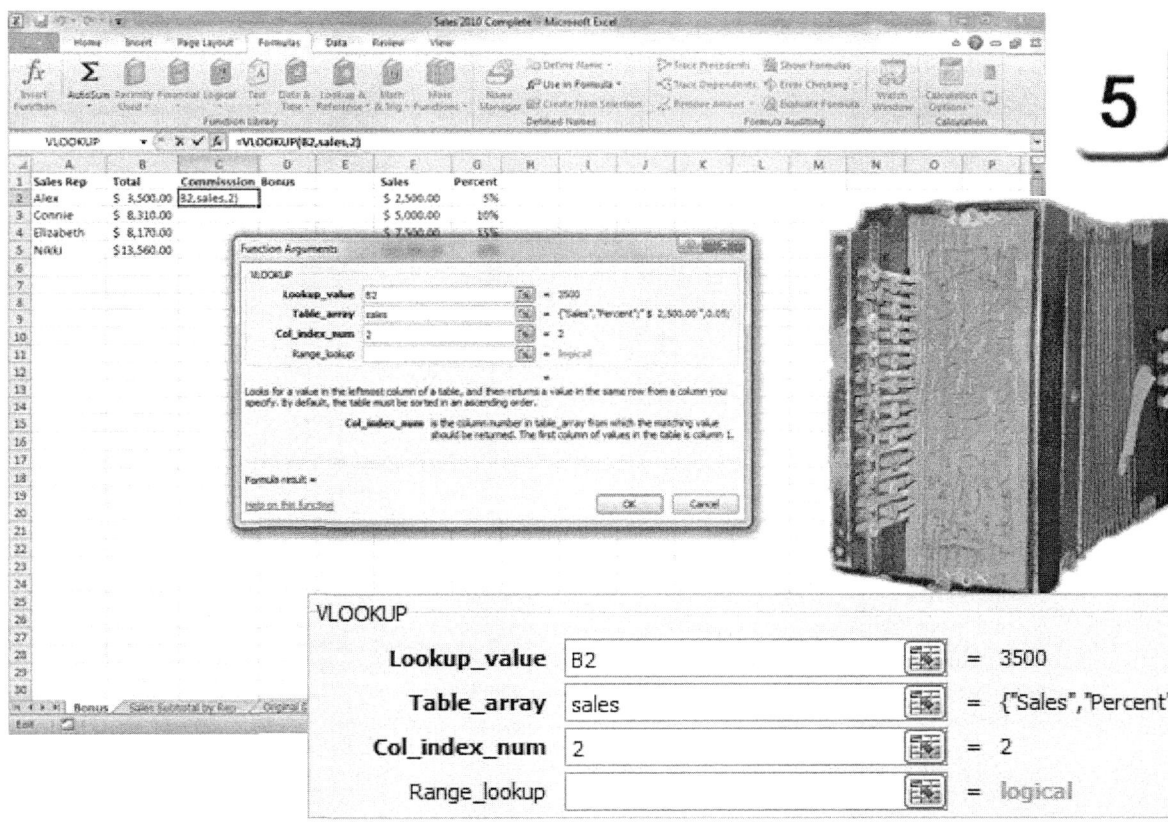

5

	VLOOKUP		
Lookup_value	B2		= 3500
Table_array	sales		= {"Sales","Percent"
Col_index_num	2		= 2
Range_lookup			= logical

Exam 77-882: Microsoft Excel 2010 Core
5. Applying Formulas and Functions
5.1. Create formulas: VLookup

Take Two

Autofill the VLookup

6. Try This: AutoFill the Formula
Select Cell C2.
Use the **AutoFill** handle to copy to formulas to Cells C3 through C5.

What Do You See? The VLookup function compares how much our sales rep made and determines the best percent for the commission.

The equation in Cell C5 would be:
=VLOOKUP(B5,Sales,2)

Memo to Self: This is a good place to **Save** your work. Please name the spreadsheet: Sales 2010 Complete.

Insert -> Function ->VLookup

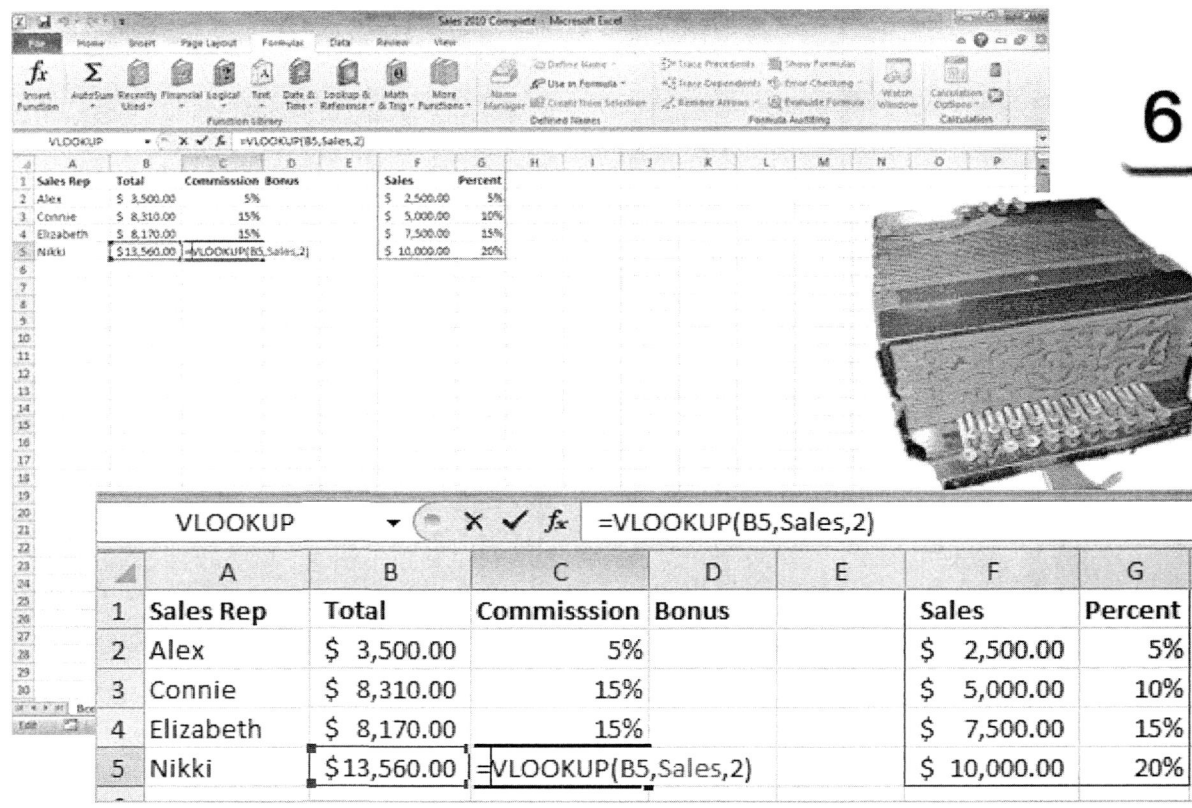

	A	B	C	D	E	F	G
1	Sales Rep	Total	Commisssion	Bonus		Sales	Percent
2	Alex	$ 3,500.00	5%			$ 2,500.00	5%
3	Connie	$ 8,310.00	15%			$ 5,000.00	10%
4	Elizabeth	$ 8,170.00	15%			$ 7,500.00	15%
5	Nikki	$13,560.00	=VLOOKUP(B5,Sales,2)			$ 10,000.00	20%

Exam 77-882: Microsoft Excel 2010 Core
5. Applying Formulas and Functions
5.1. Create formulas: VLookup

Calculate the Bonus

Now, we can calculate the bonus for each sales rep. Each sales rep's **Total** is entered in Column B. The **VLookup** formula looks up the right **Commission** in the Sales table.

7. Try it: Calculate the Bonus
Select Cell D2.
Enter the following equation:
=B2*C2

Try This, Too: AutoFill the Formula
Select Cell D2.
Use to **AutoFill** handle to copy the formula from Cell D3 through D5.

What Do You See? The formula in Cell D5 is =B5*C5.

Memo to Self: ### means you have too much money. Technically, the column is not wide enough to display the numbers correctly You can make the column wider if you wish.

VLOOKUP ▼ ● X ✓ fx =B5*C5

	A	B	C	D	E	F	G
1	Sales Rep	Total	Commisssion	Bonus		Sales	Percei
2	Alex	$ 3,500.00	5%	$ 175.00		$ 2,500.00	5
3	Connie	$ 8,310.00	15%	$1,246.50		$ 5,000.00	10
4	Elizabeth	$ 8,170.00	15%	$1,225.50		$ 7,500.00	15
5	Nikki	$13,560.00	20%	=B5*C5		$ 10,000.00	20

7

Exam 77-882: Microsoft Excel 2010 Core
5. Applying Formulas and Functions
5.3. Apply cell references in formulas: Use Relative Cell References

Chart Tools->Design->Chart Styles

Insert a Chart

People have a difficult time seeing what the numbers mean. Make it easier: let's create a chart. This example begins by using the Control key on the keyboard to select two ranges that are not connected.

1. Try it: Insert a Chart

Select A1 through A5. Hold your Control key on the keyboard and select D1 through D5, too.
Go to **Insert->Charts->Columns.**
Select the a **3D Column** template.

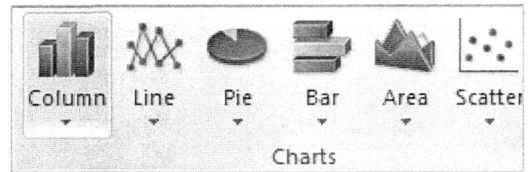

What Do You See? Microsoft Excel will create a new Chart. When the Chart is selected, the Chart Tools should be available. Keep going...!

Memo to Self: There are three Chart Ribbons: Design, Layout and Format.

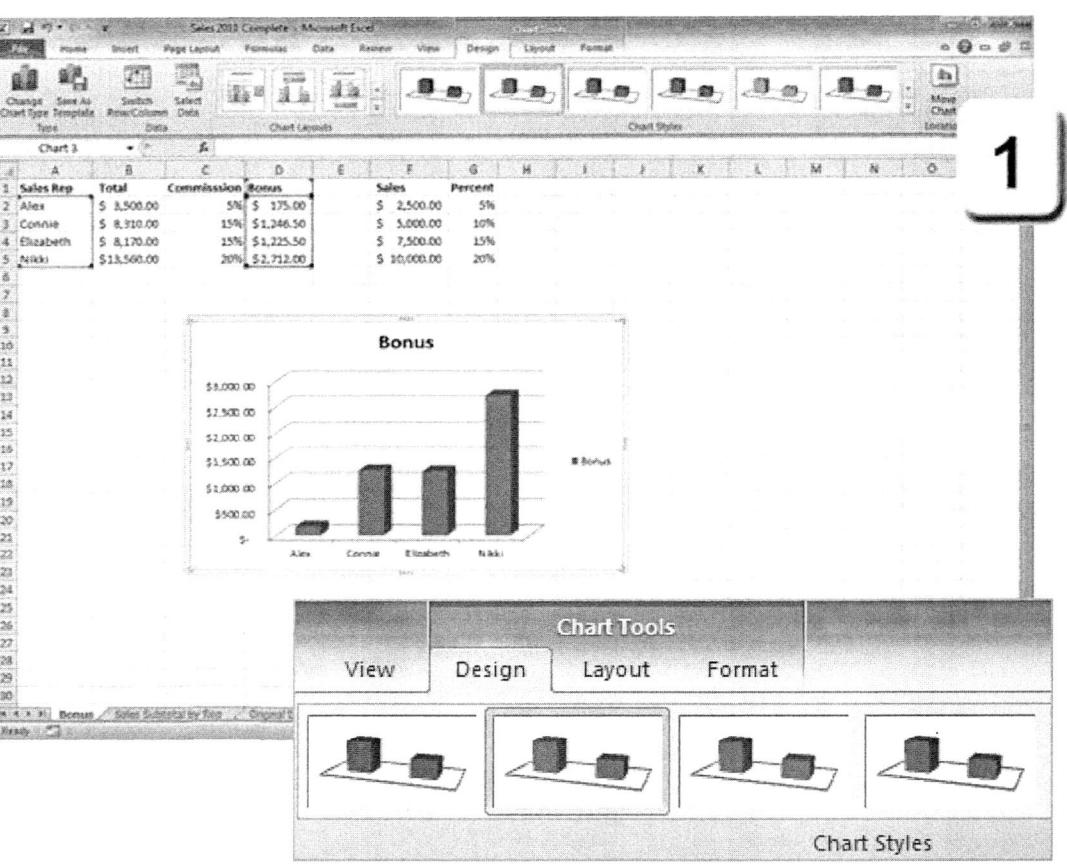

Exam 77-882: Microsoft Excel 2010 Core
6. Presenting Data Visually
6.1. Create charts based on worksheet data

Chart Tools -> Layout -> Labels-> Legend

Modify the Chart

A chart should tell the story in 3 seconds or less. The **Chart Legend** is not the most effective way to teach the numbers. It is "one step away" from your data. In our example, the legend is redundant. You can use the Chart Tools to remove the Legend.

2. Try it: Remove the Legend
Select the Chart and go to **Chart Tools**.
Go to **Layout->Labels-> Legend**.
Select: **None**.

Keep going...

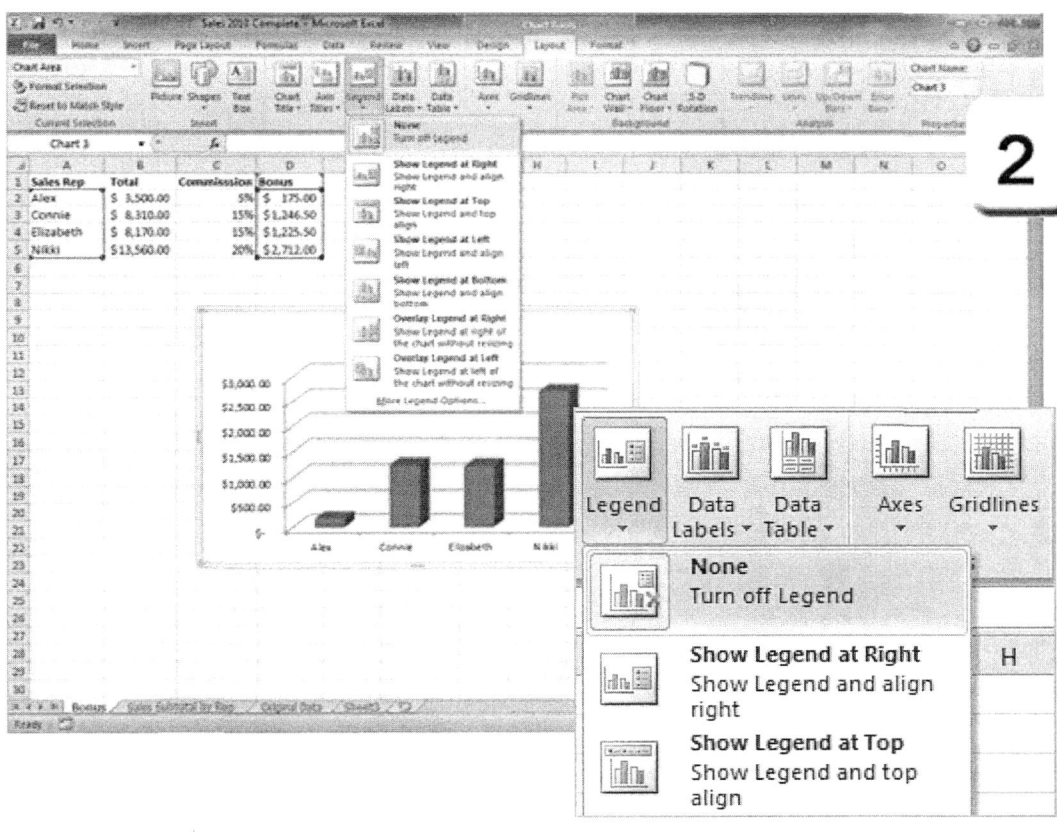

Exam 77-882: Microsoft Excel 2010 Core
6. Presenting Data Visually
6.1. Create charts based on worksheet data: Modify the Layout

Format the Chart
Formatting the data in the chart by color and position helps to tell the story. Here are some options.

3. Try This: Format the Chart Style
Select the Chart and go to **Chart Tools.**
Go to **Chart Tools -> Design.**
Go to **Chart Styles.**
Choose a **Style.**

What Do You See? The Chart in this example is formatting with a Chart Style.

The column that has the most sales has been formatted with a picture by using the **Shape Fill** on the Chart Tools->Format Ribbon. Very good. This works.

Save, save, save.

Chart Tools -> Design -> Chart Styles

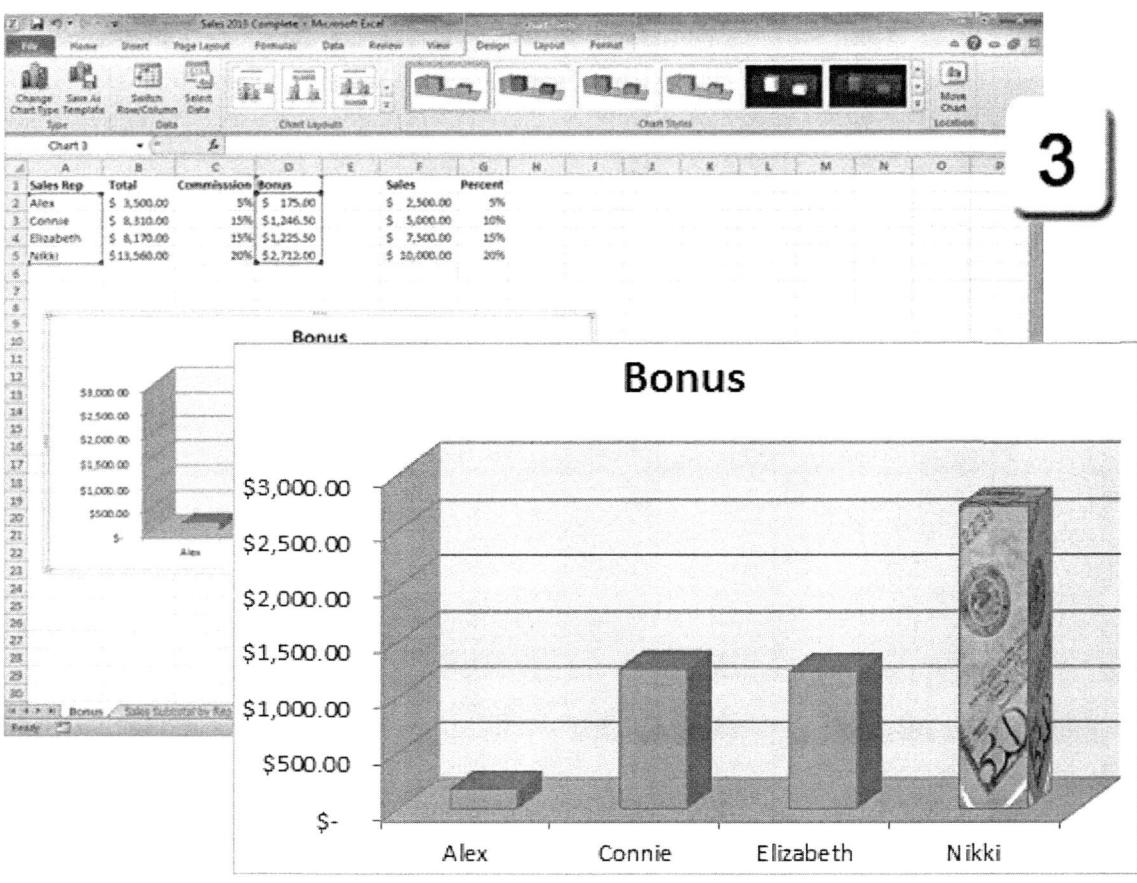

Exam 77-882: Microsoft Excel 2010 Core
6. Presenting Data Visually
6.1. Create charts based on worksheet data: Modify the Design

The HLookup Function

The previous example demonstrated the **VLookup** function. "V" is for vertical. The VLookup finds the answers in the columns. The **HLookup** function searches for the answers in the rows.

1. Try it: Create the Customers Sheet

Go to a new blank spreadsheet.
Double-click the tab.
Rename the spreadsheet: Customers.

Add the following labels:
Select Cell A1 and type: Category.
Select Cell B1 and type: Total.
If these are labels (and they are) they need to be formatted BOLD.
Select Cells A1:B1.
Go to **Home->Font->Bold**.

Add some data:
Select Cell A2 and type: Corporate
Select Cell A3 and type: Educational
Select Cell A4 and type: Government
Select Cell A5 and type: Private
Keep going...

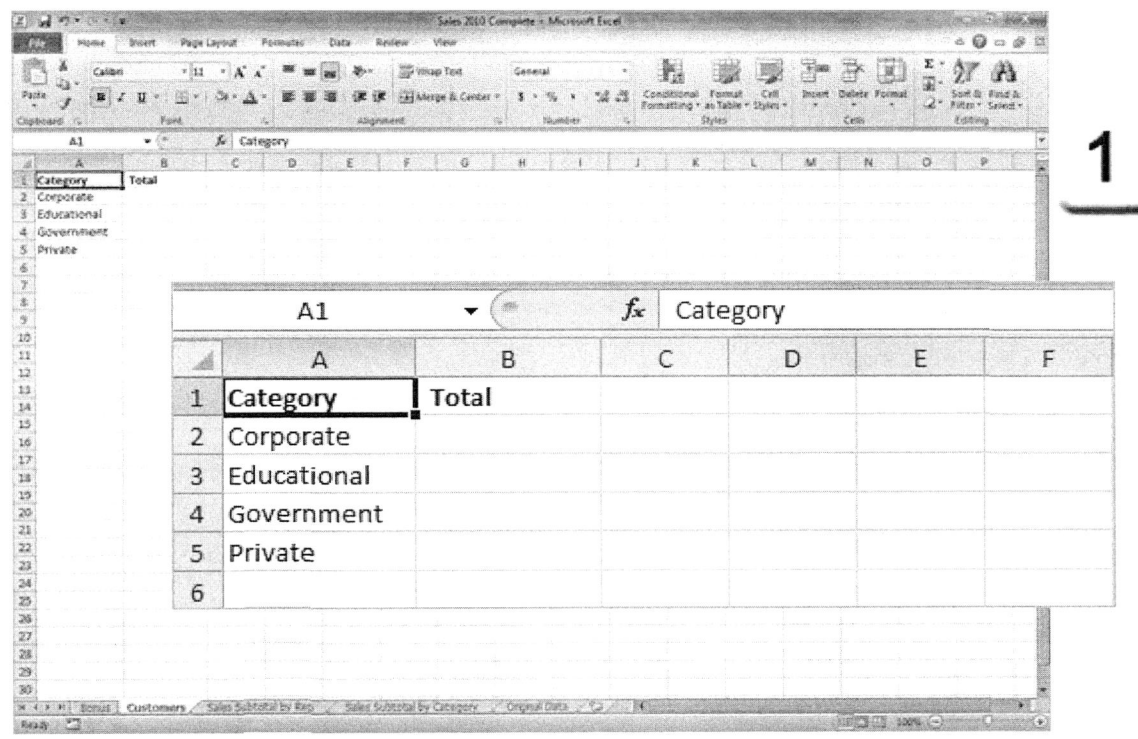

*You can use the **sample spreadsheet** or enter your own data if you wish.*

Exam 77-882: Microsoft Excel 2010 Core
2. Creating Cell Data
2.1. Construct cell data

Still Before You Begin...

2. Try it: Add Sample Data
Select Cell B2 and type: 2,850
Select Cell B3 and type: 8,180
Select Cell B4 and type: 21,470
Select Cell B5 and type: 1,050

Select Column D and format the numbers.
Go to **Home->Numbers->Accounting.**

Keep going...

Memo to Self: You can use the **sample spreadsheet** or enter your own data. If you use the sample spreadsheet, you can link the sales data to the spreadsheet called Sales Subtotal by Category,

Home->Numbers->Accounting

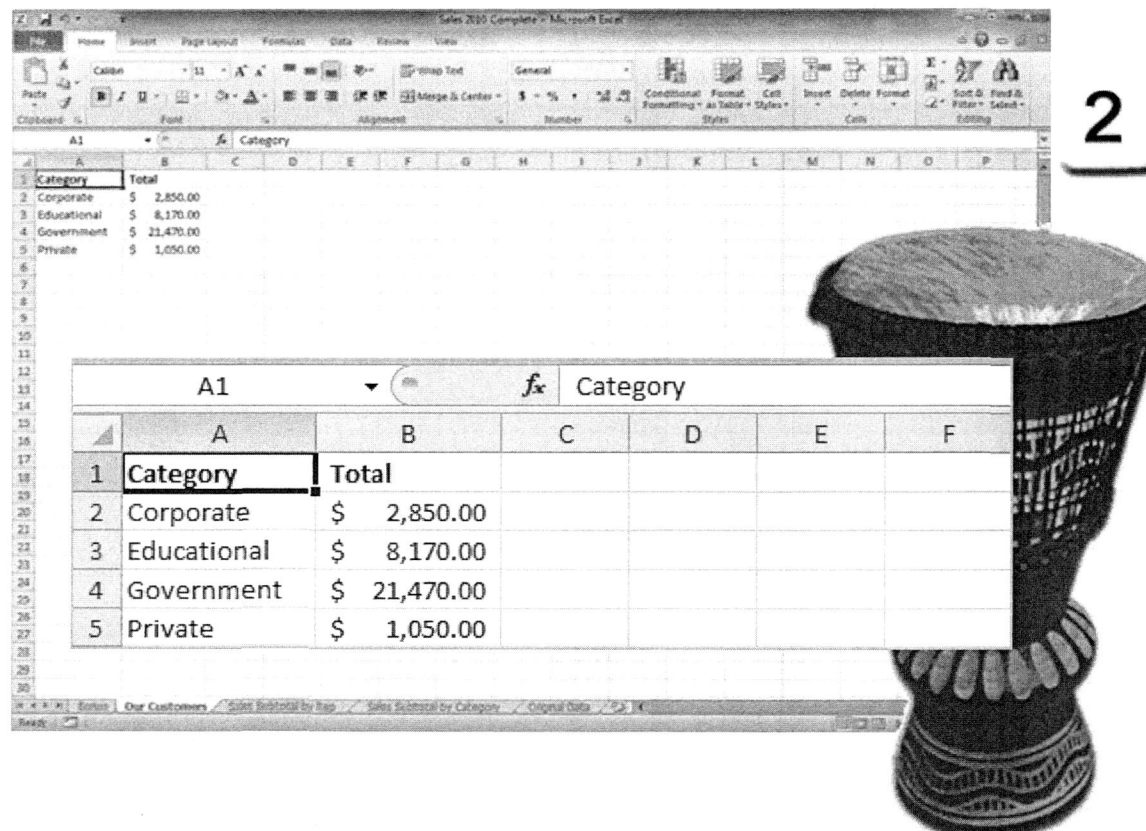

	A	B	C	D	E	F
1	Category	Total				
2	Corporate	$ 2,850.00				
3	Educational	$ 8,170.00				
4	Government	$ 21,470.00				
5	Private	$ 1,050.00				

Exam 77-882: Microsoft Excel 2010 Core
3. Formatting Cells and Worksheets
3.1. Apply and modify cell formats

Create the Lookup Table

This Lookup table will calculate when the invoices will be paid based on the aging: 30. 60, 90 days. The Lookup Table will determine the aging by the amount owed in the Total column.

3. Try it: Create the Lookup Table
Select Cell G1 and type: Amount.
Select Cell G2 and type: Net Pay.
If these are labels (and they are) then they should be formatted BOLD.

Select Cell H1 and type: 1,000
Select Cell I1 and type: 5,000
Select Cell J1 and type: 10,000
Select Cell K1 and type: 20,000
Select H1:K1 and format the numbers for accounting. ($)

Select Cell H2 and type: 30
Select Cell I2 and type: 45
Select Cell J2 and type: 60
Select Cell K2 and type: 90

Keep going...!

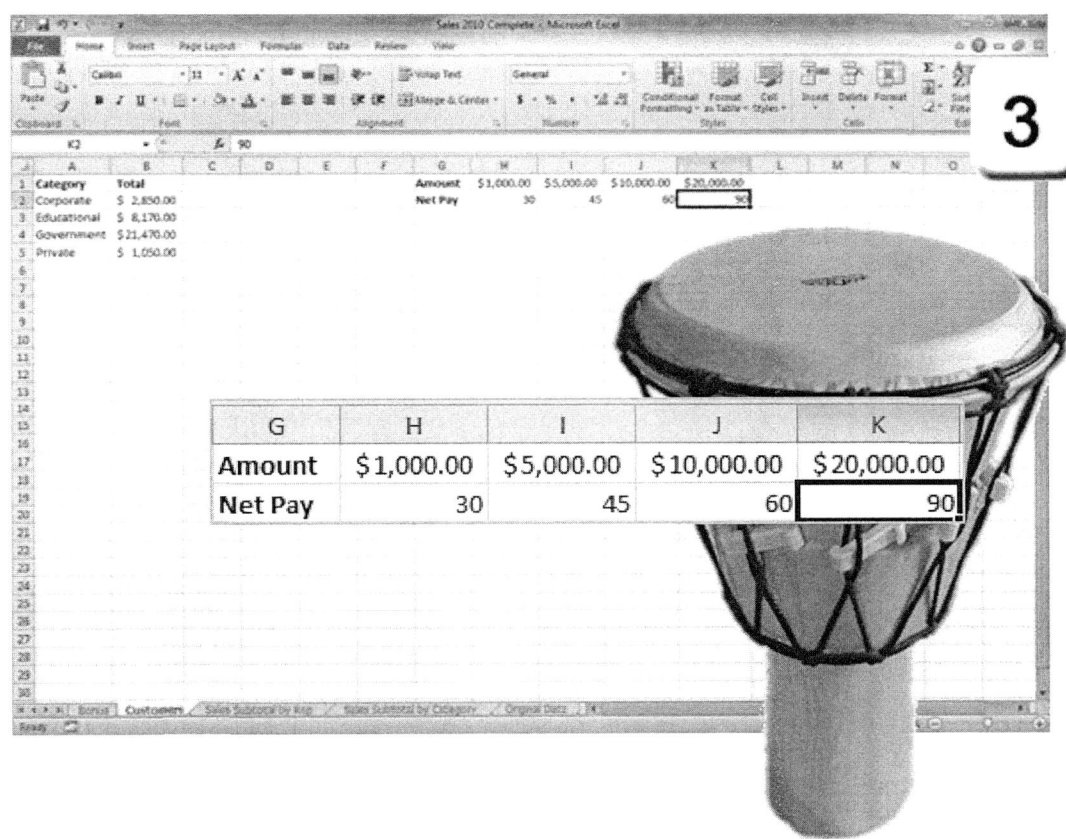

G	H	I	J	K
Amount	$1,000.00	$5,000.00	$10,000.00	$20,000.00
Net Pay	30	45	60	90

Exam 77-882: Microsoft Excel 2010 Core
5. Applying Formulas and Functions
5.1. Create formulas: HLookup

Name the Range

4. Try it: Create a Named Range
Select the RANGE G1:K2.
Go to **Formulas->Defined Names**.
Click on **Define Name**.

What Do You See? Microsoft Excel will prompt you
to enter the following information:
Name: Terms
Refers to: =Customers!$G$1:$K$2

Keep going...!

Memo to Self: The **Scope** means this Defined Name
is available to every sheet in this Excel workbook.
You can limit the scope to one specific worksheet if
you wish.

Formulas->Defined Names->Define Name

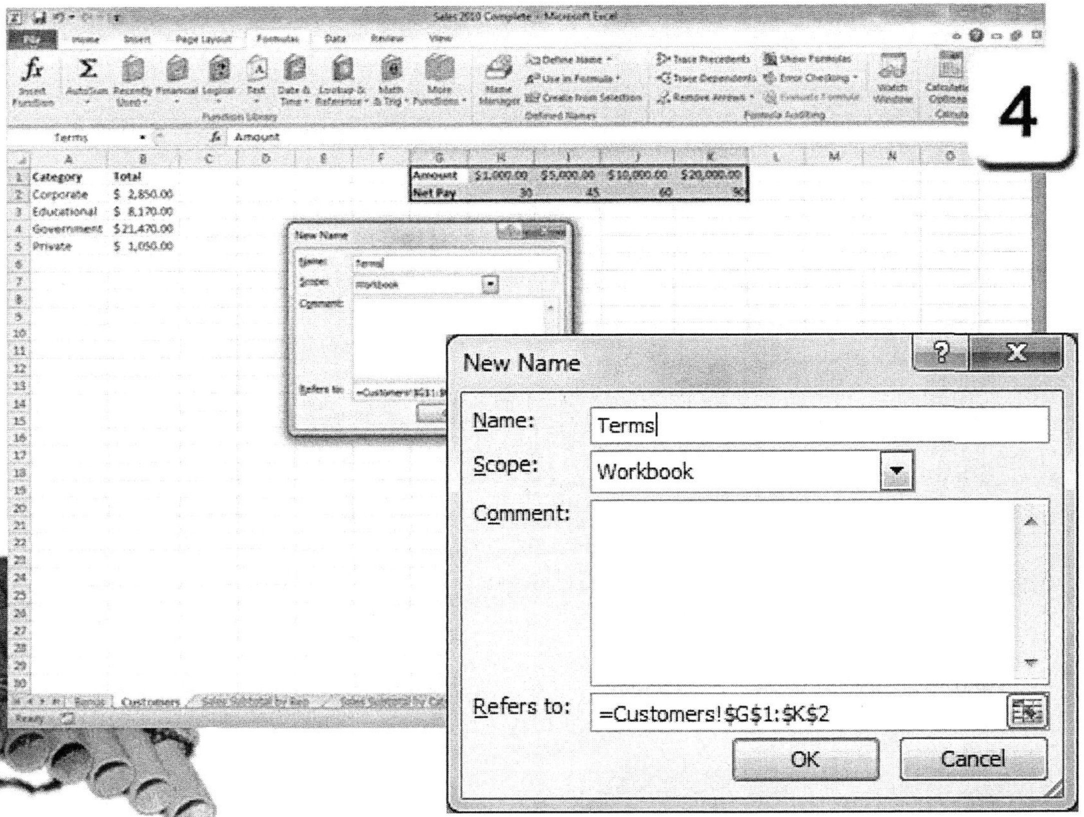

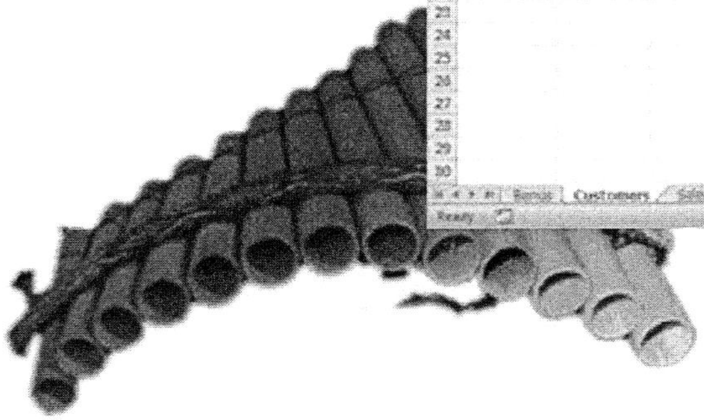

Exam 77-882: Microsoft Excel 2010 Core
5. Applying Formulas and Functions
5.5. Apply named ranges in formulas

Formulas -> Function Library ->Lookup and References ->HLookup

5

HLookup Arguments

Now that you have a name for the reference list, you can use that name in a formula.

5: Try This: Use the HLookup Function
Select: Cell C1 and type: Net Days.
Format Cell C1 BOLD, this is a label.

Select Cell C2 and create the formula:
Go to **Formulas-> Function Library.**
Go to **Lookup and References.**
Click on **HLookup.**

What Do You See? Microsoft Excel will prompt you to fill in the **HLOOKUP Arguments:**
Lookup_value: B2
Table_array: Terms
Row_index_num: 2

Click on OK. Keep going, please.

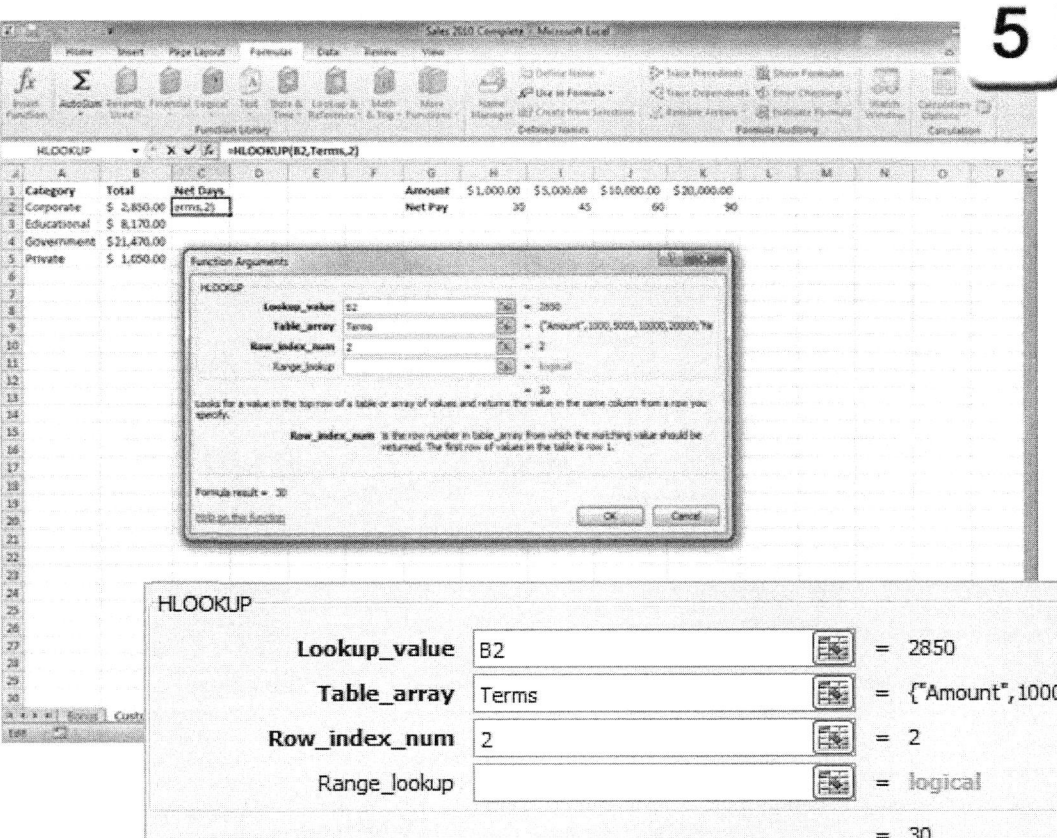

Exam 77-882: Microsoft Excel 2010 Core
5. Applying Formulas and Functions
5.1. Create formulas: HLookup

6

HLookup Results
The HLookup compared the data with the reference cells in the Lookup Table and determined an appropriate value.

6. Fill Down the Formula
Select: Cell C2.
Autofill the equation in Cells C3:C5.

The formula in Cell C5 in this example is:
=HLOOKUP(B5,Terms,2)

Memo to Self: You should SAVE your work at this point...especially if the formula works!

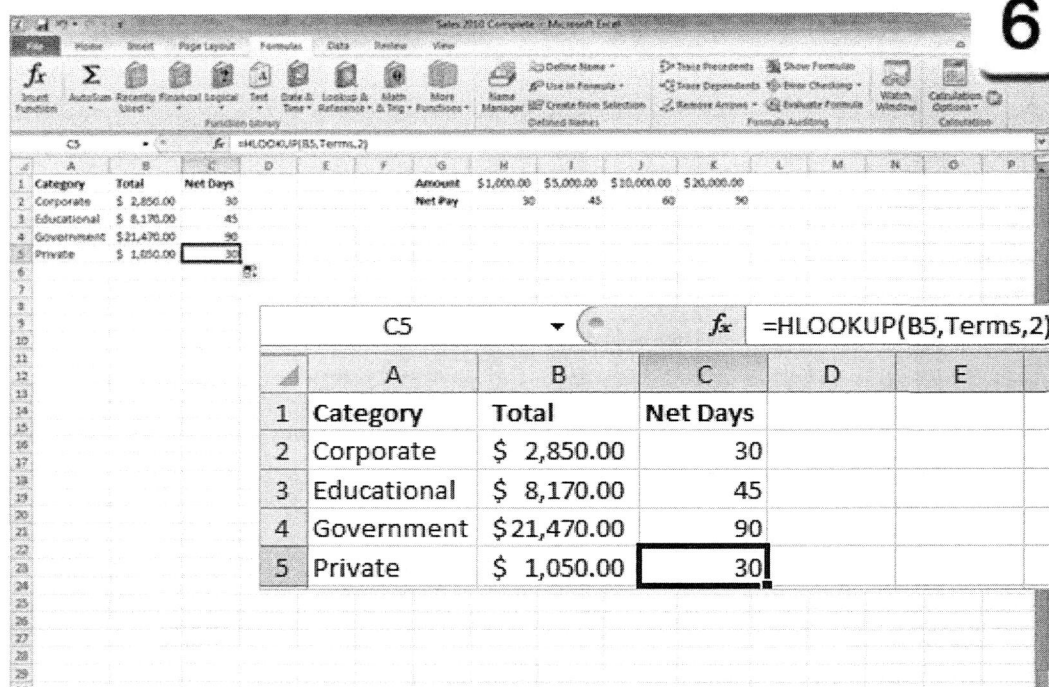

| C5 | ▼ | f_x | =HLOOKUP(B5,Terms,2) |

	A	B	C	D	E
1	Category	Total	Net Days		
2	Corporate	$ 2,850.00	30		
3	Educational	$ 8,170.00	45		
4	Government	$21,470.00	90		
5	Private	$ 1,050.00	30		

Exam 77-882: Microsoft Excel 2010 Core
5. Applying Formulas and Functions
5.1. Create formulas: HLookup

HOME

Working with Logical Formulas

The previous pages demonstrated how to create, name and use Lookup tables. Another useful set of Functions are the **Logical** formulas.

A Logical formula is binary. There are only two answers: True/False, Yes/No. It begins with a **Logical Test**. Say you wanted to calculate how much money would be paid in **less than 60** days? You could use a **Logical** equation here.

1. Try it: Create a Logical Formula
Select Cell D1 and type: Pay in 60
Select Cell D1 and format the label BOLD.

Select Cell D2.
Go to **Formulas->Function Library ->Logical.**
Click on **IF**
What Do You See? Microsoft Excel will prompt you to fill in the Arguments.
Logical Test: C2<60
Value_if_true:B2
Value_if_false: 0 (that's a zero)
Please click OK. Keep going...!

Formulas ->Function Library ->Logical ->IF

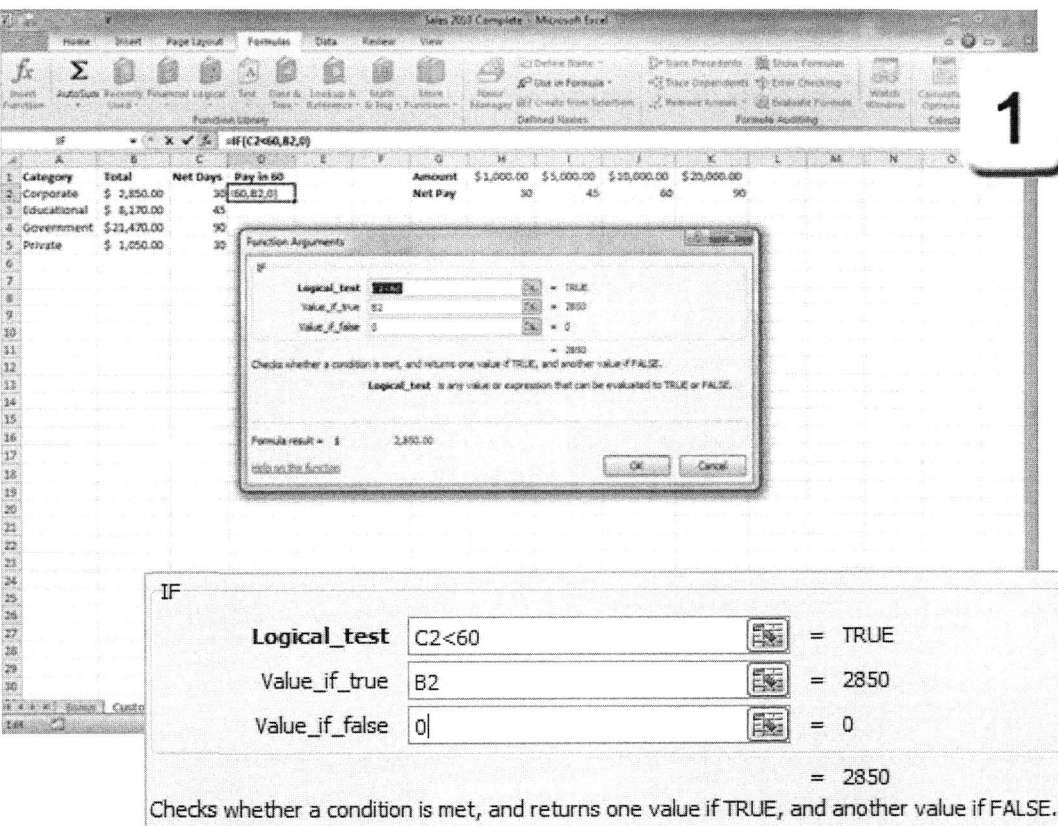

IF			
Logical_test	C2<60		= TRUE
Value_if_true	B2		= 2850
Value_if_false	0		= 0
			= 2850

Checks whether a condition is met, and returns one value if TRUE, and another value if FALSE.

Exam 77-882: Microsoft Excel 2010 Core
5. Applying Formulas and Functions
5.4. Apply conditional logic in a formula (<,>,=)

The Logical Formula Results

The Logical formula **IF** asked if the data in Column C, the Net Days calculated from the Lookup table, was less than 60. If it was **less than 60**, than look up the Total in Column B. If not than, enter a zero.

2. Fill Down the Formula
Select: Cell D2.
Autofill the equation in Cells D3:D5.

The formula in Cell D4 in this example is:
=IF(C4<60,B4,0)

Formulas ->Function Library ->Logical ->IF

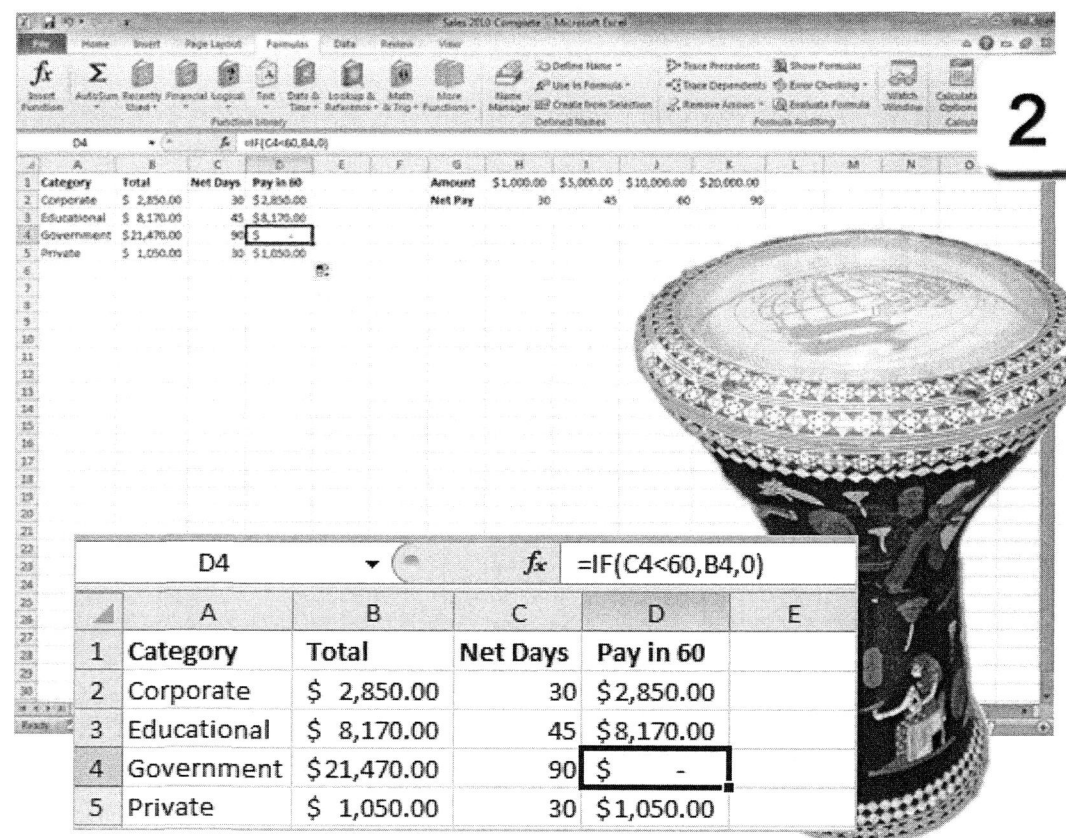

	A	B	C	D	E
1	Category	Total	Net Days	Pay in 60	
2	Corporate	$ 2,850.00	30	$2,850.00	
3	Educational	$ 8,170.00	45	$8,170.00	
4	Government	$21,470.00	90	$ -	
5	Private	$ 1,050.00	30	$1,050.00	

Exam 77-882: Microsoft Excel 2010 Core
5. Applying Formulas and Functions
5.4. Apply conditional logic in a formula (<,>,=)

Logical Functions: AND

Conditional Logic uses the following expressions: AND, OR, and NOT. The following pages will show some examples of how you can use these functions.

1. Try it: Create a Logical Formula
Select Cell E1 and type: Big Pay in 120
Select Cell E1 and format the label BOLD.

Select Cell E2.
Go to **Formulas->Function Library ->Logical**.
Click on **AND**.
What Do You See? Microsoft Excel will prompt you to fill in the Arguments.
Logical1: C2<120
Logical2: B2>5000

Please click OK. Keep going...!

Memo to Self: You can add up to 255 Logical Arguments in the AND Function.

Formulas ->Function Library ->Logical ->AND

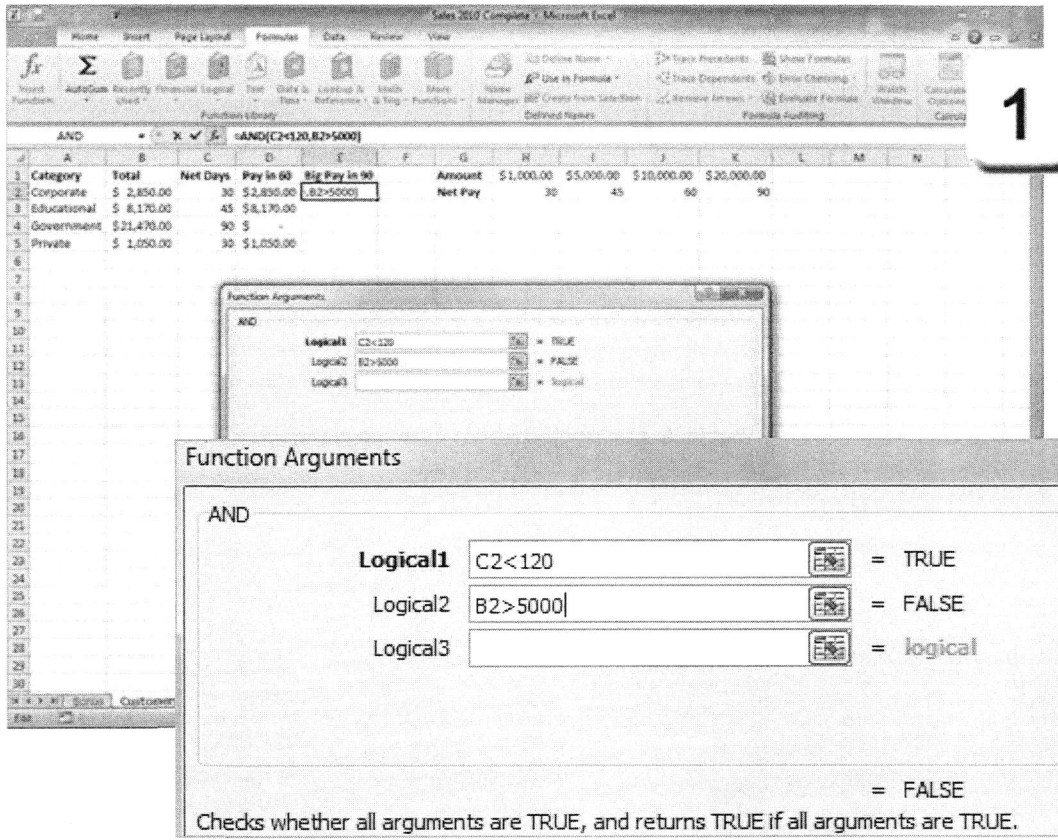

Exam 77-882: Microsoft Excel 2010 Core
5. Applying Formulas and Functions
5.4. Apply conditional logic in a formula (<,>,=)

Intermediate Excel 2010 Page 133 of 230

HOME

Formulas ->Function Library ->Logical ->AND

AND Function Results

The Logical formula **AND** asked if the data in Column C, the Net Days, is less than 120 **AND** if the data in Column B is greater than 5000.

2. Fill Down the Formula
Select: Cell E2.
Autofill the equation in Cells E3:E5.

The formula in Cell E5 in this example is:
=AND(C5<120,B5>5000)

What Do You See? The answer in this example is either TRUE or FALSE.

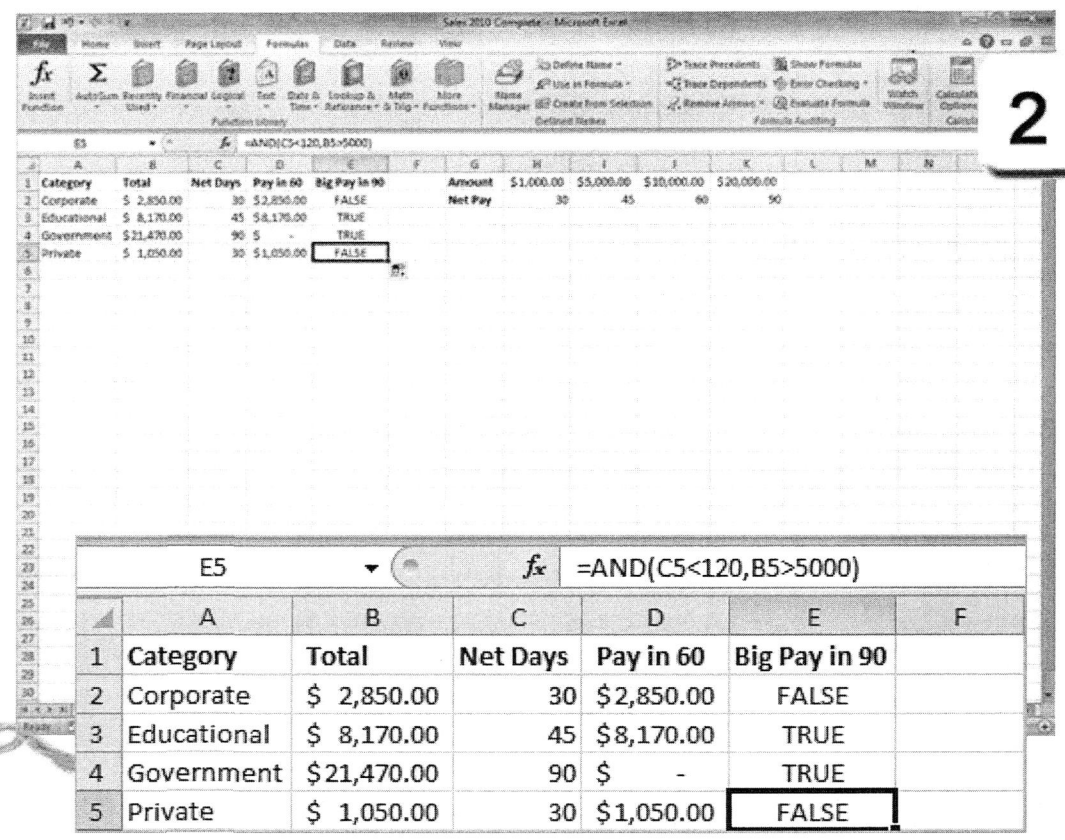

	A	B	C	D	E	F
	E5			f_x	=AND(C5<120,B5>5000)	
1	Category	Total	Net Days	Pay in 60	Big Pay in 90	
2	Corporate	$ 2,850.00	30	$2,850.00	FALSE	
3	Educational	$ 8,170.00	45	$8,170.00	TRUE	
4	Government	$21,470.00	90	$ -	TRUE	
5	Private	$ 1,050.00	30	$1,050.00	FALSE	

Exam 77-882: Microsoft Excel 2010 Core
5. Applying Formulas and Functions
5.4. Apply conditional logic in a formula (<,>,=)

HOME

Logical Functions: OR

The **OR** function answers True if ANY of the conditions are true. The OR function will only return FALSE if ALL of the logical arguments are FALSE. This is **Conditional Logic.**

1. Try it: Create a Logical Formula

Select Cell F1 and type: Little Pay in 60.
Select Cell F1 and format the label BOLD.

Select Cell F2.
Go to **Formulas->Function Library ->Logical.**
Click on **OR.**
What Do You See? Microsoft Excel will prompt you to fill in the Arguments.
Logical1: C2<60
Logical2: B2<5000

2. Fill Down the Formula

Select: Cell F2.
Autofill the equation in Cells F3:F5.
The answer should be **TRUE or FALSE.**

Formulas ->Function Library ->Logical ->OR

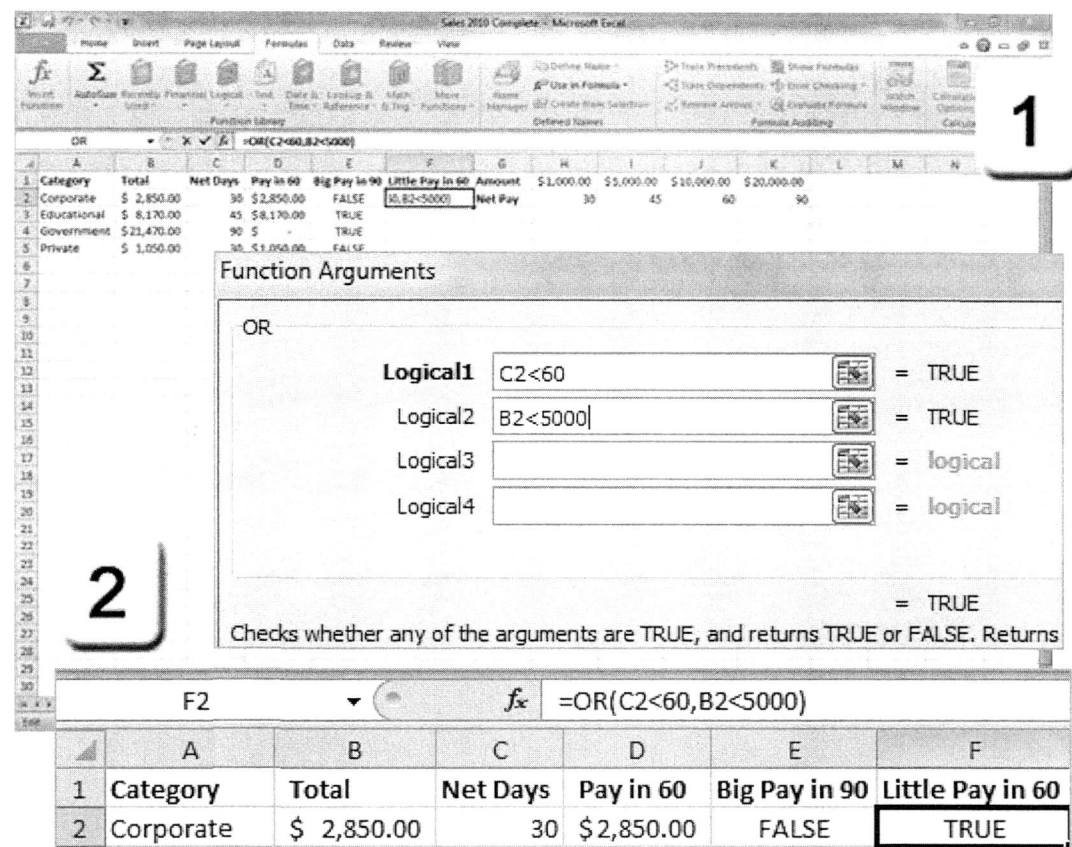

▲	A	B	C	D	E	F
1	Category	Total	Net Days	Pay in 60	Big Pay in 90	Little Pay in 60
2	Corporate	$ 2,850.00	30	$2,850.00	FALSE	TRUE

Exam 77-882: Microsoft Excel 2010 Core
5. Applying Formulas and Functions
5.4. Apply conditional logic in a formula (<,>,=)

Logical Functions: NOT

The NOT function returns the opposite answer: changes FALSE to TRUE or vice versa.

Before You Begin: Add Another Column
Select Column H.
Go to **Home->Cells->Insert.**
There should a new, blank Column G.

1. Try it: Create a Logical Formula
Select Cell G1 and type: Won't Pay in 30.
Select Cell G1 and format the label BOLD.

Select Cell G2.
Go to **Formulas->Function Library ->Logical.**
Click on **NOT.**

What Do You See? Microsoft Excel will prompt you to fill in the Arguments.
Logical1: C5=30

2. Fill Down the Formula
Select: Cell G2.
Autofill the equation in Cells G3:G5.
The answer should be **FALSE or TRUE.**

Formulas ->Function Library ->Logical ->NOT

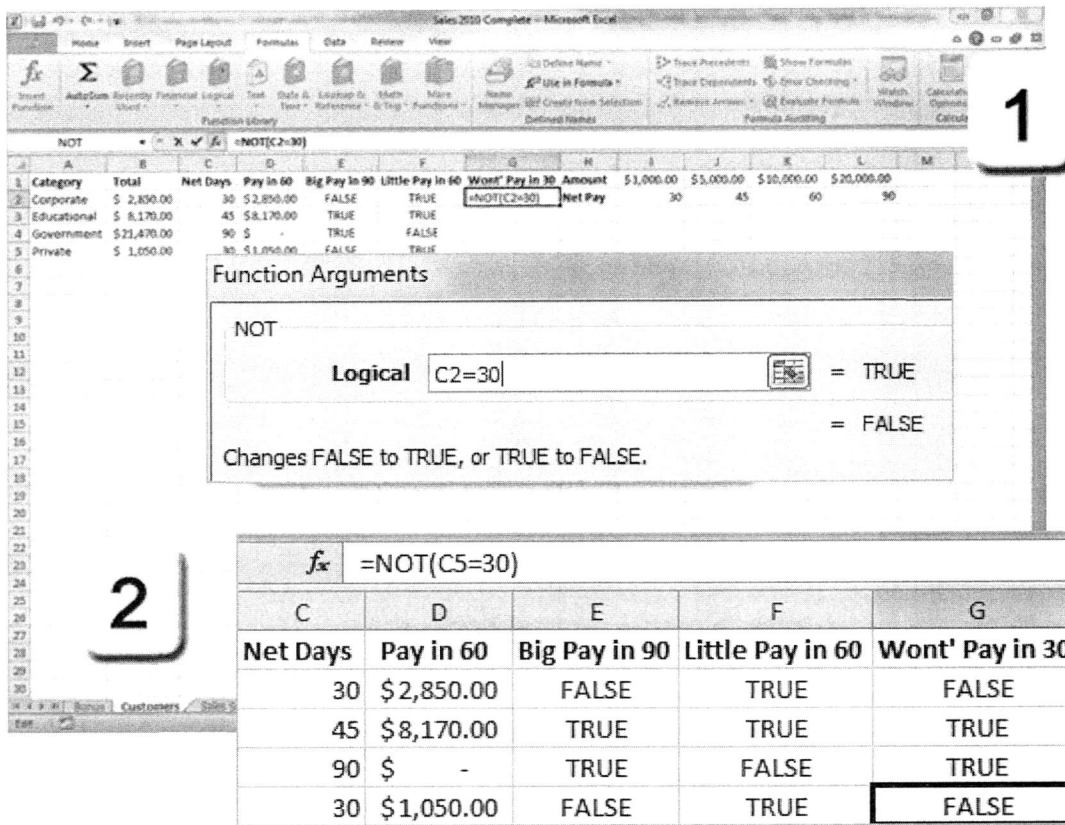

fx	=NOT(C5=30)			
C	D	E	F	G
Net Days	Pay in 60	Big Pay in 90	Little Pay in 60	Wont' Pay in 30
30	$2,850.00	FALSE	TRUE	FALSE
45	$8,170.00	TRUE	TRUE	TRUE
90	$ -	TRUE	FALSE	TRUE
30	$1,050.00	FALSE	TRUE	FALSE

Exam 77-882: Microsoft Excel 2010 Core
5. Applying Formulas and Functions
5.4. Apply conditional logic in a formula (<,>,=)

Take Two

Logical Functions: IFERROR

The **IFERROR** function determines if there are any problems with the data. Here are a few of the problems that can be found:

#N/A (not enough data),
#VALUE! (different data types, such as adding a number to a date),
#REF! (a lost cell reference),
#DIV/0! (a divide by zero error)
#NAME? Where's the Named Range)
or #NULL!. (an empty cell with no data).

Before You Begin: Add Another Column
Select Column E.
Go to **Home->Cells->Insert**.
There should a new, blank Column E.

1. Try it: Create a Logical Formula
Select Cell E1 and type: IFERROR.
Select Cell E1 and format the label BOLD.

Keep going...

Formulas ->Function Library ->Logical ->IFFERROR

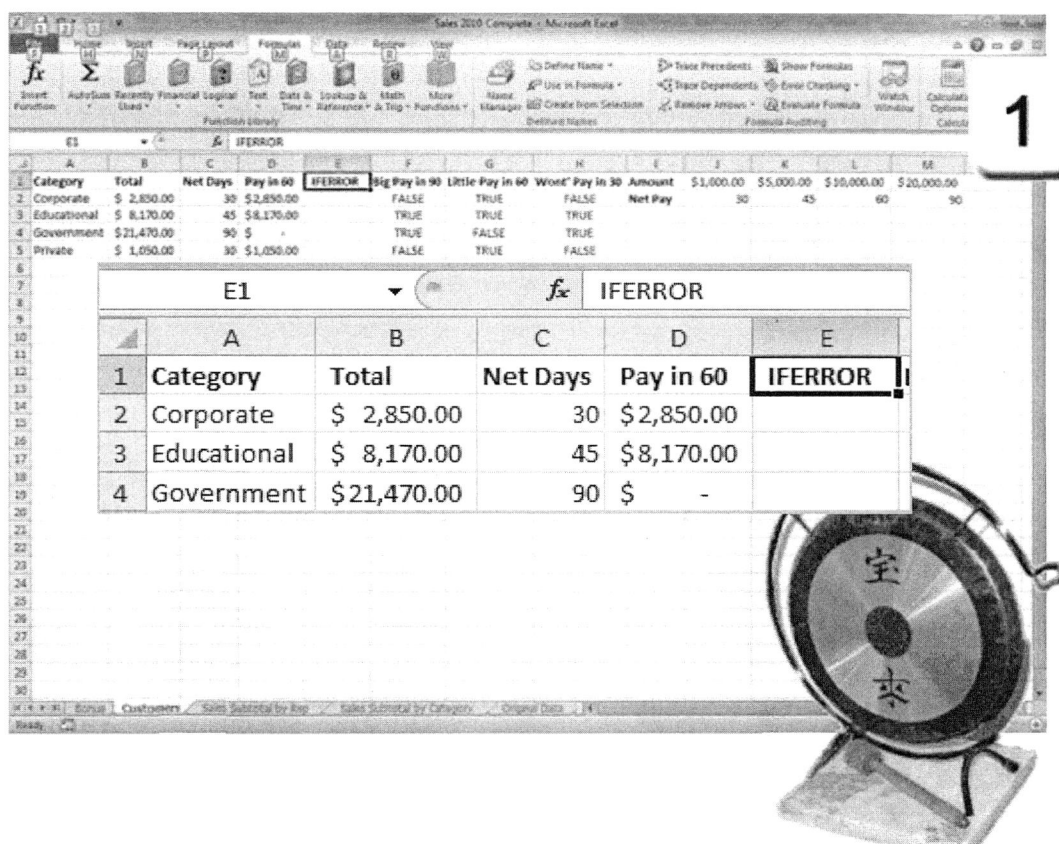

Exam 77-882: Microsoft Excel 2010 Core
5. Applying Formulas and Functions
5.4. Apply conditional logic in a formula (<,>,=)

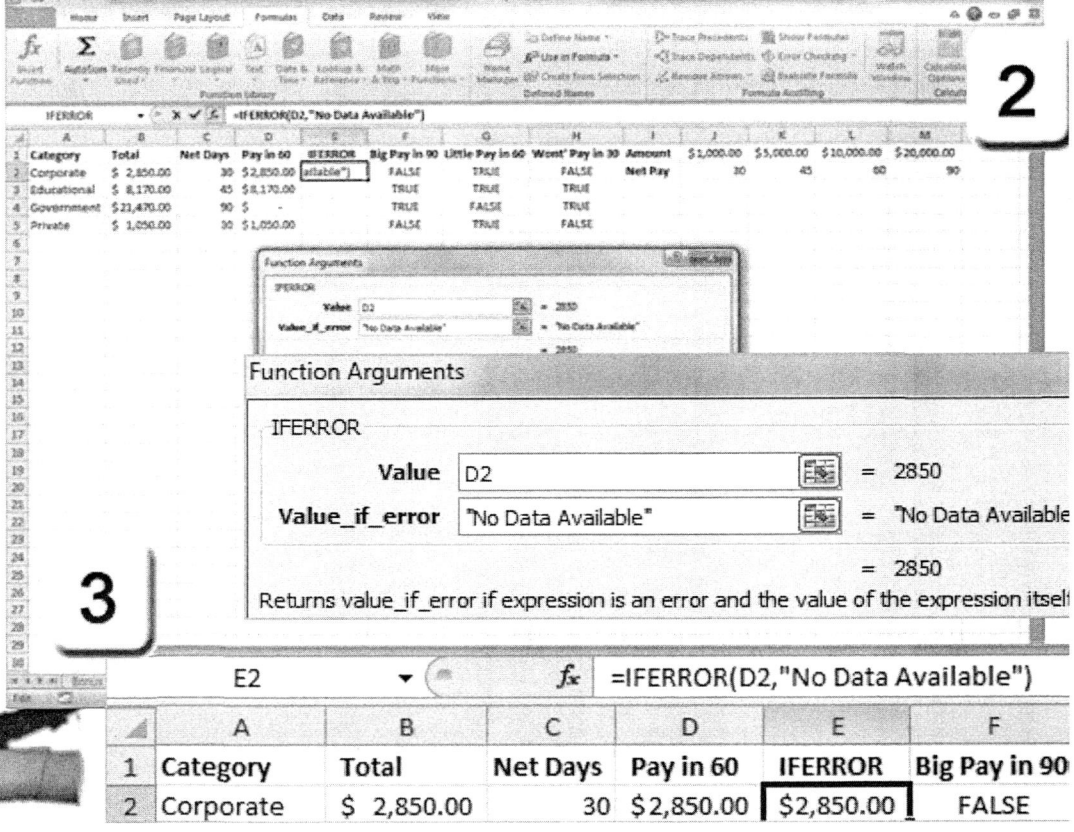

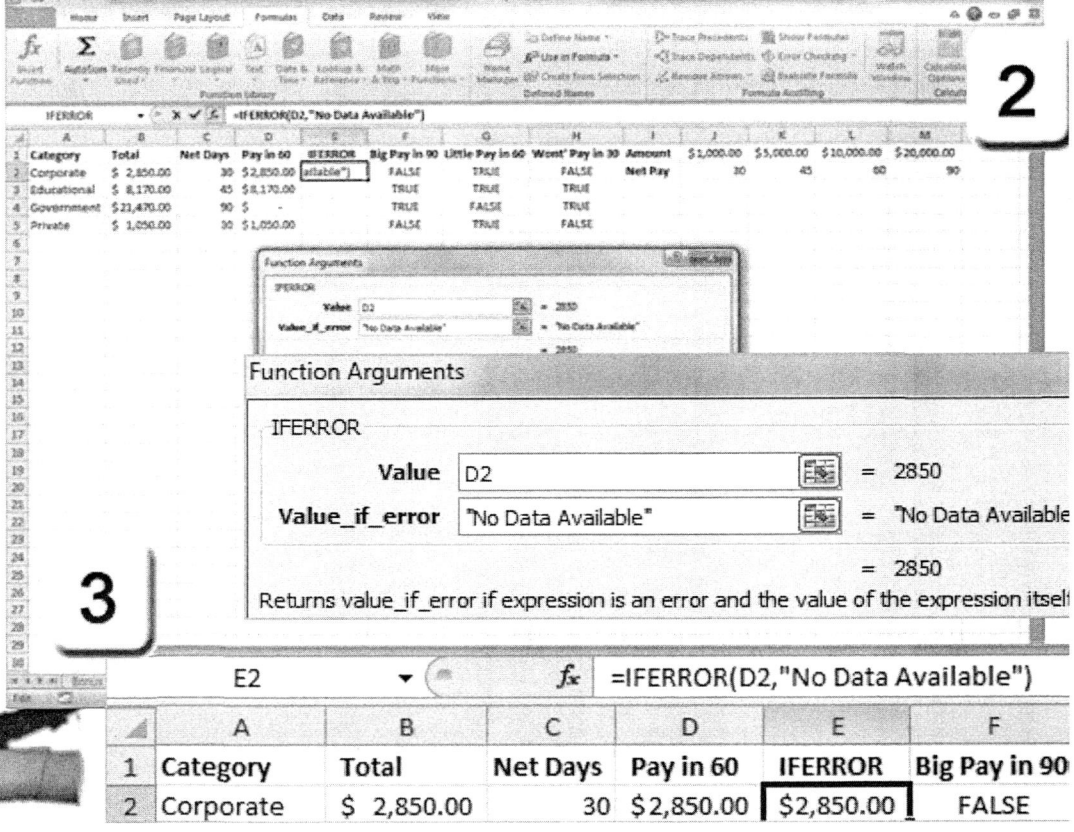

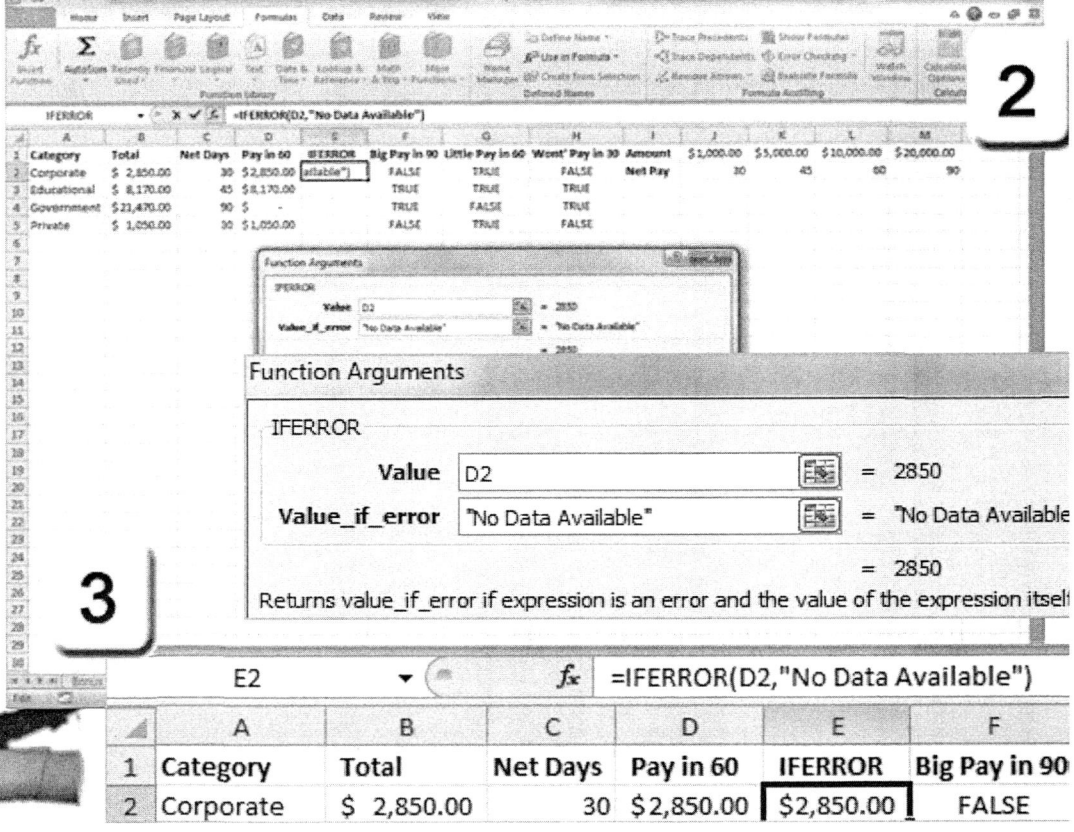

Formulas ->Function Library ->Logical ->IFERROR

IFERROR Functions

2. Try This: The IFERROR Function
Select: Cell E2.
Go to **Formulas ->Function Library ->Logical.**
Click on **IFERROR.**
Value: D2
Value_if_error: "No Data Available"

The formula in this example is:
=IFERROR(D2,"No Data Available")

What Do You See? The answer should be the data in Cell D2. If there is no data, then the result will be our error message: No Data Available.

3. Fill Down the Formula
Select: Cell E2.
Autofill the equation in Cells E3:E5.
Keep going...

Function Arguments

IFERROR

Value	D2	= 2850
Value_if_error	"No Data Available"	= "No Data Available"

= 2850

Returns value_if_error if expression is an error and the value of the expression itself

E2 f_x =IFERROR(D2,"No Data Available")

	A	B	C	D	E	F
1	Category	Total	Net Days	Pay in 60	IFERROR	Big Pay in 90
2	Corporate	$ 2,850.00	30	$2,850.00	$2,850.00	FALSE

Exam 77-882: Microsoft Excel 2010 Core
5. Applying Formulas and Functions
5.4. Apply conditional logic in a formula (<,>,=)

Make a Mistake

So, there is a Logical formula in Column E. **IFERROR** Logical formulas are binary. They only have two answers: **Value if TRUE**, **Value_If_Error**. This formula shows the data from Cell B2, the **Value if TRUE**. What do you see if there is a mistake?

4. Try it: Make a Mistake

Select Cell C2. The HLOOKUP formula should be available in the Formula Bar. Edit the Name: Change Terms to Term

5. What Do You See? Changing the Named Range created an error in Cell C2. By definition, #NAME? means that Excel cannot find that Name in the Name Manager.

What Else Do You See? The IFERROR Formula in Cell E2 now shows the Value_If_Error: No Data Available.

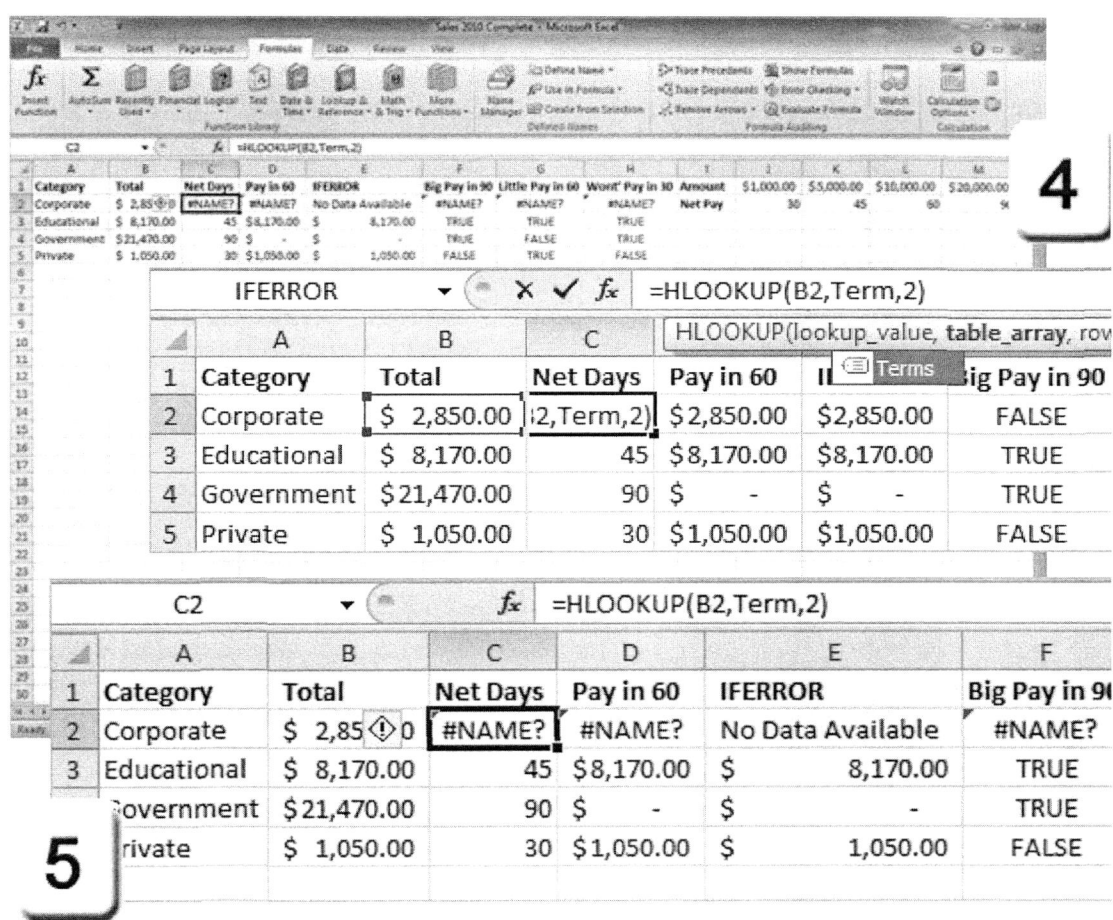

C2   ✓ fx | =HLOOKUP(B2,Term,2)

HLOOKUP(lookup_value, **table_array**, row

	A	B	C	Pay in 60	Terms Big Pay in 90
1	Category	Total	Net Days	Pay in 60	Big Pay in 90
2	Corporate	$ 2,850.00	2,Term,2)	$2,850.00	$2,850.00	FALSE
3	Educational	$ 8,170.00	45	$8,170.00	$8,170.00	TRUE
4	Government	$21,470.00	90	$ -	$ -	TRUE
5	Private	$ 1,050.00	30	$1,050.00	$1,050.00	FALSE

C2   fx | =HLOOKUP(B2,Term,2)

	A	B	C	D	E	F
1	Category	Total	Net Days	Pay in 60	IFERROR	Big Pay in 9(
2	Corporate	$ 2,85⟨!⟩0	#NAME?	#NAME?	No Data Available	#NAME?
3	Educational	$ 8,170.00	45	$8,170.00	$ 8,170.00	TRUE
4	Government	$21,470.00	90	$ -	$ -	TRUE
5	Private	$ 1,050.00	30	$1,050.00	$ 1,050.00	FALSE

Summary

This lesson focused on how to find the right answer in a Lookup Table. The key to making the Lookup Formulas work is naming the Lookup Table. Our lesson demonstrated how to use the Lookup Table in the formula.

We also investigated the Logical Formulas: IF, AND, OR, NOT and IFERROR.

Very good. You get two cookies.

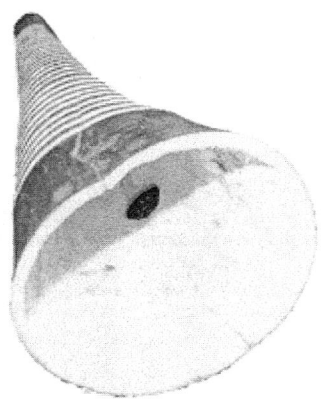

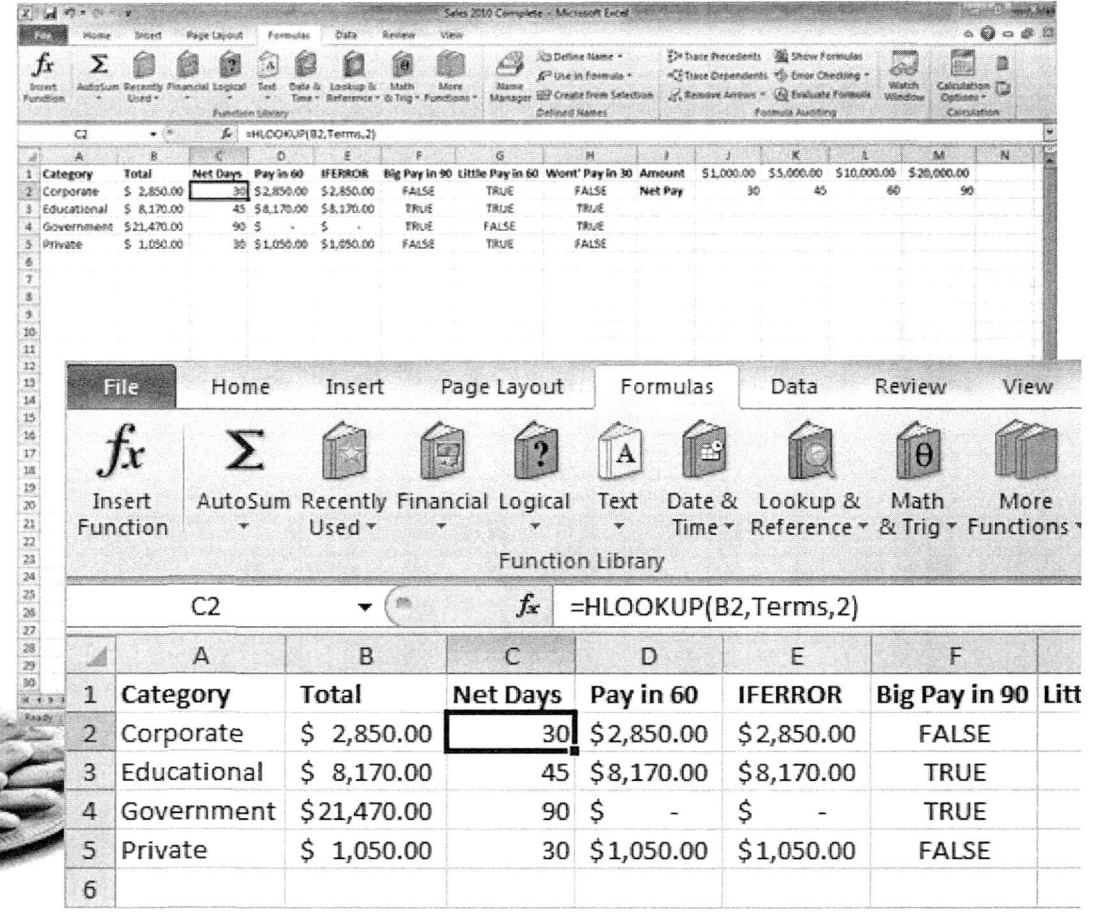

	A	B	C	D	E	F	
1	Category	Total	Net Days	Pay in 60	IFERROR	Big Pay in 90	Litt
2	Corporate	$ 2,850.00	30	$2,850.00	$2,850.00	FALSE	
3	Educational	$ 8,170.00	45	$8,170.00	$8,170.00	TRUE	
4	Government	$21,470.00	90	$ -	$ -	TRUE	
5	Private	$ 1,050.00	30	$1,050.00	$1,050.00	FALSE	
6							

C2 =HLOOKUP(B2,Terms,2)

Practice Activities

Lesson 4: Sound Advice

Try This: Do the following steps
1. Open the spreadsheet: Student Records.xlsx

2. On Sheet 2, create an VLOOKUP table with the following grading scale. Put the **percentages** in Colum A and the **letter grade** in Column B.

3. Select the grading scale and Name the Range: GRADES.

0	E
62	D-
65	D
69	D+
72	C-
75	C
79	C+
82	B-
85	B
89	B+
92	A-
100	A

4. Rename Sheet 2: Grading Scale

5. On Sheet 3, create an HLOOKUP table for the Homeroom Teacher. Put the **Class** in Row 1 and the **Teacher** in Row 2. Enter the following information:
Students in the class of 2010 have Mr. Green.
Students in the class of 2011 have Mr. Plum.
Students in the class of 2012 have Mrs. White.
Students in the class of 2013 have Ms. Scarlett.

6. Name the HLOOKUP Table TEACHER

7. On Sheet 1, use the HLOOKUP function in Column E to return the appropriate Homeroom Teacher.

8. Rename Sheet 1 as Student Records

Save your work as YOUR NAME Sound Advice Practice.

Test Yourself

1. Which of the following is true?
(Select all correct answers)
a. VLOOKUP uses values in columns
b. VLOOKUP uses values in rows
c. HLOOKUP uses values in columns
d. HLOOKUP uses values in rows
Tip: Intermediate Excel, page 115

2. Lookup functions are found on the formula ribbon under Lookup & Reference
a. True
b. False
Tip: Intermediate Excel, page 118

3. What does Col_index_num refer to?
a. Which column in the range has the data
b. Which column the data will be put into
c. There is an error in the formula
Tip: Intermediate Excel, page 119

4. It is possible to select two, non-connected ranges in Excel
a. True
b. False
Tip: Intermediate Excel, page 122

5. The Scope of a defined range refers to whether the selected Defined Name is available to one or all sheets in the workbook.
a. True
b. False
Tip: Intermediate Excel, page 128

6. Which of the following are Logic Functions? (Select all correct answers.)
a. IF
b. AND
c. OR
d. NOT
Tip: Intermediate Excel, page 133

7. Match the Error messages with their meaning.
a. #N/A
b. #VALUE
c. #REF!
d. #DIV/0!
e. #NAME!
f. #NULL!
g. ######

i. Can't find the named range
ii. Column too narrow
iii. Different data types, such as adding a number to a date
iv. Divide by zero error
v. Lost cell reference
vi. Not enough data
vii. Refers to an empty cell with no data
Tip: Intermediate Excel, 137

Excel 2010: Excel in Print

Print and Page Layout Options

Take One

Intermediate Excel Objectives

In this lesson, you will learn how to:

1. Use the Page Layout options to prepare a professional print out

2. Edit the Page Setup including the Orientation, Margins, Size, Background, and Titles

3. Create custom Headers and Footers with different Odd and Even pages

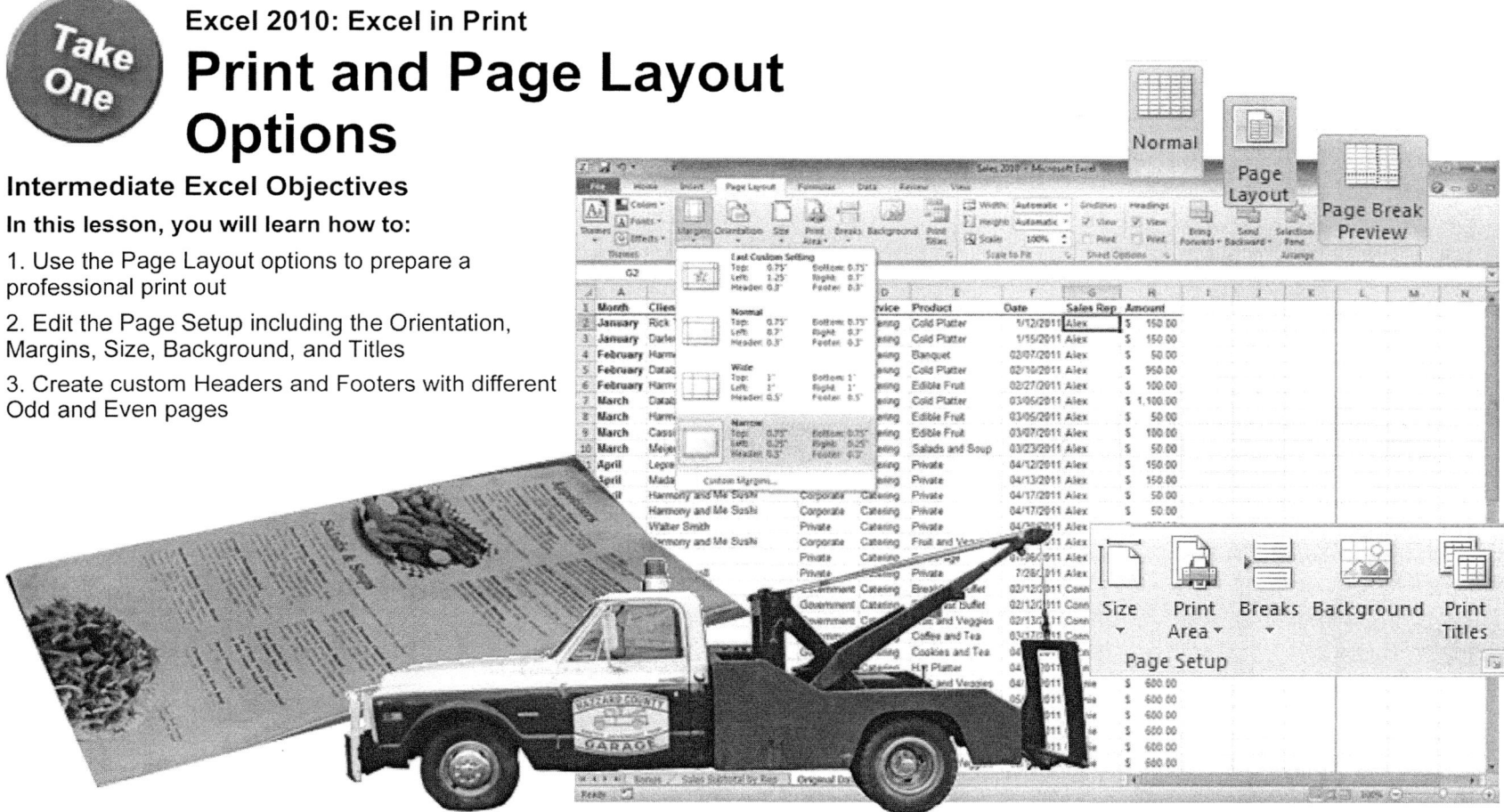

Lesson 5: Excel in Print

1. Readings

Read Lesson 5 in the Intermediate Excel guide, page 143-169.

Project

A sample project that investigates the options for Page Layout and Printing.

Downloads

Sales 2010.xlsx

2. Practice

There is no Practice Activity in this lesson.

3. Assessment

Review the Test questions, page 170.

Page Layout

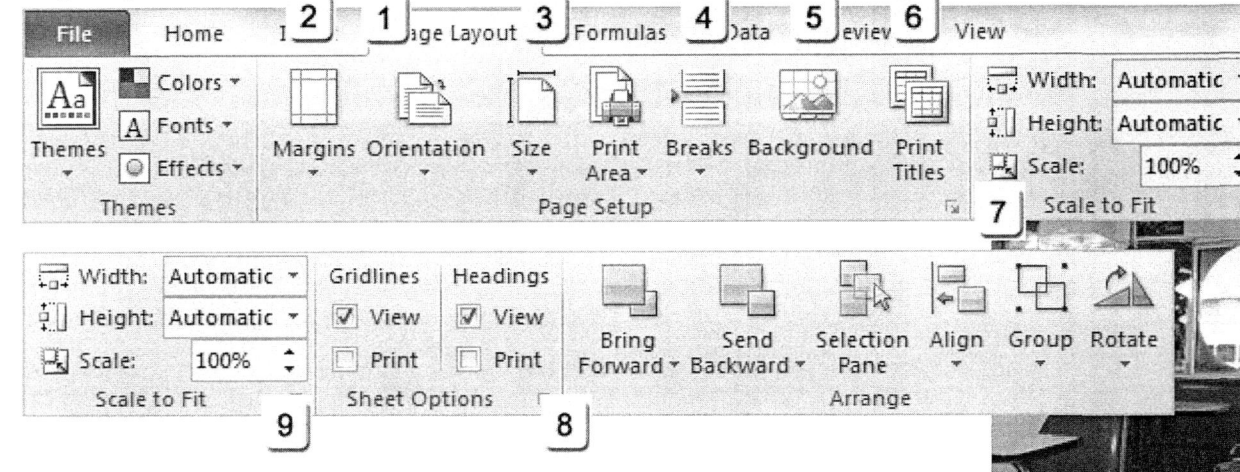

Menu Maps

This lesson shows the **Page Layout** Ribbon.

1. Page Layout -> Page Setup ->Orientation, page 149
2. Page Layout -> Page Setup ->Margins, page 150
3. Page Layout -> Page Setup ->Size, page 152
4. Page Layout -> Page Setup ->Breaks, page 153
5. Page Layout -> Page Setup ->Background, page 155
6. Page Layout -> Page Setup ->Print Titles, page 156
7. Page Layout -> Page Setup ->More->Header/Footer, page 159
8. Page Layout -> Sheet Options, page 165
9. Page Layout: Scale to Fit, page 166

Excel: In Print

Even spreadsheets need to get dressed up and printed sometimes. Menus, price sheets, delivery schedules and shipping lists are all part of customer service. If it is going to be in your customers' hands, it should look good in print. The spreadsheet should include a name and number, too....just in case your customers want to buy something.

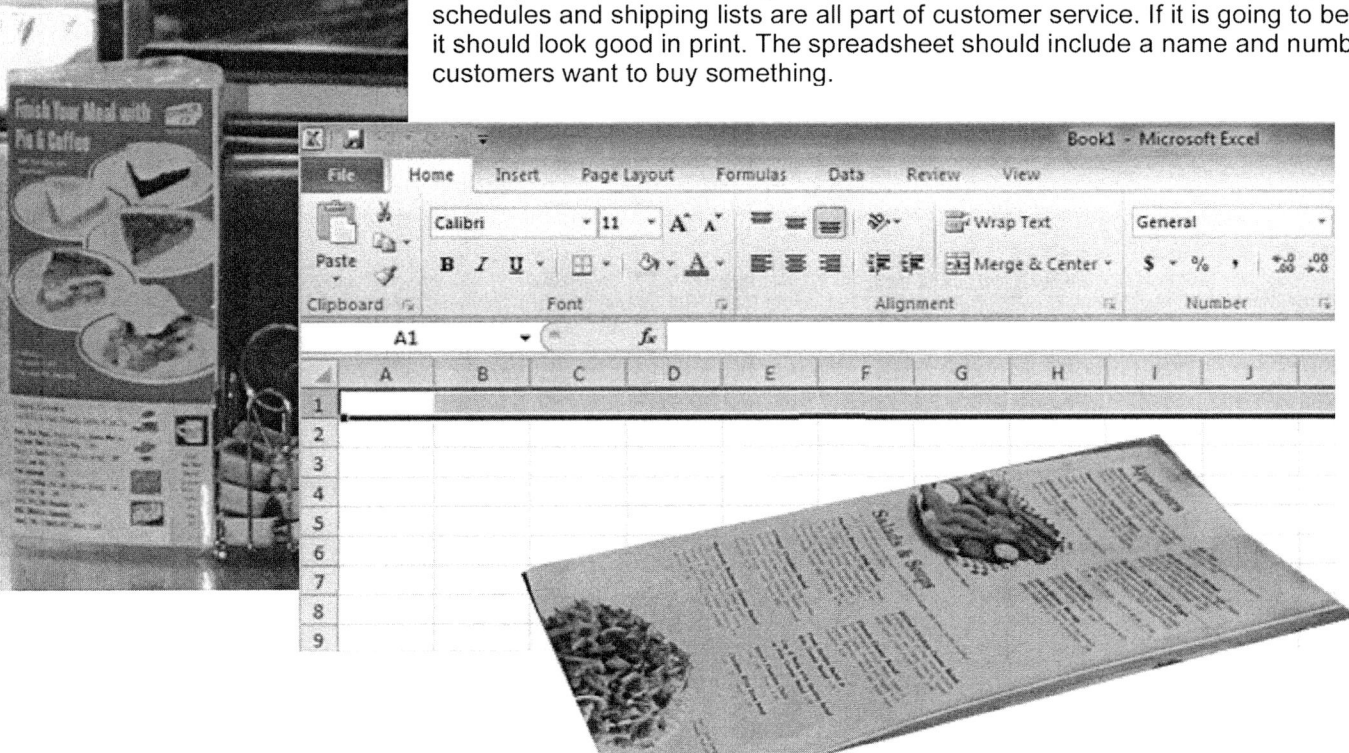

So, Start Microsoft Excel. What do you see? Is there a **Title Bar** that says Microsoft Excel? Yes.

Is there a **Home Ribbon** with the Clipboard, Font and Number **Groups**? Yes.

If your screen looks similar to the example on this page, then you are ready to get started.

Before You Begin
The purpose of this lesson is to demonstrate the **Page Setup** and **Print** Options in Microsoft Excel. You can use the spreadsheet that you created in an earlier lesson or download a new sample if you wish.

1. Try This: Open a Sample Spreadsheet
Open a sample spreadsheet: Sales2010.xlsx
Go to the Original Data sheet.

What Do You See? This sheet shows the product sales for Charlotte' Website. The first row is BOLD: it is the Header Row. There are many rows of data.

Memo to Self: You do not have to MATCH the numbers shown on these pages. It is more important that you begin with some data and understand the options.

File -> Open

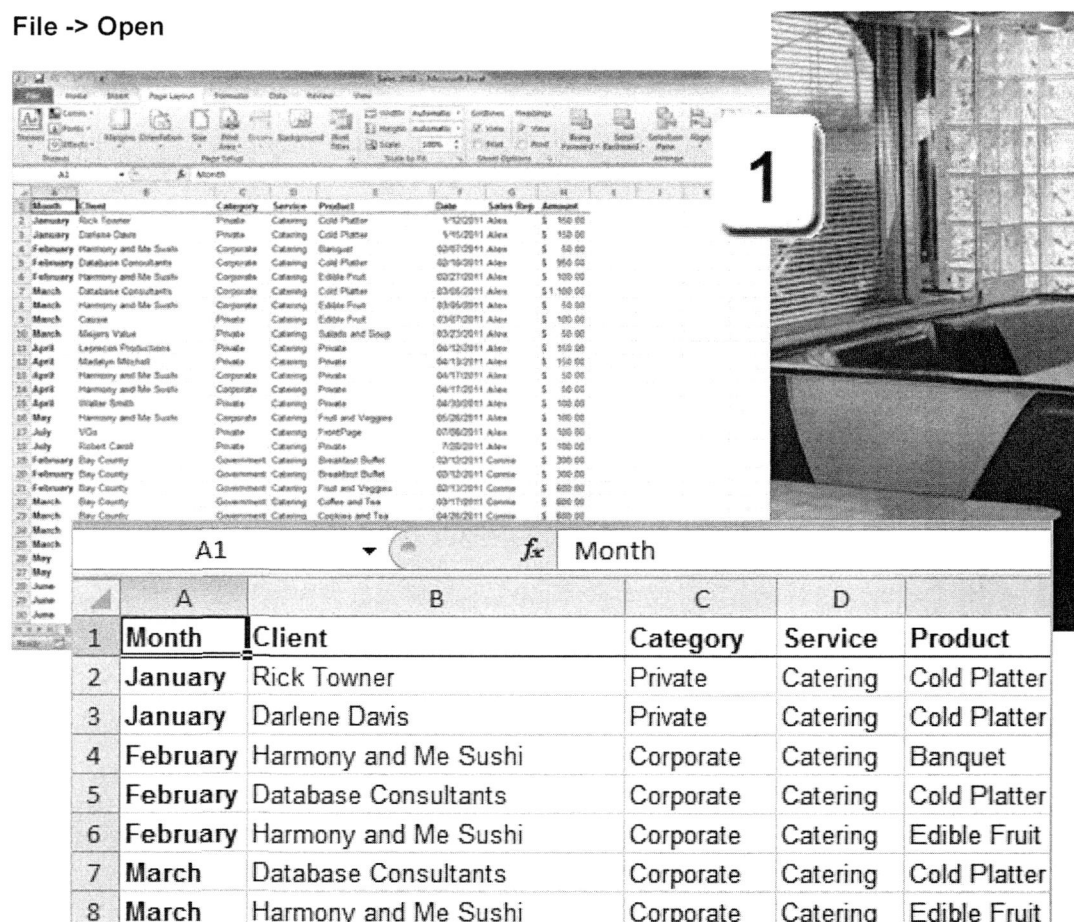

	A	B	C	D	
1	Month	Client	Category	Service	Product
2	January	Rick Towner	Private	Catering	Cold Platter
3	January	Darlene Davis	Private	Catering	Cold Platter
4	February	Harmony and Me Sushi	Corporate	Catering	Banquet
5	February	Database Consultants	Corporate	Catering	Cold Platter
6	February	Harmony and Me Sushi	Corporate	Catering	Edible Fruit
7	March	Database Consultants	Corporate	Catering	Cold Platter
8	March	Harmony and Me Sushi	Corporate	Catering	Edible Fruit

Workbook Views

2. Try This: View the Page Layout
Go to **View -> Workbook Views**.
Click on **Page Layout**.

What Do You See? The **Page Layout**
shows how the spreadsheet would look
when it is printed. This spreadsheet has
"Widows and Orphans." The sales numbers
are "orphaned" on page 2, separated from
the product and customer data on page 1.

Keep going, please...

View -> Workbook Views ->Page Layout

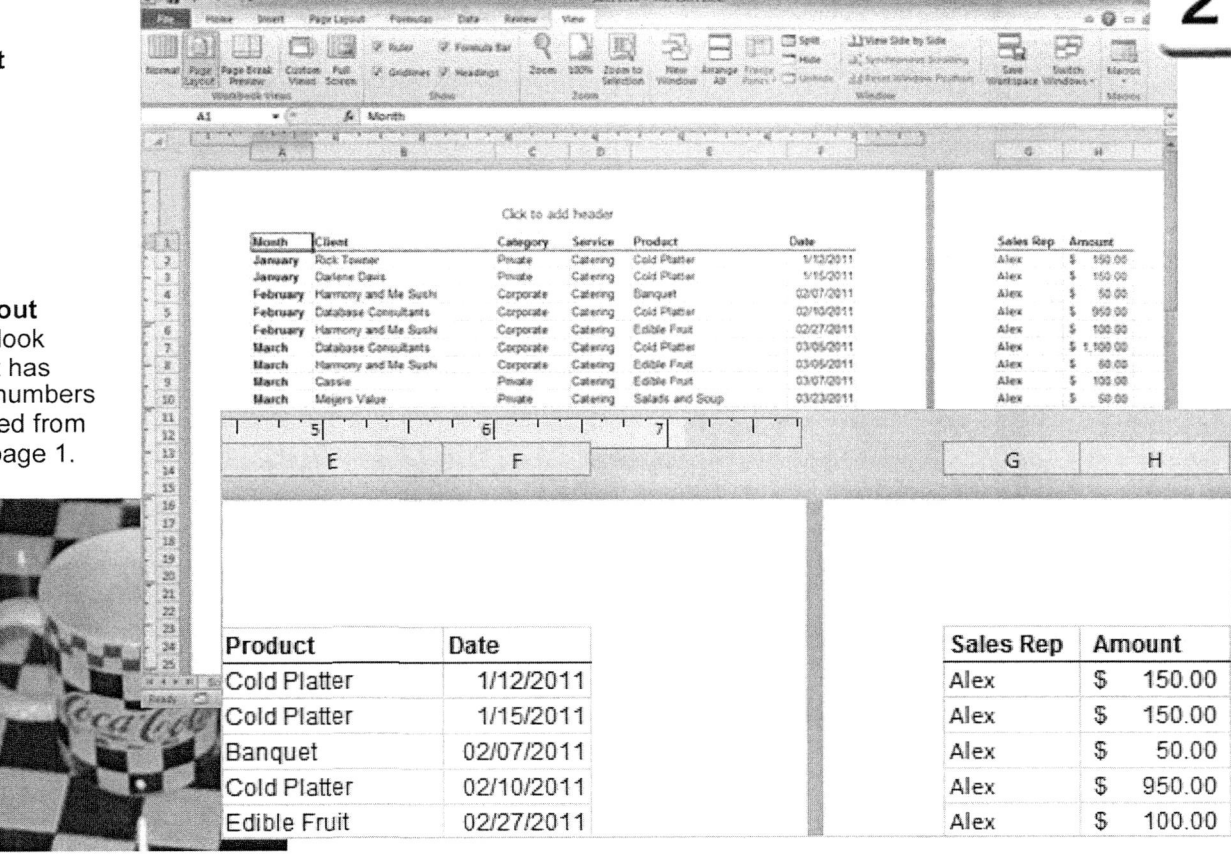

Product	Date		Sales Rep	Amount
Cold Platter	1/12/2011		Alex	$ 150.00
Cold Platter	1/15/2011		Alex	$ 150.00
Banquet	02/07/2011		Alex	$ 50.00
Cold Platter	02/10/2011		Alex	$ 950.00
Edible Fruit	02/27/2011		Alex	$ 100.00

Exam 77-882: Microsoft Excel 2010 Core
4. Managing Worksheets and Workbooks
4.3. Manipulate workbook views

View -> Workbook Views ->Normal

Return to Normal View

3. Try This: Return to the Normal View
Go to **View -> Workbook Views**.
Click on **Normal**.

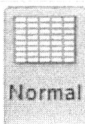

What Do You See? There should be a
dashed line that indicates where the Page
Break would be. In the example on this page,
the Page Break is between Column F and G.

Keep going...

Memo to Self: The Computer Mama sez,
"Don't get me started on what's "Normal..."

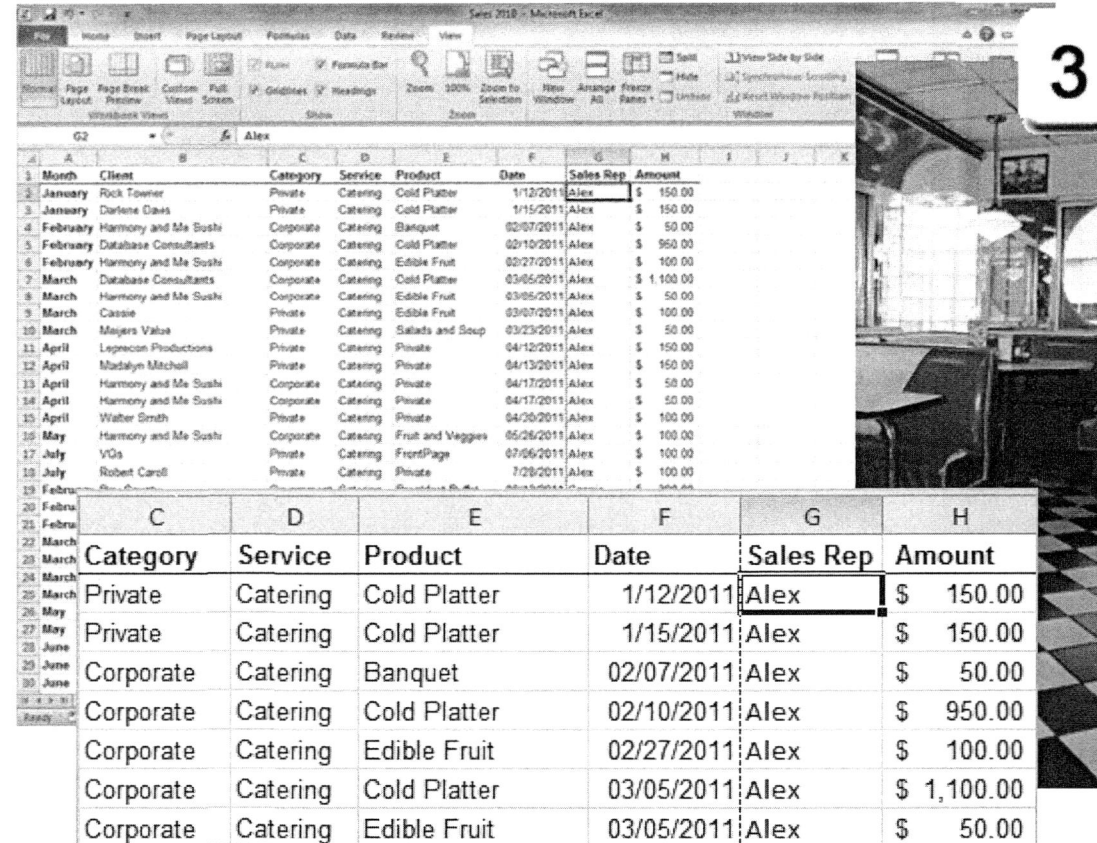

Category	Service	Product	Date	Sales Rep	Amount
Private	Catering	Cold Platter	1/12/2011	Alex	$ 150.00
Private	Catering	Cold Platter	1/15/2011	Alex	$ 150.00
Corporate	Catering	Banquet	02/07/2011	Alex	$ 50.00
Corporate	Catering	Cold Platter	02/10/2011	Alex	$ 950.00
Corporate	Catering	Edible Fruit	02/27/2011	Alex	$ 100.00
Corporate	Catering	Cold Platter	03/05/2011	Alex	$ 1,100.00
Corporate	Catering	Edible Fruit	03/05/2011	Alex	$ 50.00

Exam 77-882: Microsoft Excel 2010 Core
4. Managing Worksheets and Workbooks
4.3. Manipulate workbook views: Normal View

HOME

Take One

Page Layout -> Page Setup ->Orientation

Edit the Page Setup
There are several things that can be changed before this spreadsheet is sent to the printer. You can use the **Page Layout** Ribbon to make improvements. Most of the tools can be found in the **Page Setup** Group.

1. Try This: Change the Orientation
Go to **Page Layout -> Page Setup.**
Click on **Orientation.**
Select **Landscape**.

What Do You See? There should be a dashed line indicating the page breaks. In this example, the line is between Column I and J when the orientation is **Landscape**.

Keep going...

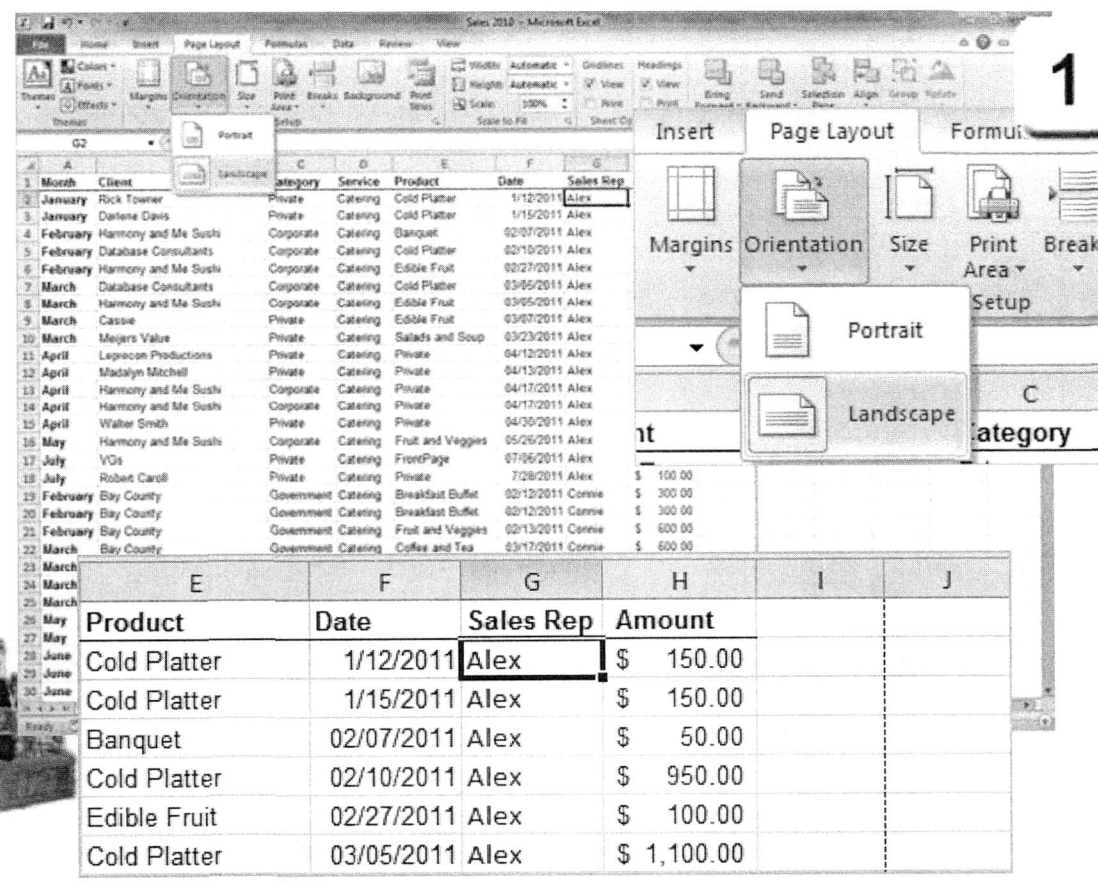

	E	F	G	H	I	J
	Product	**Date**	**Sales Rep**	**Amount**		
	Cold Platter	1/12/2011	Alex	$ 150.00		
	Cold Platter	1/15/2011	Alex	$ 150.00		
	Banquet	02/07/2011	Alex	$ 50.00		
	Cold Platter	02/10/2011	Alex	$ 950.00		
	Edible Fruit	02/27/2011	Alex	$ 100.00		
	Cold Platter	03/05/2011	Alex	$ 1,100.00		

Exam 77-882: Microsoft Excel 2010 Core
3. Formatting Cells and Worksheets
3.5. Manipulate Page Setup options for worksheets: Orientation

Page Setup: Margins

By default, the **Normal Margins** in an Excel Spreadsheet are set at:
Top and Bottom: 0.75"
Left and Right Sides: 0.7"
The **Header and Footer** are 0.3" from the edges of the paper.

2. Try This: Format the Margins
Go to **Page Layout -> Page Setup.**
Go to **Margins.**
Click on **Narrow.**

What Do You See? The **Narrow Margins** are:
Top and Bottom: 0.75 inches
Left and Right Sides: 0.25 inches
The **Header and Footer** are 0.3 inches from the edges of the paper.

Keep going...

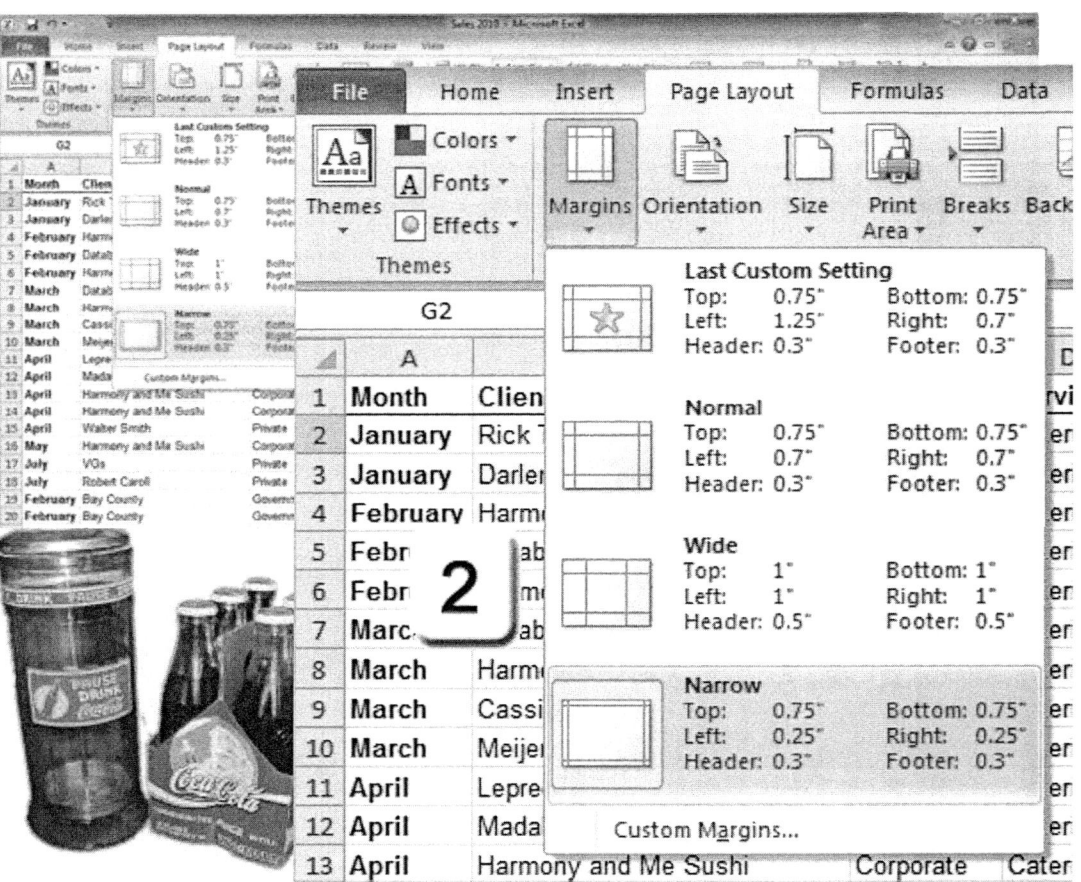

Exam 77-882: Microsoft Excel 2010 Core
3. Formatting Cells and Worksheets
3.5. Manipulate Page Setup options for worksheets: Margins

Page Setup: Custom Margins
You can create **Custom Margins** as well.

Page Layout -> Page Setup ->Margins->Custom Margins

3. Try This, Too: Custom Margins
Go to **Page Layout -> Page Setup.**
Go to **Margins->Custom Margins.**

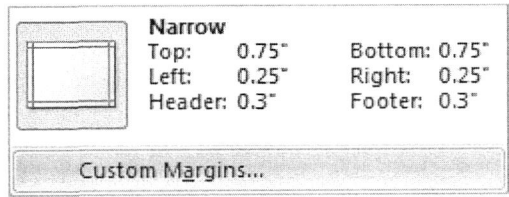

What Do You See? You can edit any of the Margins if you wish. The Left/Right and the Top/Bottom do not have to be the same size.

What Else Do You See? This is the page that lets you **Center** your data on the page.

Memo to Self: Printers have design limits. Most printers cannot bleed: print all the way to the edge of the paper, even if Excel does let you make the Margins 0.0" (zero inches.)

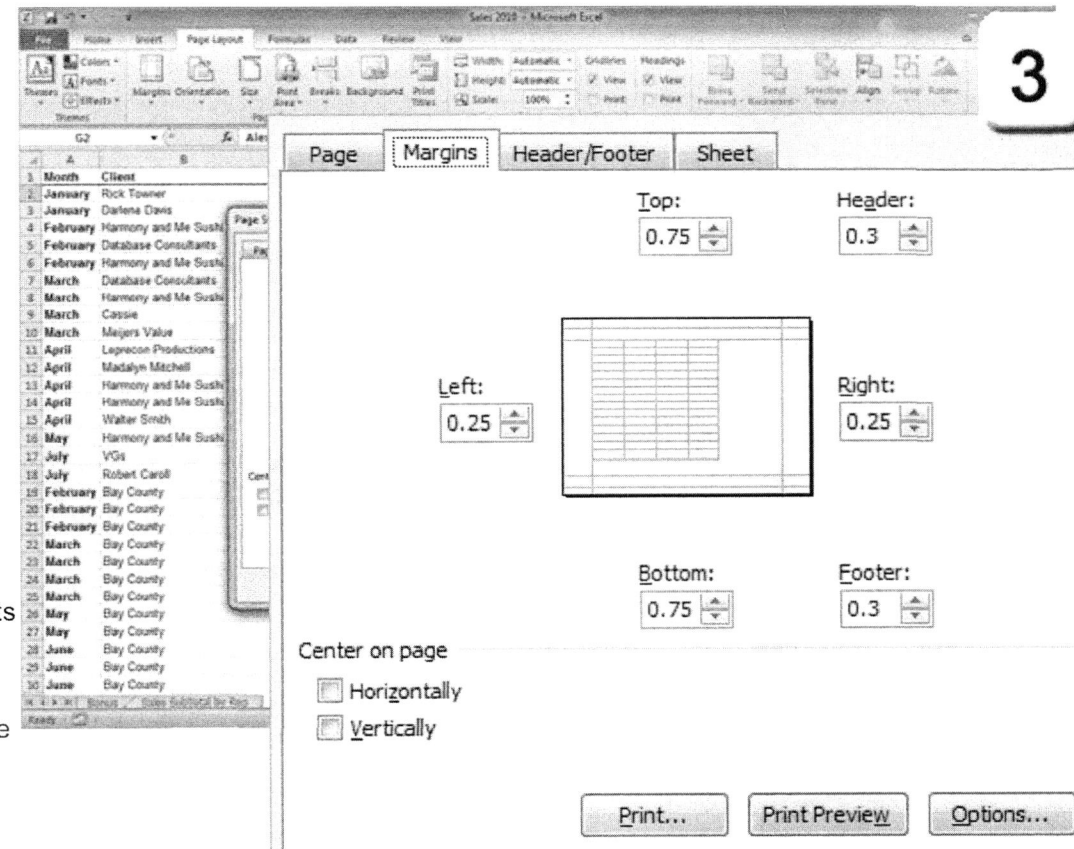

Exam 77-882: Microsoft Excel 2010 Core
3. Formatting Cells and Worksheets
3.5. Manipulate Page Setup options for worksheets: Margins

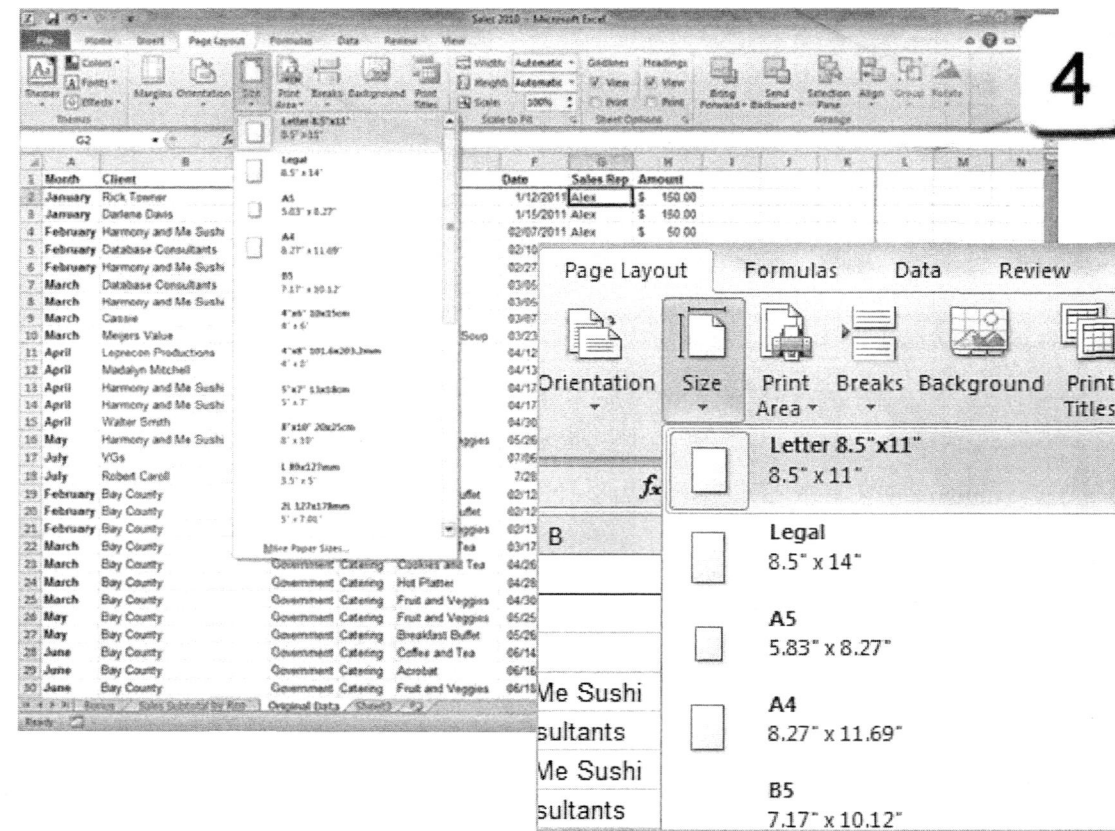

Page Layout -> Page Setup ->Size

Page Setup: Size

What size is this spreadsheet? By default, a spreadsheet is Letter: **8.5" x 11"**.

4. Try This: Review the Page Size
Go to **Page Layout -> Page Setup**.
Go to **Size**.
What Do You See? The **Sizes** also include **Legal, 8.5" x 14"** which may be helpful if you need to print a very wide spreadsheet with many months.

What Else Do You See? Letter and Legal are standard American page dimensions. A5, A4, B5 etc were designed with Metric page dimensions. The numbers are simple in the Metric system, but they look funny displayed as American dimensions, huh?

Keep going...

Exam 77-882: Microsoft Excel 2010 Core
3. Formatting Cells and Worksheets
3.5. Manipulate Page Setup options for worksheets: Size

Page Setup: Breaks

There are two ways to change the **Page Breaks.** Here are the options on the **Page Layout** Ribbon.

5. Try This: Add a Break
Select Row 19 in the sample spreadsheet.
Go to **Page Layout -> Page Setup.**
Click on **Breaks**.

What Do You See? The Break will be inserted above the row that you selected. The Break looks like a dashed line.

What Else Do You See? You can use the same menu to **Remove Page Breaks** or **Reset All Page Breaks**.

Keep going, there are more Page Setup options to consider...

Page Layout -> Page Setup ->Breaks

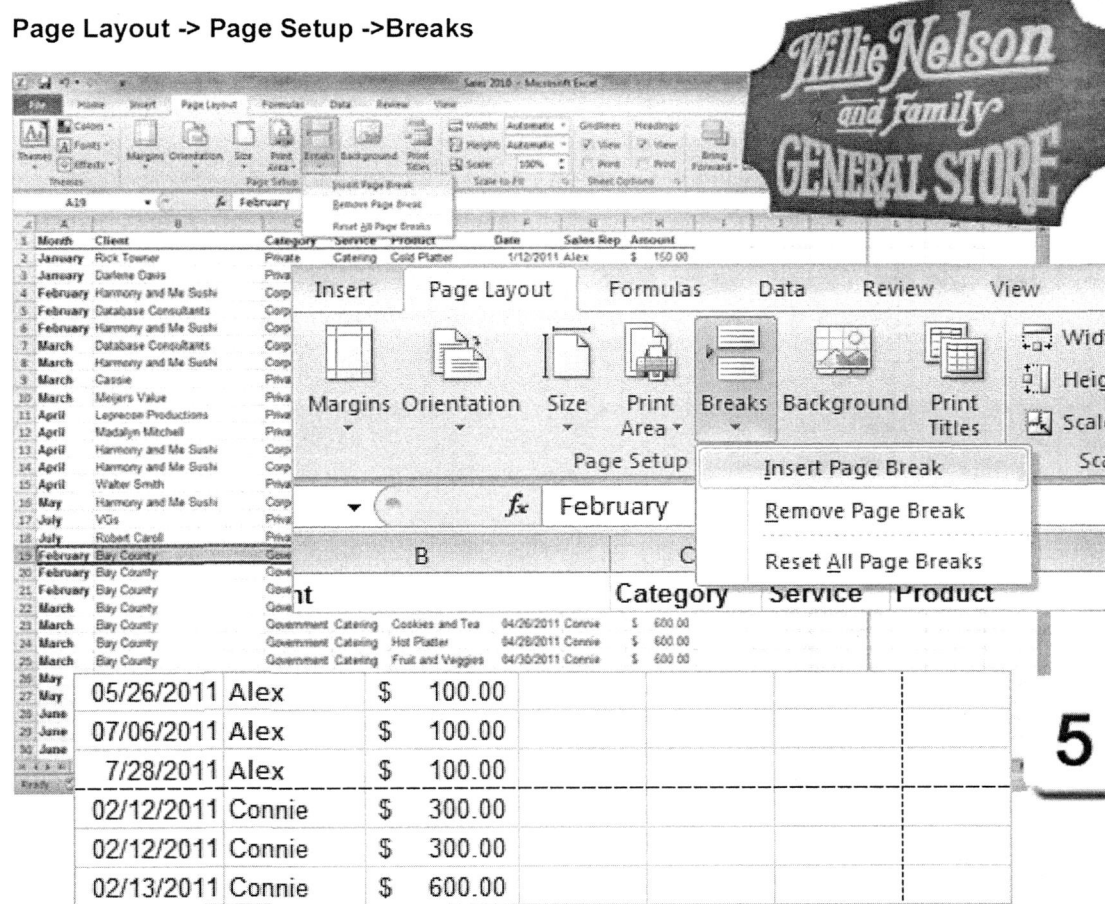

Exam 77-882: Microsoft Excel 2010 Core
3. Formatting Cells and Worksheets
3.5. Manipulate Page Setup options for worksheets: Breaks

Another Way to Edit the Breaks
The **View Ribbon** also has a Page Break preview. Let's compare the options.

Try This, Too: Page Break Preview
Go to **View -> Workbook Views**.
Click on **Page Break Preview.**

What Do You See? The Page Breaks are shown as thick, blue lines. Each page is identified by a watermark.

Did You Know...? You can reposition the **Page Breaks** by dragging the blue lines to a different Column or Row.

Please go to **View -> Workbook Views.**
Click on **Normal** to return to the default view for Microsoft Excel.

Keep going...

View -> Workbook Views ->Page Break Preview

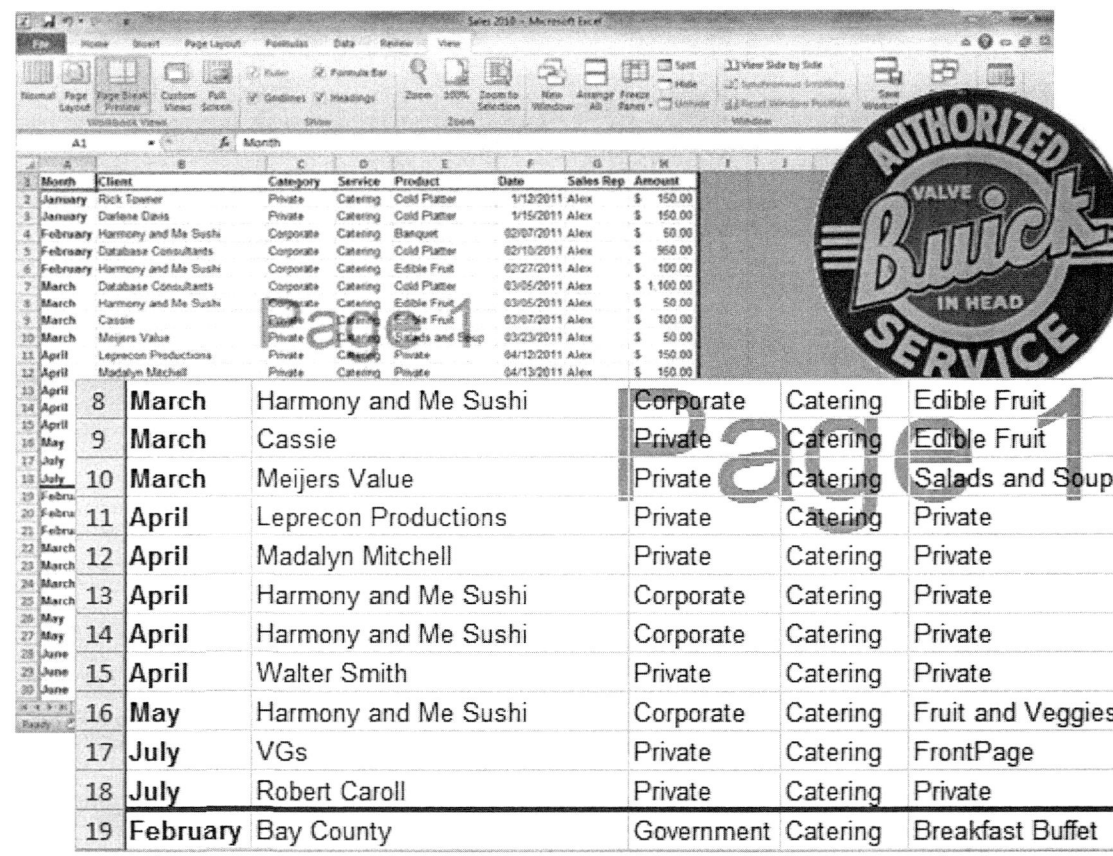

Exam 77-882: Microsoft Excel 2010 Core
4. Managing Worksheets and Workbooks
4.2. Manipulate window views

Take
One

Page Setup: Background

You can add color and watermarks to the spreadsheet background. This is one more way to add your company name and images to a price sheet.

6. Try it: Format Worksheet Background
Go to **Page Layout-> Background**.

Background

Browse to a folder with your pictures and double click to select one.

What Do You See? Your picture may Tile, or repeat, in the background of your spreadsheet.

Can you read the data? Background images may be stunning, but the purpose of the spreadsheet is the present the data.

Please **Remove Background** and continue.

Page Layout -> Page Setup ->Background

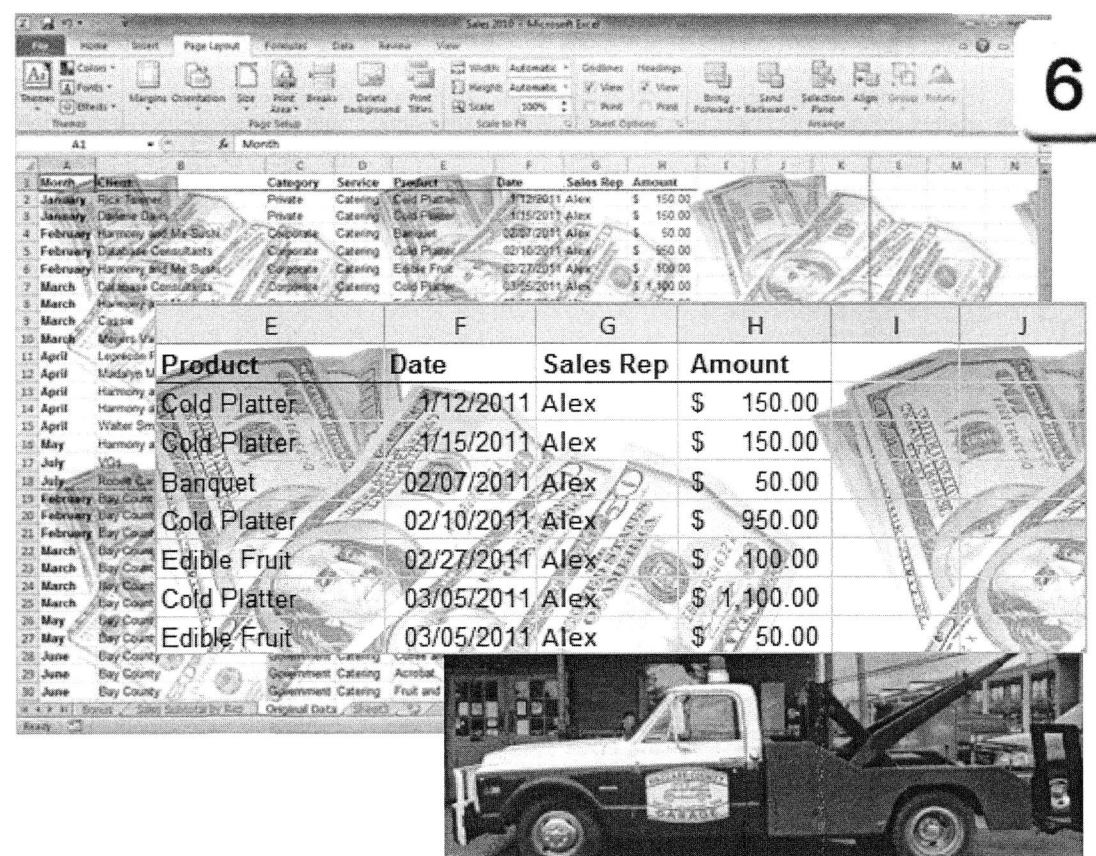

E	F	G	H	I	J
Product	**Date**	**Sales Rep**	**Amount**		
Cold Platter	1/12/2011	Alex	$ 150.00		
Cold Platter	1/15/2011	Alex	$ 150.00		
Banquet	02/07/2011	Alex	$ 50.00		
Cold Platter	02/10/2011	Alex	$ 950.00		
Edible Fruit	02/27/2011	Alex	$ 100.00		
Cold Platter	03/05/2011	Alex	$ 1,100.00		
Edible Fruit	03/05/2011	Alex	$ 50.00		

Exam 77-882: Microsoft Excel 2010 Core
3. Formatting Cells and Worksheets
3.5. Manipulate Page Setup options for worksheets: Background

Page Setup: Print Titles

You can select which **Titles** you wish to print on your spreadsheet.

7. Try This: Print Titles
Go to **Page Layout -> Page Setup**.
Click on **Print Titles**.

What Do You See? The Page Setup window will open. You will be prompted to select which Row you would like to repeat at the top of each page in your print out.

What Else Do You See? You can select if you would like to **Print** the following:
Gridline
Black and White
Draft quality
Row and column headings.

Try This, Too: Select the Rows to Repeat
Go to **Rows to repeat at top**.
Select Row 1.
Excel will enter $1:$1 in the blank.

Keep going...

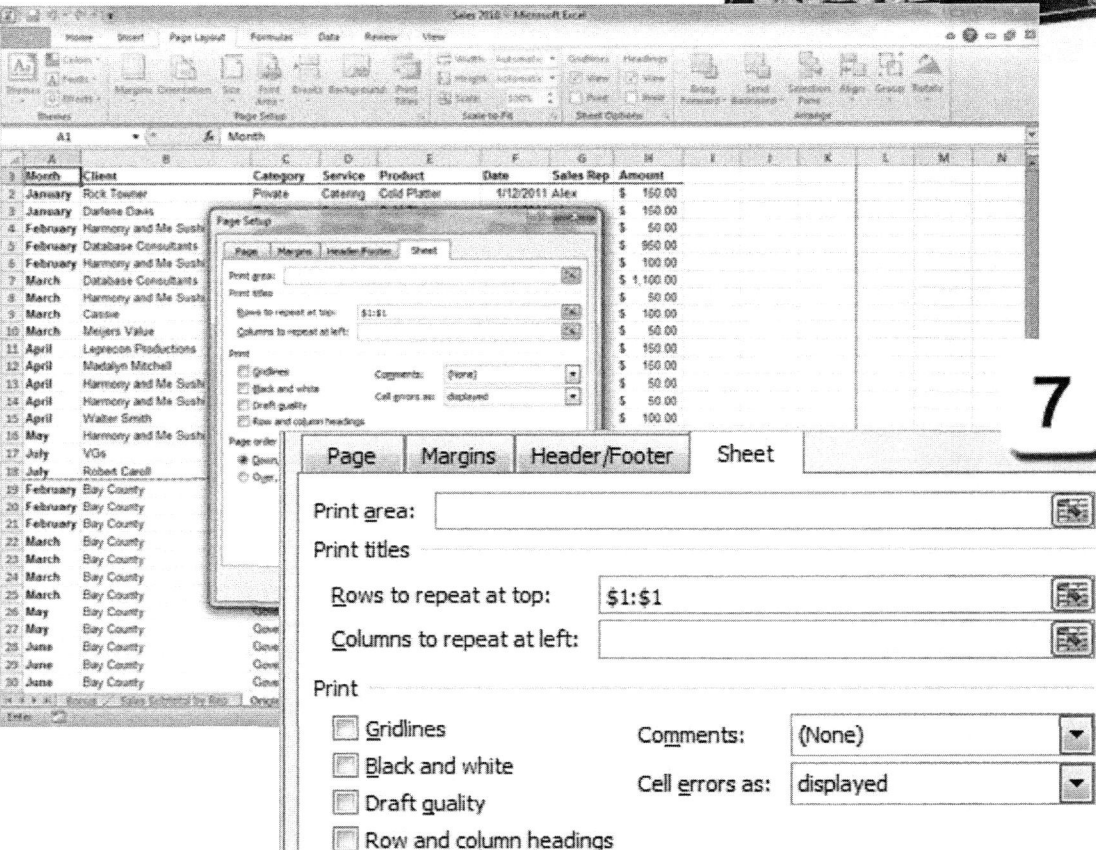

Exam 77-882: Microsoft Excel 2010 Core
3. Formatting Cells and Worksheets
3.5. Manipulate Page Setup options for worksheets: Print Titles

Print Preview

So, what does it look like when Excel repeats the titles at the top of each page? You can use **Print Preview** to proof your work.

Try This, Too: Print Preview
Go to **File->Print**.

What Do You See? The new **Backstage** view has a very detailed **Print Preview**. On the left you can choose which printer and edit the printer **Settings**.

On the right side of the Backstage view is the **Print Preview**. You can use the navigation buttons at the bottom to turn the pages and see if the **Titles** are repeated.

So far, so good. Click on the **Page Layout** Ribbon and keep going, please...

File-> Print

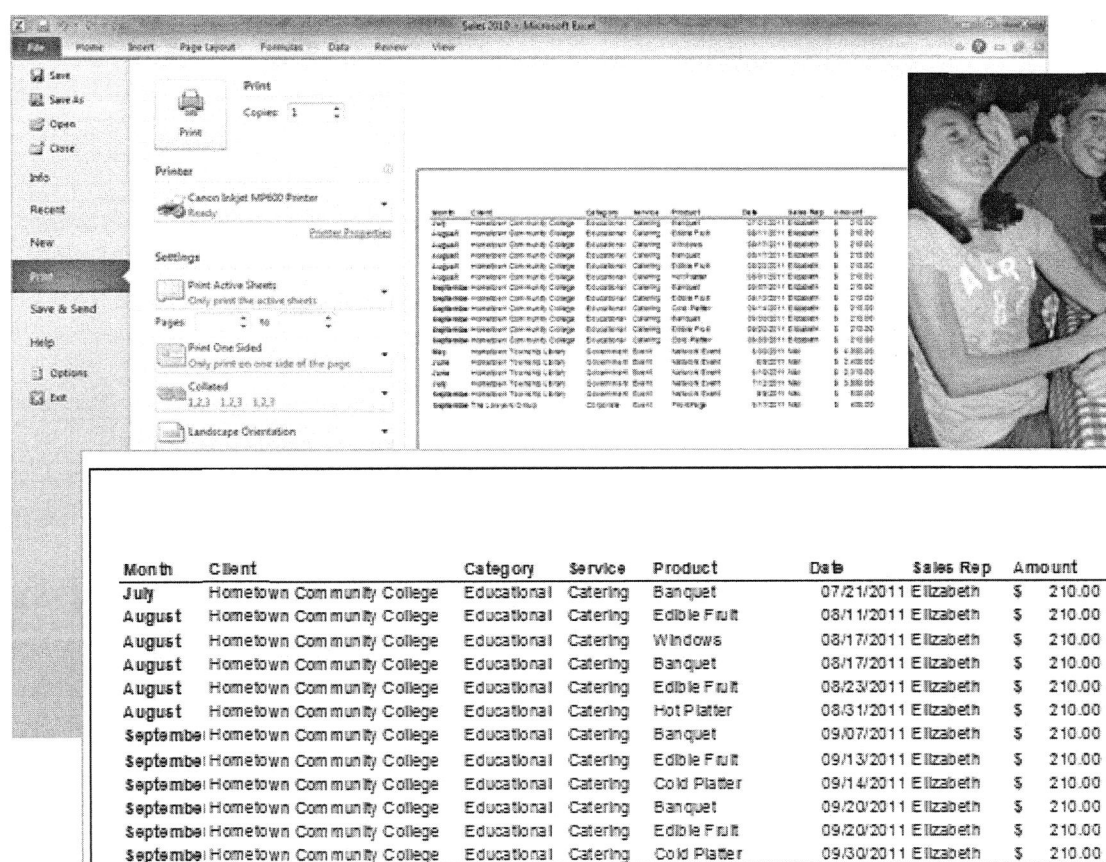

Month	Client	Category	Service	Product	Date	Sales Rep	Amount
July	Hometown Community College	Educational	Catering	Banquet	07/21/2011	Elizabeth	$ 210.00
August	Hometown Community College	Educational	Catering	Edible Fruit	08/11/2011	Elizabeth	$ 210.00
August	Hometown Community College	Educational	Catering	Windows	08/17/2011	Elizabeth	$ 210.00
August	Hometown Community College	Educational	Catering	Banquet	08/17/2011	Elizabeth	$ 210.00
August	Hometown Community College	Educational	Catering	Edible Fruit	08/23/2011	Elizabeth	$ 210.00
August	Hometown Community College	Educational	Catering	Hot Platter	08/31/2011	Elizabeth	$ 210.00
September	Hometown Community College	Educational	Catering	Banquet	09/07/2011	Elizabeth	$ 210.00
September	Hometown Community College	Educational	Catering	Edible Fruit	09/13/2011	Elizabeth	$ 210.00
September	Hometown Community College	Educational	Catering	Cold Platter	09/14/2011	Elizabeth	$ 210.00
September	Hometown Community College	Educational	Catering	Banquet	09/20/2011	Elizabeth	$ 210.00
September	Hometown Community College	Educational	Catering	Edible Fruit	09/20/2011	Elizabeth	$ 210.00
September	Hometown Community College	Educational	Catering	Cold Platter	09/30/2011	Elizabeth	$ 210.00

Exam 77-882: Microsoft Excel 2010 Core
3. Formatting Cells and Worksheets
3.5. Manipulate Page Setup options for worksheets: Print Preview

HOME

Take One

Page Setup: More

1. Try This: Find More Page Setup Options
There are more options in the Page Setup Group. These options can be found by clicking on the **Option arrow** in the lower right corner.

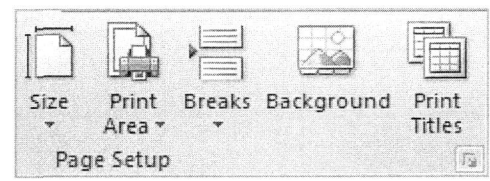

What Do You See? This window summarizes the Page Setup options on four tab: Page, Margins, Header/Footer, and Sheet tabs.

Keep going...

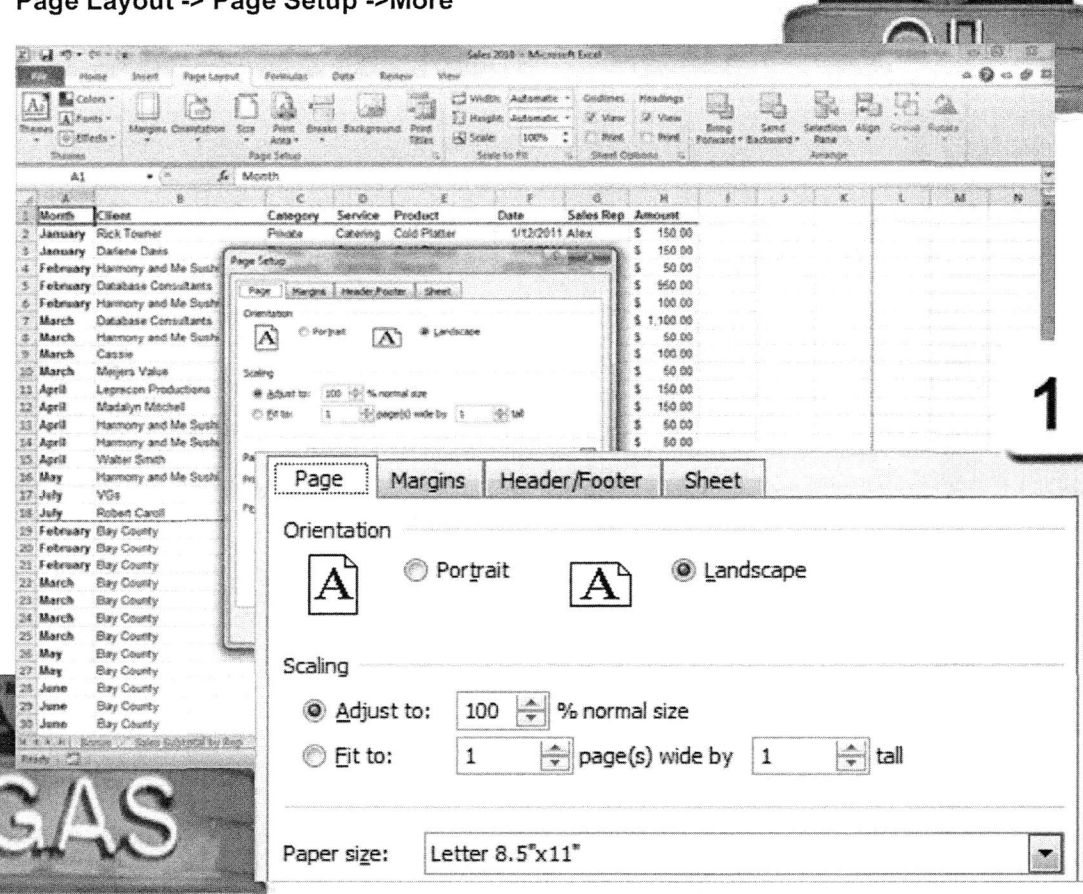

GAS

Exam 77-882: Microsoft Excel 2010 Core
3. Formatting Cells and Worksheets
3.5. Manipulate Page Setup options for worksheets: Page

Take One

Page Setup: Headers and Footers

Headers and Footers are placed at the top and bottom of a page. The Header and Footer can include the name of your company as well as the number or address for contacting you: the call to action.

2. Try This: Review the Headers and Footers
Go to **Page Layout -> Page Setup ->More**.
Click on the **Header/Footer** tab.
Select a **Header**.

What Do You See? Microsoft Excel has several Header and Footer templates. The templates can include the name of the spreadsheet, the date as well as the page number.

Keep going...

Page Layout -> Page Setup ->More->Header/Footer

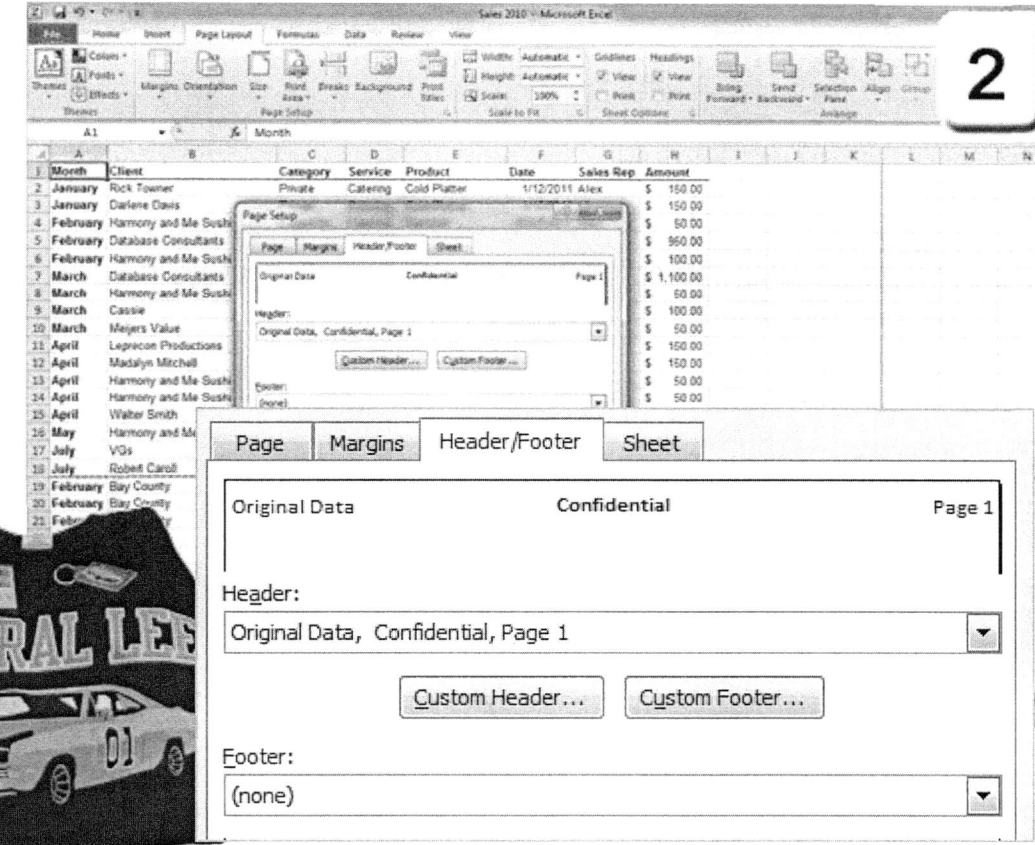

Exam 77-882: Microsoft Excel 2010 Core
3. Formatting Cells and Worksheets
3.5. Manipulate Page Setup options for worksheets: Header/Footer

Page Layout -> Page Setup ->More->Header/Footer->Custom Footer

Page Setup: Custom Footer

3. Try This: Create a Custom Footer
Go to **Page Layout -> Page Setup ->More.**
Click on the **Header/Footer** tab.
Select **Custom Footer.**

Type the following:
Left Section: Charlotte's Website
Center Section: Questions? Call 810.555.1212
Right Section click on the Date button.

What Do You See? When you click on the
Date button, Excel will insert **&[Date].** This is
code that updates the date to the current date
when the spreadsheet is opened.

Click **OK**. You will return to the Page Setup
window. Please keep going...

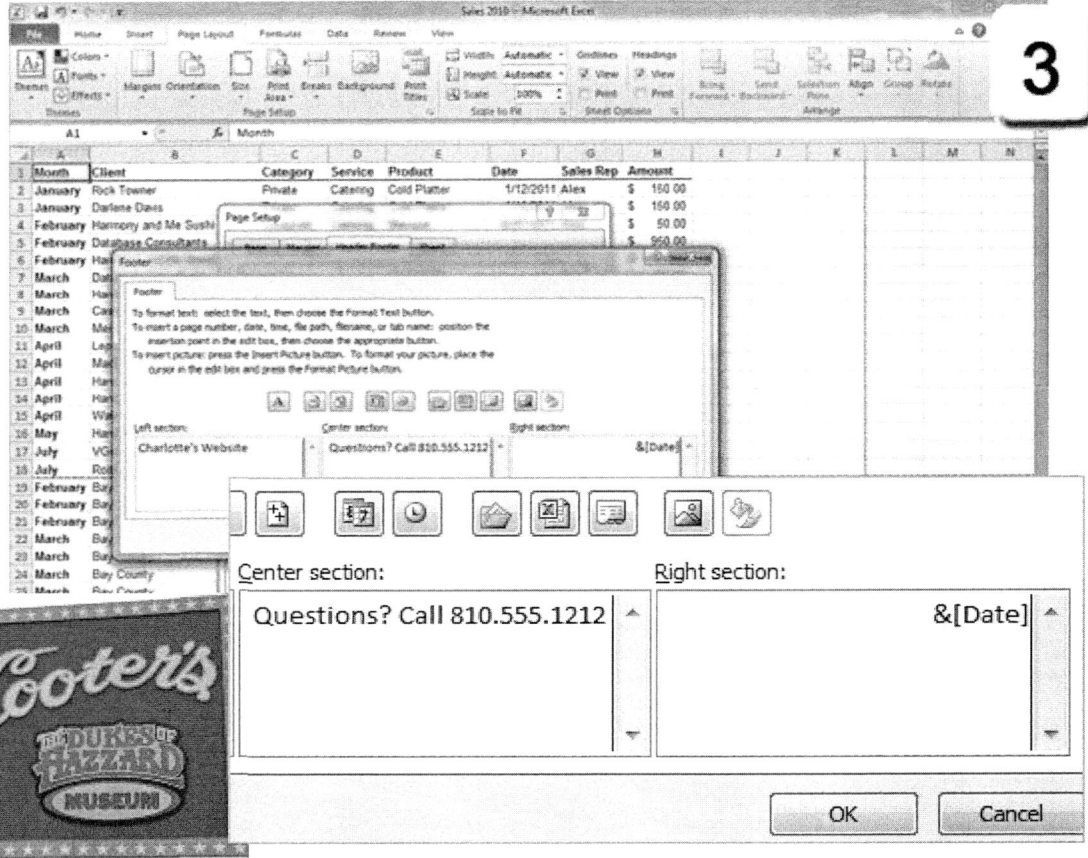

Exam 77-882: Microsoft Excel 2010 Core
3. Formatting Cells and Worksheets
3.5. Manipulate Page Setup options for worksheets: Header/Footer

Page Setup: Header/Footer

4. What Do You See? Look at the bottom for:
Different odd and even pages: in a book the even pages are on the right side. They usually have the name of the Chapter. The odd pages are on the left side. The odd headers show the name of the lesson.

Different first page: The first page is like a report cover. The Header and Footer may be blank or there may be a disclaimer.

Scale with document: The Header and Footer can resize (scale) if you print the spreadsheet at, say, 90%.

Align with page margins: By default, the Header and Footer align with the page margins.

Click **OK** to close the Page Setup window. Keep going..!

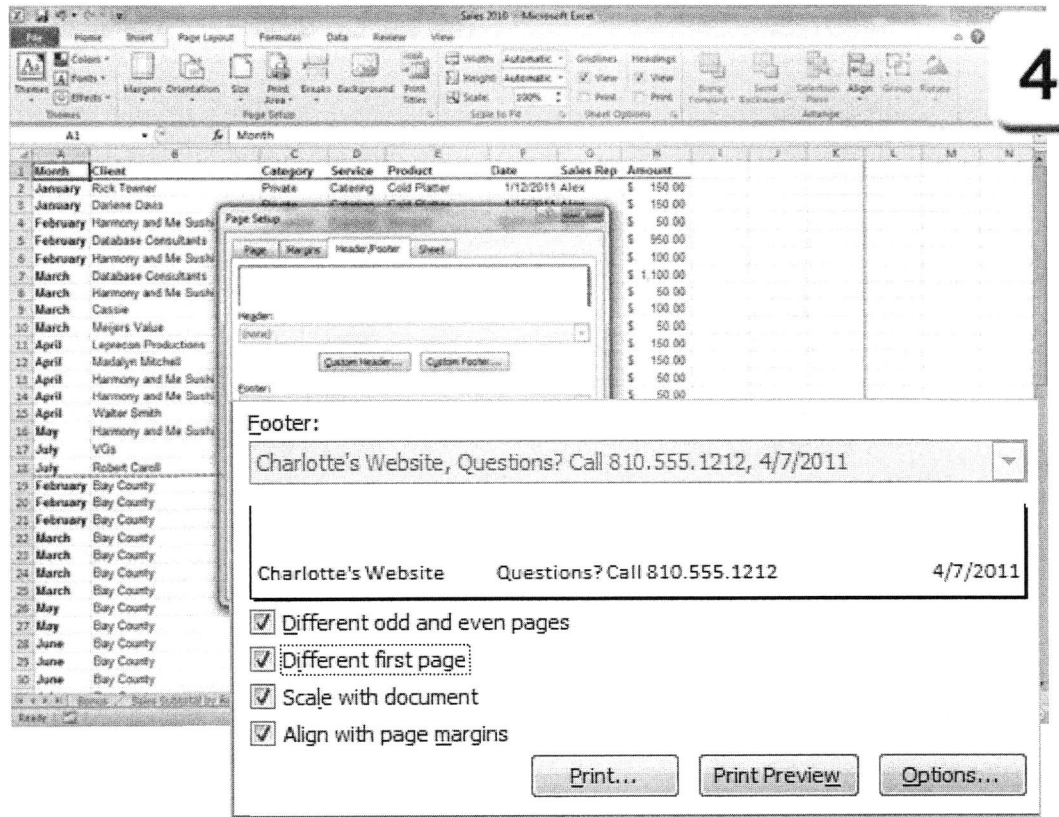

Exam 77-882: Microsoft Excel 2010 Core
3. Formatting Cells and Worksheets
3.3. Create row and column titles: Different titles on odd or even pages

Header & Footer Tools

Before You Begin: Change the View
Go to **View->Page Layout**.

Find the Header/Footer Ribbon
Click on the Header. The **Header & Footer** Ribbon should be available.

What Do You See? Look at the top of the first page in the document. There should be a tag in the left corner that says **First Page Header**.

5. Try This, Too: Edit the Header
Click on the First Page Header.
Type: Charlotte's Website
Keep going...

View -> Page Layout

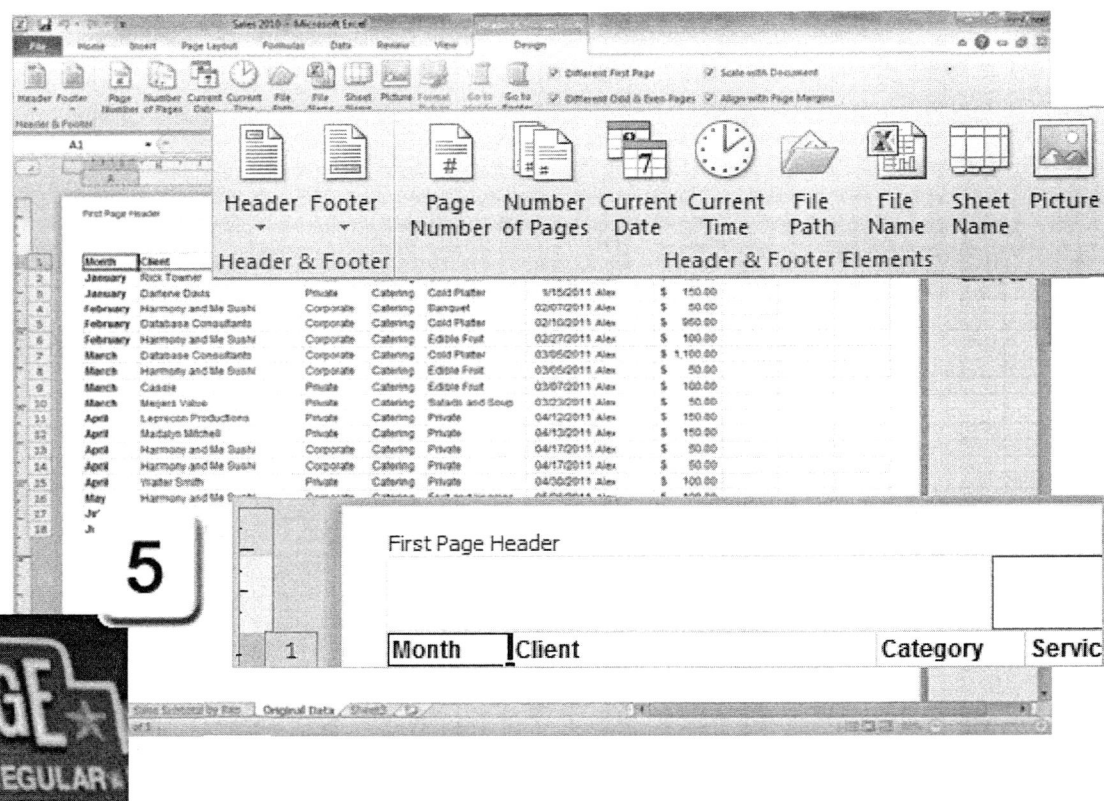

Exam 77-882: Microsoft Excel 2010 Core
3. Formatting Cells and Worksheets
3.3. Create row and column titles: Different titles on odd or even pages

HOME

Take One

Header & Footer Elements

Before You Begin: Scroll down to Page 2 in this spreadsheet. Click on the Header. The **Header & Footer** Ribbon should be visible.

What Do You See? There should be a tag that says Even Page Header.

6. Try This: Edit the Even Page Header
Even Page Header: First Quarter Sales
Click **ENTER** on the keyboard to create a new line of type.
Go to **Header & Footer -> Design.**
Go to **Header & Footer Elements.**
Click on **Current Date.**

Keep going...

Header & Footer -> Design ->Header & Footer Elements

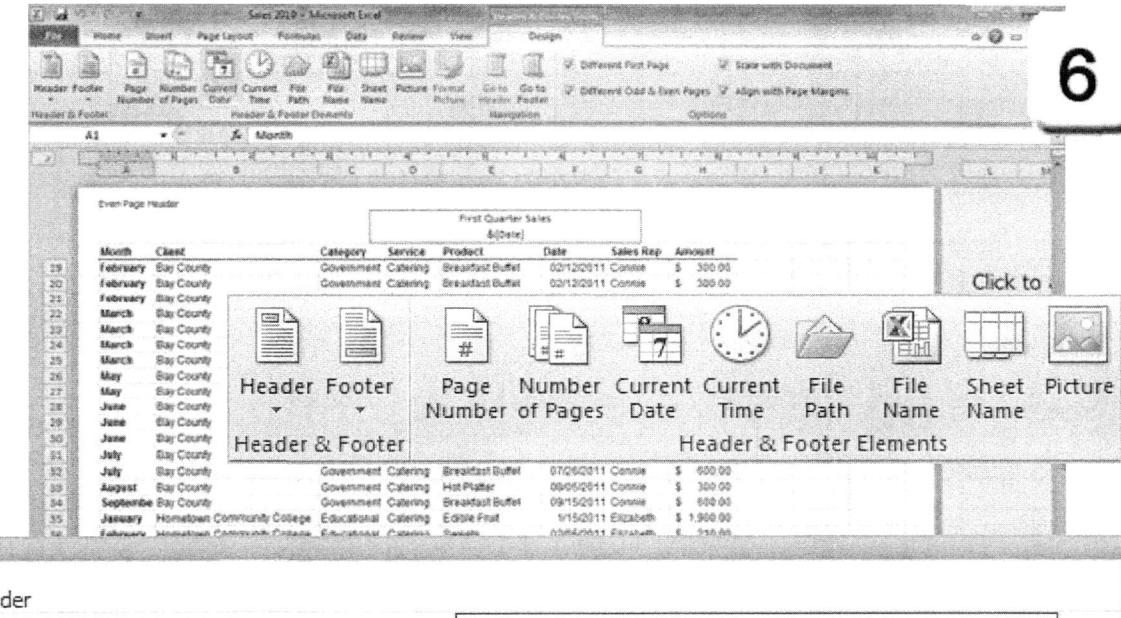

Even Page Header

| | | First Quarter Sales |
| | | &[Date] |

Month	Client	Category	Service	Product	Date	Sales Rep
February	Bay County	Government	Catering	Breakfast Buffet	02/12/2011	Connie
February	Bay County	Government	Catering	Breakfast Buffet	02/12/2011	Connie
February	Bay County	Government	Catering	Fruit and Veggies	02/13/2011	Connie
March	Bay County	Government	Catering	Coffee and Tea	03/17/2011	Connie

Exam 77-882: Microsoft Excel 2010 Core
3. Formatting Cells and Worksheets
3.3. Create row and column titles: Different titles on odd or even pages

First, Odd, and Even Headers.

What Do You See?
When you scroll up and down through the sheets in **Page Layout View** you should see the three Headers that we created in this spreadsheet.

Very good.
Go to **View->Normal** and keep going,

View-> Page Layout

First Page Header

| | | | | | Charlotte's Website | | |

Month	Client			Category	Service	Product		Date	Sales Rep

Even Page Header

| | | | | First Quarter Sales &[Date] | | |

Month	Client		Category	Service	Product	Date	Sales Rep
February	Bay County		Government	Catering	Breakfast Buffet	02/12/2011	Connie
February	Bay County		Government	Catering	Breakfast Buffet	02/12/2011	Connie
February	Bay County		Government	Catering	Fruit and Veggies	02/13/2011	Connie
March	Bay County		Government	Catering	Coffee and Tea	03/17/2011	Connie

Odd Page Header

| | | | | For More Information call: 810.555.1212 | | |

Month	Client	Category	Service	Product	Date	Sales Rep
July	Hometown Community College	Educational	Catering	Banquet	07/21/2011	Elizabeth
August	Hometown Community College	Educational	Catering	Edible Fruit	08/11/2011	Elizabeth
August	Hometown Community College	Educational	Catering	Windows	08/17/2011	Elizabeth

Exam 77-882: Microsoft Excel 2010 Core
3. Formatting Cells and Worksheets
3.3. Create row and column titles: Different titles on odd or even pages

Page Layout: Sheet Options

When you look at a spreadsheet on a computer you see the Headings for the Rows and Columns. You also see the gridlines. You can print your spreadsheet the same way.

1. Try This: Edit the Sheet Options
Go to **Page Layout->Sheet Options**.

What Do You See? There are check marks to print the Gridlines as well as the Headings.

2. Try This, Too: More Sheet Options
When you click on the **Option** arrow in the bottom right corner of the Sheet Options group you will return to the **Sheet** tab in the Page Setup Summary.

OK. Sheet options...almost done with the Page Layout options.

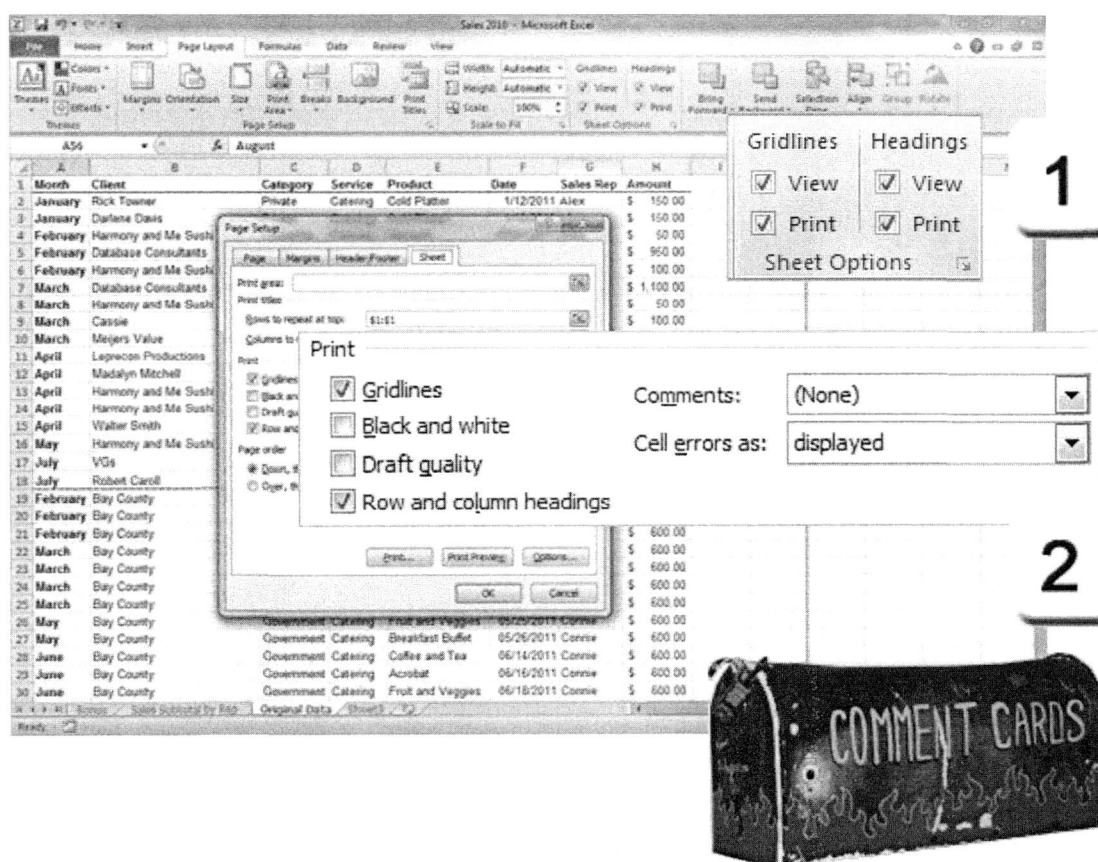

Exam 77-882: Microsoft Excel 2010 Core
3. Formatting Cells and Worksheets
3.3. Create row and column titles: Print Row and column Headings

Page Layout: Scale to Fit

You can print the spreadsheet smaller if you wish. You can force the printout to fit 1-9 pages wide or tall. You can also scale the printout by percentage.

1. Try This: Scale to Fit Options
Go to **Page Layout->Scale to Fit**

What Do You See? There are combo boxes for the Width and the Height. You can choose a percent for Scale or type your own.

2. Try This, Too: More Page Options
When you click on the **Option** arrow in the bottom right corner of the Scale to Fit group you will return to the **Page** tab in the Page Setup Summary.

Memo to Self: About half of the population (including your boss) wears bifocals and cannot see a spreadsheet that prints very small to make it all fit on one sheet.

Who is your audience! Can they read it?

Page Layout -> Scale to Fit

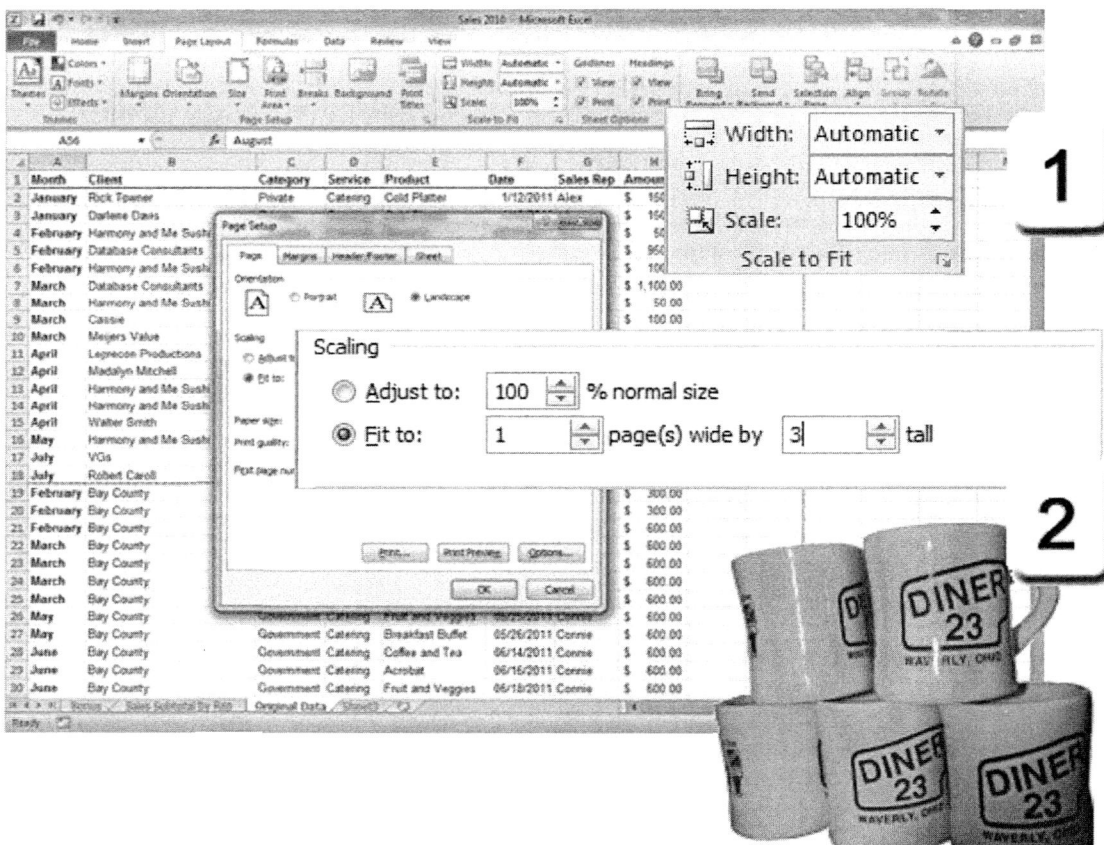

Exam 77-882: Microsoft Excel 2010 Core
1. Managing the Worksheet Environment
1.2. Print a worksheet or workbook

File -> Print

Print a Worksheet

The **Print** options are part of the new Microsoft Office **Backstage**. In the following pages we will look at printing a Worksheet, printing the entire Workbook or printing just the cells you selected. Let's start with the **Settings**.

1. Try This: Print a Worksheet
Go to **File->Print**.

What Do You See? The **Backstage** view should display the printer and the options.

Try This, Too: Review the Settings
By default, Excel prints the Active Sheet. You can print all of the pages in the Active Sheet or just one by typing the page number.

Keep going...

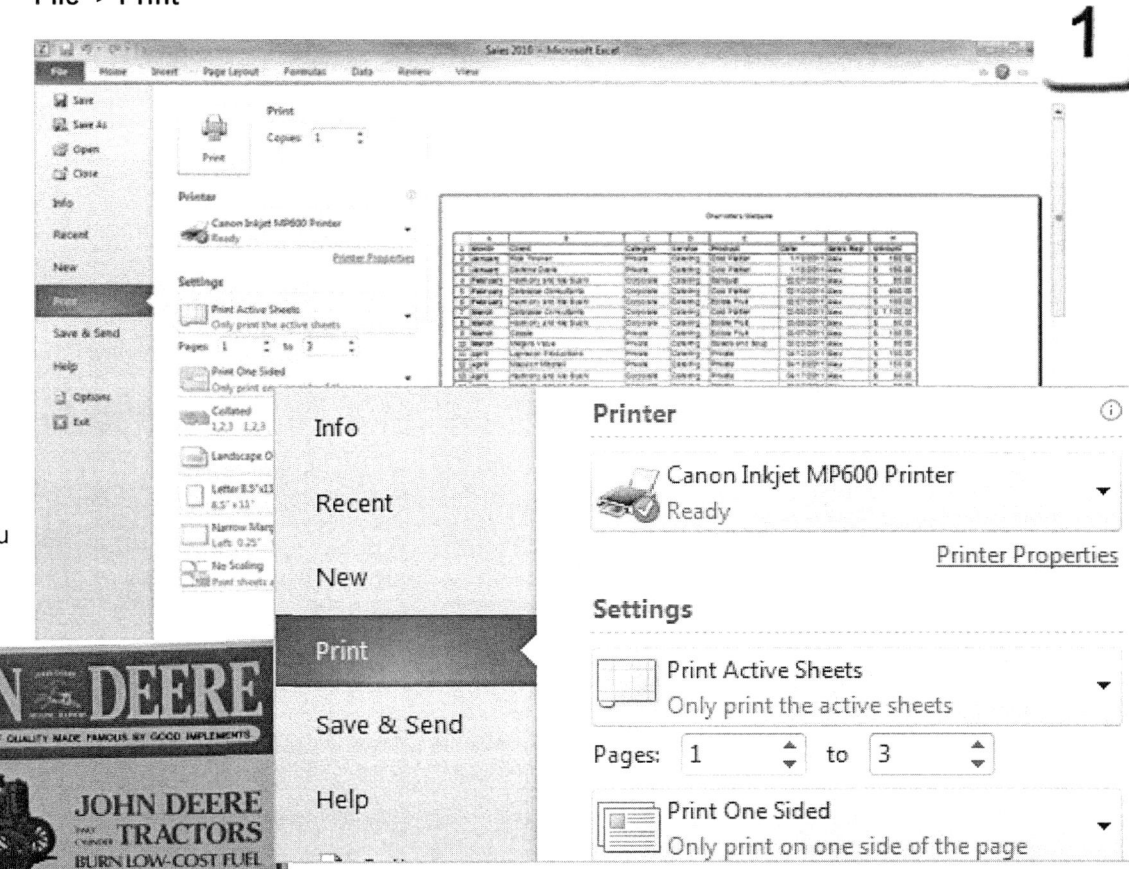

Exam 77-882: Microsoft Excel 2010 Core
1. Managing the Worksheet Environment
1.2. Print a worksheet or workbook: Selected sheets

Take One

More Print Settings
2. Try This: Print Entire Workbook
Go to **File->Print->Settings**.
Select **Print Entire Workbook**.

What Do You See? The **Print Preview** on the right side of the Backstage View will show all of the sheets in the workbook.

What Else Do You See? You can also **Print Selection**: print whatever you currently have highlighted.

File -> Print ->Settings

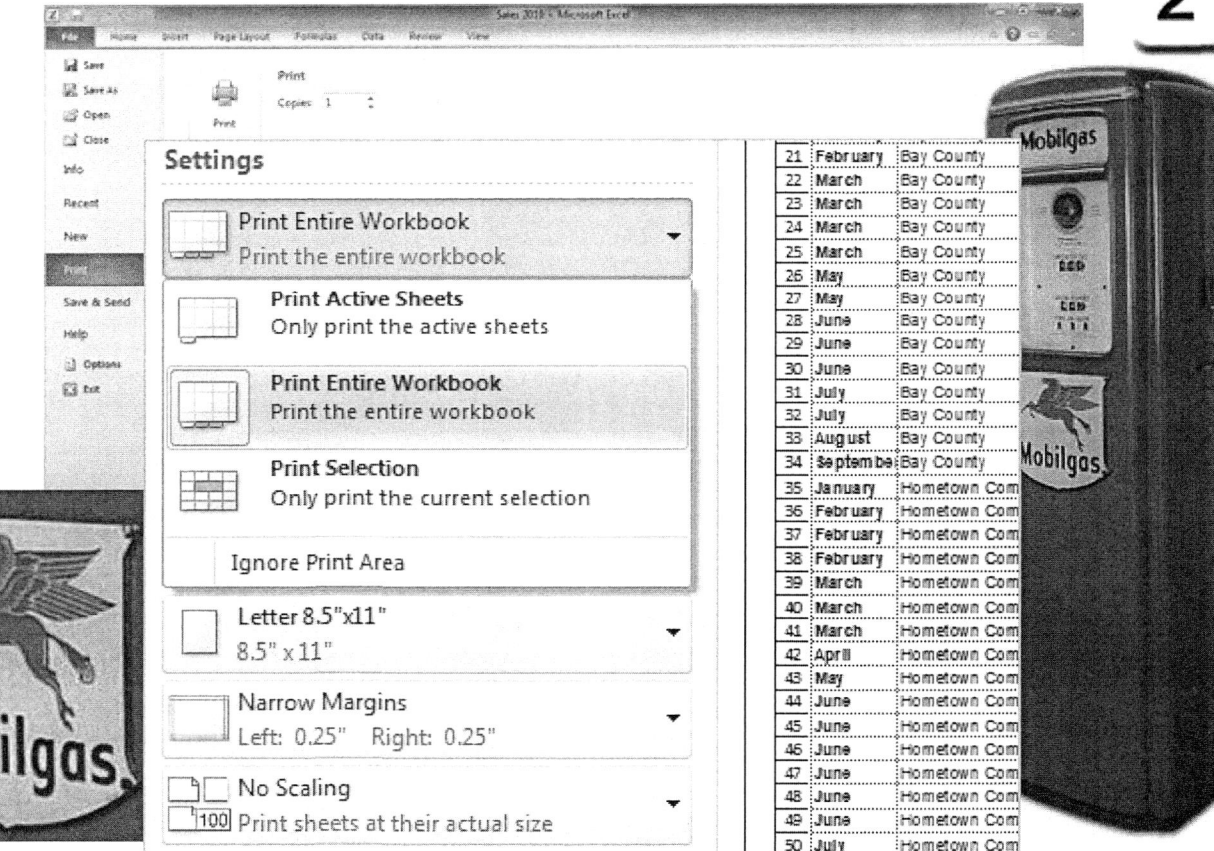

Exam 77-882: Microsoft Excel 2010 Core
1. Managing the Worksheet Environment
1.2. Print a worksheet or workbook: Entire Workbook or Selection

Summary

This lesson walked through the Page Layout Ribbon. We investigated the Page Setup, Scale to Print and Sheet Options. We used the Page Layout View to create and edit the Headers and Footers.

Finally, we reviewed the Print options in the new Microsoft Office Backstage view.

Very good. You get the cookie.

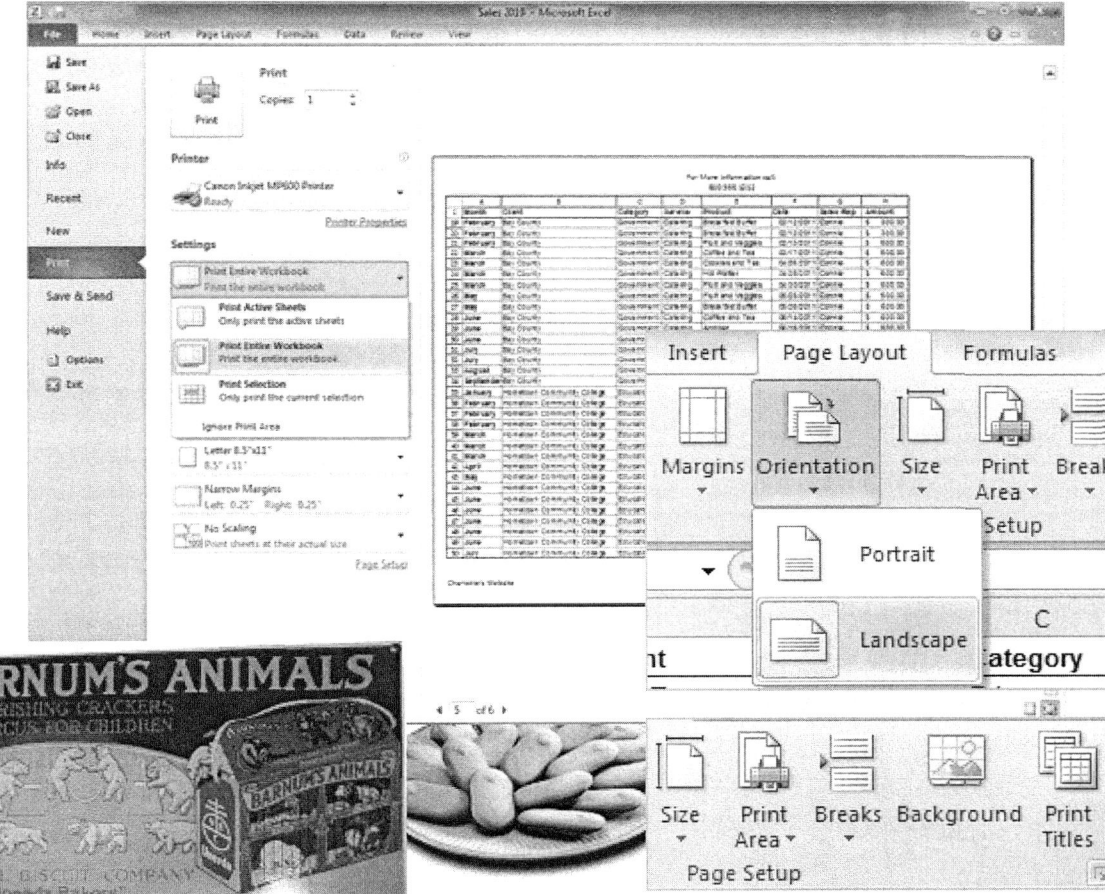

Test Yourself

1. Which Ribbon has the Workbook Views?
a. Page Layout
b. Home
c. Views
Tip: Intermediate Excel, page 147

2. Which of the following are Workbook View options?
(Select all correct answers)
a. Page Layout
b. Normal
c. Draft
d. Page Break Preview
e. Outline
Tip: Intermediate Excel, pages 148 & 154

3. What is the command for Portrait or Landscape?
a. Page Layout-> Page Setup->Orientation
b. Page View-> Page Setup->Orientations
c. Page Layout-> Change Orientation
Tip: Intermediate Excel, page 149

4. Which of the following is a Margin Option?
(Select all correct answers)
a. Narrow
b. Custom
c. Normal
d. Wide
Tip: Intermediate Excel, page 151

5. Which of the following is true about Headers? (Select all correct answers)
a. Command is Page Layout-> Page Setup-> More-> Header & Footer
b. Headers and Footers are visible in Page Layout view
c. In Page Layout View, Headers and Footers can be edited with the Header & Footer Ribbons
Tip: Intermediate Excel, page 159 &163

6. Which of the following is a printing option?
(Select all correct answers)
a. Entire workbook
b. Active Sheets
c. Print Selection
Tip: Intermediate Excel, page 168

Excel 2010: Online

Online and Open for Business

Intermediate Excel Objectives
In this lesson, you will learn how to:

1. Use the Sparkline Tools to display Line, Column and Win/Loss Sparklines

2. Format the Sparkline Line Style, Color and Markers

3. Format the Sparkline Axis

4. Use hyperlinks in a spreadsheet to link to other data in your workbook or online

	Month	Amount	
2	Click here to go to the original data shee		
3	Month	Amount	
4	January	$	2,200.00
5	February	$	2,930.00
6	March	$	4,720.00
7	April	$	710.00
8	May	$	5,510.00
9	June	$	7,770.00
10	July	$	5,490.00
11	August	$	1,350.00
12	September	$	2,860.00
13			
14	Question? Send me an email		
15			

Hyperlink

Links

Lesson 6: Online and Open for Business

1. Readings

Read Lesson 6 in your Intermediate Excel Guide, page 171-224.

Project

Format a spreadsheet so that it is as interesting and informative as a web page.

Downloads

Sales 2010.xlsx
Sales 2010 Complete.xlsx
1logo.jpg
Rainy Day Savings Training. xlsx

2. Practice

Complete the Practice Activity on page 225.

3. Assessment

Review the Test Yourself questions on page 226.

Sparkline Tools->Design

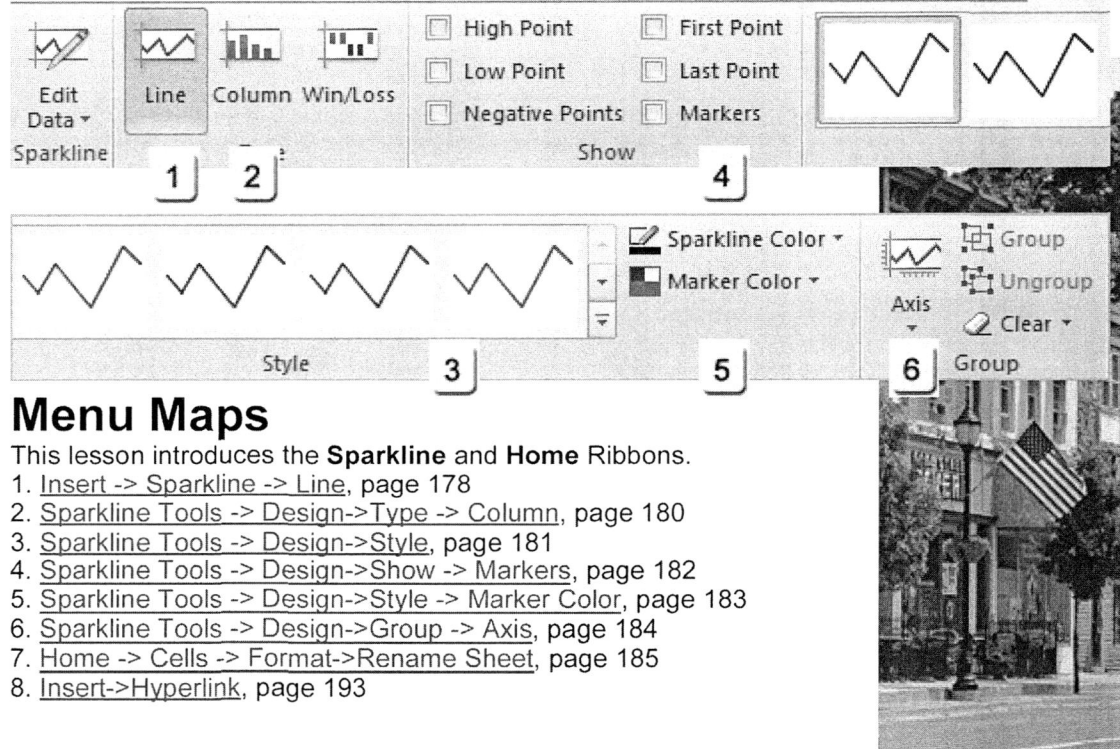

Menu Maps

This lesson introduces the **Sparkline** and **Home** Ribbons.
1. Insert -> Sparkline -> Line, page 178
2. Sparkline Tools -> Design->Type -> Column, page 180
3. Sparkline Tools -> Design->Style, page 181
4. Sparkline Tools -> Design->Show -> Markers, page 182
5. Sparkline Tools -> Design->Style -> Marker Color, page 183
6. Sparkline Tools -> Design->Group -> Axis, page 184
7. Home -> Cells -> Format->Rename Sheet, page 185
8. Insert->Hyperlink, page 193

Online and Open for Business

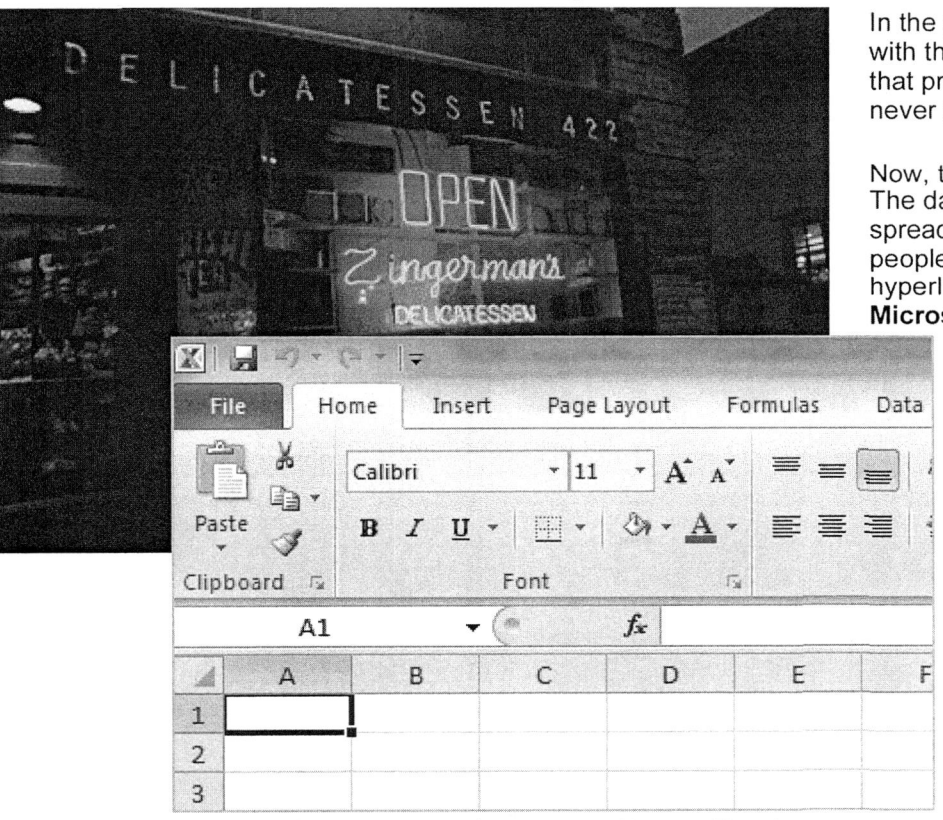

Start -> All Programs ->Microsoft Office -> Excel

In the previous lesson, the focus was on dressing up a spreadsheet with the Page Layout and Print Ribbons. We investigated the options that prepare a spreadsheet for print. However, most spreadsheets never get printed: they are simply opened, read and reviewed.

Now, think of a spreadsheet as a webpage: what would you see? The data can be presented visually with little **Sparklines**. A spreadsheet, like a webpage, can also use color and position to help people navigate through your workbook. And a spreadsheet can hyperlink to additional information or websites. Very good. **Start Microsoft Excel.**

What Do You See? Is there a Title Bar that says Book 1- Microsoft Excel? Yes.

Is there a **Home** Ribbon with the Clipboard, Font and Alignment Groups? Yes.

If your screen looks similar to the example on this page, then you are ready to get started.

Before You Begin

This discussion begins by creating a sample spreadsheet that analyzes 9 months of data-technically the first 3 quarters of sales.

1. Try This: Open a Sample Spreadsheet
Open a sample spreadsheet: Sales2010.xlsx
Go to the **Sales Subtotal by Month** sheet.

What Do You See? This sheet shows the product sales for Charlotte' Website. There are two Columns showing: Month and Amount. (The other Columns are hidden.) There is an Outline on the left side next to the names of the Months. Keep going...

Memo to Self: You do not have to MATCH the numbers shown on these pages. It is more important that you begin with some data and understand the options.

Another Memo: We will learn how to summarize data with Subtotals and PivotTable reports in the Advanced Guide to Excel 2010.

File->Open

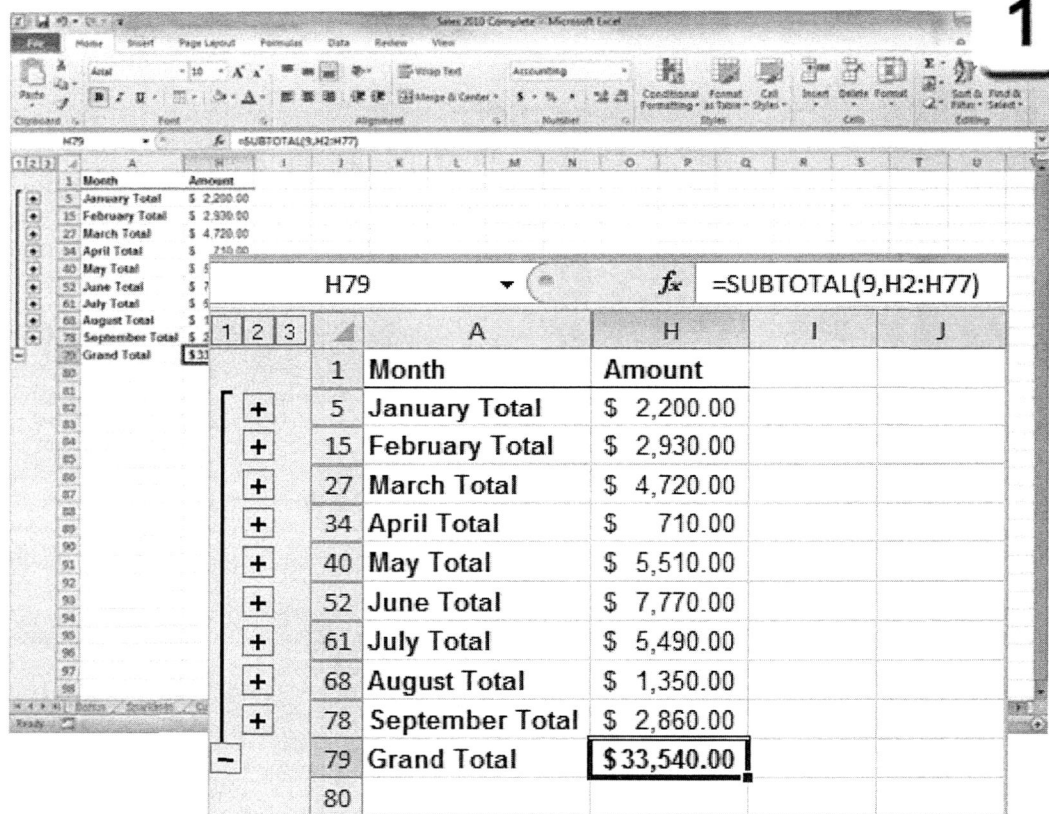

Create a New Spreadsheet

We will create a new Sparkline spreadsheet that will look up the data from the Sales Subtotal by Month spreadsheet.

2. Try it: Create a Sparkline Sheet

Go to a new blank spreadsheet.
Double-click the tab.
Rename the spreadsheet: Sparkline.

Add the following labels:

Select Cell A1 and type: Month.
Select Cell B1 and type: Total.
If these are labels (and they are) they need to be formatted BOLD.
Select Row 1. **Go to Home->Font->Bold**.

Select Cell A2 and type: January
Select Cell A3 and type: February
Select Cell A4 and type: March
Select Cell A5 and type: April
Select Cell A6 and type: May
Select Cell A7 and type: June
Select Cell A8 and type: July
Select Cell A9 and type: August
Select Cell A10 and type: September

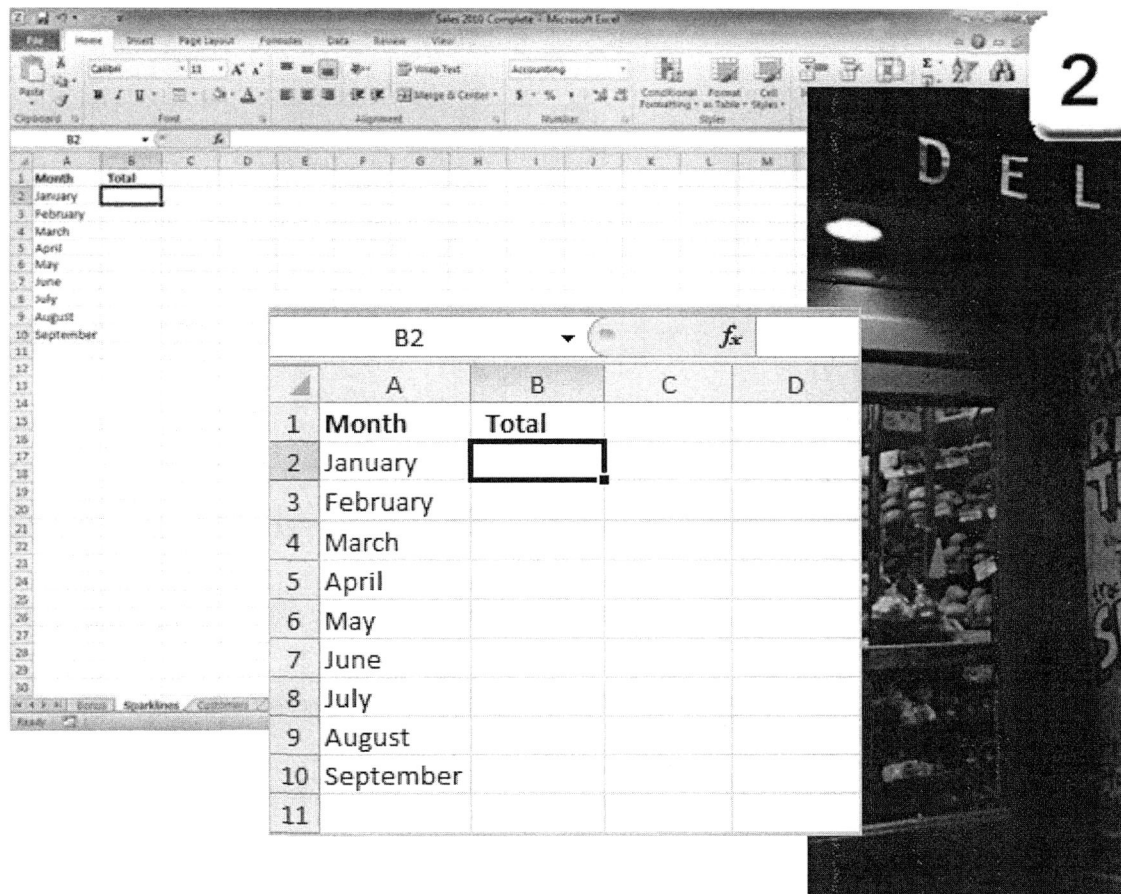

Exam 77-882: Microsoft Excel 2010 Core
2. Creating Cell Data
2.1. Construct cell data

Create the Formulas

The next steps use a formula to create a Relative Cell Reference that links data from the Sales Subtotal by Month spreadsheet that Subtotals each Month's sales.

3. Try it: Create the Formulas
Start on the **Sparkline** spreadsheet.
All equations begin with equals.

Select Cell B2 and type: =.
Go to the **Sales Subtotal by Month** sheet and click on the amount for January in Column H.

Select Cell B3 and type: =.
Go to **Sales Subtotal by Month** and click on the amount for February in Column H.

Please create formulas for the other months as well. Keep going...!

Memo to Self: *You can use the sample spreadsheet or just type the data that you see on this page if you wish.*

	A	B	C	D	E	F
1	Month	Amount				
2	January	$2,200.00				
3	February	$2,930.00				
4	March	$4,720.00				
5	April	$ 710.00				
6	May	$5,510.00				
7	June	$7,770.00				
8	July	$5,490.00				
9	August	$1,350.00				
10	September	$2,860.00				
11						

B2 = 'Sales Subtotal by Month'!H5

Exam 77-882: Microsoft Excel 2010 Core
5. Applying Formulas and Functions
5.3. Apply cell references in formulas: Use Absolute and Relative cell references

Still Before You Begin

There are a couple of formatting tasks that should be done. First, add two blank rows at the top of the spreadsheet. Next, select two cells and merge them.

4. Try This: Add Two Rows
Select Row 1.
Go to **Home->Cells->Insert**.
Click on **Insert->Insert Sheet Rows**.
There should be a new Row 1.
Repeat to add a second, blank Row.

Try This, Too: Merge Two Cells
Select Cells A2:B2.
Go to **Home -> Alignment**.
Click on **Merge and Center**.

What Do You See? When you click on Merge and Center, the two Cells that you selected will be combined into one Cell.

Do This Now: Save Your Work
Go to **File->Save As**.
Enter a new name: Sales 2010 Complete.

Home -> Alignment -> Merge and Center

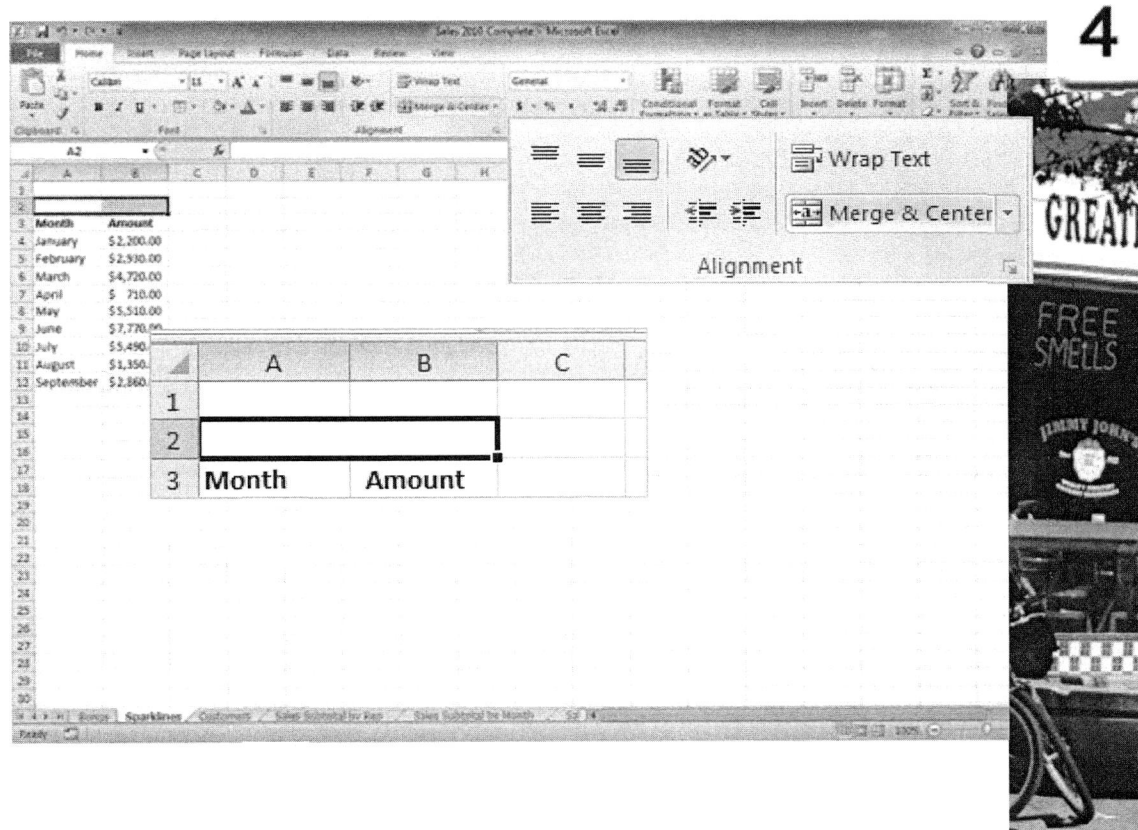

Exam 77-882: Microsoft Excel 2010 Core
3. Formatting Cells and Worksheets
3.2. Merge or split cells

Add Some Spark

Microsoft Excel 2010 has a new feature called Sparklines. A **Sparkline** is a little chart that helps people see the trends. It is another way of picturing the data.

1. Try This: Add a Sparkline

Select the new merged Cell.
Go to **Insert -> Sparkline**.
Click on **Line**.

You will be asked to select the Ranges:
Data Range: B4:B12
Location Range: $A$2.

Keep going...

What If It Doesn't Work? Look at the Location Range. You may have noticed that the Location Range was listed as $A$2:$B$2. You need to correct this or you may receive an error message about an invalid Range.

Insert -> Sparkline -> Line

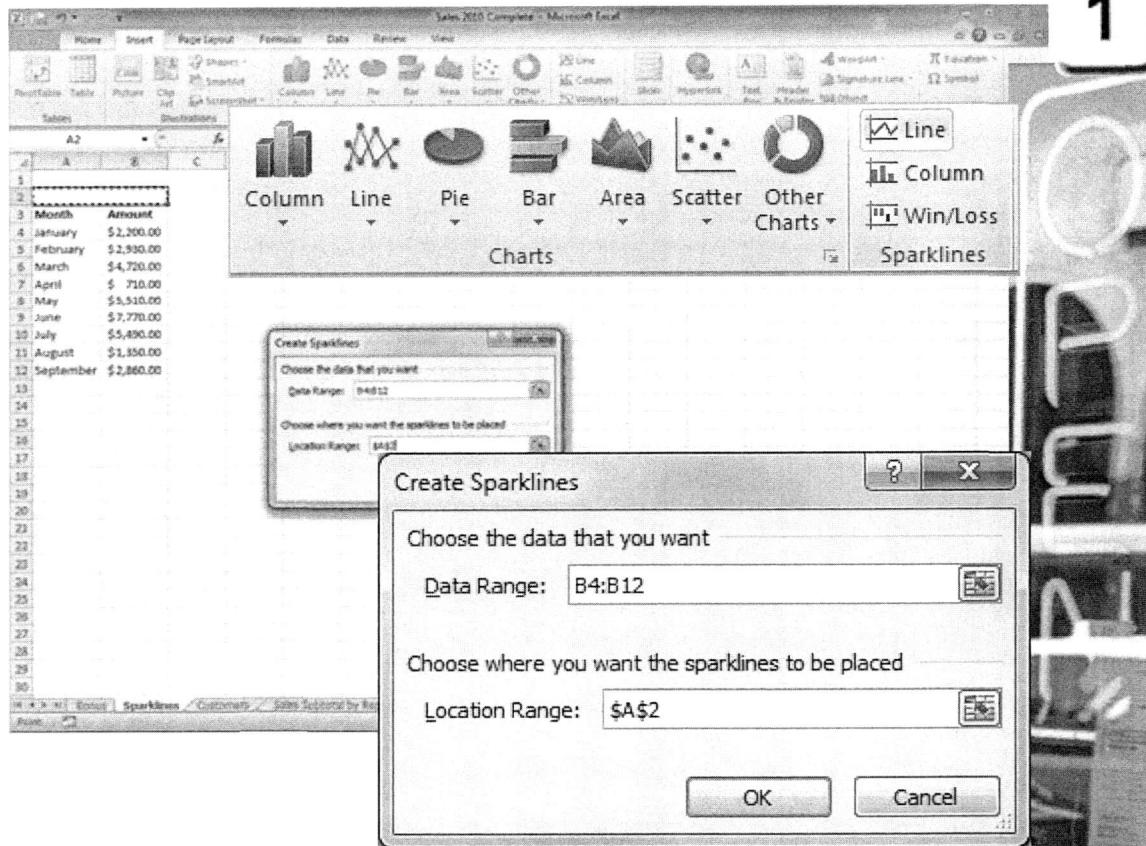

Exam 77-882: Microsoft Excel 2010 Core
6. Presenting Data Visually
6.4. Apply Sparklines

Hello, Sparkline!

2. What Do You See? There should be a new, tiny Sparkline chart. The **Sparkline** Tools should be available.

What Else Do You See? In the example on this page, Row 2 has been made taller and Column B is wider so that the Sparkline is earlier to see.

Keep going...

	Month	Amount
1		
2		
3	**Month**	**Amount**
4	January	$ 2,200.00
5	February	$ 2,930.00
6	March	$ 4,720.00
7	April	$ 710.00
8	May	$ 5,510.00
9	June	$ 7,770.00
10	July	$ 5,490.00
11	August	$ 1,350.00
12	September	$ 2,860.00
13		

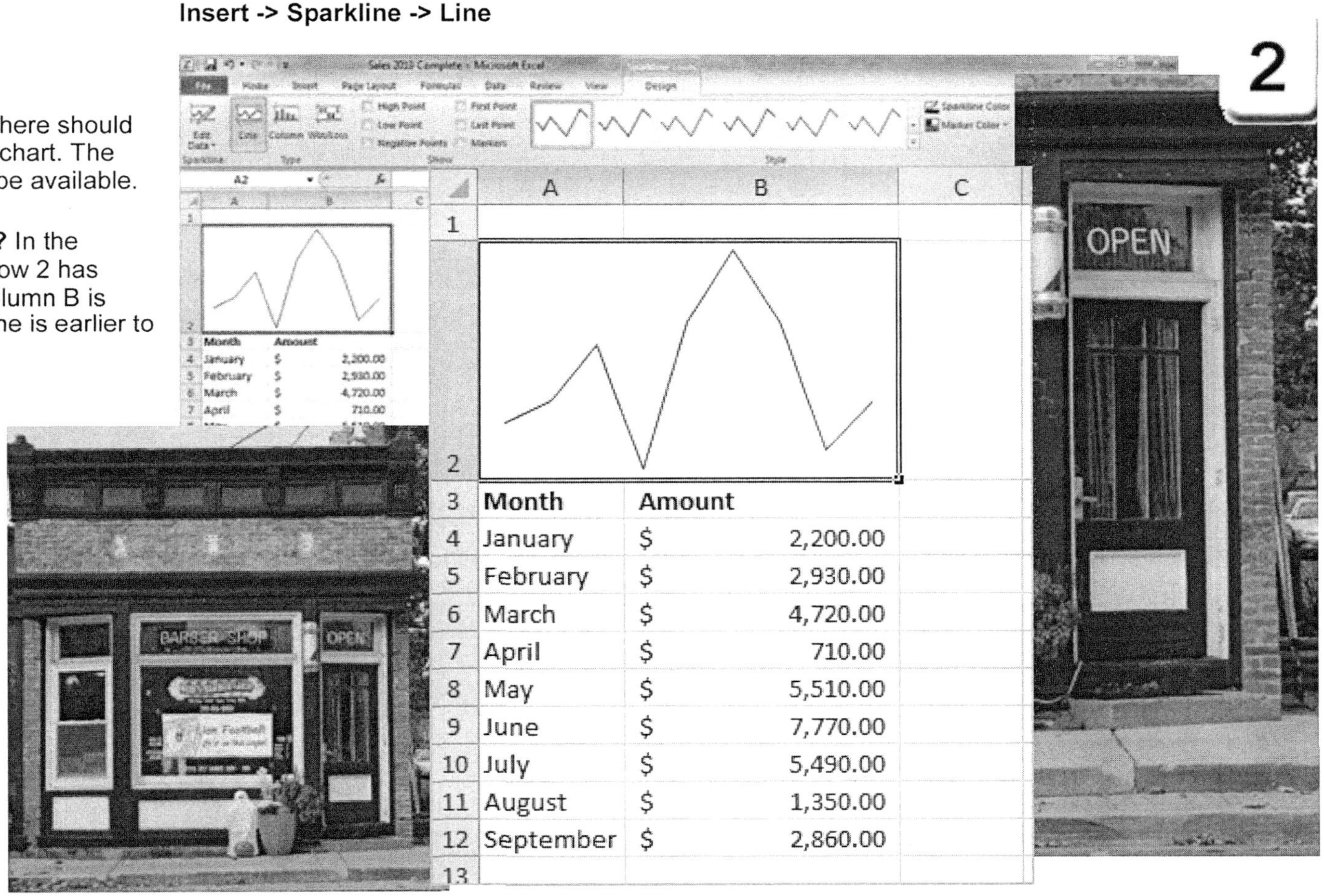

Exam 77-882: Microsoft Excel 2010 Core
6. Presenting Data Visually
6.4. Apply Sparklines

Take Two

Sparkline: Change Type

There are three types of Sparklines: Line, Column, Win/Loss. You can change the Type with the Sparkline Ribbon if you wish.

Before You Begin: Click once on the Sparkline so that it is selected. The **Sparkline Tools** should be available.

3. Try This: Change the Type
Go to **Sparkline Tools -> Design**.
Go to **Type->Column**.

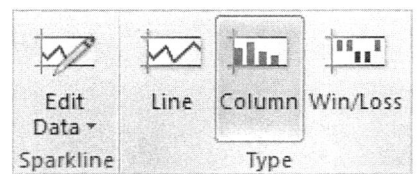

What Do You See? The Sparkline is a very tiny chart. The Column type may be easier to see the trends compared to the Line type, depending on the data. Keep going...

Sparkline Tools -> Design->Type -> Column

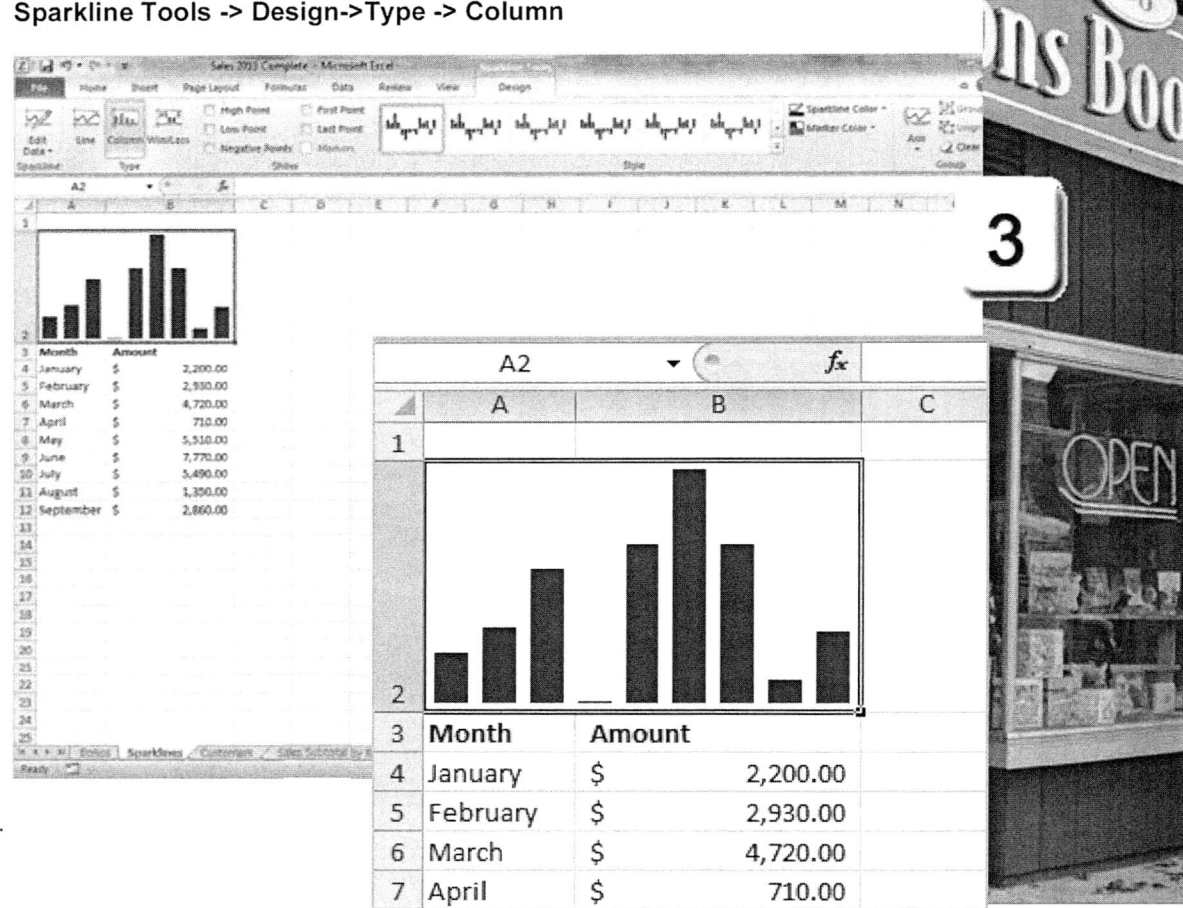

Exam 77-882: Microsoft Excel 2010 Core
6. Presenting Data Visually
6.4. Apply Sparklines: Format a Sparkline

Sparkline: Styles

Each object in Microsoft Office can be formatted with **Styles**. Sparklines have a small gallery of Styles as well.

Before You Begin: Click once on the Sparkline so that it is selected. The **Sparkline Tools** should be available.

4. Try This: Edit the Style
Go to **Sparkline Tools -> Design**.
Go to **Style**.
Click on a Style: Accent 6.

What Do You See? The Sparkline Styles are simple compared to the Chart Styles.

Keep going...

Sparkline Tools -> Design->Style

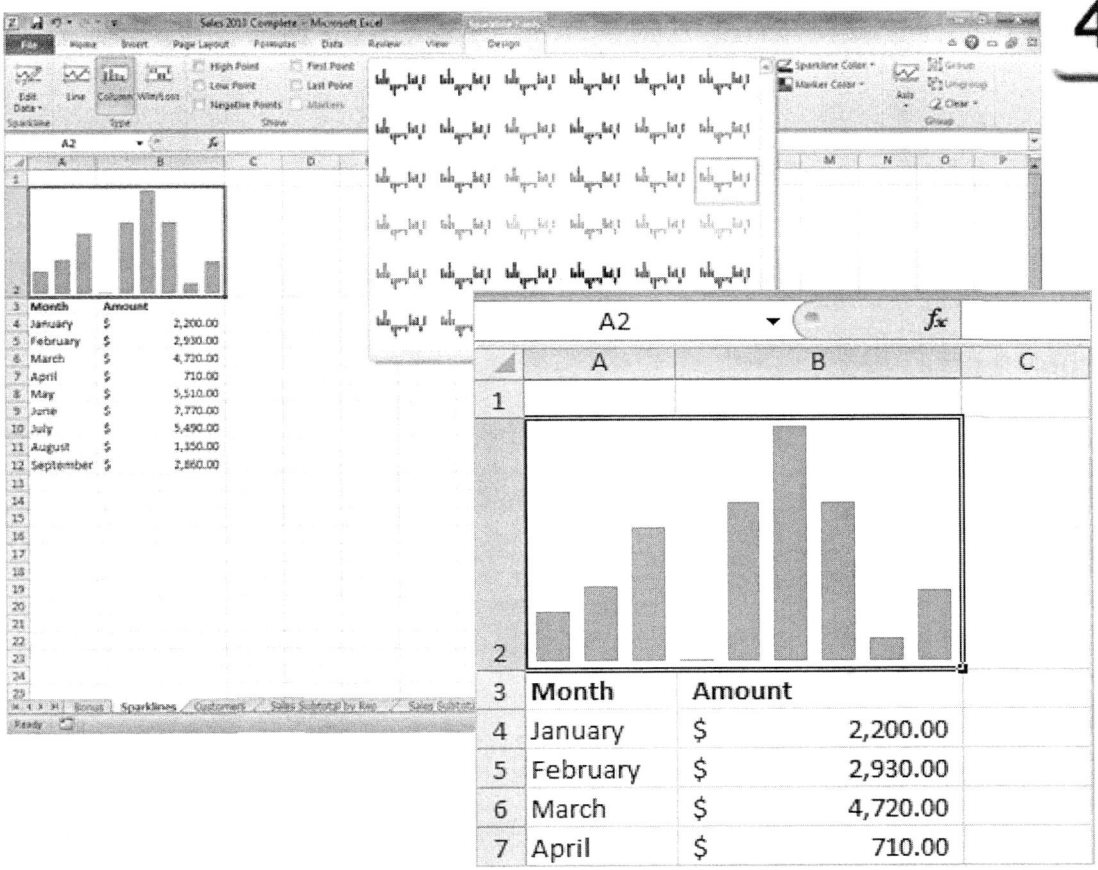

Exam 77-882: Microsoft Excel 2010 Core
6. Presenting Data Visually
6.4. Apply Sparklines: Format a Sparkline

Sparkline: Data Markers

Markers are data points. You can format the points to draw attention to the data.

Before You Begin: Click once on the Sparkline so that it is selected. The **Sparkline Tools** should be available. Go to **Sparkline Tools->Design->Type**. Click on **Line**.

5. Try This: Show the Markers
Go to **Sparkline Tools -> Design->Show..** Click on **Markers**.

What Do You See? The Markers include:
High Point
Low Point
Negative Points
First Point
Last Point

Keep going...

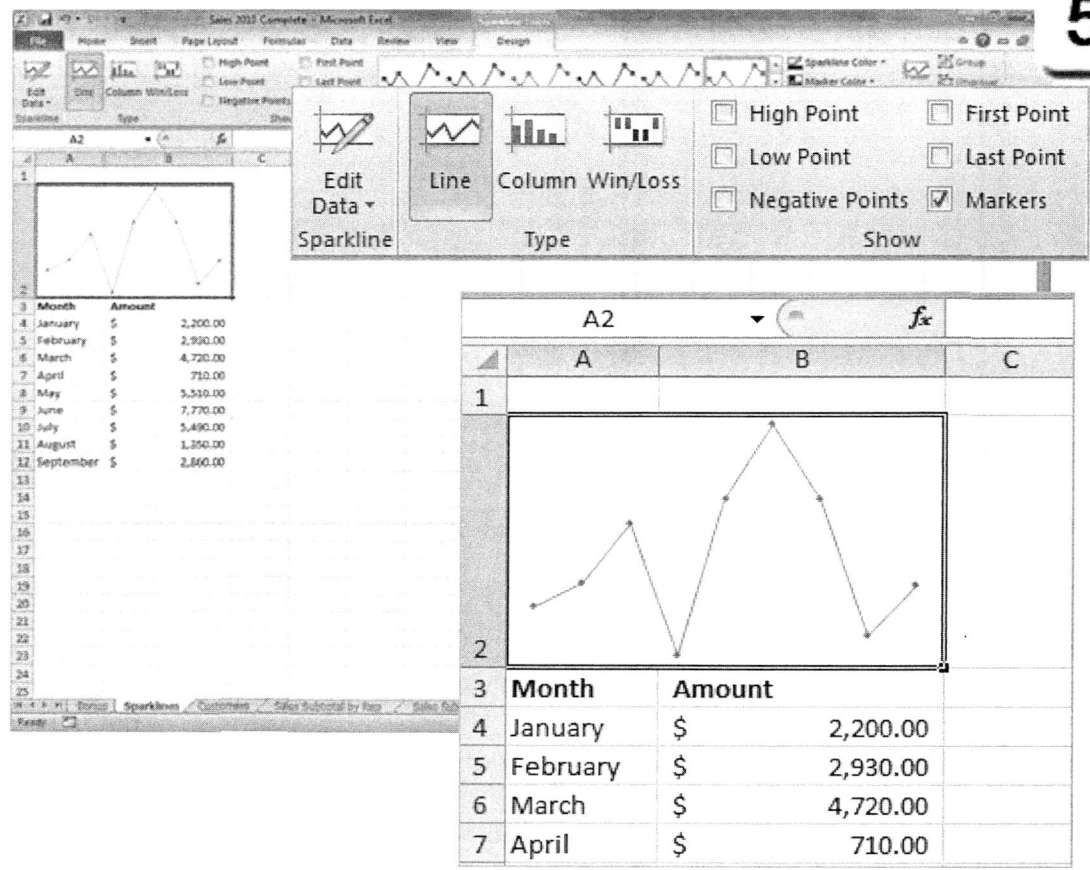

Exam 77-882: Microsoft Excel 2010 Core
6. Presenting Data Visually
6.4. Apply Sparklines: Show the Data Markers

Sparkline: Marker Color

The purpose of the Sparkline is to visualize the data. You can format the Markers to make the points more obvious.

Before You Begin: Click once on the Sparkline so that it is selected. The **Sparkline Tools** should be available.

6. Try This: Format the Marker Color
Go to **Sparkline Tools -> Design**.
Go to **Style->Marker Color**.
Click on a Theme Color: Orange.

What Do You See? You can choose a different **Marker Color** for the points.

Keep going...

Memo to Self: If you have a Column Sparkline, the whole Column changes color when you format the Markers.

Exam 77-882: Microsoft Excel 2010 Core
6. Presenting Data Visually
6.4. Apply Sparklines: Show the Data Markers

Sparkline: Format Axis

There are some basic **Axis** options that you can choose.

Before You Begin: Click once on the Sparkline so that it is selected. The **Sparkline Tools** should be available.
Go to **Sparkline Tools->Design->Type**.
Click on **Column**.
The **High Point Marker** is Purple.

7. Try This: Format the Axis
Go to **Sparkline Tools -> Design->Group**.
Click on **Axis**.

What Do You See? By default **Axis** options show the Maximum and Minimum Values for the Horizontal and Vertical Axis.

Very Good. That's a lot for a little chart.
Save. Save. Save.

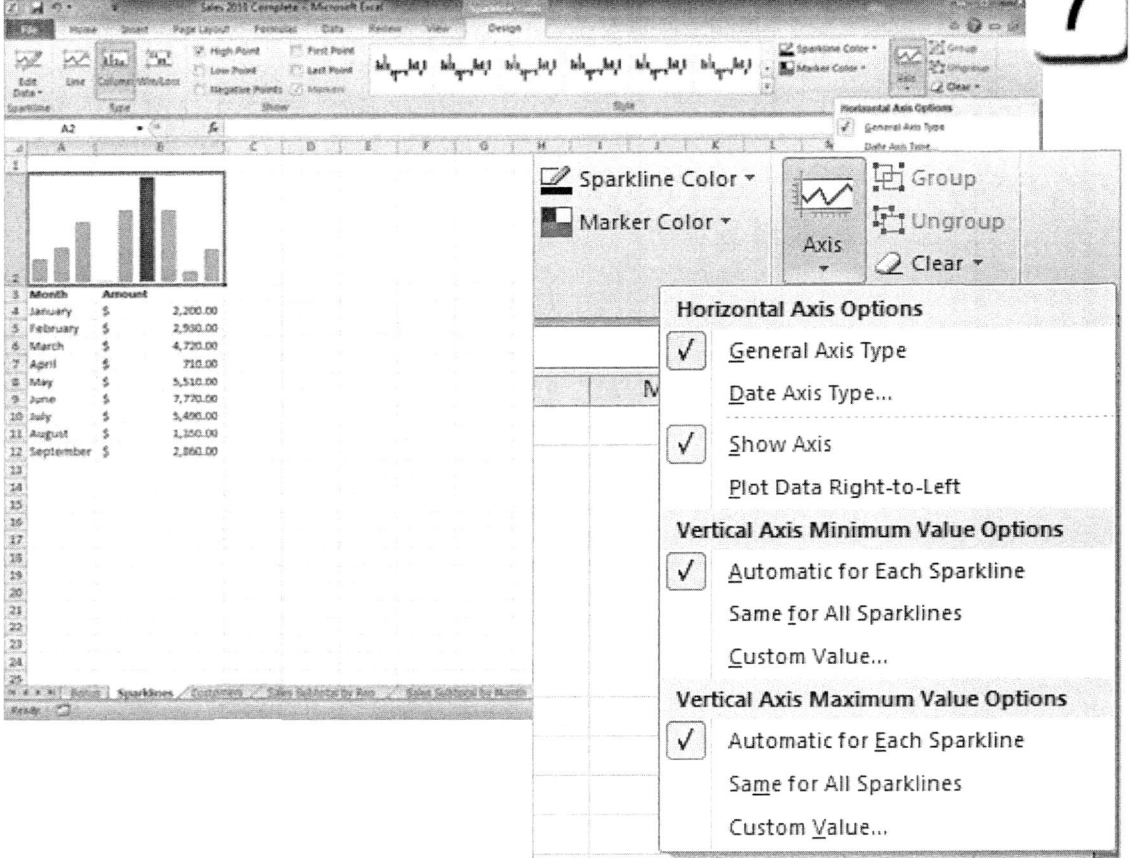

Exam 77-882: Microsoft Excel 2010 Core
6. Presenting Data Visually
6.4. Apply Sparklines: Customize Sparklines

Formatting Worksheets

Technically, a spreadsheet is just one sheet in a an Excel Workbook file. Each sheet can be named so it is easier to find the information. You can use Color, Position and Grouping to manage the spreadsheets as well.

This lesson begins with a review of how to **Rename** a Worksheet. The example shown on these pages is the same one from the previous pages.

1. Try This: Rename the Worksheet
Click on the Sparklines tab.
Go to **Home -> Cells -> Format**.
Click on **Rename Sheet**.
The Name in the tab should be highlighted black. Type: Sparklines 2
Click ENTER on the keyboard.

Keep going...

Memo to Self: You can also **Rename** the sheet by right-clicking the tab.

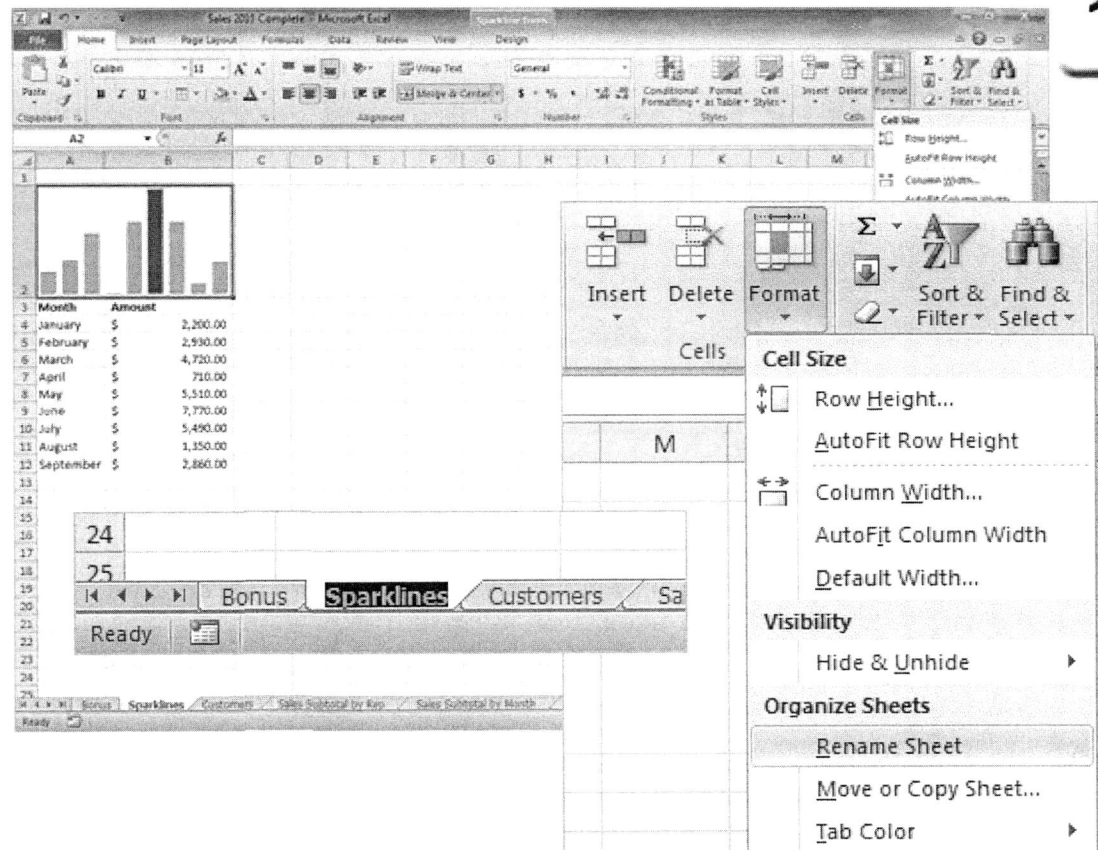

Exam 77-882: Microsoft Excel 2010 Core
4. Managing Worksheets and Workbooks
4.1. Create and format worksheets: Rename

Worksheets: Move

Move or Copy are on the same page. Here are the steps.

2. Try This: Move a Worksheet
Click on the Sparklines 2 tab.
Go to **Home -> Cells -> Format**.
Click on **Move or Copy Sheet**.

What Do You See? A little window will prompt you to Move selected sheet. In the example on this page the Sparklines 2 sheet will be placed before the Sales Subtotal by Rep sheet.

What Else Do You see? You could use this method to Move or Copy a sheet to a different Excel workbook.

Memo to Self: You can also **Move** the sheet by left-clicking and holding the tab. The cursor will follow your mouse as you move across the tabs. When you let go of the mouse, the page will be placed there.

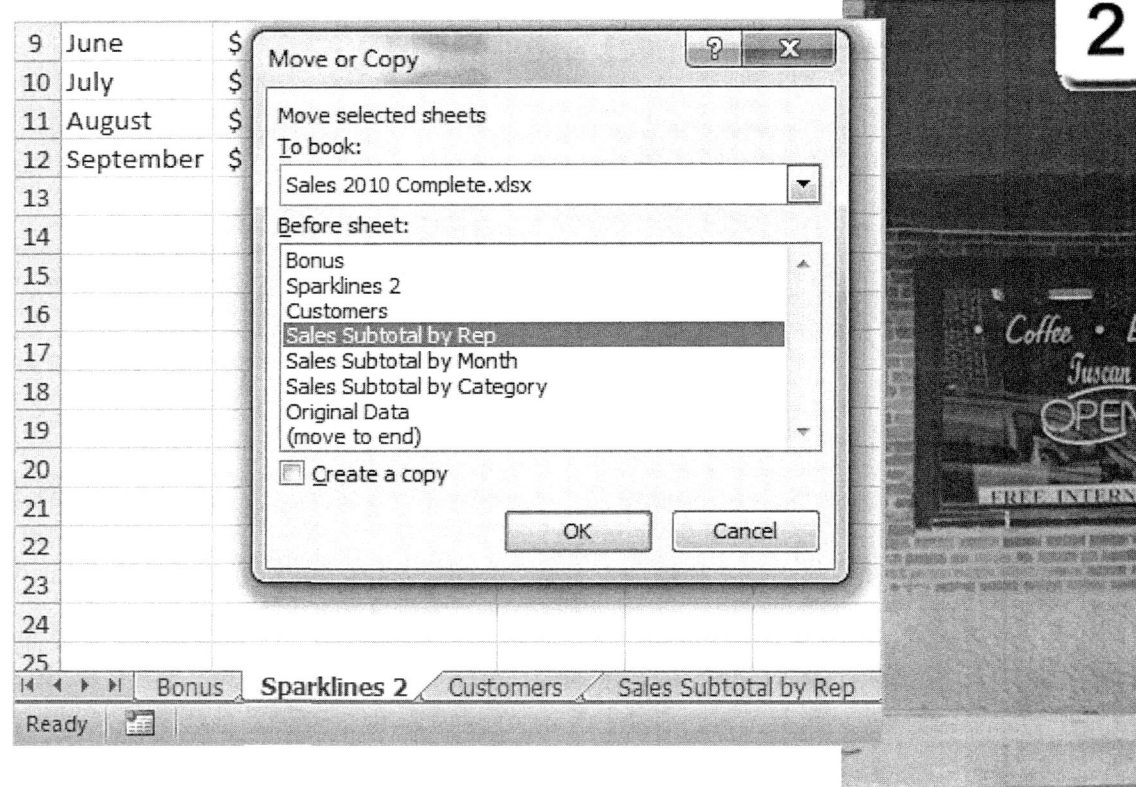

Exam 77-882: Microsoft Excel 2010 Core
4. Managing Worksheets and Workbooks
4.1. Create and format worksheets: Move or Copy Sheet

Intermediate Excel 2010 Page 186 of 230

Worksheets: Color

Color is a very important clue for navigating and locating data. The Computer Mama's first mentor used colored floppy disks: green for financials, red for priority projects, and so forth. You can color the tabs in your Workbook. Here are the steps.

3. Try This: Color the Sheet Tabs
Select any Tab in the Workbook.
Go to **Home -> Cells -> Format**.
Click on **Tab Color**,
Choose a **Theme Color**.

What Do You See? The **Tab Color** is difficult to see when it is the active sheet. The Colors are much more obvious when it is not the active sheet.

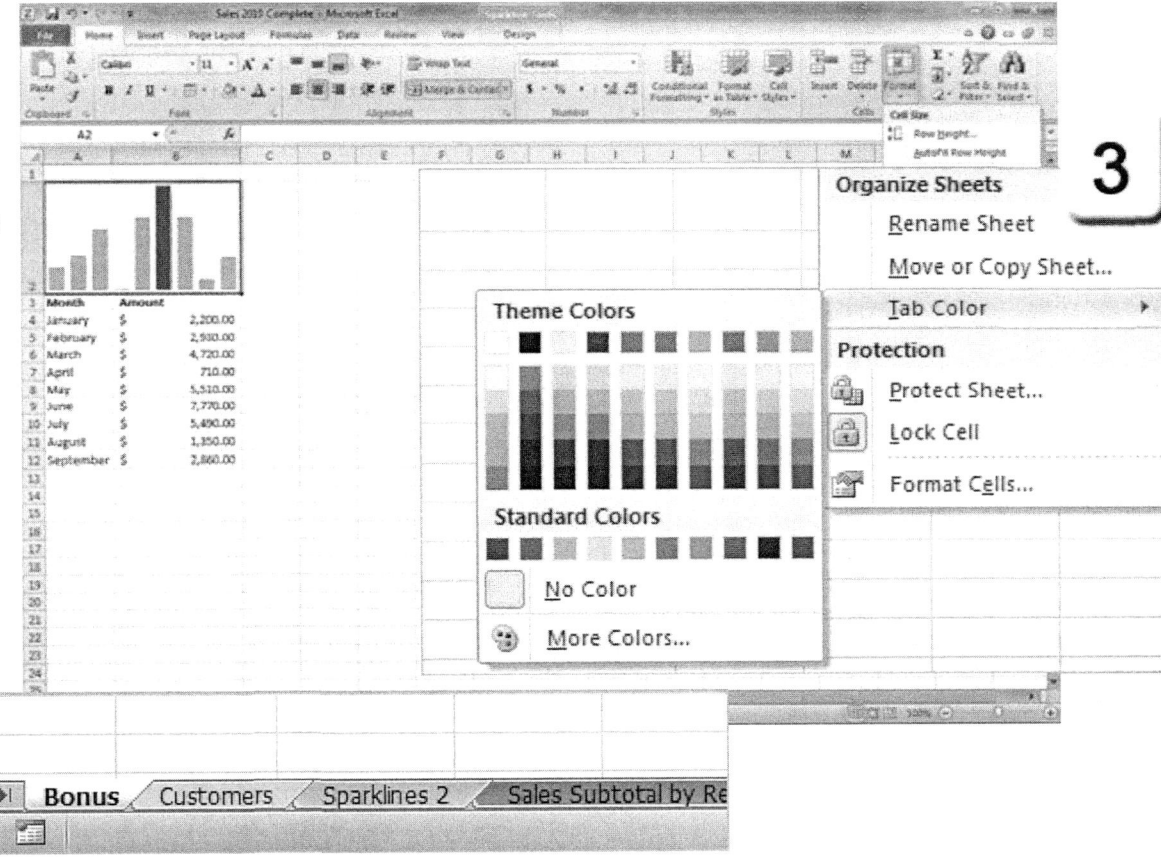

Exam 77-882: Microsoft Excel 2010 Core
4. Managing Worksheets and Workbooks
   4.1. Create and format worksheets: Move or Copy Sheet

Worksheet: Hide a Sheet

Sometimes it is helpful to **Hide** the sheets that the users don't need to edit or modify. For example you might consider hiding the the sheets with the lookup tables.

4. Try This: Hide a Spreadsheet

Select any spreadsheet. The example on this page is the Bonus spreadsheet.
Go to **Home -> Cells -> Format.**
Go on **Hide & Unhide-> Hide Sheet.**

What Do You See? "Silly wabbit! Trix are for kids." You WONT see anything. The sheet is hidden.

Keep going...

Home -> Cells -> Format->Hide & Unhide->Hide Sheet

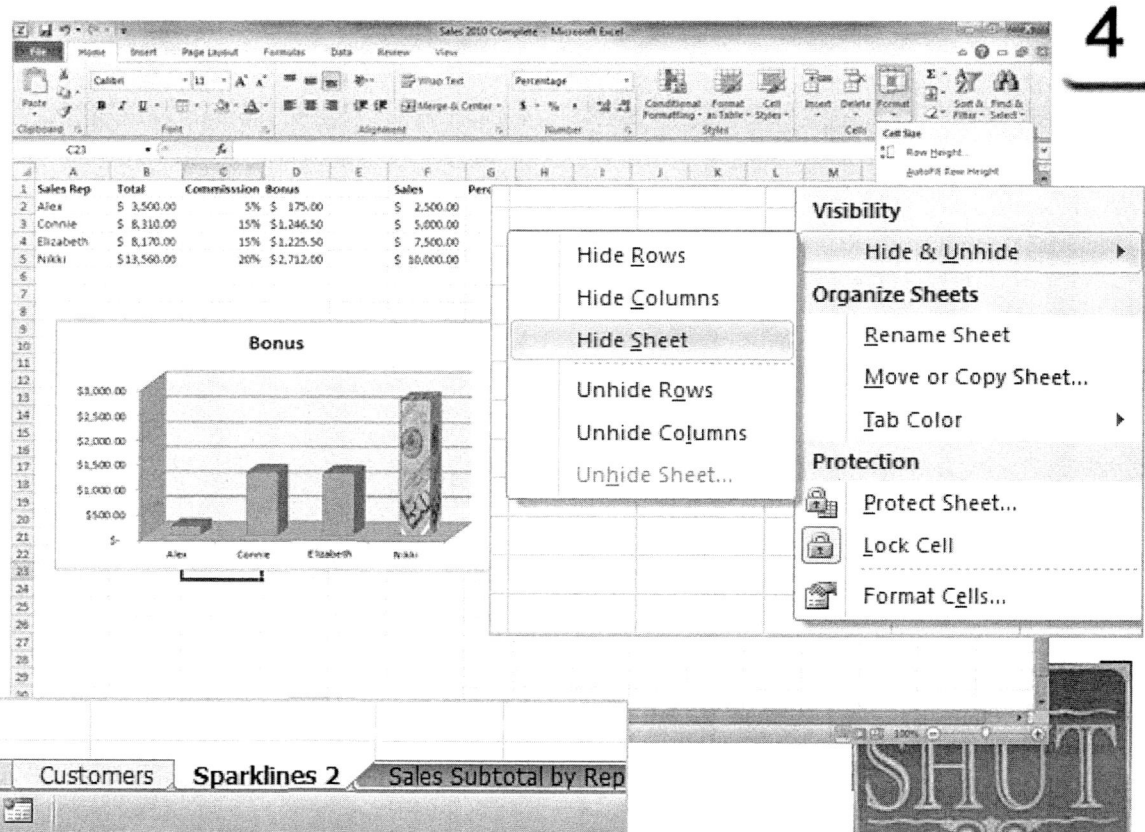

Exam 77-882: Microsoft Excel 2010 Core
4. Managing Worksheets and Workbooks
4.1. Create and format worksheets: Hide or Unhide a Sheet

Worksheet: Unhide a Sheet

5. Try This: Unhide a Spreadsheet
Go to **Home -> Cells -> Format**.
Click on **Unhide**.

What Do You See? If you have more than one hidden sheet, you will be prompted to select which one should be visible.

Please **Unhide** all of the hidden sheets.

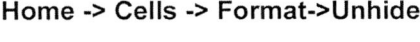

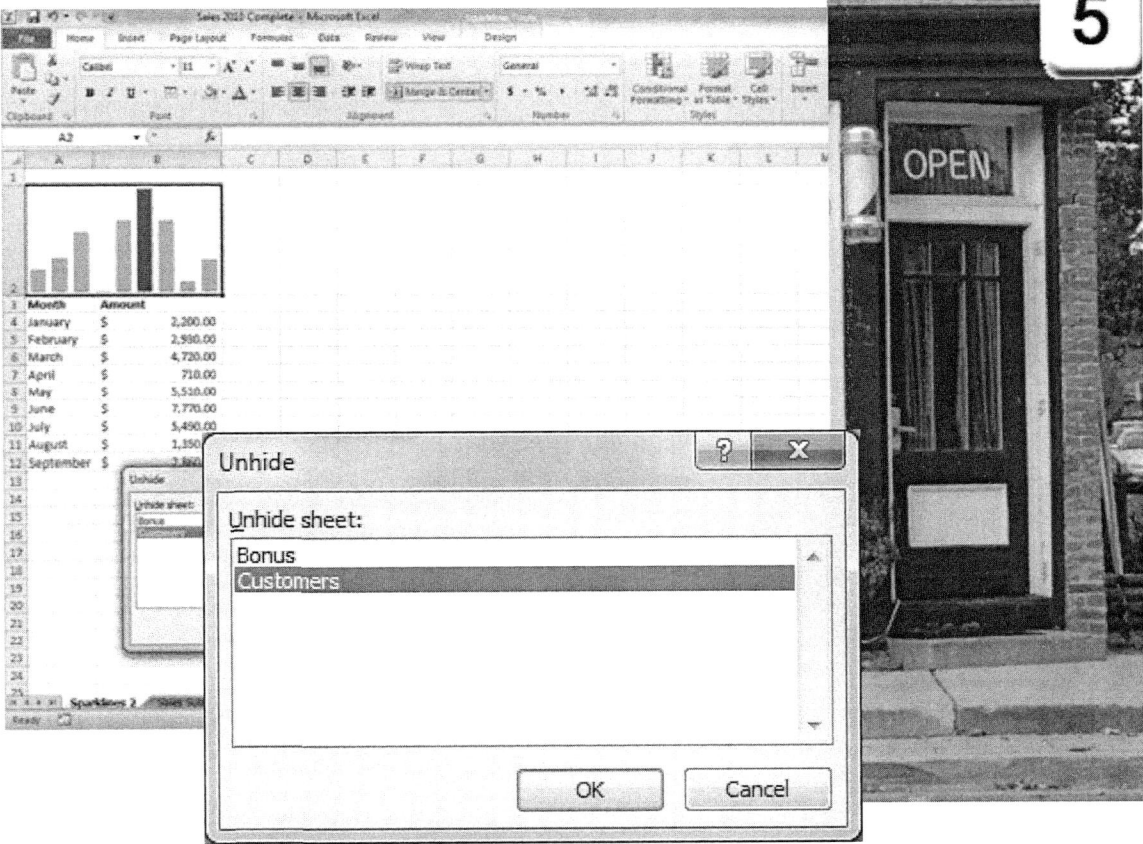

Exam 77-882: Microsoft Excel 2010 Core
4. Managing Worksheets and Workbooks
4.1. Create and format worksheets: Hide or Unhide a Sheet

Insert a Worksheet

There are two more useful worksheet commands: **Insert** and **Delete**. You probably already know them, but they complete the discussion.

6. Try This: Insert a Sheet
Select a spreadsheet.
Go to **Home -> Cells -> Insert**.
Click on **Insert Sheet**.

What Do You See? In this example, there is a new worksheet: Sheet1. Your new sheet may be Sheet2, Sheet3, or whatever the next number would be.

Memo to Self: You can also right-click the tabs and click on **Insert...**

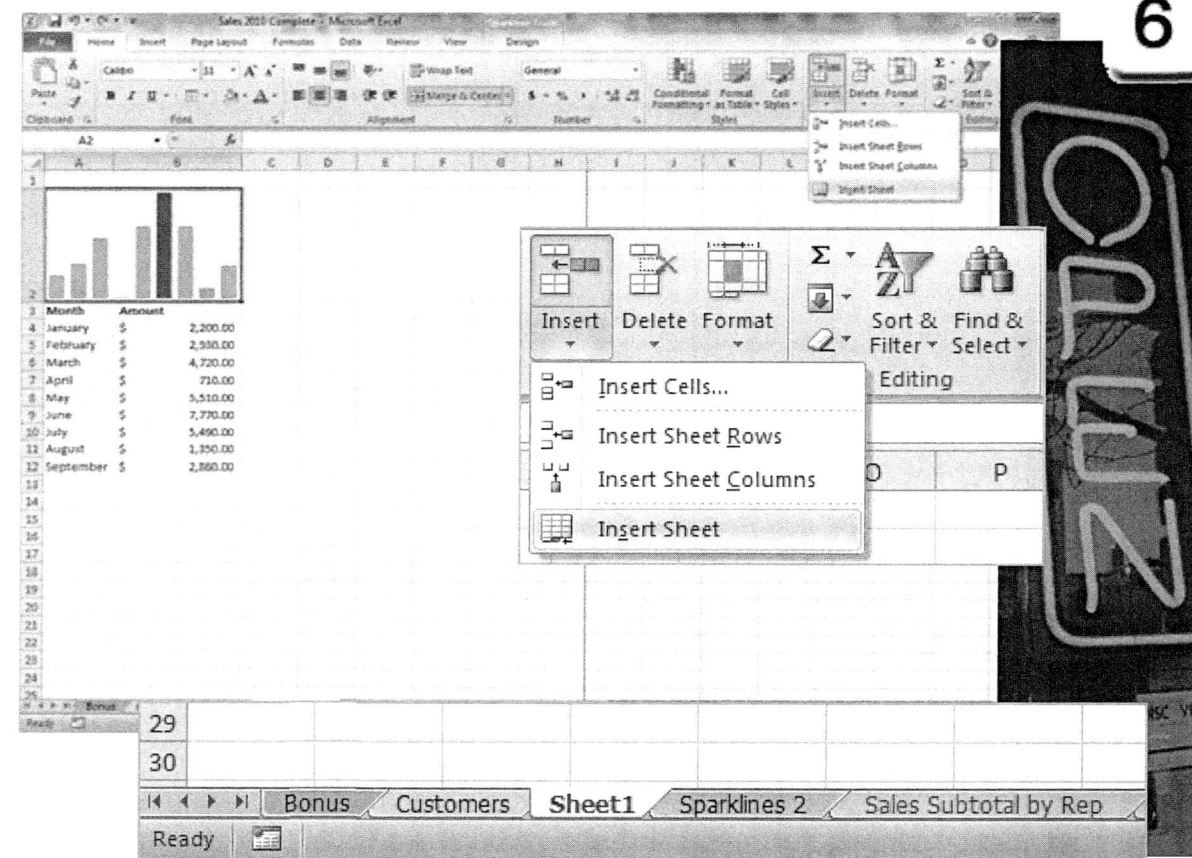

Exam 77-882: Microsoft Excel 2010 Core
4. Managing Worksheets and Workbooks
4.1. Create and format worksheets: Insert or Delete a Sheet

Delete a Worksheet

If you can Insert a spreadsheet, then you can also **Delete** a spreadsheet.

7. Try This: Delete a Sheet
Select a spreadsheet.
Go to **Home -> Cells -> Delete**.
Click on **Delete Sheet**.

But Wait...! What Do You See? If the sheet has data (text, numbers, graphics, anything) then you will be warned that the data will be deleted... **Permanently**.
There is no Undo.

Click **CANCEL**. Do NOT delete the sheet.

Memo to Self: When you delete a blank spreadsheet, you will not lose any data so you may not see the warning message.

Home -> Cells -> Delete->Delete Sheet

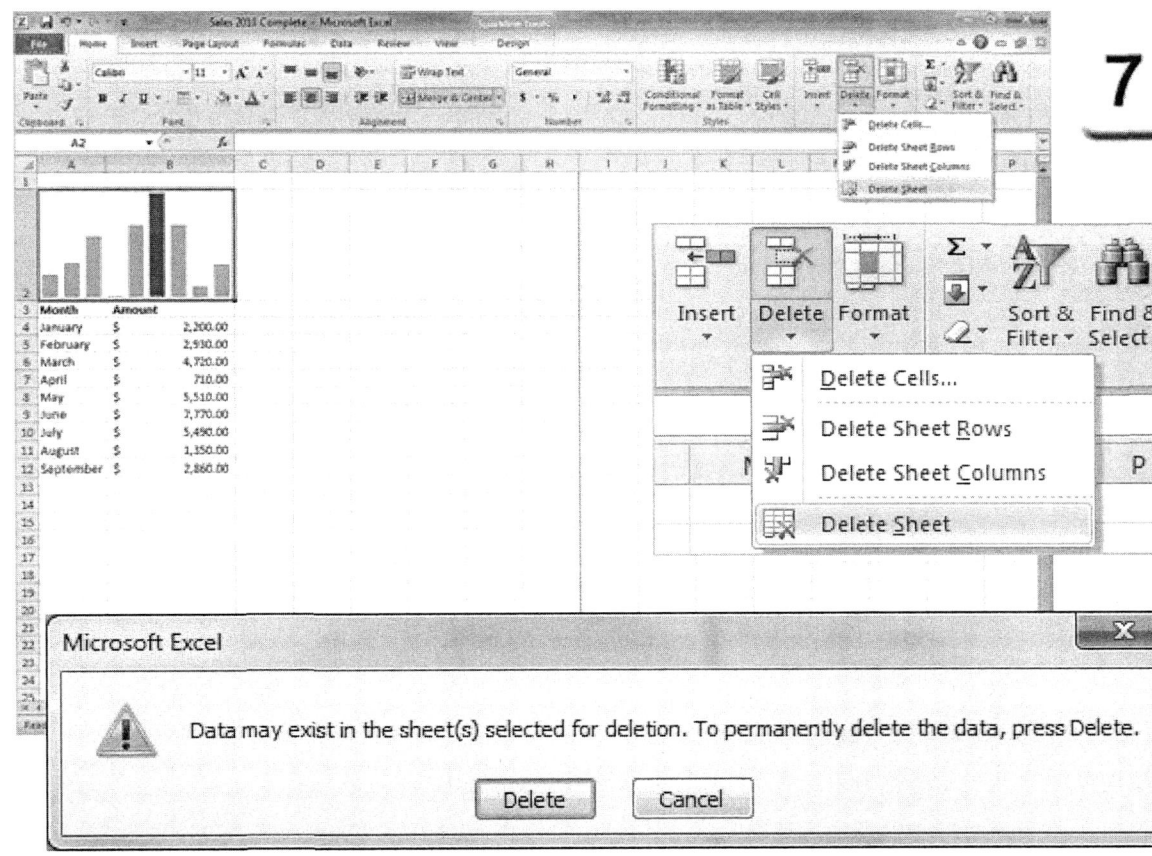

7

Exam 77-882: Microsoft Excel 2010 Core
4. Managing Worksheets and Workbooks
4.1. Create and format worksheets: Insert or Delete a Sheet

Group the Worksheets

One last example. Say you have a collection of sheets that belong together. There is a new **Group** function in Microsoft Excel that allows you to manage those sheets together.

Try This: Group Many Sheets
This sample workbook has several sheets.
Select the first sheet.
Hold the CONTROL key on the keyboard.
Select the second, third and fourth sheets.

What Do You See? This set of sheets is now a Group. When you **Move** one, you Move them all together. A cursor and a stack of pages will follow your mouse as you move across the tabs.

Try This, Too: Ungroup the Sheets
Right click the Group.
Click on **Ungroup Sheets**.
The Sheets will be independent, again.

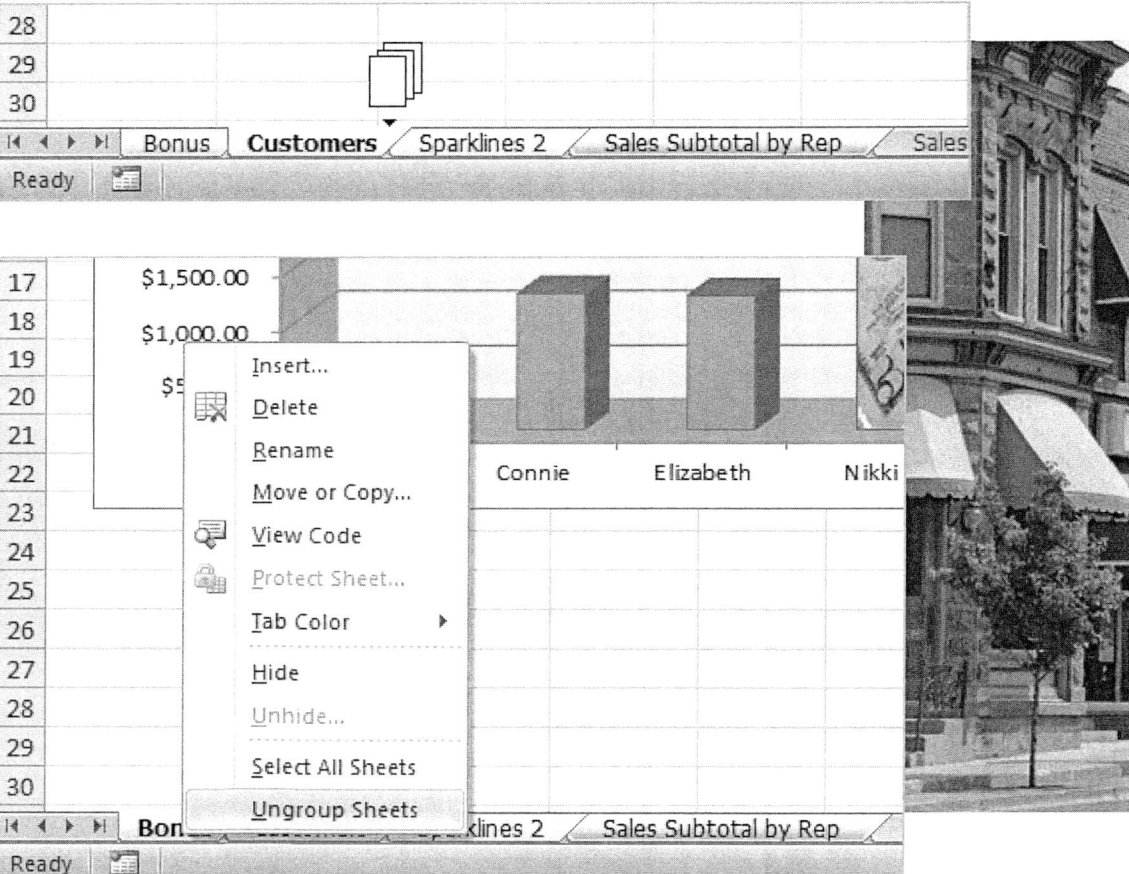

Exam 77-882: Microsoft Excel 2010 Core
4. Managing Worksheets and Workbooks
4.1. Create and format worksheets: Group or Ungroup a Sheet

Home -> Alignment -> Merge and Center

Links and Hyperlinks

A spreadsheet can include **Hyperlinks** to additional information. The hyperlinks can take you to a website or they can link to other spreadsheets.

A hyperlink can be added to text as well as graphics. This lesson will begin by adding a picture to the Sparkline sheet.

1. Before You Begin: Edit the Spreadsheet
The example begins on the Sparkline sheet. Select Cell A1:B1.

Go to **Home -> Alignment**.
Click on **Merge and Center**.

What Do You See? Cells A1 and B1 are merged together. In the example on this page Row 1 has been made taller.

Keep going...

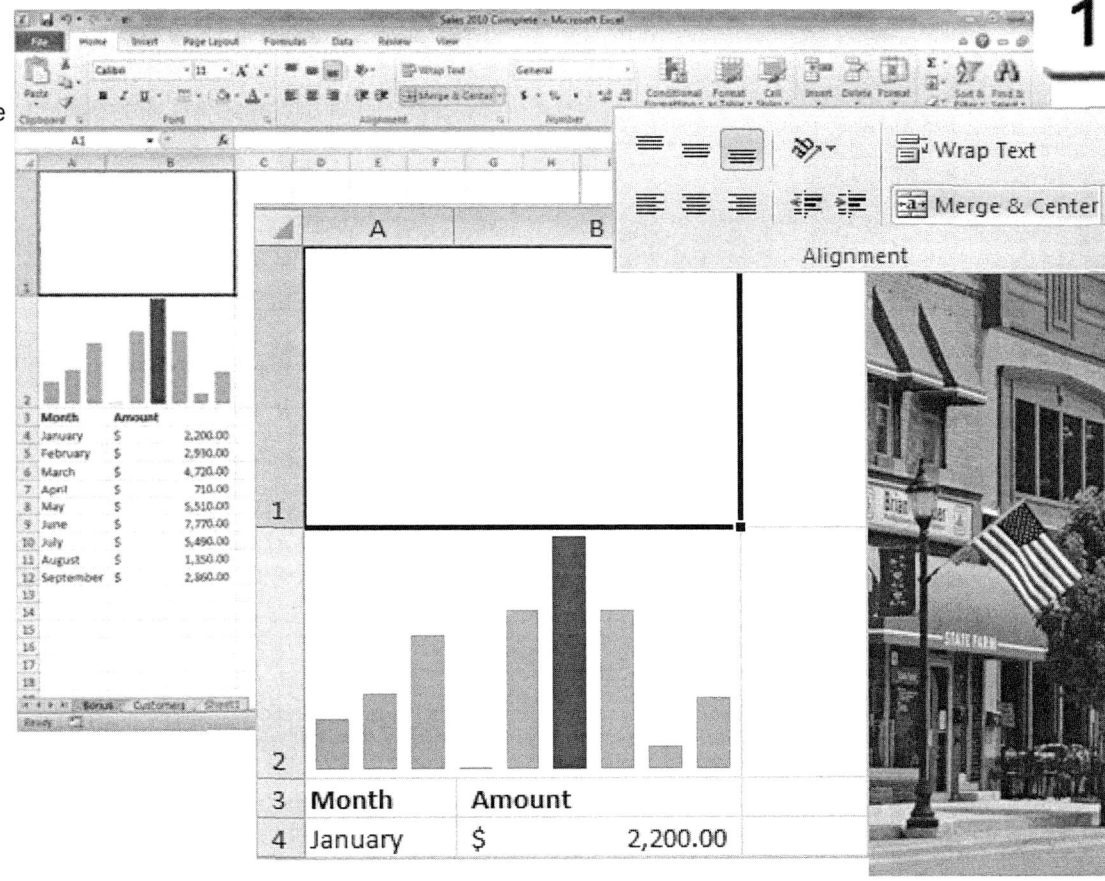

Exam 77-882: Microsoft Excel 2010 Core
3. Formatting Cells and Worksheets
3.2. Merge or split cells

Insert a Picture

2. Try This: Insert a Picture
Select the new merged cell.
Go to **Insert ->Picture**.
Browse for a picture: 1logo.jpg
Double click to add the picture to this spreadsheet.

What Do You See? The Picture Tools should be available when the picture is selected. You can resize the logo to fit the merged cell.

Keep going...

Memo to Self: You do not have to MATCH the example on this page. You can use the sample picture, **1logo.jpg,** or your own picture if you wish.

Insert ->Picture

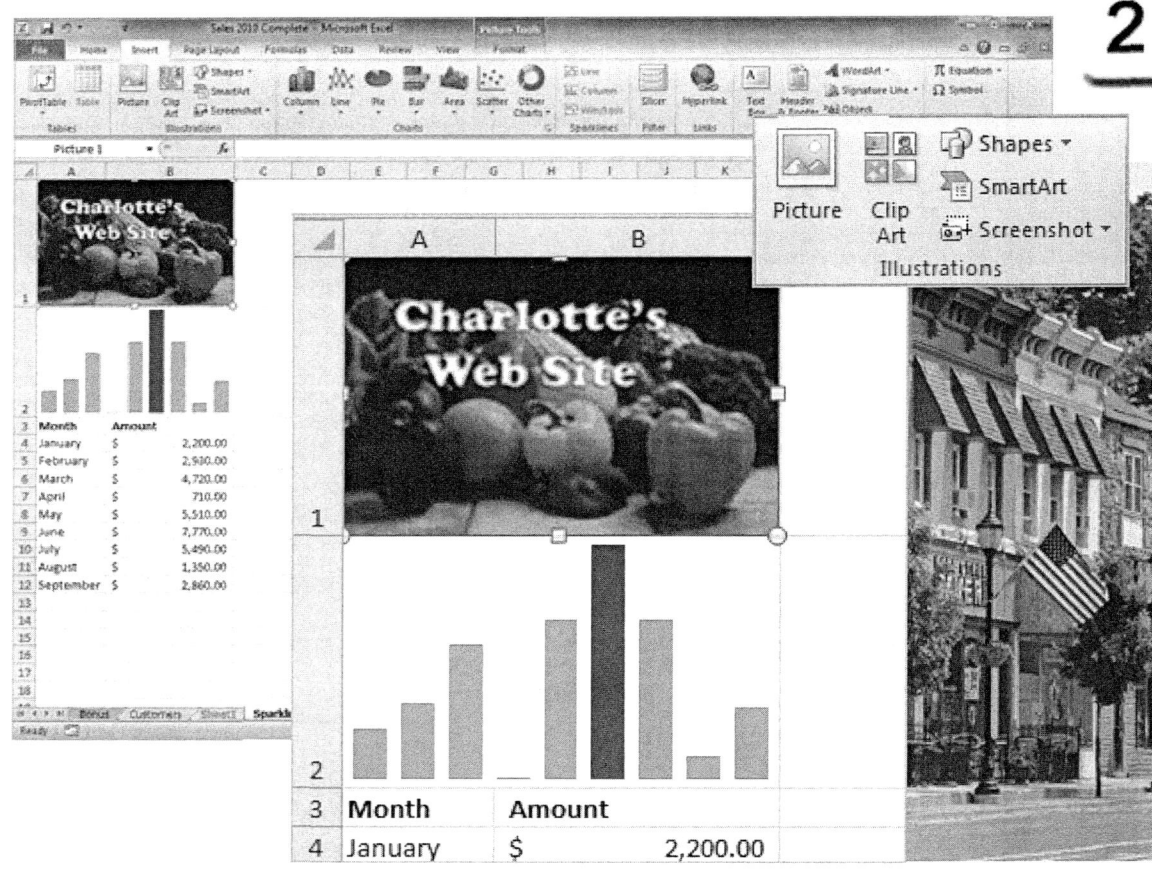

Exam 77-882: Microsoft Excel 2010 Core
5. Applying Formulas and Functions
5.3. Apply cell references in formulas: Use Absolute and Relative cell references

Take Two

Insert ->Links-> Hyperlink

3

Insert a Hyperlink

Where do you want the **hyperlink** to go? You can link to a place in the same document, link to the Internet, create a new document, even open an email. This lesson will add hyperlinks to a picture, a Sparkline, as well as text.

3. Try This: Insert a Hyperlink
Click once on the picture to select it.
Go to **Insert -> Links-> Hyperlink**.

Hyperlink

Links

What Do You See? When you click on **Existing File or Web Page**, you can link to a file on your computer. You can also type the address for a webpage.

Type an Address: www.comma2010.com
(Excel may add the http:// stuff.)
Click **OK**. Keep going.

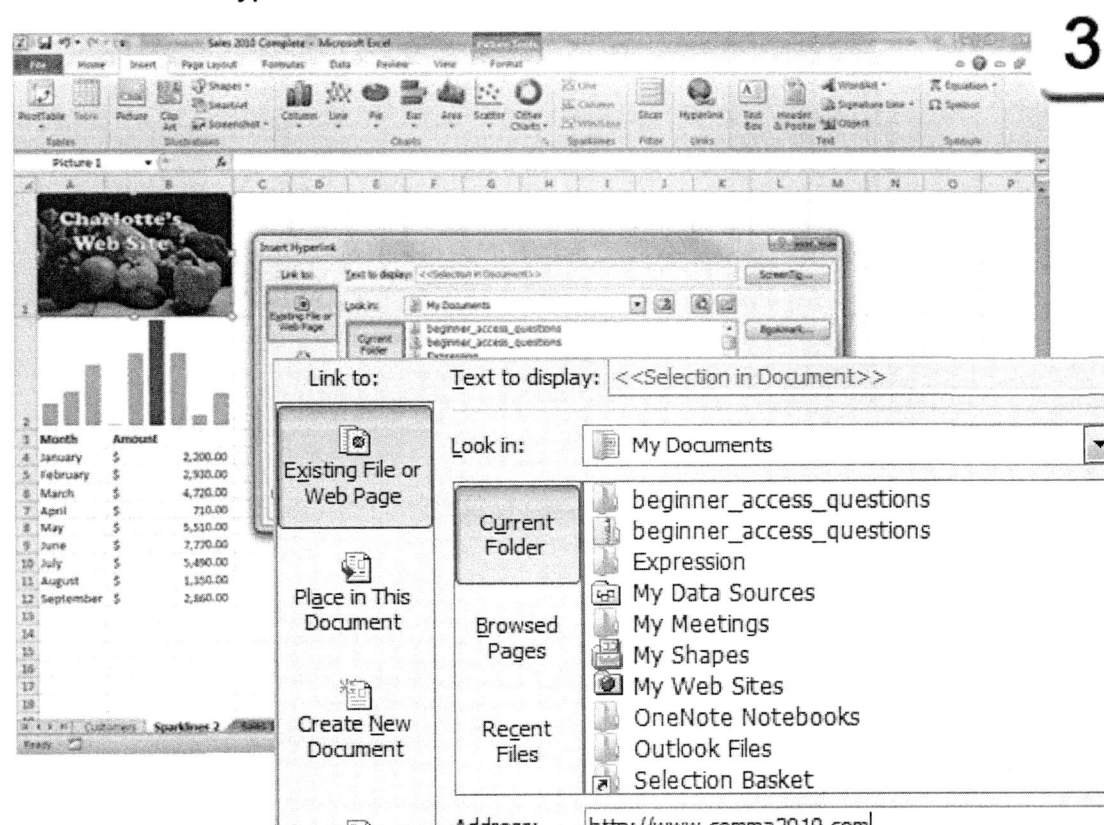

Exam 77-882: Microsoft Excel 2010 Core
2. Creating Cell Data
2.3. Apply and manipulate hyperlinks

Insert -> Links-> Hyperlink

Try the Hyperlink
So, what does a hyperlink look like to someone using your Excel spreadsheet?

4. Try This: Find the Hyperlink
Run your mouse over the picture that has the hyperlink, please.

What Do You See? When you run the mouse over a hyperlink, you should see the "finger." You should also see where the link will go.

Try This, Too: Try the Hyperlink
Click on the picture.
Did the website open in your browser?

In the example on this page, the hyperlink will go to www.comma2010.com, our course online.

Keep going...

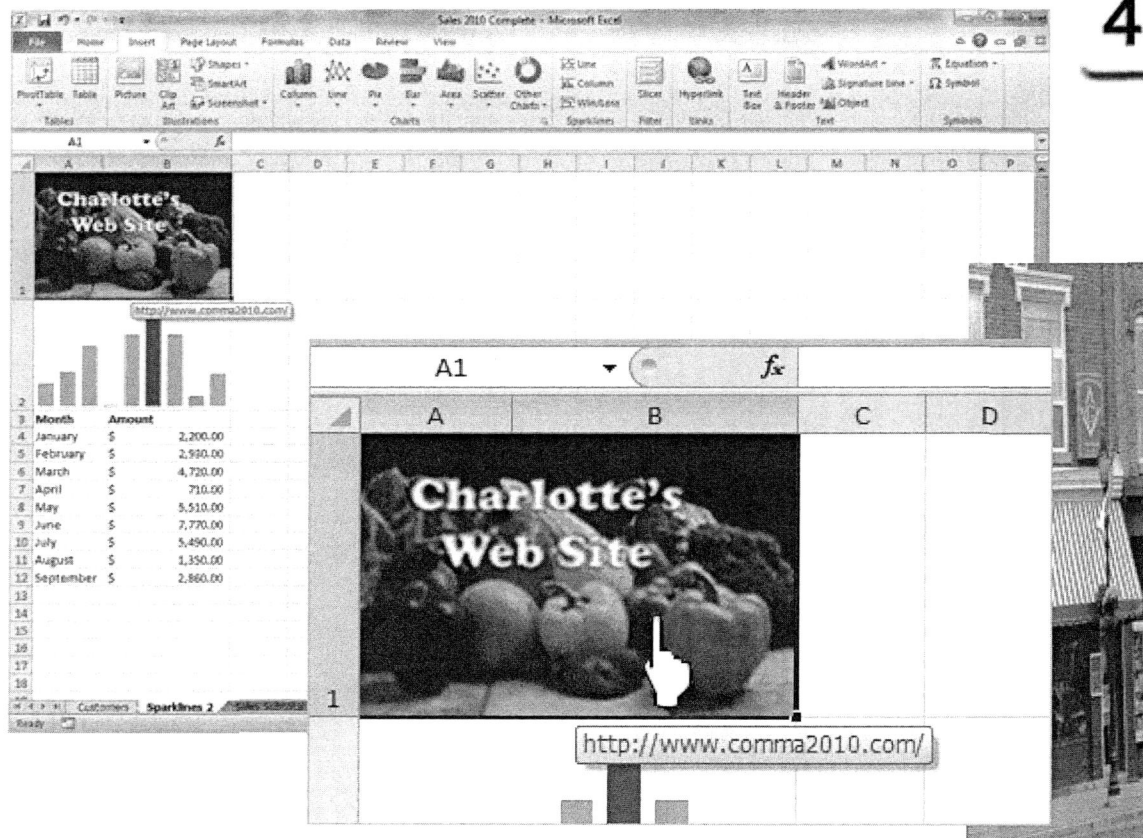

Exam 77-882: Microsoft Excel 2010 Core
2. Creating Cell Data
2.3. Apply and manipulate hyperlinks

Insert ->Links-> Hyperlink

Link to a Spreadsheet
Say you wanted to link to the original data sheet. You can create a hyperlink that goes to another sheet in this workbook.

Before You Begin: This lesson shows the **Sales 2010 Complete.xlsx** file. This workbook has a sheet named Original Data as well as the Sparkline that we created earlier.

5. Try This: Link to a Sheet
Click on the Sparkline.
Go to **Insert-> Links-> Hyperlink**.
Select: **Place in the Document.**
Click on the **Original Data** spreadsheet.

What Do You See? When you choose **Place in This Document** you should see a list of Sheets and Defined Names that you can link to.

Click **OK** and keep going...

Where Have You Seen This Before? In Microsoft Word, you can hyperlink to the text or picture that has a **Bookmark**.

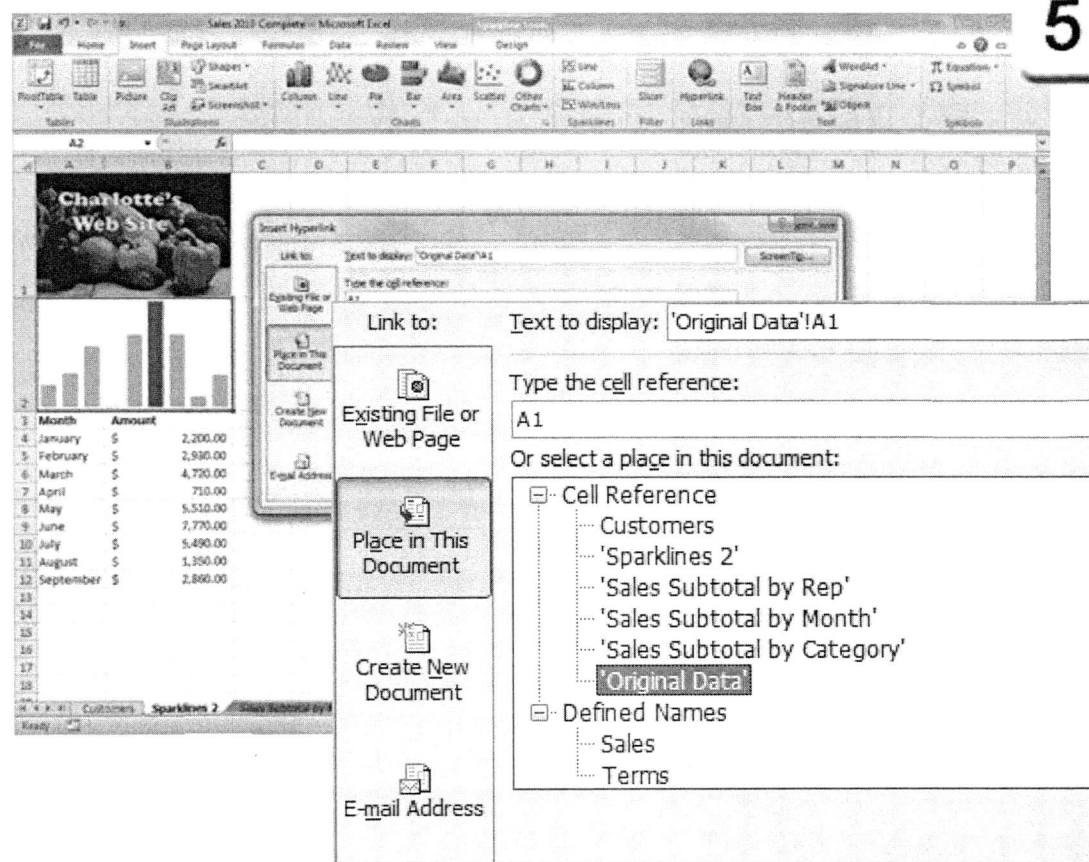

Exam 77-882: Microsoft Excel 2010 Core
2. Creating Cell Data
2.3. Apply and manipulate hyperlinks: Create a Hyperlink in a Cell

Insert-> Links-> Hyperlink

Try This Hyperlink, Too

Every good programmer tests the links and buttons. Test, test, test.

6. Try This: Test the Hyperlink

Run your mouse over the Sparkline that has the hyperlink, please.

What Do You See? You should see the "finger." that indicates a hyperlink.

Try This, Too: Try the Hyperlink

Click on the Sparkline. Did the link take you to the Original Data sheet?

What Else Do You See? The hyperlink, **Original_Data!A1** is displayed on the Sparkline. While this is accurate--that's where the hyperlink goes-it is confusing.

We can do better. Keep going...

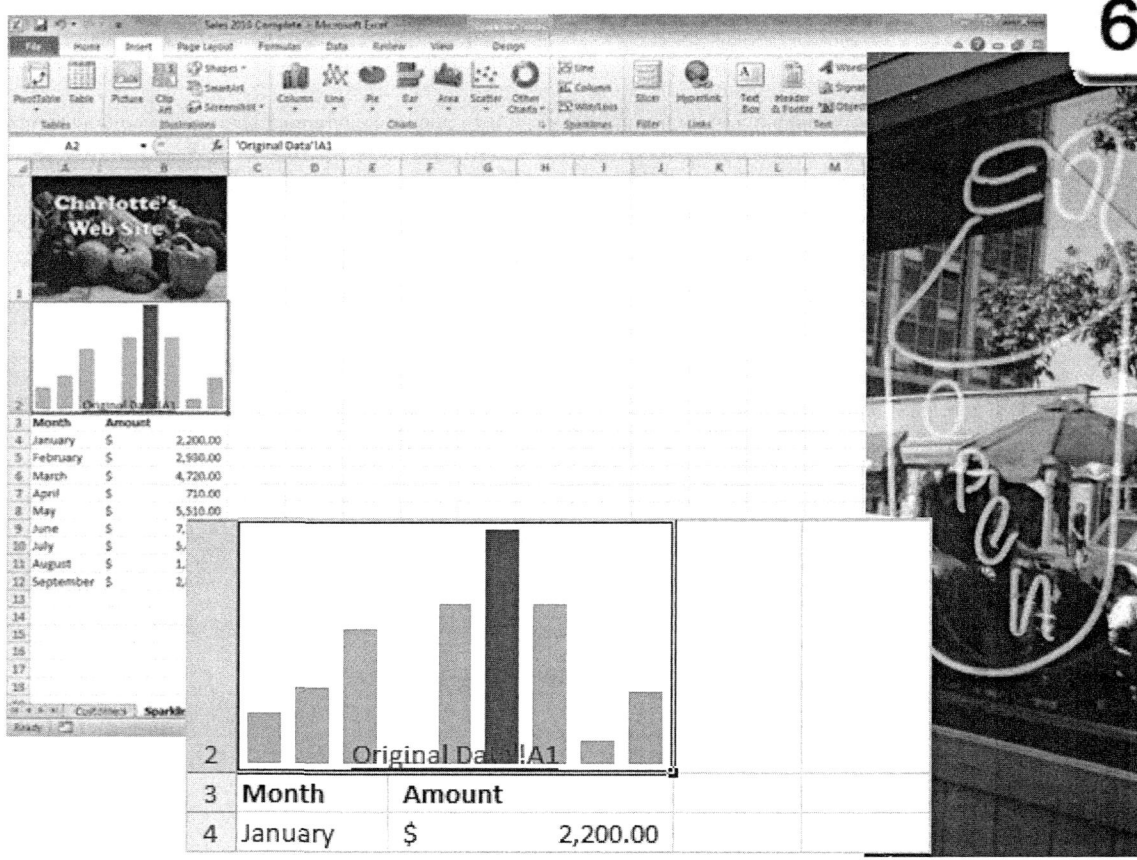

Exam 77-882: Microsoft Excel 2010 Core
2. Creating Cell Data
2.3. Apply and manipulate hyperlinks: Create a Hyperlink in a Cell

Modify a Hyperlink

In this example, the hyperlink was applied to the Cell. You can modify the hyperlink properties if you wish.

7. Try This: Modify a Hyperlink
Click once on Cell A2 to select it.
Go to **Insert-> Links-> Hyperlink**.

What Do You See? The **Edit Hyperlink** window will open, again.

What Else Do You See? You can delete a hyperlink by clicking on **Remove Link**.

Keep going...

Insert-> Links-> Hyperlink

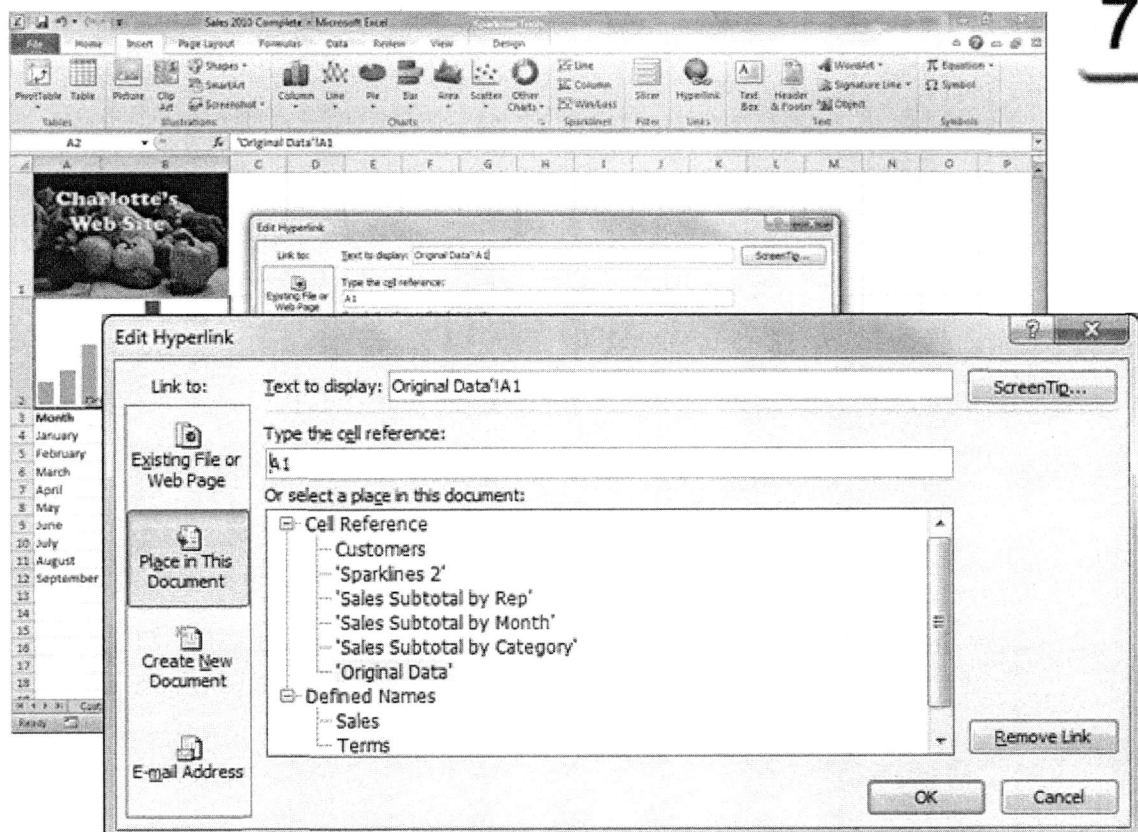

Exam 77-882: Microsoft Excel 2010 Core
2. Creating Cell Data
2.3. Apply and manipulate hyperlinks: Modify Hyperlinks

Take Two

Improve the Hyperlinks

Insert-> Links-> Hyperlink

Hyperlinks on web pages give the user hints and suggestions. Before you click on any link, the **Screen Tip** tells you what will happen. Spreadsheets can be "User Friendly," too.

8. Try This, Too: Edit the Text to Display
Go to **Insert-> Links-> Hyperlink**.
You should be on Pace in this document.
Go to **Text to display.**
Delete: Original Data'!A1
Type: Click here to go to the original data sheet

Click **OK** to save these changes to the hyperlink.
So, did that work?

Keep going...there's one more hyperlink you really want to consider.

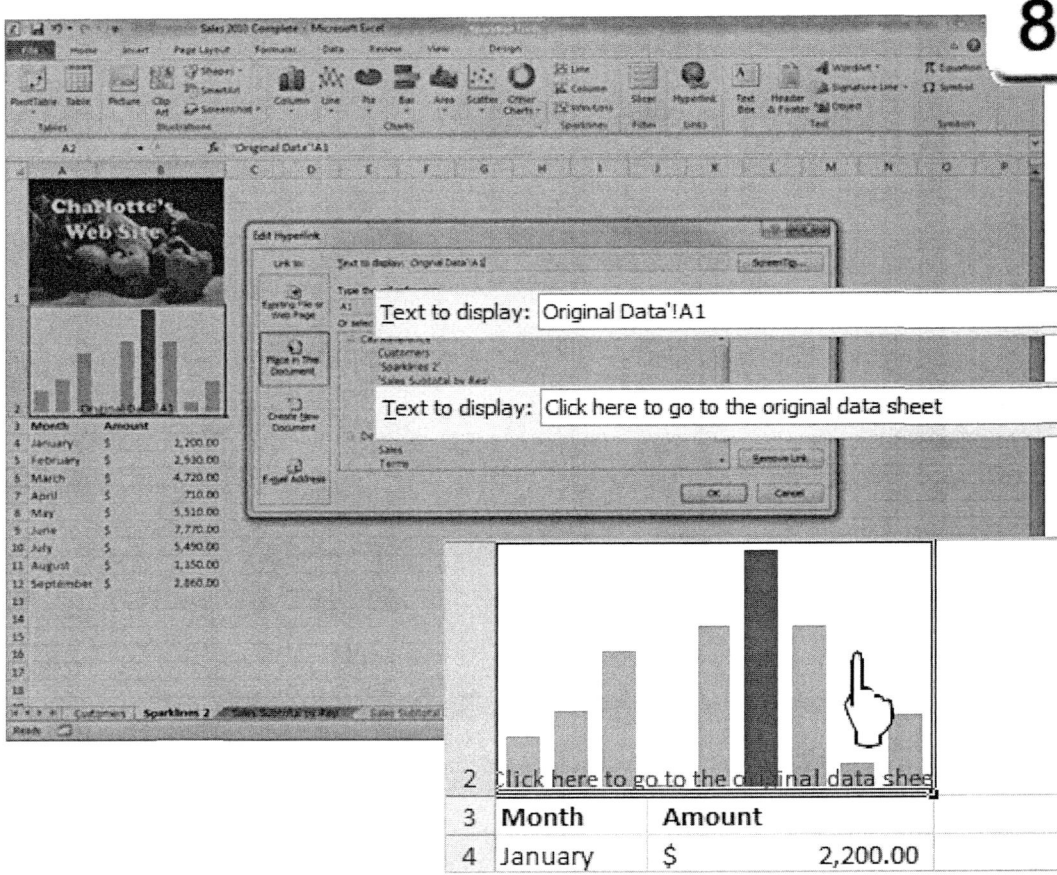

Exam 77-882: Microsoft Excel 2010 Core
2. Creating Cell Data
2.3. Apply and manipulate hyperlinks: Modify Hyperlinks

Insert-> Links-> Hyperlink

One More Useful Hyperlink

One of the best hyperlinks automatically opens an email message, adds your email address and even fills in the subject line.

9. Try This: Create an Email Link
Select Cell A14:B14
Go to **Home->Alignment-> Merge and Center**.
You should see a merged Cell in Row 14.
Type: Questions? Send me an email.

Go to **Insert-> Links-> Hyperlink**.
Click on **E-mail Address**.

Enter the E-mail address:
thecomputermama@hotmail.com
Excel will add "mailto:"

Enter the Subject:
Charlotte's Website Monthly Sales
Click **OK** to finish the link.

What Do You See? If you have Microsoft Outlook, the hyperlink should open an email that has an email address and subject. Very good....

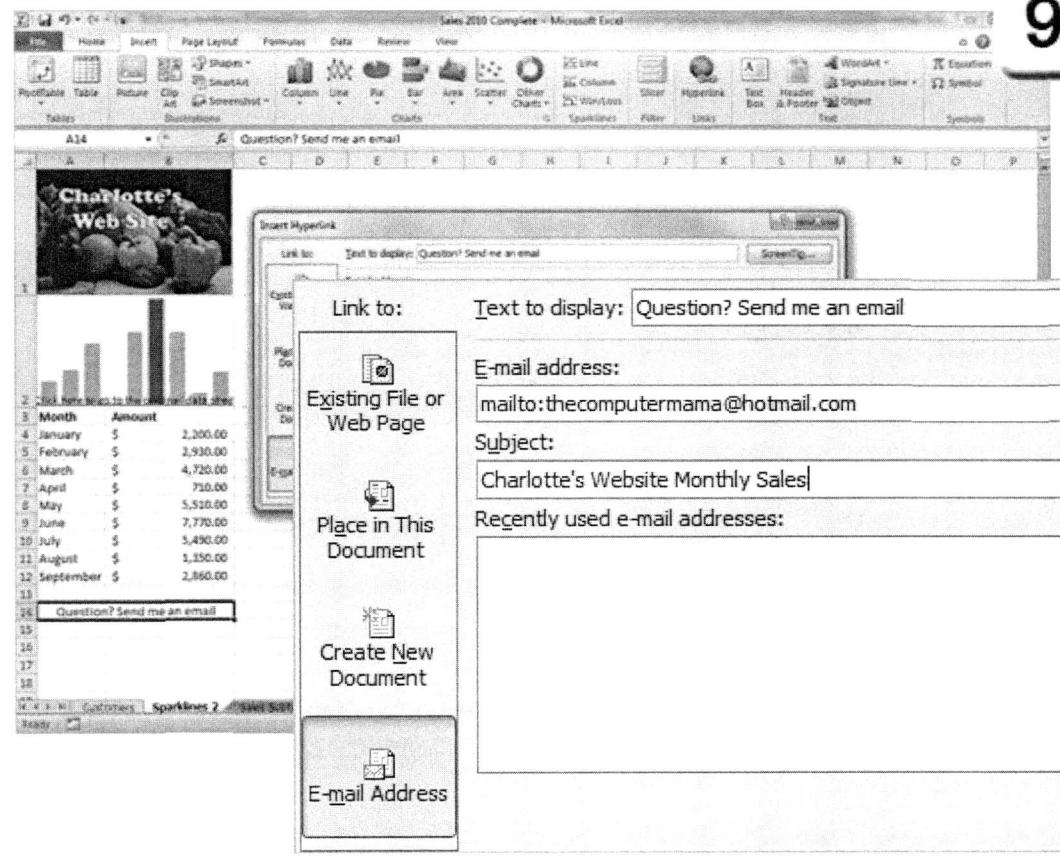

Exam 77-882: Microsoft Excel 2010 Core
2. Creating Cell Data
2.3. Apply and manipulate hyperlinks

Save As Template

Say this spreadsheet has everything you want: data, formulas, hyperlinks, even a company logo. You can save this file as a **template**.

What Is A Template? A template is a document, spreadsheet or even a form that has custom information and formatting. Templates allow you to start at a very high level of completeness, instead of opening a blank sheet. Templates save time.

Before You Begin: You can use the same Excel file you saved in the previous lesson or any sample spreadsheet if you wish.

1. Try This: Save As Template
Go to **File->Save As**.

Keep going...

File ->Save As

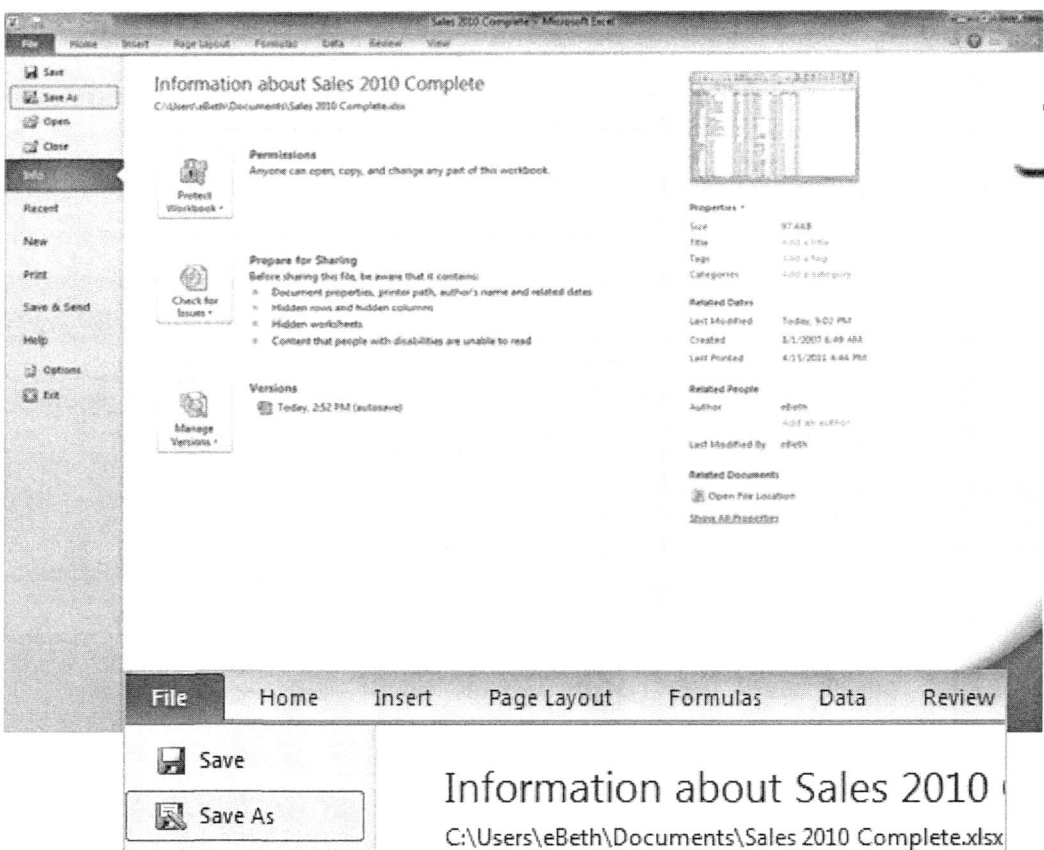

1

Exam 77-888: Microsoft Excel Expert 2010
1. Sharing and Maintaining Workbooks
1.1. Apply workbook settings, properties, and data options: Save as Template

File ->Save As-> Excel Template

Save As a Template

2. What is the File Name?
Type: Sales Template

3. What is the File Type?
By default, the file type for Excel 2007 and 2010 is Excel Workbook. A template is a different File Type. You need to choose **Excel Template** from the extensive list of file types that Microsoft Office supports.

An Excel Template is an *.xltx file type.

4. Where are you saving it? When you choose **Save as Type: Excel Template**, then Excel will switch to the default location for Templates.

Click on **Save**, please. Keep going...

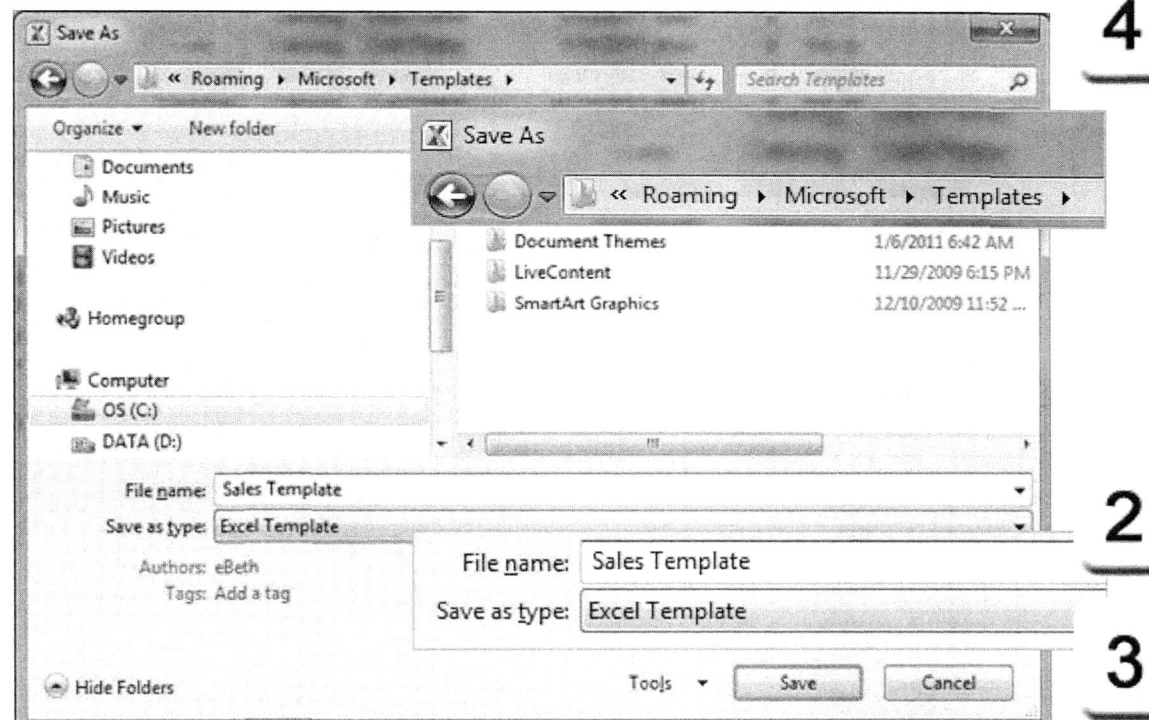

Exam 77-882: Microsoft Excel 2010 Core
7. Sharing worksheet data with other users
7.1. Share spreadsheets by using Backstage: Change File Type

Use Your Template

So, how do you use your own template?
Here are the steps.

1. Try it: Find the Templates
Go to **File->New**.
The new **Backstage** window will open.

2. What Are Your Choices?
The list of Available Templates includes:
Blank workbook
Recent Templates
Sample Templates
My Templates
New from existing

Click on **My Templates**.
Keep going...

File->New ->Templates-> My Templates

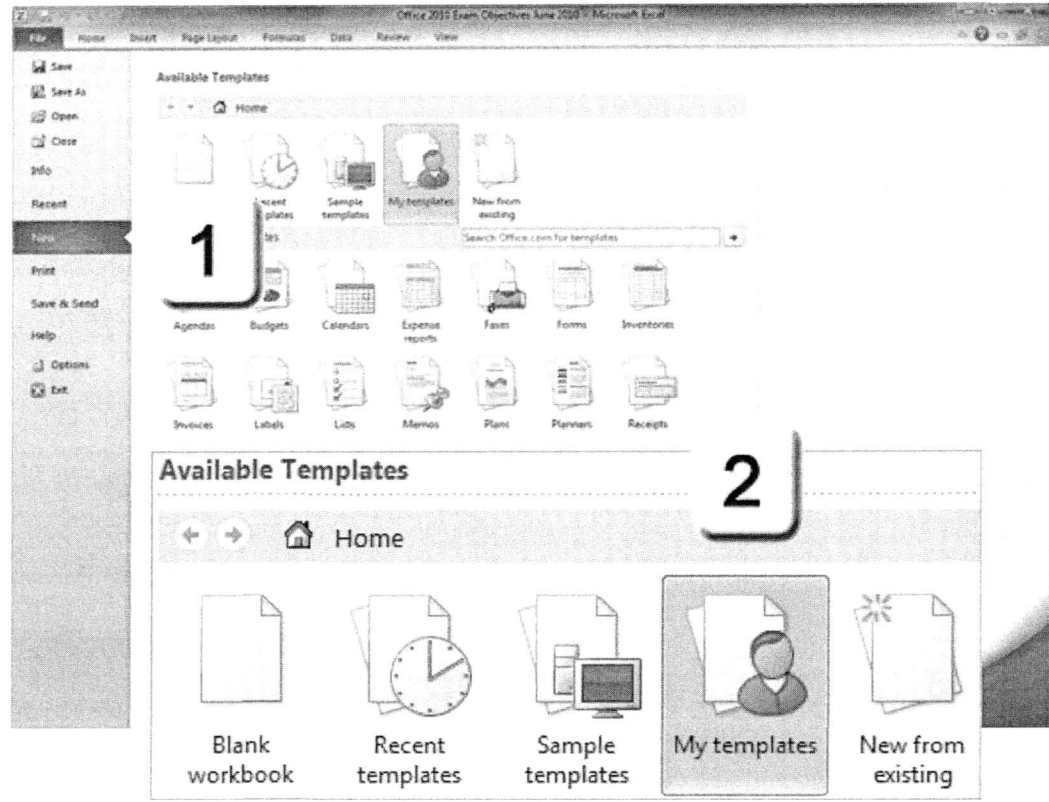

Exam 77-888: Microsoft Excel Expert 2010
1. Sharing and Maintaining Workbooks
1.1. Apply workbook settings, properties, and data options: Save as Template

A New Workbook

3. Try it: Choose a Personal Template
When you saved your own spreadsheet as a template, by default your template was saved in the Templates folder.

Now, when you go to **File->New** and click on **My Templates**, you should see your own templates the **Personal Templates**.

Double click the Sales Template to open it. Keep going...!

File->New ->Templates-> My Templates

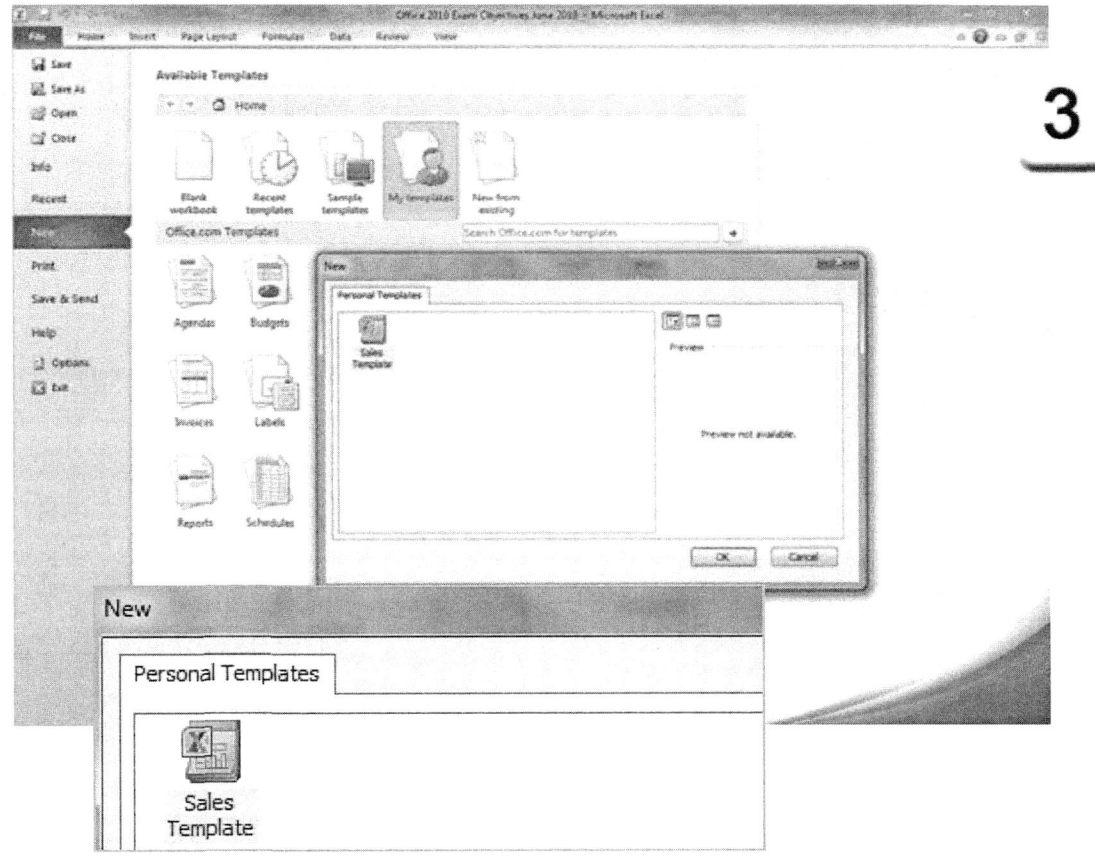

3

Exam 77-888: Microsoft Excel Expert 2010
1. Sharing and Maintaining Workbooks
1.1. Apply workbook settings, properties, and data options: Save as Template

Working with Templates

4. What Do You See? When you select your template, you will open a new workbook that is fairly complete including data, Sparklines and even a company logo that links to the website.

What Else Do You See? Look again at the Title Bar on this workbook. Does it say Sales Template1?

Sales Template1 - Microsoft Excel

This is your clue that you are working on a new workbook which you can save when you are ready.

OK, that was a good introduction to Templates. Our discussion continues with other Backstage methods for sharing this spreadsheet digitally.

Memo to Self: It may or may not say Sales Template1: it depends on how many other files you opened at this time. ;-)

File->New ->Templates-> My Templates

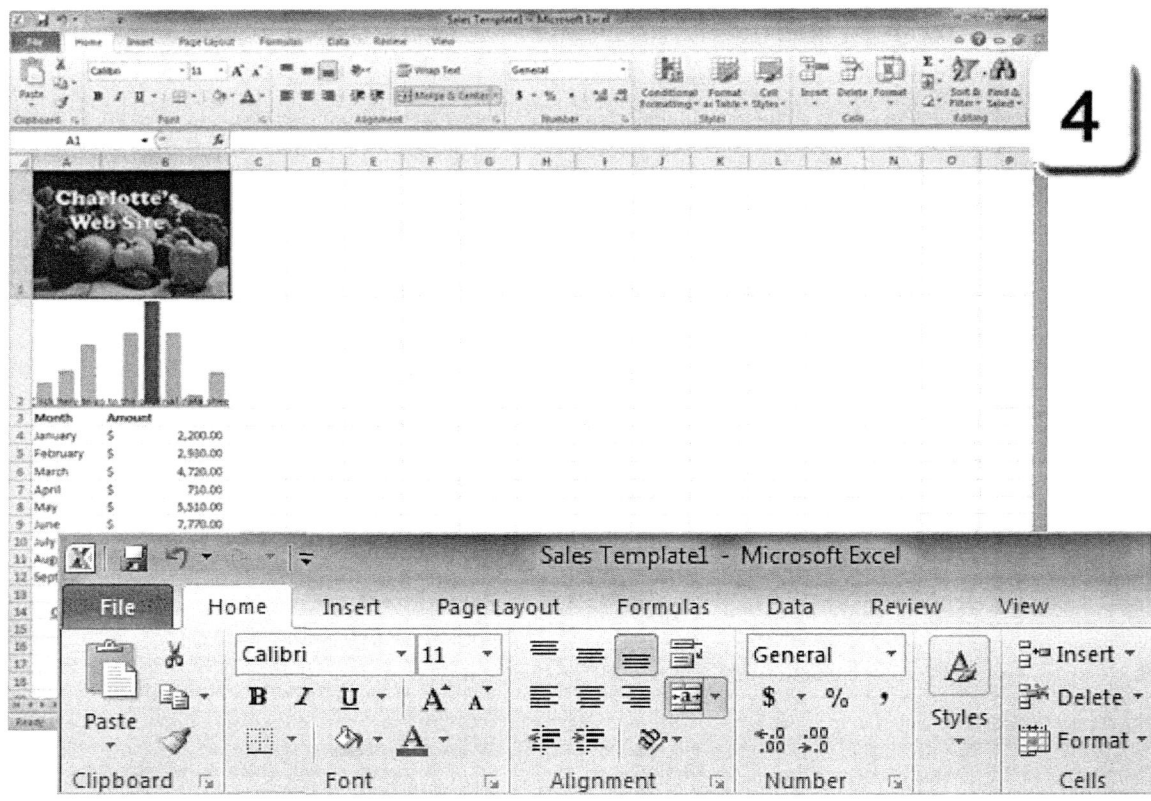

Exam 77-888: Microsoft Excel Expert 2010
1. Sharing and Maintaining Workbooks
1.1. Apply workbook settings, properties, and data options: Save as Template

Save and Send Options

The theme of this lesson is "Online and Open for Business." Microsoft Office 2010 has significantly improved the **Save and Send** options. The new Backstage makes it easier to publish and share your spreadsheets.

Online: There are several online formats that you can create with the Save As commands. We will walk through the steps to create Templates, PDF and XPS files.

Open for Business: You can also use Excel to Send your work by email.

Before You Begin: You can use the same Excel file you saved in the previous lesson or any sample spreadsheet if you wish.

Keep going...!

File ->Save and Send

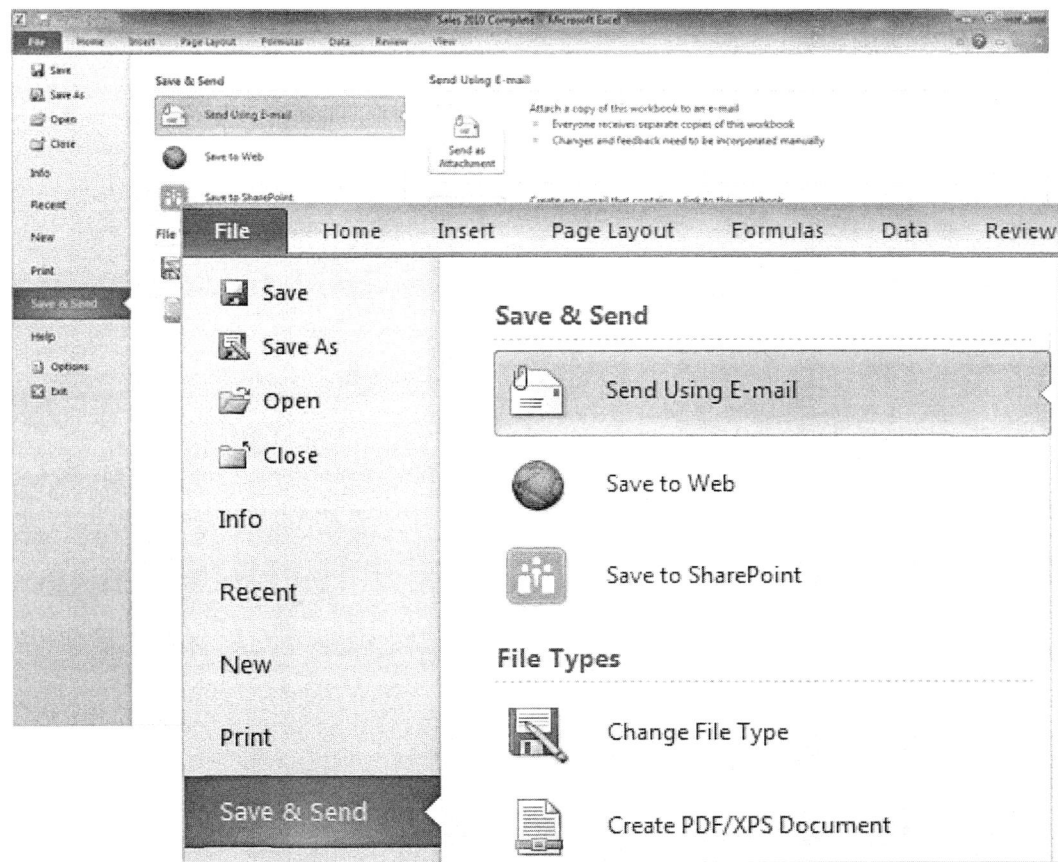

Exam 77-888: Microsoft Excel Expert 2010
4. Working with Macros and Forms
4.1. Create and manipulate macros.

Send Using E-mail

The easiest way to share your spreadsheet is to Send Using E-mail. Here are the steps.

This This: Send Using E-mail
Go to **File ->Save and Send.**
Click on **Send Using E-mail.**

What Do You See? The options include:

Send as Attachment adds this file to the email as an attachment.

Create Link is useful if this spreadsheet is shared online in a folder everyone can access, say a SharePoint Portal.

Send as PDF converts your spreadsheet into an Adobe Acrobat format.

Send as XPS converts your spreadsheet into the new Microsoft version of a PDF.

Send as Internet Fax creates a Fax using an Internet Fax service.

File ->Save and Send-> Send Using E-mail

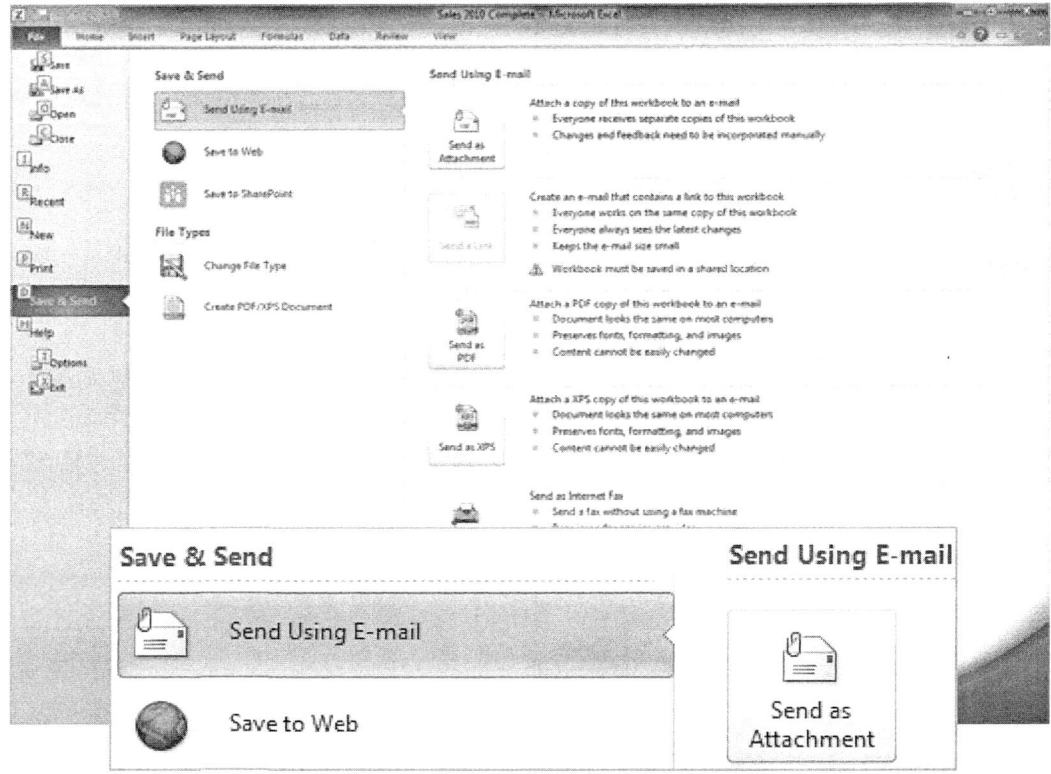

Exam 77-882: Microsoft Excel 2010 Core
7. Sharing worksheet data with other users
7.1. Share spreadsheets by using Backstage: Send Using E-Mail

Send as Attachment

Try it: Send as Attachment
Go to **File ->Save and Send.**
Go to **Send Using E-mail.**
Click on **Send as Attachment.**

What Do You See? When you choose **Send as Attachment**, a new message will open with the spreadsheet included.

Memo to Self: The screen capture on this page shows a new message in Microsoft Outlook 2010. The option to Send as Attachment may not work if you use webmail (such as Gmail, Yahoo mail or AOL) as your default email program.

File ->Save and Send-> Send Using E-mail->Send as Attachment

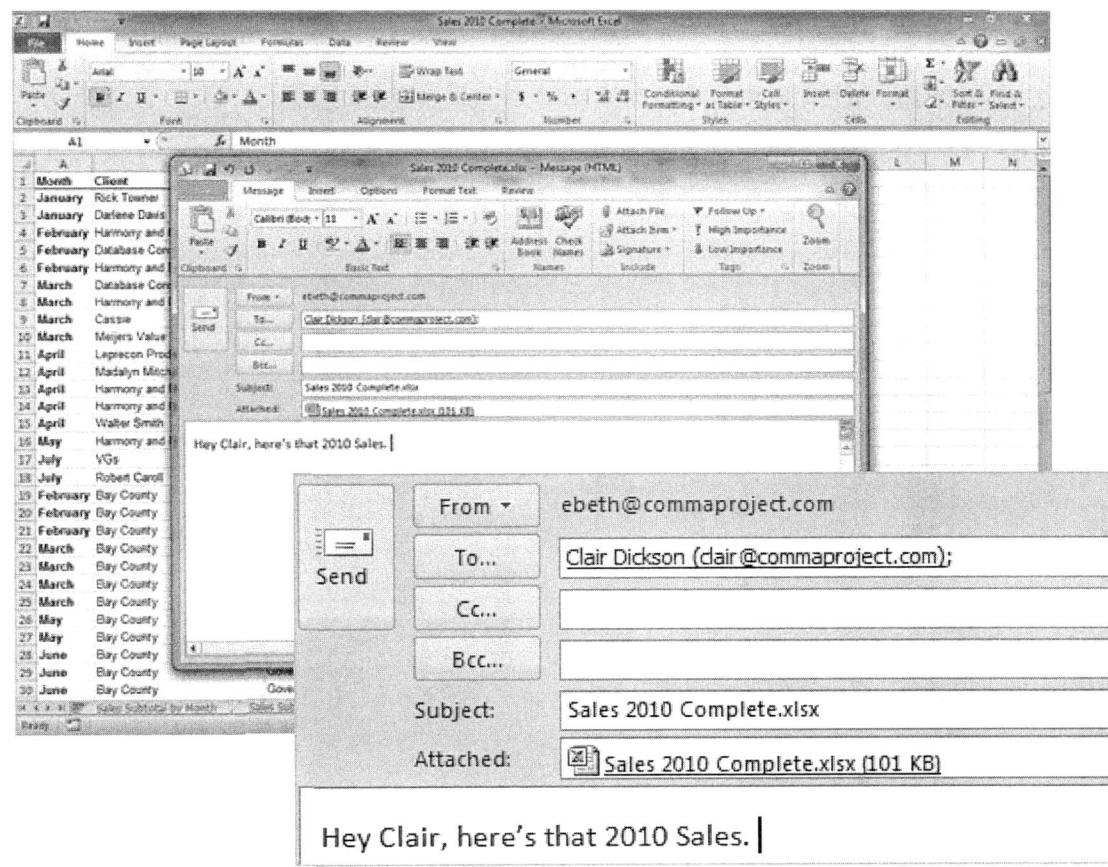

Exam 77-882: Microsoft Excel 2010 Core
7. Sharing worksheet data with other users
7.1. Share spreadsheets by using Backstage: Send Using E-Mail

Send as Internet Fax

A Fax machine sends a facsimile of the original document. It may be a contract or a legal document that has been signed. A Fax uses telephone technology. Many businesses still have a dedicated phone line for the fax machine.

Say you needed to Fax this spreadsheet, but your business runs on cell phones-no dial-up phones. You can still fax the spreadsheet even if you don't have a fax machine. Here are the steps.

1. Try it: Send as an Internet Fax
Go to **File ->Save and Send.**
Go to **Send Using E-mail.**
Click on **Send as Internet Fax.**

Keep going...

File ->Save and Send-> Send Using E-mail->Send as Internet Fax

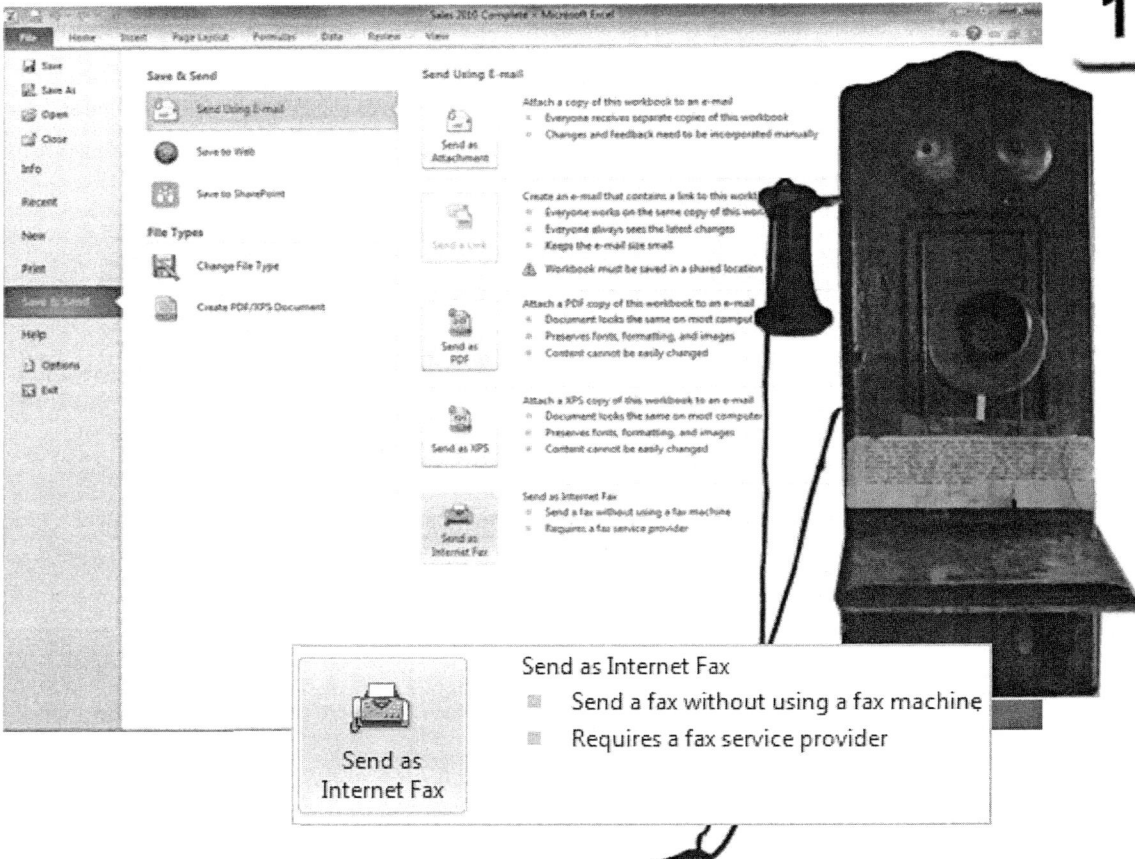

Exam 77-882: Microsoft Excel 2010 Core
7. Sharing worksheet data with other users
7.1. Share spreadsheets by using Backstage: Send as Internet Fax

Internet Fax Options

2. What Do You See? The first time you try to send an Internet Fax you will be prompted to set up an **Internet Fax Service Provider**.

Microsoft Office Marketplace offers links to the **Internet Fax Service Providers** who specialize in faxing from Microsoft Office.

All of these services have a Free Trial so you can test this option and see if it worth the monthly service fees.

File ->Save and Send-> Send Using E-mail->Send as Internet Fax

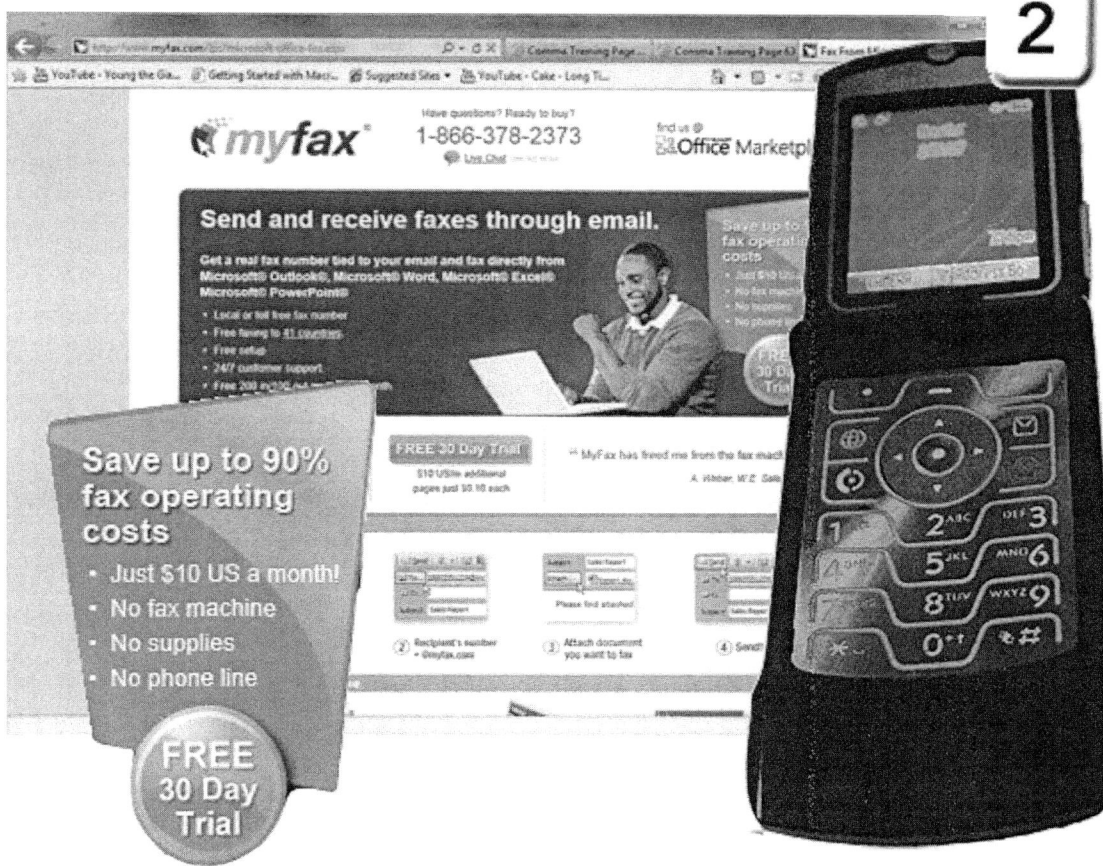

Exam 77-882: Microsoft Excel 2010 Core
7. Sharing worksheet data with other users
7.1. Share spreadsheets by using Backstage: Send as Internet Fax

Save to Web

Cloud computing gives people and businesses the option of saving their work on an Internet server. Many businesses already use cloud computing such as Gmail for their email.

The benefit of saving to the web is backup, backup, backup. Your data is stored on a commercial server that you can access from any computer if your hardware melts down.

Microsoft Office has an option to save your workbooks to the Web in private, secure folders that you can choose to share. It is called **SkyDrive**. Here are the steps.

1. Consider This: Save to the Web
Go to **File ->Save and Send.**
Go to **Send Using E-mail.**
Click on **Save to Web.**

2. What Would You See? You will be prompted to authenticate yourself with a Windows Live ID. You can use a Hotmail, Messenger or Xbox password. You can also create a new account. Keep going..

File ->Save and Send-> Send Using E-mail->Save to Web

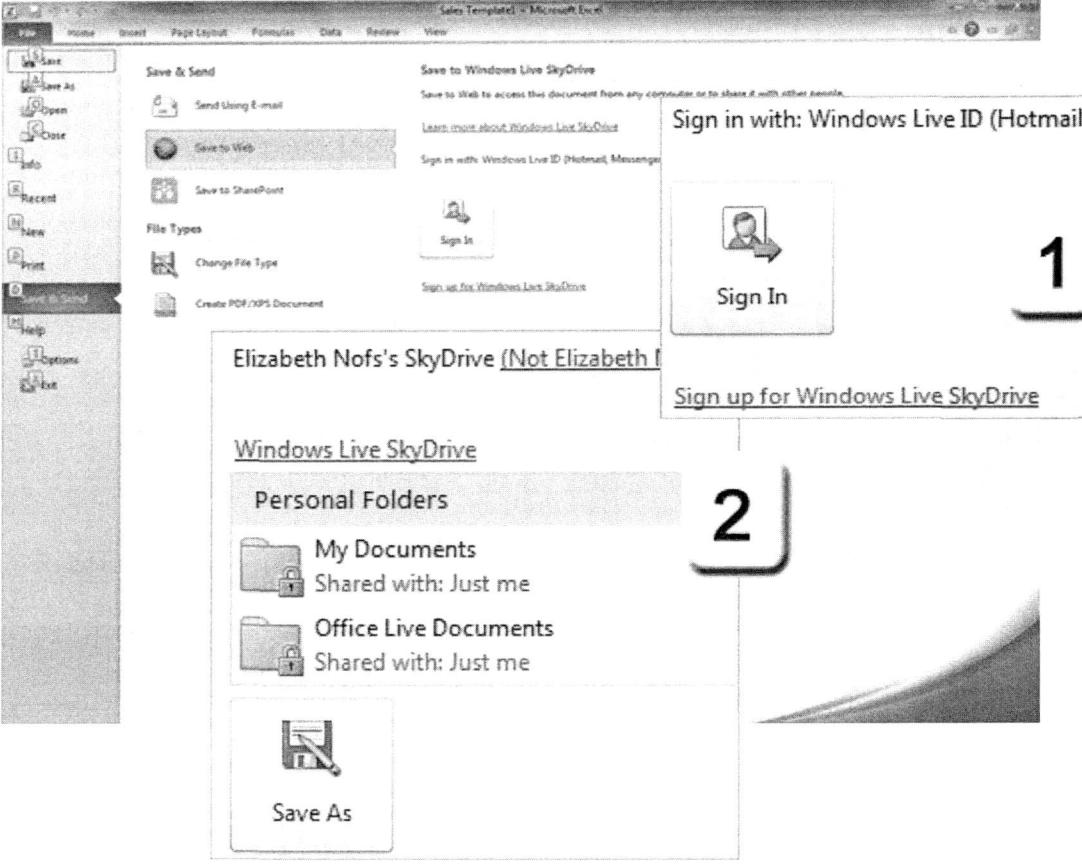

Exam 77-882: Microsoft Excel 2010 Core
7. Sharing worksheet data with other users
7.1. Share spreadsheets by using Backstage: Save to Web (SkyDrive)

Using SkyDrive

SkyDrive, like webmail, can be accessed from any computer, anywhere. Your data is stored on a robust commercial server, so if your laptop goes up in smoke, your work would still be available.

3. Consider This, Too: Log into SkyDrive

In the example on this page, the workbook was saved to SkyDrive with a Windows Live ID password from Hotmail. When this author logged into Hotmail, SkyDrive was one of the Windows Live options.

Memo to Self: By default, the SkyDrive folders are private. I can choose to create a separate folder for Work which can be shared with my team.

File ->Save and Send-> Send Using E-mail->Save to Web

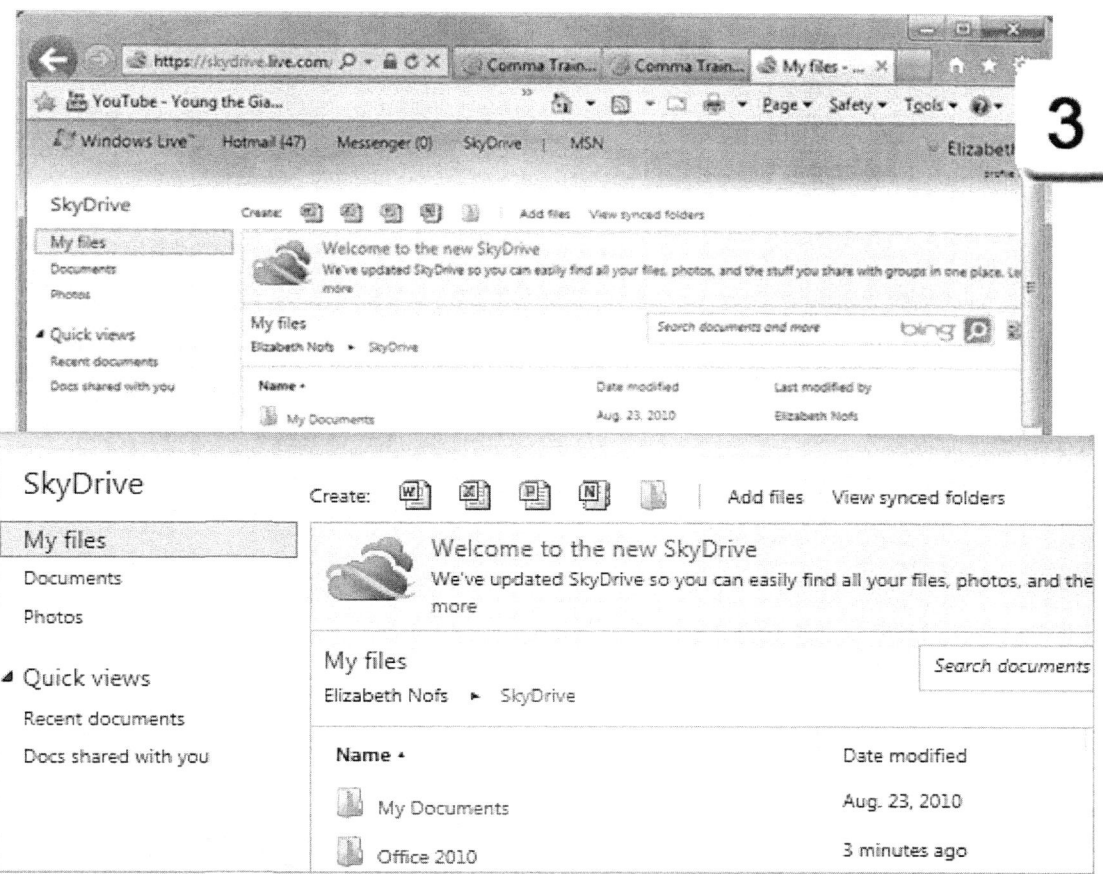

Exam 77-882: Microsoft Excel 2010 Core
7. Sharing worksheet data with other users
7.1. Share spreadsheets by using Backstage: Save to Web (SkyDrive)

Change File Type

When you share your work with people in other companies, sometimes even different countries, you may need to save your work in a different file format. Microsoft Excel can convert your workbook into many new and legacy file formats.

Try it: Sample
Go to **File ->Save and Send**.
Click on **Change File Type**.

The Workbook File Types are:
Workbook
OpenDocument Spreadsheet
Macro-Enabled Workbook
Excel 97-2003 Workbook
Template
Binary Workbook

The Other File Types are:
Text (Tab delimited)
Formatted Text (Space delimited)
CSV (Comma delimited)
Save as Another File Type

File ->Save and Send-> Change File Type

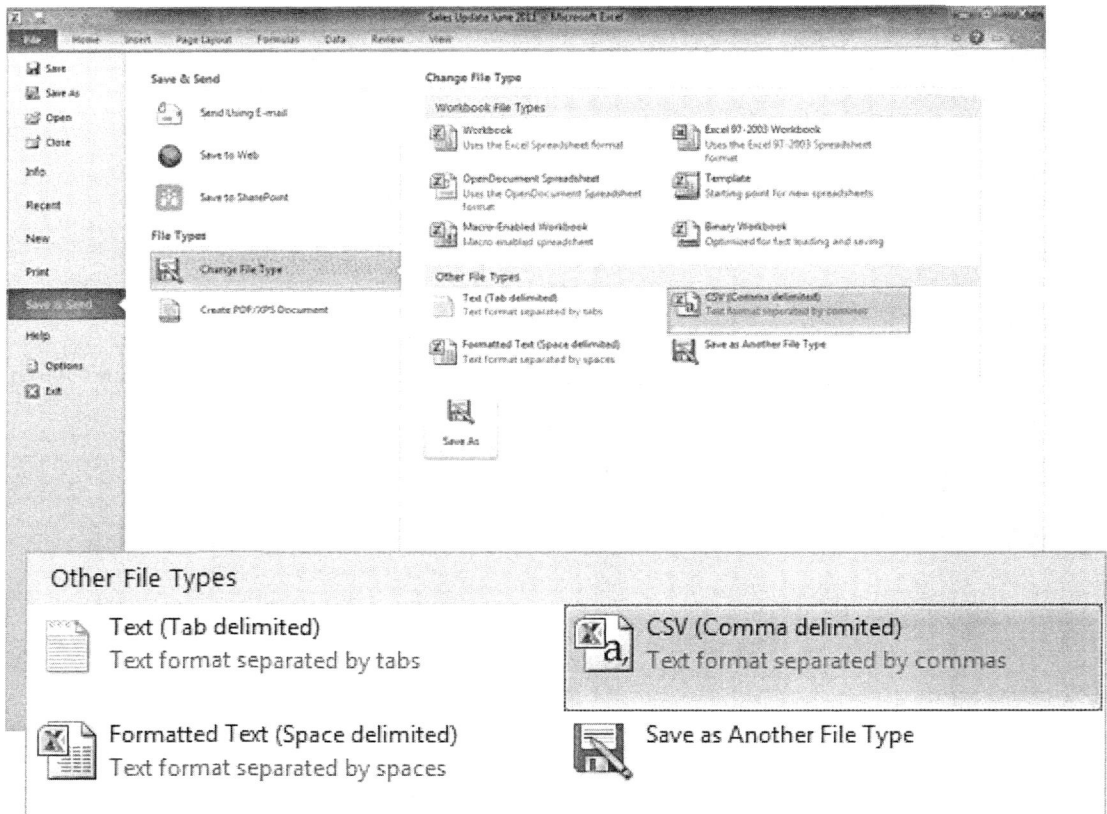

Exam 77-882: Microsoft Excel 2010 Core
7. Sharing worksheet data with other users
7.1. Share spreadsheets by using Backstage: Change File Type

HOME

Take Two

Save as PDF

PDf means **Portable Document File**. The PDF format was developed by Adobe Systems in 1993 as a way to represent documents in a way that was independent of which program created the document or which operating system might be running on your computer-today or 20 years ago.

XPS means **XML Paper Specification**. XPS is the open source format developed by Microsoft in 2009. It is also independent of software or operating system.

1. Try it: Save as PDF or XPS
Go to **File ->Save and Send**.
Go to **Send Using E-mail**
Click on **Create PDF/XPS**.

Keep going.. let's look at the options.

File ->Save and Send-> Send Using E-mail->Create PDf/XPS

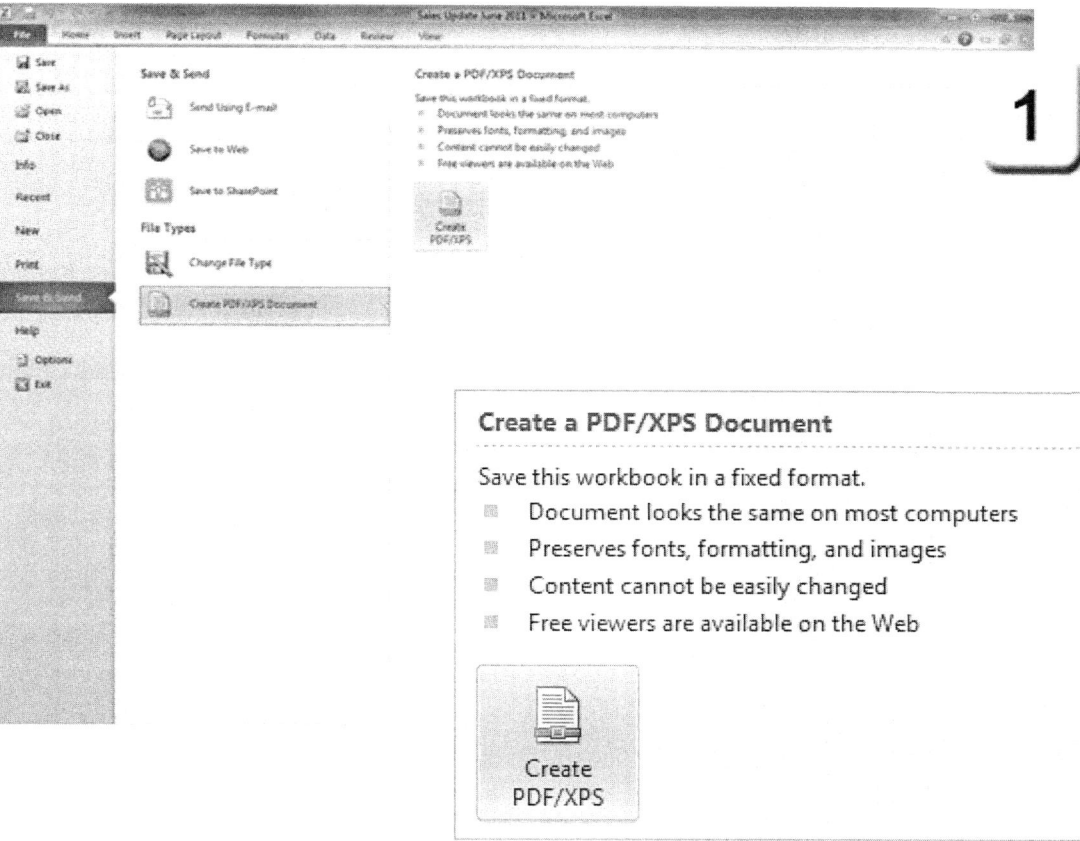

Create a PDF/XPS Document

Save this workbook in a fixed format.

- Document looks the same on most computers
- Preserves fonts, formatting, and images
- Content cannot be easily changed
- Free viewers are available on the Web

Create PDF/XPS

Exam 77-882: Microsoft Excel 2010 Core
7. Sharing worksheet data with other users
7.1. Share spreadsheets by using Backstage: Create PDF/XPS

File ->Save and Send-> Send Using E-mail->Create PDf/XPS

Simple PDF Options

When you save a spreadsheet as a PDF, you will be prompted to browse to a folder to save your new PDF file. Here are the options

2. Try This: Edit the PDF Options
Save as type: PDF (*.pdf)

Optimize the PDF

Microsoft Excel offer two levels of resolution for the PDF file: **Standard** and **Minimum**. The **Standard** format has a higher resolution for graphics so that the images will print well. The **Minimum** format compromises on image size and quality to reduce the file size and make the downloads faster.

The completed PDF file will open in Adobe Acrobat, a free reader program that is installed on all PCs.

Memo to Self: A workbook that was saved as a PDf file will NOT open in Excel, again.

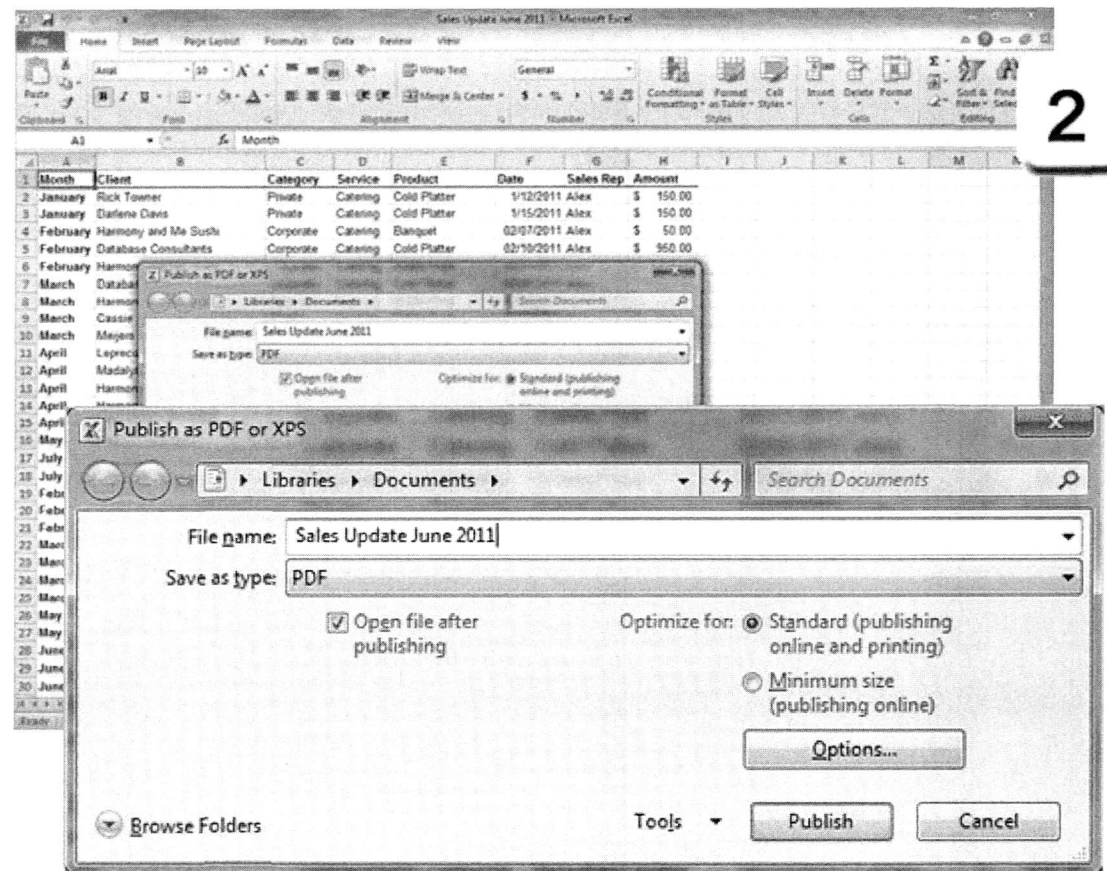

Exam 77-882: Microsoft Excel 2010 Core
7. Sharing worksheet data with other users
7.1. Share spreadsheets by using Backstage: Create PDF/XPS

Send as XPS

You can convert a workbook to a PDF or an XPS file and then send it as an email attachment. It is a "one-click" process that works rather effectively. Here are the steps.

Try it: Save as PDF or XPS
Go to **File ->Save and Send.**
Go to **Send Using E-mail**
Click on **Send as PDF/XPS.**

What Do You See? When you choose **Send as PDF/XPS**, a new message will open with the XPS file attached.

Another Reminder: The image on this page shows a new email in Microsoft Outlook 2010. The option to **Send as Attachment** may not work if you use webmail (such as Gmail, Yahoo mail or AOL) as your default email.

File ->Save and Send-> Send Using E-mail->Send as XPS

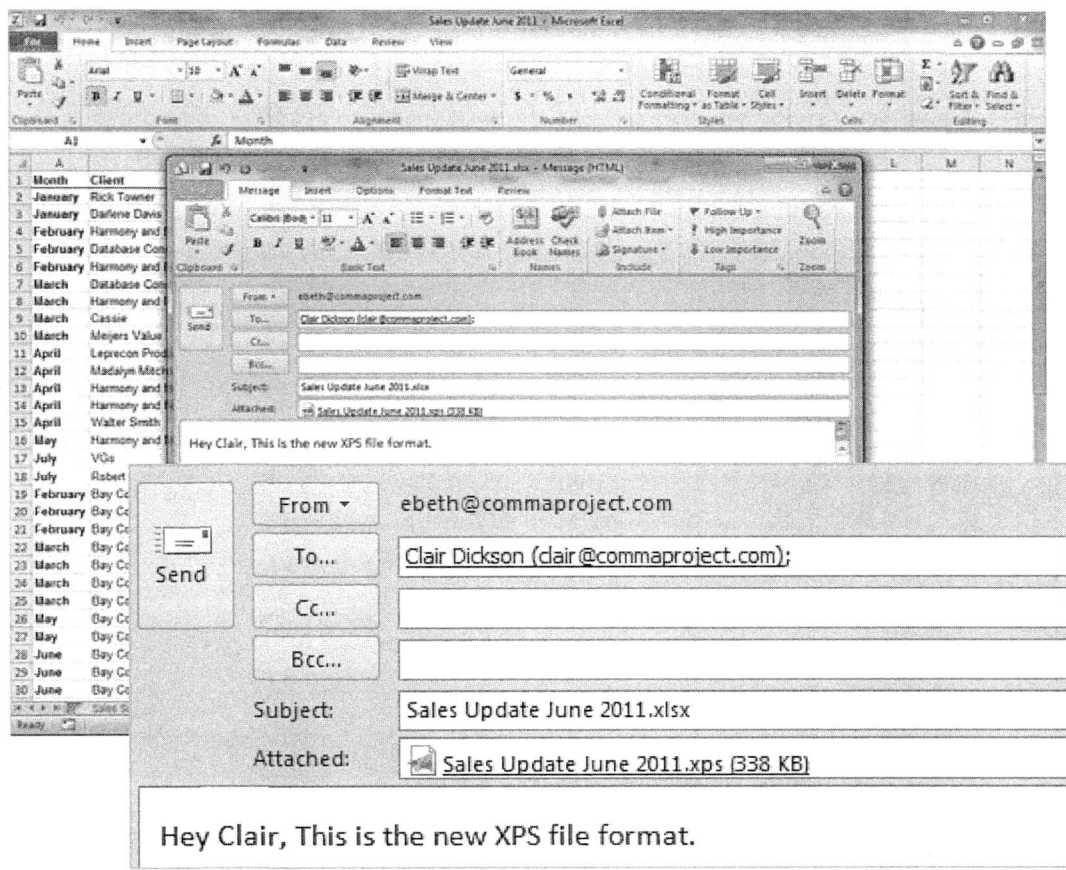

Exam 77-882: Microsoft Excel 2010 Core
7. Sharing worksheet data with other users
7.1. Share spreadsheets by using Backstage: Create PDF/XPS

Extra for Experts: Formulas

The *Intermediate Guide to Microsoft Excel 2010* demonstrated a dozen or so essential formulas.

Many spreadsheets use recursive or very complicated math functions, such as computing energy or figuring out the cost per unit of an area or volume. You may have wondered what can you do to make sure the math is right.

PEMDAS is an acronym that was invented to help folks remember the Oder of Operations. All equations follow PEMDAS, no matter how complex or simple the formula may be.

1. Consdier This: The Order of Operation
(P) Parentheses, first
(E) Exponents (or Powers)
(M) Multiplication
(D) Division
(A) Addition
(S) Subtraction

Keep going...

Formulas ->Formula Auditing

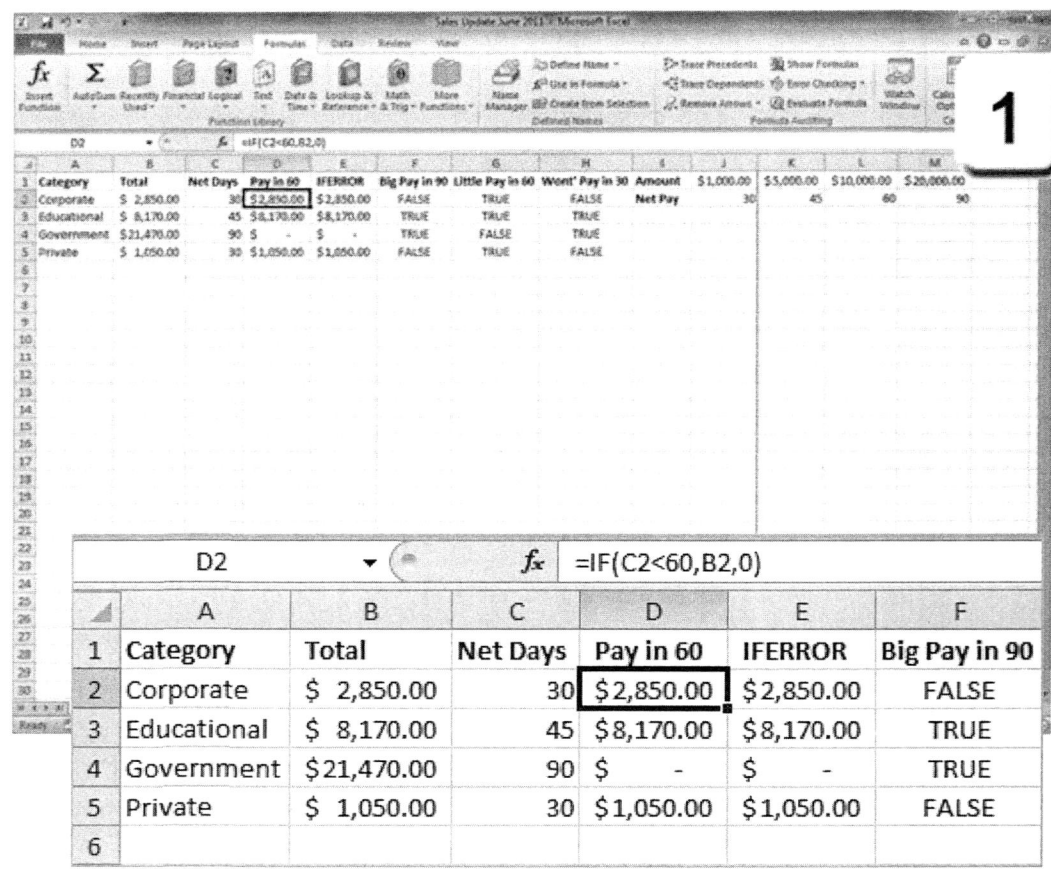

	A	B	C	D	E	F
1	Category	Total	Net Days	Pay in 60	IFERROR	Big Pay in 90
2	Corporate	$ 2,850.00	30	$2,850.00	$2,850.00	FALSE
3	Educational	$ 8,170.00	45	$8,170.00	$8,170.00	TRUE
4	Government	$21,470.00	90	$ -	$ -	TRUE
5	Private	$ 1,050.00	30	$1,050.00	$1,050.00	FALSE
6						

D2 f_x =IF(C2<60,B2,0)

Exam 77-882: Microsoft Excel 2010 Core
5. Applying Formulas and Functions
5.2. Enforce precedence: Precedence of operators

Order of Precedence

By default, Microsoft Excel evaluates formulas based on this Order of Precedence:
1. Reference operators: Colon, space, comma
2. Negation: For example a negative number -1
3. Percentage: Percent (%)
4. Exponentiation: Raising to a power (^)
5. Multiply (*) and Divide (/)
6. Plus (+) and Minus (-)
7. Concatenation: Combining text (&)
8. Comparison: Equals, Less than, Greater than.

2. Consider This: Review the Math
Look at the simple equation on this page. Microsoft Excel reads a formula from Left to Right. This equation has Multiplication and Addition. The answer will be quite different, depending on how you solve the equation.

So, how would Excel solve this problem?
PEMDAS: add up whatever is between the parenthesis. Then multiply the sum of the numbers by 0.25.

Keep going...

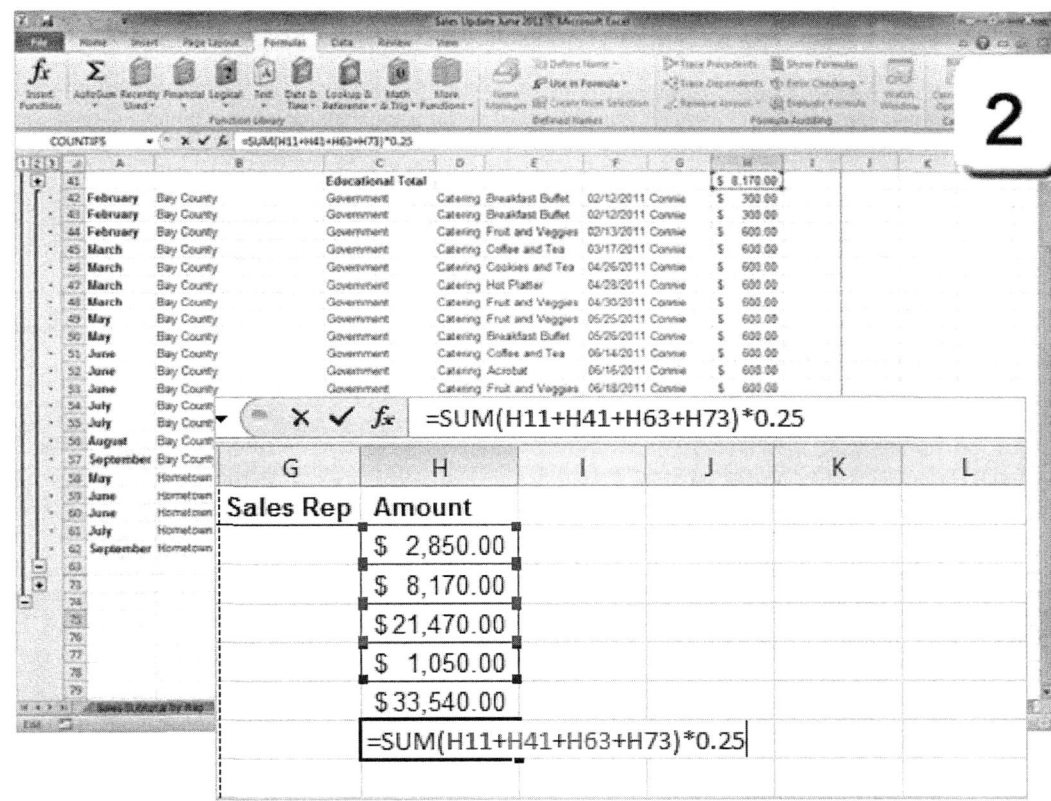

G	H	I	J	K	L
Sales Rep	Amount				
	$ 2,850.00				
	$ 8,170.00				
	$21,470.00				
	$ 1,050.00				
	$33,540.00				
	=SUM(H11+H41+H63+H73)*0.25				

=SUM(H11+H41+H63+H73)*0.25

Exam 77-882: Microsoft Excel 2010 Core
5. Applying Formulas and Functions
5.2. Enforce precedence: Precedence using parenthesis

Evaluating Formulas
You can evaluate formulas in Microsoft Excel. The little formula auditing tool has some interesting capabilities.

3. Consider This: Evaluate a Formula
In the example on this page, the formula refers to several cells that are calculated in a different spreadsheet. When a cell reference, such as Cell H11, is highlighted, you can **Step Into** the cell and look at the formula that goes with it.

Way cool technology.

Formulas ->Formula Auditing->Evaluate Formula

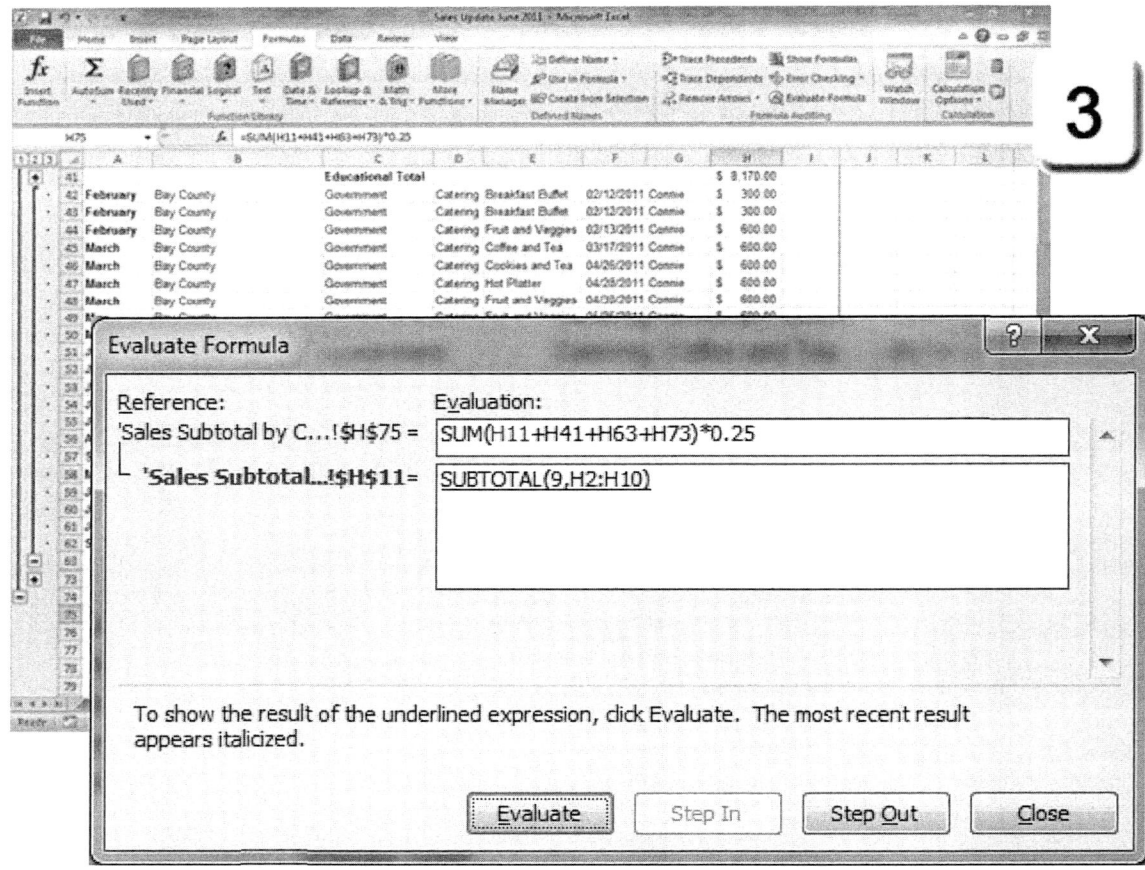

Exam 77-882: Microsoft Excel 2010 Core
5. Applying Formulas and Functions
5.2. Enforce precedence: Order of Evaluation

Take Two

Formula Calculations

These lessons have focused on formulas and more formulas. By default, the workbook calculations are automatic.

Try it: Enable the Calculations
Open any sample spreadsheet you created in the previous lessons.

Go to **Formulas ->Calculation**.
Click on **Calculation Options**.

What Do You See? The options include:
Automatic
Automatic Except for Data Table
Manual

What Else Do You See? The little buttons to the right of Calculation Options are:
Calculate Now
Calculate Sheet

These buttons are useful when the Calculation is set to Manual.

Formulas ->Calculation->Calculation Options

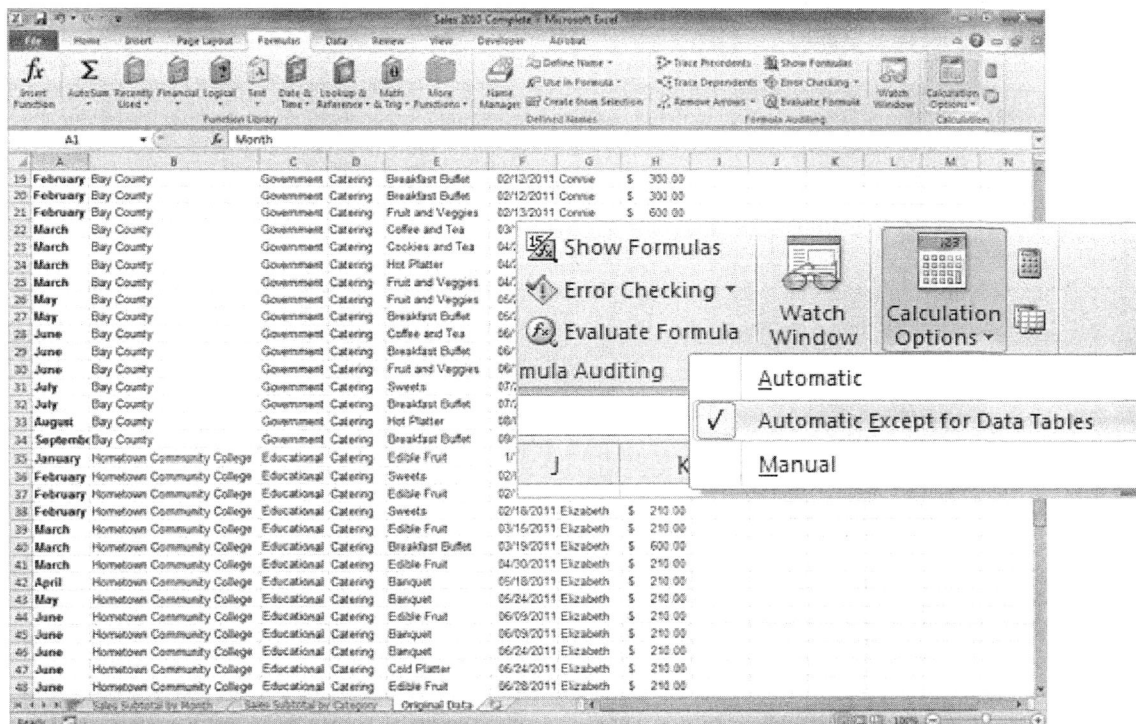

Exam 77-888: Microsoft Excel Expert 2010
2. Applying Formulas and Functions
2.2. Manipulate formula options: Enable Automatic Calculation Options

Take Two

Iterative Calculations

How many times does Excel repeat a calculation? Once? Twice? Say you make a mistake, a circular reference that adds itself to itself, then the computer would calculate the same formula forever. You can set the **iterative calculation** in the Backstage.

Try it: Set iterative Calculation Options
Open any sample spreadsheet you created in the previous lessons.

Go to **File ->Options->Formulas.**
There is a check mark for Enable iterative calculation. The default settings are:
Maximum Iterations: 100
Maximum Change: 0.001

The Maximum Change is the smallest change that you will accept between calculations. The smaller the number, the more accurate the result and the more time Excel needs to recalculate a worksheet

File ->Options-> Formulas

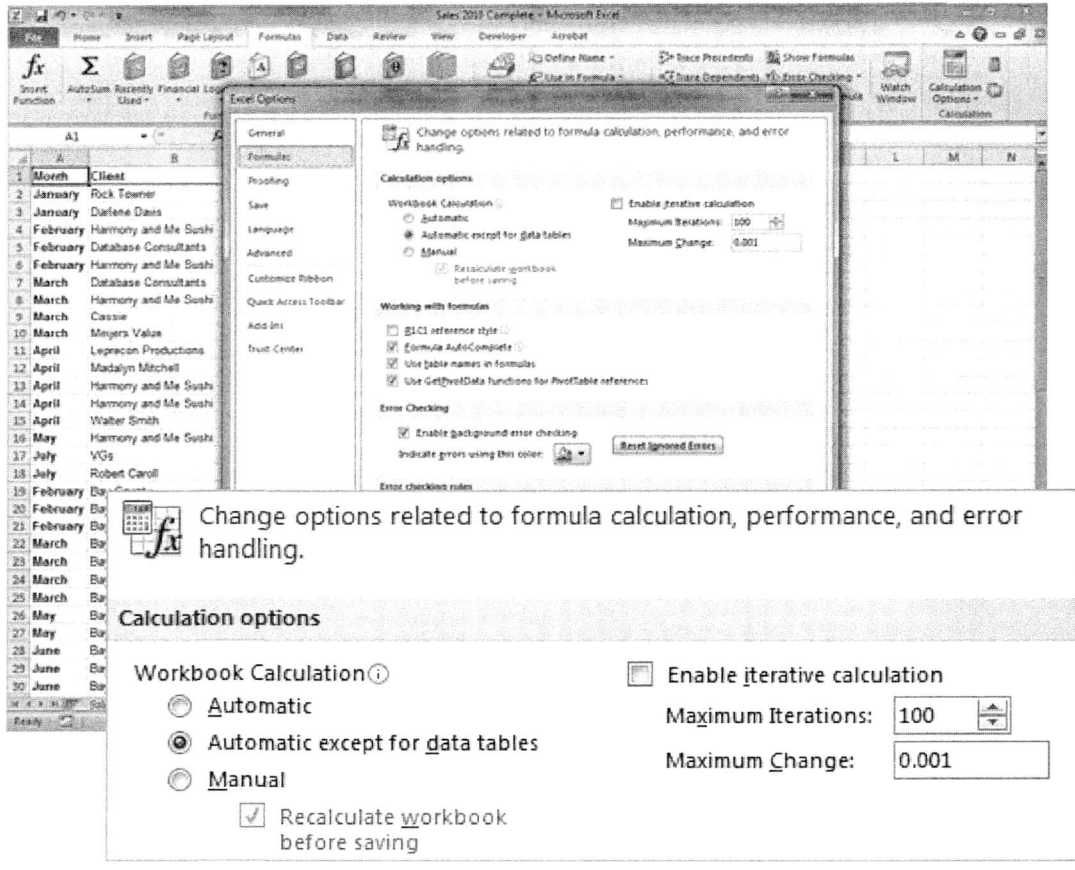

Exam 77-888: Microsoft Excel Expert 2010
2. Applying Formulas and Functions
2.2. Manipulate formula options: Set Iterative Calculation Options

Intermediate Excel 2010 Page 222 of 230

Summary

The goal of this lesson was to create a spreadsheet that is as interesting and informative as a web page. We began by creating little Sparklines that would visualize the data.

In addition to the Sparklines, we focused on improving **navigation** by formatting the Sheet tabs with color, position, grouping and **hyperlinks**. Finally, we looked at several **Save and Send** options.

This completes the Intermediate Guide to Excel. In many ways, the Intermediate examples are much more difficult that the Advanced ones: probably all that math and formula stuff...eeep.

Well, you done real good. Say you got a whole bunch of cookies and shared them with your friend.

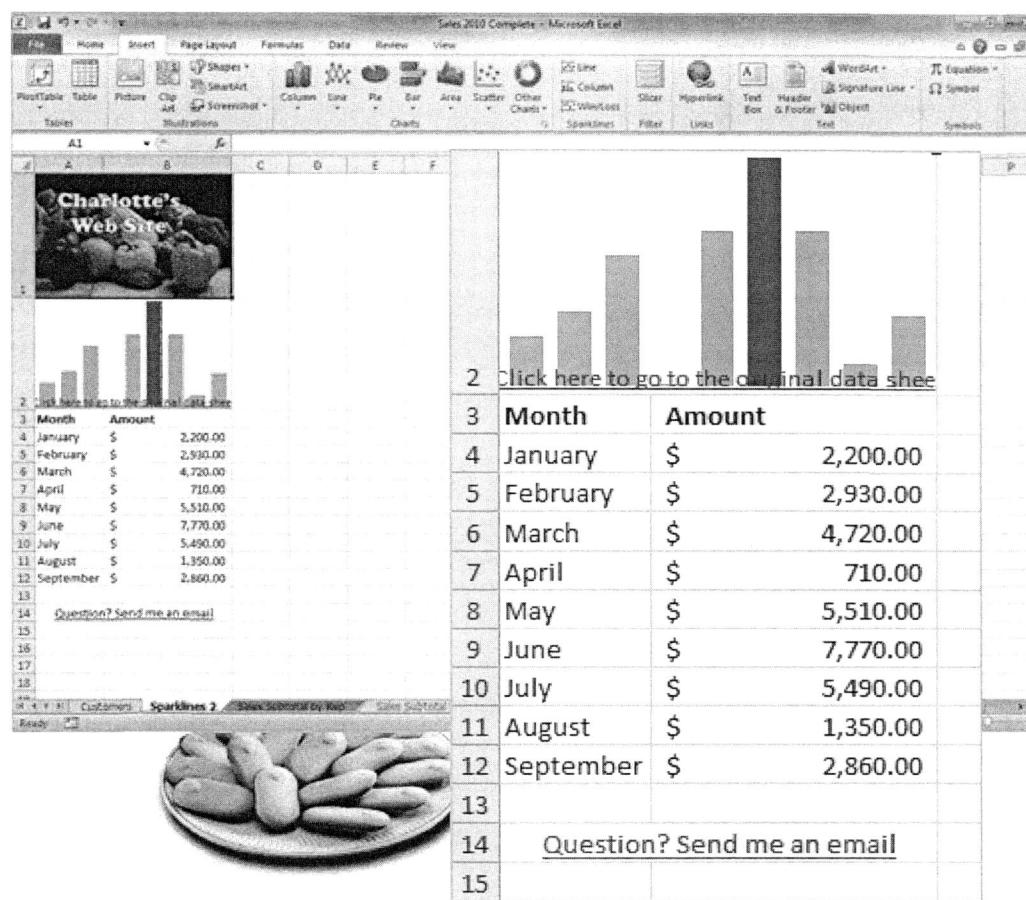

Appendix: Hot Keys

Hot Keys and **Short Cut Keys** are quick, efficient ways of using the keyboard to complete a task. **Hot Keys** are a new set of options that are available in Office 2010.

Short Cut Keys are Legacy Commands from the old days.

Hot Keys begin by typing ALT
The Home Ribbon uses H.
The File Menu uses F.

Short Cut Keys begin by typing CTRL
These commands go back to when computers did not always have a mouse! So, how did they select the Cells without a mouse? Here are the steps.

Try It: Select Cells with a Keyboard
Go to top-left Cell of the range.
Press **F8** on the keyboard.
Go to bottom-left Cell of the range.
Press **ESC.**

Hot Key	Pathway
ALT+HVP	Home->Clipboard->Paste
ALT+HX	Home->Clipboard->Cut
ALT+HC	Home->Clipboard->Copy
ALT+HP	Home->Clipboard->Format Painter
ALT+HII	Home→Insert→Insert Cells
ALT+HIR	Home→Insert→Insert Sheet Rows
ALT+HIC	Home→Insert→Insert Sheet Columns
ALT+HIS	Home→Insert→Insert Sheet
ALT+HDD	Home→Cells→Delete->Delete Cells
ALT+HDR	Home→Cells→Delete->Delete Rows
ALT+HDC	Home→Cells→Delete->Delete Columns
ALT+HDS	Home→Cells→Delete->Delete Sheet
ALT+HEA	Home→Editing→Clear->Clear All
ALT+HEF	Home→Editing→Clear->Clear Formats
ALT+FS	File→Save
ALT+FA	File→Save As
ALT+FO	File→Open
ALT+FC	File→Close
ALT+FN	File→New
ALT+FD	File→Save and Send

Short Cut	Pathway
CTRL+O	File->Open
CTRL+S	File->Save
CTRL+W	File->Close
CTRL+D	File->Properties
CTRL+P	File→Print
CTRL+Q	File→Exit
CTRL+X	Edit→Cut
CTRL+C	Edit→Copy
CTRL+P	Edit→Paste
CTRL+Z	Edit→Undo!

Keyboard	Function
CTRL+A	Select All
CTRL+HOME	Select First Cell
CTRL+End	Select Last Cell
CTRL+Down Arrow	Go to Last Cell in the Column
CTRL+Up Arrow	Go to First Cell in the Column
CTRL+Right Arrow	Go to Last Cell in the Row
CTRL+Left Arrow	Go to First Cell in the Row

Exam 77-882: Microsoft Excel 2010 Core
3. Formatting Cells and Worksheets
3.1. Apply and modify cell formats: Hot Keys

Practice Activities

Lesson: Excel-Online

Try This: Do the following steps

1. Open the Spreadsheet: <u>**Rainy Day Savings Training. xlsx**</u>

2. Insert 2 blank lines at the top of the Office Training sheet.

3. Insert a column Sparkline showing the attendance for training in January of 2008.

4. Insert a hyperlink on the heading Microsoft Office Training to www.microsoft.com

5. Go to the Ethics training sheet. Insert 2 blanks links at the top.

6. Insert a Sparkline showing the attendance of Ethics Training for day 1 for all of 2008

7. Recolor the Sparkline chart to be gray

8. Resize the Sparkline chart to be taller

9. Go to the Sales training sheet. Insert 2 blank lines at the top.

10. Insert a Sparkline showing the attendance of Sales Training for the entire period shown.

Save the file as Your Name Excel Online Practice

Test Yourself

1. A Sparkline is a little chart that helps people to see trends.
a. True
b. False
Tip: Intermediate Excel, page 178

2. Where is the command for Sparklines?
a. Insert-> Sparkline
b. Insert-> Chart-> Sparkline
c. View-> Sparklines
Tip: Intermediate Excel, page 178

3. Which is a type of Sparkline? (Select all correct answers)
a. Line
b. Column
c. Win/Loss
Tip: Intermediate Excel, page 180

4. Sparklines have Styles
a. True
b. False
Tip: Intermediate Excel, page 181

5. A Sparkline chart has many of the formatting options of a regular chart.
a. True
b. False
Tip: Intermediate Excel, page 184

6. Which is the way to rename a Spreadsheet? (Select all correct answers)
a. Double-click the spreadsheet tab, then type a new name
b. Right click the tab and select Rename Sheet
Tip: Intermediate Excel, page 185

7. Which is the command to insert a new sheet in a workbook?
(Select all correct answers)
a. Home-> Cells-> Insert-> Insert sheet
b. Page Layout-> Insert-> Sheet
c. Right-click the sheet tabs and select Insert Sheet
Tip: Intermediate Excel, page 190

8. A hyperlink can link to which of the following (Select all correct answers.)
a. A website
b. Another spreadsheet
c. A specific sheet in a workbook
d. An email address
Tip: Intermediate Excel, page 195

Intermediate Excel Skill Test

Please do the following steps:

1. Open a new blank spreadsheet.
   In Cell A1 type: April
   In Cell B1 type: May
   Use the Autofill to enter the labels from June through October

2. Add the following values to your spreadsheet:
   A2=3.4
   B2=2.7
   C2=1.8
   D2=.75
   E2=.5
   F2=6.4
   G2=3.4

3. Select the Range from A1 through G2.
   Create a Chart using this Range.
   Select the Cylinder Chart type and remove the legend.
   Place the Chart on the same spreadsheet as your data

4. Select the Chart and format the CHART COLUMN fill color to red.
   Format the CHART COLUMN for September yellow.

5. Select the chart WALL (behind the Chart columns)
   Format the fill to be the Waterdrop texture.

6. Select the text on the AXIS of the Cylinder chart
   Format the type to be 9pt.

7. Select the labels (the month names in the first Row)
   Apply the CELL STYLE: Accent 6

8. Rename the spreadsheet SHEET 1 to be Rainfall Graph

9. Select SHEET 2 and add the following labels:
   A1=Expenses
   A2=Rent
   A3=Phone
   A4=Electricity

10. Rename SHEET 2 to be Expenses

11. Select Sheet 2 and add the following data:
    B1=Amount
    B2=1,500
    B3=545
    B4=130

12. Format Column B for currency.

13. Create a 3D pie chart from the Expense data.

14. Change the Options to show: Category name and Percentage.

15. Save the file as Your Name Excel Intermediate Skill Test.
    Please submit the Skill Test online.

Microsoft Excel 2010: Index
Microsoft Office Specialist (MOS): Exam 77-882 and 77-888 for Excel 2010

Intermediate Microsoft Excel 2010: Glossary
Microsoft Office Specialist (MOS): Exam 77-882 and 77-888 Excel 2010

Absolute reference—a reference that refers to a target cell by its exact location on the spreadsheet. This type of reference is not affected by moving cells *pg.37*

AutoFill—function that fills data, usually in a series such as predefined increments or months *pg.18*

AVERAGE—function that finds the average in a group of values *pg.103*

Chart legend—indicates what the colors or marks on a chart represent *pg.123*

Chart— visual representation of data *pg.122*

Circular reference—an equation or function that refers to itself *pg.106*

Concatenate—function that combines data from two cells, including text and numbers *pg.61*

Conditional summary—filters data based on specific criteria *pg.97*

COUNT—function that counts and shows many cells have either text, numbers, or any content *pg.101*

Footer— material separate from the document contents that appears at the bottom of the page *pg.159*

Header—material separate from the document contents that appears at the top of the page *pg.159*

HLOOKUP—a reference table with data arranged in rows to return values based on set criteria *pg.115*

Hyperlinks— how to get from one web page to another, links the pages *pg.193*

Logical formulas—a formula that asks a yes-or-no question about the target data, returns the value as specified. Also known as the IF function *pg.131*

Lookup table—a reference table to return values based on set criteria. (See also VLOOKUP and HLOOKUP) *pg.127*

Margins—the white space around the edge of a page *pg.150*

Mixed reference—a reference that uses both absolute and relative references *pg.40*

Orientation— which direction on the paper is "up." Can be portrait, which is narrower than tall, or landscape which is wider than tall. *pg.149*

Page Layout View— shows how the spreadsheet will appear as a printed page *pg.164*

Range—a group of cells *pg.22*

Reference cell— a cell that formulas refer to *pg.32*

Relative reference—a Relative Reference refers to the target cell by Row and by Column. A Relative Reference that is used in an equation will adjust when the formula is Filled Down. This type of reference is affected by moving cells pg.34

SkyDrive— online storage space available from Microsoft, available wherever you have Internet access *pg.212*

Sparklines—small, simple charts to quickly convey information *pg.178*

SUM—function that adds the numbers in selected cells together *pg.24*

Template—a document, spreadsheet or form that has custom information or formatting *pg.202*

Title bar— the bar at the top of a program that includes the program name and, if applicable, the current file name *pg.13*

VLOOKUP—a reference table with data arranged in columns to return values based on set criteria *pg.115*

Workbook— a collection of spreadsheets in Excel *pg.197*

Worksheet—a single spreadsheet in Excel *pg.96*